D1564052

Januarius MacGahaN

J. A. MACGAHAN, THE CORRESPONDENT.

Januarius MacGahan in Bulgarian days, by C. deGrimm. (Mac-Gahan Papers)

Januarius MacGahan

The Life and Campaigns of an American War Correspondent

DALE L. WALKER

OHIO UNIVERSITY PRESS
ATHENS

Library of Congress Cataloging-in-Publication Data

Walker, Dale L.
  Januarius MacGahan, the life and campaigns of an American war
correspondent / by Dale L. Walker.
    p.   cm.
  Bibliography: p.
  Includes index.
  ISBN 0-8214-0894-1
  1. MacGahan, J. A. (Januarius Aloysius), 1844-1878.
2. Journalists—United States—Biography.   3. War correspondents—
United States—Biography.   4. Franco-German War, 1870-1871.
5. Russo-Turkish War, 1877-1878.   6. Spain—History—Carlist War,
1873-1876.   7. Bulgaria—History—1762-1878. I. Title.
PN4874.M17W35   1988
070.4'33—dc19   88-1632
                                                                                CIP

Ohio University Press books are printed on acid free paper. ∞

Contents

List of Illustrations

" . . . the New and Honorable Fraternity of war correspondents, who all possess the inalienable right of doing as much work as they can and getting as much for it as Providence and their owners shall please. To these things are added in time, if the brother be worthy, the power of glib speech that neither man nor woman can resist . . . the eye of a horsecoper, the skill of a cook, the constitution of a bullock, the digestion of an ostrich, and an indefinite adaptability to all circumstances. But many died before they attained to this degree."

Rudyard Kipling, *The Light That Failed* (1890)

Foreword

Among the outriders of nineteenth-century imperialism, and often the most combative and vociferous, were those intrepid gentlemen known to millions of readers of the penny press as "our special correspondent." In their heyday, from the Crimean War to the end of the century, a period of roughly fifty years, these venturesome young "specials" roamed the globe, sustained by little more than a sense of mission and a letter of credit. They wrote without bylines, yet incongruously in first person, and many developed a decided high-handedness, particularly in upbraiding and second-guessing commanders in the field. It was said, figuratively of course, that in every war correspondent's knapsack there was hidden a field marshal's baton, and a celebrated cartoon in the English humor magazine *Punch* in 1880 illustrated this. Captioned "An assault of arms between General Sword and General Pen," it depicted the eminent William Howard Russell of the *Times* of London engaged in a quill-pen bayonet charge against the peerless colonial soldier Sir Garnet Wolseley. Sir Garnet, sword *en garde*, was trying to fend Russell off. The scene was not altogether hyperbolic.

At the crest of the imperialistic tide, during the decades when the British were pushing into Africa and Asia, the United States into the Pacific, and Russia into Turkestan and Eastern Europe, there were no more doughty and self-assured standard-bearers than these correspondents. They were the representatives of the only news medium of their day, as familiar to the times as the agents of Trade, Cross, and Flag: self-proclaimed ministers-without-portfolio, through whom the designs of the decision makers at Whitehall and on Pennsylvania Avenue were transmitted to the people.

Januarius MacGahan, like virtually all of his war correspondent contemporaries, had a fame as transitory as the daily newspapers that employed him. Only a rare specialist today—perhaps among that dwindling crew of old-school, green-eyeshade-and-arm garter editors still occasionally found puzzling over their video display terminals in American city rooms—will know the name and the effulgence it once cast. The two great papers MacGahan represented are long dead. The books he wrote between "campaigns" are difficult to find in an American library. The stories he followed—the Bulgarian atrocities; the Russian incursion into central Asia; the lost Franklin Arctic Expedition;

the Franco-Prussian, Carlist, and Russo-Turkish wars—are subjects
for upper-level history classes.

Yet he helped preside at the dawn of a communications age when
the magnetic telegraph was being used extensively for the first time,
when the transoceanic cable had just become a reality—an era which
would radically change humankind's concepts of itself and its poten-
tials.

And too, he was a practitioner of the kind of "advocacy" journalism
that a hundred years later became a catchword in the new era of "the
media"—plural. MacGahan admitted, for example, that when con-
fronted by the inhumanity of tyrannical governments, he became an
advocate and an activist, rather than a coldly detached observer. "I fear
I am no longer impartial," he wrote in his first dispatch from the ravaged provinces of the Balkans in 1876, "and I am certainly no longer
cool. There are certain things too horrible to allow anything like calm
inquiry; things, the vileness of which the eye refuses to look upon, and
which the mind refuses to contemplate."

Januarius MacGahan is the finest American exemplar of that dimly
remembered time which Kipling portrayed in *The Light That Failed*, that
era when bold young correspondents, in Archibald Forbes's phrase,
"rode on the cannon thunder" in the most savage corners of the world,
hazarding life and limb to get the story their editors decided would sell
newspapers. There is an absorbing adventure tale as well as a history
lesson in looking back at a time before correspondents became slaves
to communications technology, when they moved about unfettered
either by their editors' directives or on the short tethers of videocam
and microphone cords. In MacGahan's day, a newspaper correspondent was a resplendent figure who could hold the public in thrall,
shake a government to its foundations, and influence history. Today,
more often than not, presidents, prime ministers, and prime news
makers everywhere speak to cameras and mikes and tend to ignore the
man or woman with pad and pencil. Modern print reporters too often
find themselves pushing forward through a tangle of cables and elec-
tronic paraphernalia, frantically picking at crumbs of information,
most of them destined to be hopelessly stale by the time they get them
to their readers.

In MacGahan's day, newspaper correspondents were outriders; today they are too often in the rearguard.

Then too, consider that Januarius MacGahan is a name virtually
vanished from the fickle historical annals of his own country, while in
the People's Republic of Bulgaria, over a century after his death, he is

remembered—indeed, revered. Masses have been sung to his memory in the church at the foot of Shipka Pass in the central Balkans near where he rode in the van of Gourko's grim, gray-clad army. There is a MacGahan street in Sofia, another in Plovdiv; his portrait and bust can be found in museums in such remote Balkan villages as Pazardzhik and Batak; his life, written almost as hagiography, can be found in P. M. Mateev's *Eliki Blagodeteli na Bulgarskia Narod* (Great Benefactors of the Bulgarian People). And, in a 1966 centennial translation of the harrowing dispatches MacGahan wrote from the sundered Ottoman provinces, the Bulgarian editor depicts the American not only as "the most brilliant journalist of the XIX Century," but as "a martyr to his sense of duty and fellowship."

But the whole truth is that Januarius MacGahan's story simply begs telling. In a time when it is fashionable to lament, "Where are the heroes of today?" we might benefit in learning about the unsung heroes of yesterday.

And who can resist the story of an Ohio farmboy who earned an epitaph which, in four words, credits him as liberator of a nation?

—Dale L. Walker
El Paso, Texas
January 2, 1987

Acknowledgments

When I began following MacGahan's trail in 1969, it did not take long to discover how that path had been obscured in the ninety-one years since the correspondent's death in Constantinople. No biography of him existed; indeed, with the exception of F. Lauriston Bullard's excellent chapter in *Famous War Correspondents* (1914), nothing of any length or substance had ever been published on this extraordinary man. Bullard, and the scattered, obscure memoirs of Archibald Forbes, the great London *Daily News* "special," have been the sources of most of the infrequent references to MacGahan over the past century.

Significantly, not even Bullard, whose chapter on MacGahan is generally factual, looked at Bulgarian sources and the signally important matter of MacGahan's stature in that country. In this respect, I have had the good fortune of assistance from the embassy of the People's Republic of Bulgaria in Washington, D. C. Ambassadors Luben Guerassimov and Konstantin Grigorov enabled me to receive invaluable help from Sofia. This information came to me in the form of a splendid work, written in 1970 by Dobrimir Chilingirov, entitled "The Bulgarians about MacGahan." I have made liberal use of this unpublished monograph and cannot adequately express my gratitude for having this thoroughly documented work at my disposal.

Theodore Delchev Dimitrov of Geneva, Switzerland, was also of enormous assistance, sending me his 1966 English-Bulgarian edition of MacGahan's *The Turkish Atrocities in Bulgaria*. And another Bulgarian contact has been Bozidar Kuntschev of Sofia, a student in philology when I first wrote him at the suggestion of the late Joan London Miller, daughter of the famed American writer, Jack London. Mr. Kuntschev, using the resources of the University of Sofia, answered my questions faithfully and unstintingly.

No writer could be more fortunate in dealing with the descendants of a biographical subject than I have been, specifically in working with Januarius MacGahan's grandsons, John A. MacGahan in Pennsylvania and upstate New York and William H. MacGahan in New Jersey. A glance at the Manuscripts listing in the Sources section of this book will give the reader an idea of the extent of the MacGahan family papers and why it is inconceivable that a book about the correspondent could be written without them and without the assistance and trust of his heirs.

At the University of Texas at El Paso, Prof. Z. Anthony Kruszewski found translators for some letters in the Bulgarian language and as-sisted with the difficult matter of Slavic place and proper names. (On a visit to Sofia in 1984, Prof. Kruszewski asked a taxi driver to take him to "MacGahan Street" and was whisked away there, taking time to photograph the modest street sign for me.) I am also grateful to Hugh Treadwell for providing me a number of expert translations from the French of Barbara MacGahan's longhand letters, to Prof. Joseph R. Smiley for his valuable help in linguistic matters, and to Prof. David A. Hackett for his invaluable critique of the manuscript.

Among writer-friends who have read portions of the manuscript and who gave me good advice are Alvin S. Fick, Elroy Bode, Leon C. Metz, Nancy Hamilton, Loren D. Estleman, Richard Wheeler, and James Stowe. The late Brig. Gen. S. L. A. Marshall, war correspondent and eminent military historian, gave me a priceless critique of the Franco-Prussian, Carlist, and Russo-Turkish war episodes in the book and gave me in addition an even more treasured friendship and encouragement.

Similarly, I would never forget my great friend and mentor, the late Richard O'Connor of Ellsworth, Maine. In 1967, O'Connor and I wrote a biography of the American radical journalist John Reed, pub-lished as *The Lost Revolutionary*. My interest in MacGahan was an out-growth of that Reed work; indeed, the two men had much in common: separated in time by less than a half century, each found a career as a newspaper correspondent, each (though vastly different philosophi-cally) had revolutionary ideals, each wrote in a richly partisan style, the fate of each was inextricably bound with Russia, and each died young in a foreign land. Dick O'Connor was enthusiastic about a book on MacGahan from the start. He knew MacGahan's era well, having documented those times in numerous books including a wonderful biography of MacGahan's nemesis, the owner of the New York *Herald*, James Gordon Bennett.

Just before his sudden death of a heart seizure in 1975, O'Connor wrote me, after reading an early draft of the book, "It's a helluva tale, ol' Dale, and high time it was told."

Mrs. Fae Chappelear of the *Perry County Tribune* in New Lexington, Ohio, was of immense help in digging through the morgue of her newspaper for MacGahan clippings; the late James E. Sisson III of Berkeley, California, uncovered some rare periodical items for me; and the Public Information Office of the Ohio State Historical Society in Columbus patiently gave time and effort in locating fugitive Mac-Gahan documents in their files.

The El Paso Public Library and the libraries of the University of

Texas at El Paso and the University of Kansas were invariably helpful in permitting me to use their collections, microforms, and interlibrary loan services.

Lastly, I want to mention the quiet patience and encouragement of my wife, Alice McCord Walker, who has lived with Januarius as long as I have. The other Walkers—Dianne, Eric, Chris, Mike, John—started out snickering over that grandly rolling name and ended up saying, "My dad's writing a book about a famous war correspondent."

Part I

I

Up from Pigeon Roost Ridge

1
"Liberator of Bulgaria"

On July 1, 1911, New Lexington, seat of Perry County, Ohio, launched its homecoming celebration. Former residents returned to the town from all over the East and Midwest, finding the streets draped with patriotic bunting and scented with baking pies, sawn lumber, and fireworks. That Saturday and the following day were devoted to informal reunions, to strolling around and touching old landmarks, and to remembering with pride the county's two most illustrious sons: Philip H. Sheridan, the dashing Civil War cavalry leader and later Commanding General of the U.S. Army, lived in nearby Somerset as a youth; and the celebrated foreign correspondent J. A. MacGahan had been born just a few miles from New Lexington sixty-seven years earlier.

On Independence Day, New Lexington's homecoming gaiety would soon take a momentarily somber turn: the commemoration of a tomb for MacGahan.

The year 1911 was one of the last of what historians have labeled the Age of Innocence, that time before America struck the Faustian bargains binding on the status of a world power. New Lexington's homecoming was a manifestation of all the homely enthusiasms of an American spirit which still truly resided, everyone believed as an article of faith, in its small towns. There was a presentation to dignitaries of the key to the city and the reading of odes composed by local poets. (Among these was the effort by Col. William A. Taylor, which began, "Bulgaria in the wine press of the Turk, / Gave blood and tears and groaned upon the rack . . .") Also on the program was a soprano's rendition of an original song, titled "Perry County Home Sweet Home," and other numbers by the Kintz Mandolin Orchestra of Somerset.

At a banquet in the armory on the eve of the unveiling of Mac-Gahan's tomb, the toastmaster and the county's most formidable orator, Judge Maurice H. Donohue, ruminated at length on the significance of MacGahan's humble birth. The judge intoned:

> If on the twelfth day of June, 1844, a message had been sent to the Turk, whose domain then extended not only to the banks of the Danube, but whose suzerainty stretched from the Carpathians, that a little child had been born in the hills of Ohio who would some day change the map of his empire, he would have scorned the prophecy and challenged its fulfillment. But such a message would have been true . . .

Turks and Bulgarians, blood and tears, the map of empire—what had these to do with the placid assemblage of Ohioans fanning themselves in the July heat?

Dawn of the Fourth was shattered by a thirteen-gun cannon salute followed by a fusillade of hundreds of long strings of firecrackers, ignited by sticks of punk in the hands of every small boy in the town. By noon, ten thousand people, the largest gathering in Perry County history, milled around the streets listening to the martial airs played by the Seventh Regiment and Perry County concert bands. A parade led by part of the Seventh (National Guard) Regiment from Zanesville proceeded to the New Lexington cemetery where hundreds of homecomers managed an appropriate solemnity as they crowded around the flag-draped marker. Among the honored guests were Paul MacGahan, only son of the correspondent, and Colonel Taylor, who read his ode to MacGahan's memory in much the same voice as he had twenty-seven years earlier, in 1884, when MacGahan's body, transported from Constantinople, had been reburied in his native soil in this very cemetery.

Following Colonel Taylor's reading, the band struck up spirited renditions of the "Star-Spangled Banner" and another air—one as unfamiliar to the patient crowd as the white, green, and red flag which, with the Stars and Stripes, covered the marker.

Then Paul MacGahan stepped forward and pulled the lanyard, unveiling his father's tomb.

Beneath the shroud of flags was revealed an austere marble block resting on a massive plinth. It still stands in the Catholic section of tranquil, tree-lined Maplewood Cemetery, on the southwest side of New Lexington. The inscription on the severe marble, in hand-high raised letters, reads

MACGAHAN

LIBERATOR OF BULGARIA

How often casual visitors to the graveyard even today must be startled by that curious proclamation: an Irish-American, born and buried in a small Ohio town, the liberator of a Balkan nation?

2
"A book that will bring me fame"

Perry County, Ohio, (named for the Battle of Lake Erie hero, Oliver Hazard "We-have-met-the-enemy-and-they-are-ours" Perry) and its seat at New Lexington had some small eminence at the time of Mac-Gahan's birth. Settled in 1802, chiefly by Scotch-Irish immigrant farmers, the area could claim the distinction of being on a main thoroughfare between the eastern and western states. Until the period of steamboat navigation, a continuous stream of settlers flowed westward in their wagons, many of them through the town James Comly had laid out in 1817. By the 1840s New Lexington had a population of 200; Perry County, 20,000.

One thing people remembered about the New Lexington countryside was the great spring and fall pigeon migrations, their flights darkening the sky, the trees all about limed from their roosting, the crops ruined by their voracity. Local legend had it that there were so many pigeons a youngster could throw a stick into a tree and fell half a dozen at a time.

On May 24, 1844, from the U.S. Supreme Court chambers at the Capitol building in Washington, D. C., an artist and inventor named Samuel Finley Breese Morse, using a code of dots and dashes, tapped out a message—"What hath God wrought"—on an electrical "telegraph" he had invented. The message was received by Morse's assistant at a railroad office in Baltimore and successfully transmitted back.

And, on June 12, 1844, nineteen days after this momentous experiment, was born one who would make historic use of Morse's work: Januarius Aloysius MacGahan.* Born on what was then known as Pigeon Roost Ridge, an old farm about six miles southwest of New Lexington, Ohio, MacGahan was the first child of the second marriage of James MacGahan, a native of King's County, Ireland, "where the River Shannon flows." Little is recorded of James's youth, but family tradition has it that he served in the Royal Navy before coming to America and that he had at least one memorable moment of service in being posted as a seaman on the *Northumberland*, the vessel which had taken Napoleon to exile on St. Helena in 1815. James had settled in Perry County in 1825 and soon after married Elizabeth Dimond whose family came from northern Ireland, settling first in Johnstown, Pennsylvania, and in the mid-1830s, in Ohio. Two children were born of this union, and one of them, William, was well established in the newspaper business in St. Louis by the 1860s. Elizabeth died about 1840, and the following year, in St. Patrick's Church in New Lexington, James married Esther Dempsey, called "Hetty" by the family.

At the time of his second marriage, James was past fifty and Esther about thirty. Januarius (among family and friends, "Jan" from his childhood on) was the first of their three children to survive to adulthood.

James MacGahan died in 1850, leaving his family all but destitute. In the words of a family friend, "Jan grew old enough to work very young." He hired out to tobacco farmers in Hocking, Fayette, and Fairfield counties in the spring and summer, and returned to the district school in winter. He was a bright student and in those days aspired to be an astronomer. He wrote an excellent hand, demonstrated an uncommon skill at composition, and had read far more than the average farmboy of his age.

In 1860, MacGahan applied for a district schoolmaster's job in New Lexington but was turned down as too young and soon after traveled over to Huntington, Indiana, near Fort Wayne, where some Dempsey cousins lived. There he worked as a grocer's clerk and schoolteacher and contributed some space-rate items to the daily Huntington *Demo-*

---

*The surname is generally pronounced M'GANN, less frequently M'GAY'n and M'GAY-han. The family was Roman Catholic and "Januarius" may have derived from Saint Januarius, a bishop of the church martyred in the third century A.D. who became the patron saint of Naples, Italy.

Young Januarius, about 1865. (MacGahan Papers)

Birthplace of MacGahan, "Pigeon Roost Ridge" farm, near New Lexington, Ohio. (MacGahan Papers)

crat. Since he had a well-modulated voice and good pronunciation, he even tried his hand at public readings, particularly from the works of Charles Dickens, but his cousin P. H. Dempsey recalled this venture as "not profitable." Dempsey said, "Jan seldom took in enough money to pay for the rental hall."

Dempsey also recorded an incident in which MacGahan's courage, if not his oratory, worked well for him. A group of peripatetic Protestant "dominies" gave a series of anti-Catholic lectures in Huntington, and MacGahan, among the few ardent Catholics who dared attend, stood up to challenge what he called "several perversions of fact about the Church." He demanded the speaker debate him and despite raucous sneers from the stage and a dangerously hostile audience, Dempsey said, "Jan left the hall satisfied he had won the point."

Although Indiana had held staunchly to the Union cause in the Civil War and had supported Lincoln in the 1860 election, MacGahan's single surviving remark on the war, written in a letter to his mother in September 1864, was of the "many soldiers to be seen in Huntington," and of "someone breaking up a McClellan meeting." (General George B. McClellan, whom Lincoln had removed from command of the Army of the Potomac two years before, was a candidate for the presidency that year on the Democratic ticket.) MacGahan left no record of his own attitude toward McClellan, Lincoln, or indeed the war itself, though he was by now close to twenty years old and the war was drawing to a close.

During the three years he spent in Huntington, MacGahan attended a commercial school, learning enough bookkeeping and business to land a job in St. Louis as clerk in a railroad office. By the winter of 1864, he had saved enough money to send for his mother and brothers, Patrick and John, and establish them in Huntington before taking his leave once again.

He continued his business schooling in St. Louis and after a time took a position at seventy-five dollars a month with the wholesale stationery store of John J. Daly & Co.

In later years, Walter J. Blakely, a friend of MacGahan's in this St. Louis period, recorded some recollections of his Ohio acquaintance. "Jan's circle of friends," wrote Blakely, "were chiefly literary ones." He cared little for ordinary socializing, although he was popular, a good listener and conversationalist, and had, Blakely recalled, "a strong sense of fair play." He liked the company of women but avoided cards and billiards, bowling and drinking—the clerkish passions of his male companions. Blakely said MacGahan favored wandering in the woods, reading Shakespeare and Dickens, playing chess and smoking a good cigar. He had, Blakely continued, "an innate acting sense and for a time expressed an interest in the stage as a career." He was a great devotee of Edwin Booth and was fond of practicing elocution. MacGahan told Blakely of his ambition "to write a book that will bring me fame."

Blakely described MacGahan as about 5 feet 10½ inches tall, carrying himself with a very slight bookkeeper's stoop of the shoulders, walking with hands in trouser pockets. "His laugh was unlike any other I ever heard," Blakely wrote. "It was a sort of magnetic chuckle, the effect of which was contagious." MacGahan's eyes, said Blakely, were bluish-gray and "looked one in the face whilst speaking to one." His Ohio friend was "careless of dress, rather Bohemian in some's view, but others described him as a 'natty' dresser."

Early in 1868, MacGahan met Lt. Gen. Philip H. Sheridan, only recently appointed by President Andrew Johnson to command the Department of Missouri. "Little Phil," the five-foot two-inch-tall hero of countless cavalry actions in the late war (Corinth, Boonesville, Murfreesboro, Chickamauga, Missionary Ridge), had been Grant's cavalry commander of the Army of the Potomac. He had earned a celebrated victory over J. E. B. Stuart at Yellow Tavern and had been commander of the Union forces in the Shenandoah Valley—and Sheridan even had some things in common with the young and ambitious MacGahan. Both were Perry County Ohioans (Sheridan grew up near Somerset, a few miles north of New Lexington), both were Catholic sons of Irish immigrants, and there even existed a distant blood kinship traced on mutual family trees. It seems likely that William MacGahan, who had some prominence in the newspaper business in St. Louis, introduced his half brother to General Sheridan, and it seems equally likely that Sheridan played some role in Januarius's decision, in the winter of 1868, to go to Europe. The precise nature of that role is unknown, but the general would soon again appear at a decisive moment in the young Ohioan's life.

Whatever the sequence of events, MacGahan had a few hundred dollars saved and wrote his mother of his intention to "go to the continent" to study either languages or the law. He visited the family in Huntington, then traveled by train to New York, sailing for Ostend in December.

3

"The air is full of rumors"

Prior to his sudden and rather daring venture "to the continent," MacGahan spoke not so much of living as "existing." He had endured a static life—clerk and bookkeeper, erstwhile teacher, space-rate news-paper contributor, all geographically circumscribed in breadbasket America. He was intelligent and ambitious but thwarted by family re-sponsibilities and work-a-day drudgery. His existence as he saw it was perfectly portrayed when he wrote his mother describing to her a day's work at the Daly Stationery Company in St. Louis, followed by a night in his small room in the Daly building, reading classical literature by kerosene lamp, turning pages with one hand, swatting mosquitos with the other.

In Brussels, Paris, and at the artist's colony at Écouen, he also read the classics by kerosene lamp and swatted mosquitos, but those were the only similarities to his old mundane life.

He kept a steady correspondence flowing to his mother, to his St. Louis friend Walter Blakely, and to Blakely's sister Frances. Those let-ters which have survived are unfailingly exuberant and sublimely happy. In modern parlance, MacGahan's experiences in 1869–71 would be termed a matter of "finding himself," and indeed, this is pre-cise: for two carefree years he traveled, learned, and grew. And out of his experiences he found a career and a vibrant, far-flung life beyond his most unfettered dreams.

In the spring of 1869, MacGahan took up residence in Brussels, and from his apartment at 39 rue de Leglise, St. Gilles, he began his earnest study of the French language. "I intend to forget English as far as pos-sible," he wrote home, "that is to say, I wish to speak, to write, and even to *think* in French if I can."

The city's ancient Gothic guildhalls and churches, some dating from the eleventh century, its museums of Flemish art, its botanical gardens, the medieval and Renaissance Grand Palace square, the Broodhuis meeting place of the old States-General of the Nether-lands—all these wonders filled MacGahan's letters to Huntington and St. Louis. He wrote excitedly of spending Independence Day on the field of Waterloo, plucking yellow blossoms and clover from the or-chard at Hougoumont, blue flowers from the site of the last stand of Napoleon's Old Guard, petals from the grave of Col. Alexander Gor-don, Wellington's favorite aide-de-camp whose death from wound and rude amputation caused tears to course down the powder-blackened face of the Iron Duke.

In September 1869 in Paris, MacGahan met an American artist named J. Wells Champney who was studying painting in the artist's colony at Écouen, northwest of the capital. The two men decided to conserve their dwindling savings by sharing quarters.

The village of Écouen, MacGahan wrote Frances Blakely, was "a delightful, quaint place with old world flavor, crooked and rambling streets, running often between high walls covered with interlacing branches of old trees." He and Champney shared an airy studio on the third floor of an ancient house on a mountain slope. "An old castle frowns down on us like a grim giant," he wrote, "and I go to sleep every night watching the glowing eye in the middle of his forehead, for the place is inhabited." He spoke of the view from his window—six or seven miles of lush green countryside, copses of trees, golden fields, neat rows of homes—and of the town crier ringing his bell, and of the dance-to-midnight held every Sunday under a huge oak with lights suspended from its limbs.

"I think I was never better off in my life," he said, "and as to enjoyment, there are not two fellows in this little round old earth that know better how to find it than we . . . my friend works, I study, we fence and take gymnastics . . . We have a room apiece and a kitchen, 6 x 4 and high ceilinged. We would not exchange that cuisine for the Tuileries." He continued his smoking, he admitted, enjoying a brand of local cigar popular with the artists at Écouen.

On Sundays and Mondays, MacGahan accompanied Champney to the house of M. Frere, founder of a school of painting at Écouen, and there was brought into contact "with the World of Art" in a gathering of twenty artists and their families. In the evenings through the week he earned a few francs giving English lessons to those who needed a diversion and continued his own pursuit of French. A gifted linguist, MacGahan mastered both the spoken and written language, something that would soon give him a decided advantage in his first trial as a war correspondent.

His letters home show a thirst for news of America. He asked the Blakelys for details on the Jay Gould–Jim Fisk gold-cornering scheme and resultant "Black Friday" financial panic and Cyrus Field's new transatlantic cable. In turn, he wrote of the European furor over the opening of the Suez Canal and of the plans afoot to send an expedition to Africa to "rescue" the missionary David Livingstone.

By the end of 1869, however, MacGahan's letters were filled almost exclusively with the turbulent news from France, of the final tottering before the fall of Napoléon III's Second Empire.

"I go to Paris every week to learn the news," he wrote on November 1, "and I now know the city as well as I know St. Louis. Paris is certainly in a very strange state at present. Everyone is restless and all thinking minds expect a revolution from day to day. This condition is all the more dangerous in that there exists on the surface a certain calm and tranquility."

An air of detached excitement pervades MacGahan's letters from this period—akin to something written by a bystander at a fire or at the scene of a crime. He felt he was witness to momentous events, yet he was disturbed and confused by them and uncertain of their meaning. In this he reflected the attitude of most of the French. "The air is full of rumors," he wrote, "it is, in fact, exactly the picture of Paris of olden times, before a revolution, as Hugo pictures in *Les Misérables*."

And again: "We are upon a volcano, each moment threatening eruption . . . The other day, walking with several gentlemen in Écouen, I heard the reports of cannon. 'What is that?' I exclaimed. 'Oh, a revolution in Paris, probably,' was the careless reply."

References to Victor Hugo, in exile on Guernsey in the Channel Islands since 1855, appear frequently in MacGahan's letters, just as Hugo's name appeared frequently in the French press. "It is said that Victor Hugo, the man who is revered one might almost say to the point of idolatry, by the liberal party and especially by men of action—is on the point of returning to France," he reported.*

As 1869 ended, MacGahan knew France's drift toward war with Prussia was inexorable. Napoléon III, mentally and physically older than his sixty-two years, was guided only by the principle of preserving his dynasty; yet France was without ally, isolated, her army in the hands of incompetent officers, the working class mesmerized by the theories of Karl Marx and Mikhail Bakunin and daily joining mass strikes and febrile demonstrations.

Said the Empress Eugénie, "Unless there is a war my son will never be emperor."

4
"Voilà la guerre!"

In June 1870, about a month before Napoléon III declared war, MacGahan traveled from Écouen to Brussels, then via Liège to Aachen (Aix-la-Chapelle) near the Belgian and Dutch borders, and on to Cologne on the Rhine. At Aachen he studied the relics of Charlemagne (who was believed to have been born there in 742) and at Cologne, the Roman antiquities, medieval watchtowers, moats, and drawbridges—

---

*With the establishment of the Republic, Hugo did return, triumphantly, to Paris in September 1870.

"Everywhere poetry and romance, castles and ruins, legends and traditions, woody mountains and rocky glens haunted by ghosts and goblins"—he reflected in a long letter on June 30.

In that letter to Walter Blakely, he added his notions on the German people and the French people. For a young man who had lived, studied, and traveled in France for eighteen months and who had learned the language expertly, he had some surprisingly capricious revelations for his St. Louis friend.

"How well do I like the Germans? Much better than the French—much better . . . The French talk of 'Liberté, Fraternité, Égalité,' but the Germans *have* these qualities—they are part of the national character."

He listed a few of those characteristics, in contrast with those of the French:

> People take time to eat and sleep and drink here. Clerks on 300 thalers per year take 2-1/2 hours to dine and nobody thinks of cutting them to a beggerly half hour.
>
> Germans are religious . . . the French not. The French respect nothing; nothing is sacred in the eyes of a Frenchman.
>
> In Germany, the family is intact as it used to be in America before divorce became general.
>
> The French students have their *grisettes* and erect barricades, and the German students drink beer and fight duels.
>
> French literature is without the slightest particle of invention or novelty . . . it is always a man, married, of course, who has a mistress and a married woman who has a lover . . . all of which is interesting at first but old, old, after being seen a few times.

Journeying along the Rhine as far south as Koblenz, MacGahan was overwhelmed by the majesty of the great river and its ancient castles and legends of the *Nibelungen* and *Lorelei*.

"What a river is the Rhine!" he exulted. "Can anyone explain the interest these old castles hold for me? Churches, monuments, tombs and battlefields have each their own peculiar interest, but there is nothing so strangely fascinating as an old, old, castle."

He wrote evocatively of one old Rhine castle, Drachenfels:

> You linger about it, you know not why; you take a book, perhaps stretch yourself on the grass in sight of broken

arch and falling tower, and you find the most exciting romance tame, beside the events and creatures of your own
imagination, conjured by the sight of these hoary old
walls—which mark, more surely then any dry data could
do, the flight of centuries since human passion held sway
and human hearts have loved and sorrowed, joyed and died,
where now all is ruin and lonely desolation.

He explored Drachenfels's ruined defenses, watchtowers, subter-
ranean passages, and winding stairways of solid rock—"dungeons
black as night, splendid courts, now carpeted with richest grass,
arches, corridors and halls, but all, all in ruin and decay." And five
hundred feet below the storybook castle, he described the peaceful
village and farther off, the Rhine, "as far as the eye can reach, stretching like a sheet of molten silver; and beyond all, more mountains, more
ruins, more castles, villages and spires."

When the moon came up, bathing the woody hills in quicksilver
light, everything turned to enchantment, and he wrote: "In a deep glen
below you hear the sound of a flute, and singing perhaps, for they are
dancing away down there among the trees and in the evening stillness
the voices of young girls and children float up through the enchanted
air 'till you think that spirits are gliding to and fro in the misty moon-
shine. What a river is this *Rhine!*"

But returning to Brussels in December, nearly five months after the
war declaration, all the exuberant travelogue chatter of his letters by
now had vanished. The key battle of the war had been fought on September 1 when the French, with 130,000 men and 564 guns under the
command of Napoléon III had been forced to retire to Sedan, an old
textile town on the Meuse. There, after an attempt to fight their way
out, Napoléon III and Marshal de MacMahon had surrendered and
with that act had surrendered any further hope of winning the war.

The siege of Paris was undertaken by von Moltke on September 19,
but the city had not yet fallen, and with the emperor now held prisoner
near Kassel, Germany, the forlorn French war effort lurched on,
guided by a newly proclaimed Republican government.

And so it was with *"Voilà la guerre!"* that MacGahan began a letter to
Frances Blakely on December 5, a letter all of news, opinion, apocry-
pha, and exclamation marks. He was utterly enveloped in the war, his
letter filled with rhetorical questions and half answers, his mind teeming with news, ideas, opinions, an awe of the German strength, and a
pity for the foredoomed French:

The war? What shall I say of it? I hardly know. It is a war so strange, so subversive of all ordinary ideas, and in regard to which all predictions have been so completely upset, that one knows not what to think. Who is in the right? If France declared war, Prussia has pushed it with eagerness and is carrying it on to the death. Is it well to press a brave and heroic people to despair?

On the Prussian investment of Paris: "Paris cannot hold out very long, but Trochu [Louis Jules Trochu, governor of Paris] will make a desperate effort to get out . . . He has already tried many times. If he succeeds, the war will be prolonged indefinitely. If the Prussians carry the city, the war must soon end."

Of Léon Gambetta, the moderate member of the Chamber of Deputies: "Do you know what sort of man is this Gambetta? You will have some idea of him perhaps when I tell you that while yet young, he put out his eye because his father did not wish to grant him some request which he believed himself entitled to! He has a will of iron and in this respect at least Bismarck has found his equal!"*

"I had a few hundred dollars when I came to Europe," MacGahan wrote to Walter Blakely in the spring of 1871, "which a prudent man would have invested in United States bonds instead of flinging to the winds in what many considered a wild goose chase over the world. I have gone without dinner more than once when a franc would buy a bed, but I had made up my mind to do a certain thing and I did it."

What he had done—use his linguistic gift to learn the French language thoroughly—was now to pay dividends in the Franco-Prussian War.

Probably through the auspices of General Sheridan, who had been invited by the Prussians to "observe" the war from their headquarters, MacGahan was introduced to fellow Ohioan Murat Halstead, a veteran reporter covering the war for the Cincinnati *Inquirer*, and to Dr. George Hosmer, European agent for the New York *Herald*. Hosmer's efforts resulted in MacGahan's assignment as a "special" for the *Herald*, and in the opening week of 1871, he received his instructions to proceed to Belfort, near the Swiss border, there to report on the French Army of the East and its commander, General Bourbaki.

---

*It was Gambetta, after Sedan, who announced the fall of Napoléon III and the establishment of the Republic. With the Prussians besieging Paris, he urged his colleagues to quit the capital and conduct the government from some provincial city. His pleas were rejected, but he took his own advice and fled—spectacularly—in a hot air balloon on October 8, 1870.

II
The War Correspondent

1
"Tell the exact truth"

The profession MacGahan entered in January 1871, the one he would himself shape to a considerable degree in the years to come, was undergoing fundamental and far-reaching changes in that watershed time of the Franco-Prussian War. The paramount change was simply a speeding up of communications, specifically through increased use of that device Samuel F. B. Morse had tested only a few weeks before MacGahan's birth—the telegraph—and an undersea cable. The distance between correspondents and editors was being radically narrowed by the telegrapher's key, and suddenly *time* became synonymous with *news*. The new capacity for speed created sharpened rivalry among daily newspapers and added to their mission a new element: now it was not only a matter of providing the news that editors divined their readers wanted, but to be the *first* to give it to them. A hundred years later, when almost instant global communication is routine—when a film story of famine in Ethiopia can be broadcast by satellite to a living room in Indiana in minutes—it is perhaps difficult to see what the hullabaloo was all about.

But in the last half of the last century, foreign correspondents and their newspapers exerted an unparalleled power over public thought. In an era before governments assiduously manipulated the media, before the birth of any news medium other than the printed word, "special," foreign, or war correspondents attained a position of influence unsurpassed before or since. Statesmen and politicians stood in awe of their power and openly courted their favor; generals of great armies complained that their reportage gave valuable information to the enemy; and the public was dazzled by their romantic, far-flung exploits, even if readers could not identify the correspondents by name in the anonymous columns of their papers.

A "special's" personal views were important too, since in those days, neither correspondents nor editors made an effort to sort opinion from news. Most often the dispatches by correspondents "at the front" were written in the first person—scarcely a viewpoint for straight reportage—and they therefore had a prominent role in the news they reported that gave them an aura of crusader, critic, and authority. The public believed a correspondent to be something of an oracle and, most certainly, the correspondents believed it and cultivated it.

In time of war, even in representing a neutral nation, these newspaper oracles were rarely neutral. Indeed, in many cases, they could not even be satisfied as noncombatants. George Wilkins Kendall of the New Orleans *Picayune*, America's first professional war correspondent, not only reported the battle of Chapultepec in Mexico in 1847, but fought in it and sustained a wound under General Winfield Scott's command.

Correspondents, in their self-appointed role of infallible counsel, came to be reviled by some. The great Victorian-era British field marshal, Sir Garnet Wolseley, called newspapermen "the curse of modern armies," and in support of this contention came no less a figure than Archibald Forbes of the London *Daily News*. After William Howard Russell, this glowering Scot with his chin-warmer pipe and tamo'-shanter was probably the ablest correspondent England ever produced. Wrote Forbes: "I entirely concur in Lord Wolseley's objections to the presence of journalistic persons with an army in the field against a civilized enemy. Were I a general, and had I an independent command in war offered me, I should accept it only on condition that I should have the charter to shoot every war correspondent found within fifty miles of my headquarters."

Forbes, whose career ran parallel to MacGahan's, had a simple explanation of the "paramount duty" of the war correspondent: ". . . to transmit important information without delay, to the abandonment or postponement of every other consideration."

It was Forbes who gave the tongue-in-cheek title "War Correspon-

dence as a Fine Art" to his reminiscence on news gathering in the
Franco-Prussian War, and while neither the correspondents nor their
dispatches ever really rose to such Olympian heights, Forbes made his
point. That short, bloody conflict did see a gathering of extraordinary
talent, new and old, and technique, mostly new, which made the time
pivotal in war reporting. Of the new talent, MacGahan and Forbes
made their debut, an editor named Smalley and a correspondent
named White established the new meaning of "news," and the war's
coverage included the services of the "father of war correspondents,"
William Howard Russell.

Russell's career is particularly instructive in understanding the craft
he served so distinctively and the changes in it he met, with mixed
success, in France in 1870.

Born in Dublin in 1820, Russell became associated with the *Times* of
London in 1841, beginning as a political reporter in the House of
Commons. In 1850 he wrote his first war dispatches from the battlefield of Idstedt in the Danish war over Schleswig-Holstein and two
years later wrote magnificently on the funeral of the Duke of Wellington. But it was in 1854, when the *Times* sent him as "Our Special Correspondent" in the troopship *Golden Fleece* to Gallipoli, thence to the
Crimean mainland, that this good-natured Irishman made his indelible
mark on journalistic history. John Thaddeus Delane, the *Times* editor,
issued Russell's orders, and these were simply to report on the "progress" of the British army in the war against Russia, and to "tell the
exact truth."

Russell followed his editor's instructions to a degree neither he nor
Delane had anticipated. His service in the Crimea went leagues beyond
his immortal description of the charges of the Light and Heavy Brigades at Balaclava ("They swept proudly past, glittering in the morning sun in all the pride and splendor of war. . . . The ground flies
beneath their horses' feet—gathering speed at every stride they dash
on towards that thin red streak topped with steel"). His maddeningly
precise "letters" on the decimation of the ranks of the British common
soldier on the Crimean uplands by disease, cold, neglect, misuse, and
the sheer incompetence of his officers chilled *Times* readers to their
bones. He wrote of cholera and filth, Dantesque scenes of misery and
pain in the Army hospital at Scutari which revolted his audience. He
wrote of vacillating governmental decision makers, of sophomoric
generalship, of waste and want and bungling. He issued the challenge
which inspired Florence Nightingale and her little band of nurses to
sail for the East. And Parliament, acting in behalf of an infuriated public, overthrew the Aberdeen ministry which was held responsible for

the mismanagement of the war. Later, the duke of Newcastle (secretary for war, who himself resigned because of the suffering of the Army before Sebastopol) told Russell: "It was you who turned out the government."

Indignation, if not outrage, characterized Russell's Crimean letters. He wrote: "I would, if I could, clothe skeletons with flesh, breathe life into the occupants of the charnel house, subvert the succession of the seasons, and restore the legions which have been lost; but I cannot tell lies to make things pleasant. Any statement I have made, I have chapter, and book, and verse, and witness for."

While his active career continued for another quarter century after the fall of Sebastopol in September 1855, Russell's work in the Crimea was never surpassed. He described the capture of Lucknow in the Sepoy Mutiny in India in 1857, wrote eyewitness (and highly controversial) dispatches from First Bull Run in the American Civil War, was present at Sadowa in the Austro-Prussian War of 1866, and even did some minor work on the aftermath of the Zulu War in South Africa in 1879. His was as illustrious a career as any newspaperman ever experienced, and he deserved the title "father of war correspondents"—an honor which he acknowledged with some misgivings and humor, calling himself "the miserable parent of a luckless tribe."

By the time he took his place with the Prussian army headquarters in 1870, Russell, whose name instantly merited respect and awe (for his personal influence as well as that of his great newspaper, facts quickly grasped by Bismarck), had become something of an anomaly. The momentous changes in the profession he "fathered" were taking place all about him, and he was not, in self-confessed truth, up to them. As early as 1851, after the telegraph from London to Paris was operative, Russell said of it, "The electric telegraph quite annihilates one's speculative and inductive facilities. What's the use of trying to find out where an expedition is going to, when, long before the results of one's investigations can reach England, not only the destination but the results of that expedition will be known from John O'Groat's to Land's End?" In all the Crimean campaign, which he witnessed from the first landings to the evacuation of British troops from the peninsula—fifteen months in all—Russell sent only one wire, a few words on the fall of Sebastopol.

Nine years after the Franco-Prussian War ended, Russell was in India on assignment for the *Times* when he wrote his faithful editor Delane, "I cannot describe to you the paralyzing effect of sitting down to write a letter after you have sent off the bones of it by lightning."

"Dear Old Rolling-Stone," as Delane affectionately called Russell,

William Howard Russell of the *Times* of London. (Bullard, *Famous War Correspondents*, 1914)

W. H. Russell, Esq., L.L.D., "Our Own Correspondent —The Man for the Times". (*Punch*, Oct. 8, 1881)

"Billy" Russell and Sir Garnet Wolseley: "An Assault of Arms Between General Sword and General Pen". (*Punch*, Feb. 28, 1880)

was forever a writer of "letters"—that dignified word which precisely described the long and methodical missives the old "specials" sent by post to their newspapers, a word which, as MacGahan began his career, was being replaced by one fraught with new meaning—"dispatch." And the man whose name became as synonymous with "dispatch" as Russell's with "letter" was a man whose career would interdict MacGahan's again and again in the years to come. This was the cantankerous Scotsman, Archibald Forbes.

2
"Telegraph freely"

Forbes, who said his "earliest bias toward the profession of arms came to me from listening to a lecture on the Crimean war which William Howard Russell delivered in the Music Hall of Edinburgh in the winter of '57," seems to have instinctively understood the business of a war correspondent when he, like MacGahan, had his baptism of fire in the war in France in 1870–71. In the early days of the war, as a roving correspondent for the *Morning Advertiser* (he joined the *Daily News* staff after the battle of Sedan), he served but a brief apprenticeship. He remembered a time at Bouillon when he kindled a fire in a dry river bed and was boiling a piece of meat for lunch. Inside a nearby hotel he could see among the diners Russell of the *Times* and Hilary Skinner of the *Daily News*. Forbes recalled, "I saw them mount, and envied them from the bottom of my heart, as, trim and spruce, they cantered away from the front of the Bouillon Inn. I should not have thought of accosting them; they were the elite of the profession; I was among the novices."

Forbes was afoot then, tramping with the soldiers, a change of clothes in his knapsack, dropping his stories into the field-post wagon and hoping some miracle would deliver them to England.

His apprenticeship ended when, as the only newspaperman present at the stubborn fight at Mezieres-les-Metz on October 7, 1870, Forbes had the wherewithal, now as a *Daily News* special with access to the telegraph, for the kind of journalism that quickly became as second nature to him as it would become alien to Russell. Forbes reached a point in the war when his dispatches often appeared thirty-six hours after the events they described—an astonishing record for that era. His ingenuity, and that of other great "novices" in the field, scored news beats time and again on the *Times* and its celebrated representative.

In later years, Forbes may have had Russell in mind when he wrote,

"In modern war correspondence the race is emphatically to the swift, the battle to the strong. The best organizer of means for expediting his news, he it is who is the most successful man; not your coiner of striking phrases, your piler up of corruscating adjectives."

Thus, while Russell wrote his letters and, figuratively at least, dropped them in the field-post wagon, Forbes and his young colleagues were rewriting the whole profession, bringing into clear focus the meaning of "news" in time of war and Matthew Arnold's definition of journalism as "literature in a hurry."

The telegraph was naturally the means. While Russell could not adjust to it, others could. In 1866, the New York *Herald* paid seven thousand dollars in gold for the transmission of a speech by the King of Prussia after the battle of Sadowa. In the war in France, to cite another example of the use of Samuel Morse's invention, the New York *Tribune* paid five thousand dollars for an account of the battle of Gravelotte, fought on April 18, 1870.

The main exponent of and inventor of the correspondents' order, "telegraph freely," and indeed the man who more than any other held responsibility for the revolution in war correspondence taking place in 1870, was a Boston lawyer-turned-journalist named George Washburn Smalley. He had joined the *Tribune* at the opening of the Civil War and had scored a terrific beat with his eyewitness description of the battle of Antietam in September 1862. In 1866, the *Tribune* management sent Smalley to London as "foreign commissioner" to establish a European office for the New York paper. Early in 1870, Smalley associated his London office with the *Daily News* and had already begun ordering his correspondents not to write "letters" but to telegraph important news to London—complete stories if possible, if not, summaries. The summary writers were to get back to the home office by any expeditious means and, in person, write their dispatches—the longer and more detailed, the better. "Mere fact," Smalley said, "never contents the public. It wants the full story."

Perhaps the best examples of the implementation of Smalley's policies were two experiences of Holt White, a British special in Smalley's employ and a man new and untried in the business of journalism. White was present at one of the opening battles of the Franco-Prussian War and dutifully wired, on Smalley's standing instructions, a column or so to England. It was the first battle story of any length ever sent by telegraph to London from the Continent. As Smalley put it, "English journalism had not yet regarded the telegraph as anything but a means of transmitting results." Upon receiving White's battle piece, Smalley rewrote it and, making use of the submarine cable, transmitted the story to the New York *Tribune*. Since he now had an alliance with the *Daily News*, he took a copy of White's dispatch to John R. Robinson, editor of the famous paper founded by Charles Dickens. Robinson, dubious of the association with the American newspaperman to begin with, looked at the story "with undisguised suspicion," Smalley recalled, and this conversation ensued:

"It could not have come by post."

"No."

"Well, then, how?"

"By wire."

"A dispatch of that length? It is unheard of."

Smalley shrugged. Robinson said, "Do you expect me to print this tomorrow in the 'Daily News'?"

"Print it or not as you choose," Smalley replied. "It will certainly appear in the 'Tribune'."

The *Daily News* did print it and thus became the first English newspaper to carry a telegraphic description of a battle.

At the battle of Sedan on September 1, once again Holt White was present. So too were the likes of William Howard Russell and Archibald Forbes. Russell, who had a ringside seat at Sedan, enjoyed his status throughout the war as a guest of the Prussian King Wilhelm and the crown prince. By being with the German army, the *Times* special also found himself as a guest, ironically, of one of the most diabolical press manipulators of his time, Count Otto von Bismarck.

On the brow of a hill Russell could see, in the clear morning sunlight that September 1, French soldiers on the ramparts, citizens scurrying through the streets, and the dark masses of the Prussian infantry, the sun glinting off their bayonets and helmet spikes. Russell could turn from his note taking (he scribbled, then tore the pages from his notebook and stuffed them in a dispatch pouch) to see Bismarck talking to the American observer, General Philip Sheridan, and the king occasionally pointing out something to von Moltke. Russell was deafened by the roar of musketry and artillery and saw the armies of the crown prince and the prince of Saxony draw a noose around the French until the battle broke up into fragments, the French retreating toward Sedan. As the day waned and the ridges of the Meuse hid the skirmishing, Russell wrote: "Such was the momentous battle of Sedan, the darkest spot in the checquered annals of the military glories and disasters of France. Neither Crecy, nor Agincourt, nor Pavia, nor St. Quentin, nor Blenheim, nor Waterloo was so calamitous, and modern history seeks in vain to find a parallel for the dire disaster."

Russell's long and detailed letter, marvelous in its intensity and splendor of style, was carried by a German courier. It never reached London.

Smalley's man Holt White also saw the Thursday battle, if in less comfortable and prestigious circumstances. In the saddle from 4 A.M. to the end of the fighting that evening, he happened to be near Sheridan when the French general Reille handed the letter of surrender to the Prussian king. White then sauntered across the battlefield and set out for London, intending to file a summary by telegraph en route. He had first to pass the lines of three armies: the Prussians, who refused him a permit; the French outposts north of Sedan; and the Belgians, who were making a show of guarding their frontier and preserving their neutrality.

White could never quite explain how he got through this gauntlet, but he boarded a train for Brussels, arriving there the day after the battle. He was refused access to the telegaph, took a train to Calais, missed one boat and took the next, missed the connecting train from Dover to London, but arrived in Smalley's office in Pall Mall on Saturday afternoon, ragged, disheveled and dirty, completely exhausted and famished. As White ate a huge meal in a Pall Mall café, Smalley pumped him—particularly eager to know if any other newspaperman had traveled with him. Only the scantiest information on Sedan had reached London, and Smalley knew what was locked inside White's head.

With his hurried meal finished and barely able to keep his eyes open, he was led to a desk in the *Tribune* bureau and told to write, just as if he were at a desk on a London daily. White's handwriting was execrable, but Smalley recopied each sheet, sending them one at a time by courier to the telegraph office.

By two o'clock in London on the Sunday morning after Sedan, Holt White, having worked eight hours straight, finished his clear and vivid story, six full columns in length. It appeared in the New York *Tribune* that very morning, September 4.

When William Howard Russell reached London on September 5, a copy of his lengthy narrative of the battle in his pouch, he discovered the story of Sedan to be history.

Russell's biographer wrote that the *Times's* special "had to recognize with the best grace he could how profoundly the telegraph had altered all the conditions of war correspondence since the Crimean War." Still, the biographer continued, "there was no one in print yet [on September 5] who had seen the whole battle upon the south side of the Meuse from the beginning of the Bavarian attack at Bezeilles, who had studied the battlefield, had visited Sedan, had beheld the Emperor a prisoner, and had watched the captive French army marching away."

Whatever the case for these unique ingredients, Russell had what editors call a "second-day lead"—meaning some new peg upon which to hang an old story.

William Howard Russell, whom his Prussian hosts called their *charmant franc-tireur anglais* ["charming English partisan"], was awarded the Iron Cross by the crown prince for his "service" in the war.

George Washburn Smalley and correspondents like Holt White received no medals. They won only the news beats of the war.

By the time MacGahan, the *Herald's* newest special correspondent, reached Bourbaki's exhausted army near Belfort, close to the Swiss border, early in January 1871, what remained of the French army had fallen on its knees to await the coup de grace.

It had all begun foolishly over the candidacy of Prince Leopold of Hohenzollern-Sigmaringen for the vacant throne of Spain and the calculated ploys of Bismarck to goad Louis-Napoléon to war. Backed by enormously skillful preparedness, planning, and transport, and by the genius of the Prussian general staff and its chief, von Moltke, the Prussians were able to deliver 380,000 men to the French frontier eighteen days after Napoléon III declared war on July 19, 1870.

On the French side confusion reigned from mobilization to Sedan, his best generalship reflecting the emperor's own blind and febrile national pride. In agony over the stone in his bladder, Louis joined his grandly named "Army of the Rhine" at Metz (his officers equipped with maps of Germany but none of France) on July 28 of "l'année Terrible." From the first battle, at Wörth on August 6, the French retreated in disarray. Indecisive fights at Vionville and Gravelotte followed. Bazaine was bottled up behind defenses at Metz.

Now, with the emperor held prisoner in Germany, the war really had no further business beyond the German investment of Paris. The siege was undertaken by von Moltke on September 19.

III
Baptism of Fire

1
"Montbeliard to Switzerland"

The general whose army MacGahan followed toward the end of 1871 was a dashing veteran campaigner of Greek ancestry named Charles-Denis-Sauter Bourbaki, age fifty-five, a hero of battles in Algeria, the Crimea, Mexico, and Italy. At the time of the war declaration against Prussia, Bourbaki commanded the Imperial Guard after having served as aide-de-camp to the emperor. Indicative of his martial ardor, at the outset at least, is the story that when he heard the Prussians had withdrawn their candidate to the throne of Spain and that the war had seemingly been averted, Bourbaki hurled his sword to the ground in rage.

The previous October, the old warrior Giuseppe Garibaldi, accompanied by his two sons, landed in Marseilles to offer services to the French Republic. The minister of war, Léon Gambetta, assigned Garibaldi and his volunteer force to a relatively obscure area in southeastern France where, in November, the Garibaldians surprised everyone by capturing a German garrison close to the enemy supply artery to Paris. This exploit gave Gambetta, ever the amateur strategist, one last idea: By delivering a blow to the rail lines on the Lorraine frontier, he could sever Prussian communications and raise the siege of Paris.

Bourbaki was the man sent in mid-December with an army of

100,000 to join Garibaldi's ragtag band of francs-tireurs near Dijon. From the start, the operation seemed destined for disaster. The troops, transported in cattle cars on an overtaxed rail line to the southeast, suffered appallingly in the arctic winter, and Bourbaki himself was hounded by increasing apprehension and a sense of impending doom. As the historian Alistair Horne has written, the dashing guardsman lived up to the tradition of bad generalship France exhibited throughout the war. Bourbaki had shown some skill and great courage in fighting Algerians in Africa and Mexicans in Mexico, but wars against European powers were long passed, and ardent memories of the Crimea, of Magenta and Solferino, were not helpful now to a man who, as an undying imperialist, cared nothing for Gambetta and the Republic and saw nothing to gain in continuing a war patently lost. Bourbaki's level of confidence, Horne says, was epitomized in his grumbling to a young officer who proposed a night operation: "I am twenty years too old. Generals should be your age."

After his starving and tattered army arrived in the Dijon vicinity, incompetent staff work caused great confusion in Bourbaki's planned liaison with Garibaldi's volunteers. Yet, after fierce fighting, his army forced a temporary evacuation of the city, and when news of this setback reached Versailles, the Prussian crown prince offered a prayer that Bourbaki might be held at bay. In the meantime, the French general began showing symptoms of what one writer has called "a melancholy caution."

Files of the New York *Herald* do not give a clue to MacGahan's first published work for the paper. He had not yet been tested and would serve some months on the staff before receiving that great encomium, a mention by name in James Gordon Bennett's editorial pages as "one of our special correspondents." Stories in the *Herald* of the suffering of Bourbaki's soldiers in their freezing bivouac, huddled around sputtering campfires smouldering of green wood—these may have been MacGahan's work. Even the accounts of the small battle at Villersexel in the Vosges Mountains near Montbeliard on January 9 might have been his, but there is nothing distinguished about these islets of prose in the *Herald*'s ocean of type.

We know from his own rather offhand testimony—in which he marked his assignment with Bourbaki as "from Montbeliard to Switzerland"—that MacGahan was present as Bourbaki's army fell back to the icy slopes of the Jura Mountains of the Swiss border, the force in total disarray. And after the fall of Paris on January 27, he

The Franco-Swiss frontier, site of MacGahan's debut as war correspondent. (Map by Kathleen Rogers)
INSET: Gen. Bourbaki. (Forbes, Henty, *Battles of the Nineteenth Century*, II, 1897)

Mr Bordeaux

It was not without a feeling of
of timidity that I went to see
and talk to Victor Hugo
There is such an atmosphere
of greatness hanging about the
grand old man, there is such a
something so impressive in the
thought that one was talking to the
author of Les Miserables and
Les Chatiments, to the man who
for twenty years had the courage
to denounce and lash in such
terrible words the Great
Infamy of the century while
the whole world truckled to
it whose conscience would
have fought almost alone the
Crime of December never
and allowed him for ____
years to compromise with
the ____ wrong while ____
and promotion prompted it
and whose words have after
a lapse of twenty years found
their fulfillment in the ruin
of France. "And that could
last" said he speaking of the
Coup d'Etat. "You tell me that
will last. No no no by
the blood that rushes through
our veins it will not last.
Ah if it did ____ it would
be that was no longer a
France on the earth, no longer
a ____ in Heaven."

Page from MacGahan's journal, March [1871], from Bordeaux after his meeting with Victor Hugo. (MacGahan Papers)

probably witnessed the wraith of that army crossing into neutral territory on February 2 and laying down its arms.

We know too that he left Bourbaki's pitiful force upon receiving
instructions from London, and proceeded to Lyons, then to Bordeaux,
seat of the newly elected Assembly, where he saw the new head of the
French government, Adolphe Thiers, conduct peace negotiations with
the Prussian conquerors, a treaty ratified on March 1.

Yet a final bloody chapter remained to be written between March 18
and May 28: the rise and fall of the Commune of Paris.

2
"Courage to denounce and lash"

In a letter written from Bordeaux early in March 1871, his first personal communication after joining the *Herald* staff, MacGahan wrote:
"I had supposed it took somebody like Russell of the *Times* to be a war
correspondent and did not think it worthwhile for an unknown person
like myself to try it. From what I have seen since I have been on it I am
satisfied that I could have got $500 a month and expenses if I had
offered myself at the beginning."

He wrote that he "had a little time and some ink not yet sold to the
Herald," and proceeded: "The war is about over now. . . . I have
written up Bourbaki's campaign from Montbeliard to Switzerland;
then came to Bordeaux by way of Lyons and here found four of our
men already. . . . Every man is expected to write from half to three
columns a day, but the *Herald* does not use one-tenth of what they get."

Because of that last doleful truth, and doubtlessly too because of his
junior status among *Herald* "specials," MacGahan's early dispatches are
difficult to locate in the files of his newspaper. He provides only a few
clues himself, saying that since he spoke French better than any of the
others he was put on "heavy interpreting." MacGahan comments that
the *Herald* had twenty correspondents in Europe, several of whom
spoke neither French nor German: "How they manage to get on I do
not understand."

Of his interview assignments, MacGahan especially cherished his
conversation in Bordeaux, toward the end of February, with Victor
Hugo, recently returned from exile on the island of Guernsey to which
he was committed for his opposition to the rule of Napoléon III, and
now a member of the new Assembly. The aging Hugo (he was sixty-
nine), France's venerated man of letters—poet, dramatist, novelist—
agreed to visit with the *Herald* correspondent, and MacGahan was received in a large, airy room on the first floor of Hugo's home. He noted

the simplicity of the furnishings—a table in the center of the room stacked with books (which, judging from their titles, MacGahan deduced belonged to Hugo's housekeeper), a clock on the mantlepiece, a few chairs scattered about.

Presently, Hugo entered and shook hands warmly with the *Herald* correspondent. Some fragments of MacGahan's impressions of this eminent Frenchman survive in the notes he took as they chatted: "Not a large man, but strong and hearty for his age, white haired and bearded, with a healthy complexion. Vigorous constitution. Temperate life. Deep blue eyes. . . . Asked for news."

MacGahan, in later recalling the brief meeting, paid special tribute to Hugo's opposition to the bloody coup which had brought Louis-Napoléon to power in 1851, "to the man who for twenty years had the courage to denounce and lash in such terrible words the Great Infamy of the century . . . whose conscience never once allowed him to compromise . . . who, speaking of the *coup d'état* said, 'You tell me that it will last. No, no, no, by the blood that rushes through our veins it will *not* last. Ah, if it will, it would be that France was no longer of the Earth and God no longer in Heaven!' "

In addition to interpreting and conducting an occasional interview, MacGahan had the duty of attending Assembly meetings and reporting, whether anything was occurring or not, to fill his daily wordage quota. Thus, on March 6, in the first dispatch that can definitely be attributed to him (his handwritten copy survives in family archives), he wrote from Bordeaux: "There is nothing of importance transacted in the Assembly today. They met as usual, quarreled a little less than could have been expected, and after ratifying a few elections, went home to dinner. . . ."

The *Herald* did not print news that there was no news, but by the time this soporific story had reached London, MacGahan was taking part in an event that ensured him page-one space in his newspaper and recognition of his name even by the *Herald's* lofty proprietor, James Gordon Bennett.

The seventy-day madness of the Paris Commune erupted in March 1871 as an insurrection against the national government of Adolphe Thiers, that gnomish aristocrat, aged seventy-three, who, his detractors said, was dedicated to the principle of "peace at any price." The tocsin which sounded in the streets of Paris called for bloody resistance to the royalist leanings of the Thiers government, against the humiliating Prussian peace protocols, and against the hated enemy occupation of the capital.

At Versailles on February 26, Thiers had concluded a crushing treaty with the conquerors which ceded all of the province of Alsace and most of Lorraine to the Germans, accepted an unprecedented war indemnity, and permitted Paris to be subjected to a triumphal march through, and "possession" of, the city, a ceremony which took place on March 1 when thirty thousand Prussian soldiers filed through the Arc de Triomphe and past the newly crowned Kaiser Wilhelm.

Toward the end of February, radical elements of the Paris National Guard made a significant gesture of defiance to the Versailles agreement. Descending on artillery parks throughout the city, guardsmen removed two hundred cannon, hauling them up to the "Red" (anti-Thiers radical) stronghold of Montmartre (the anxious mayor of which was a twenty-nine-year-old physician named Georges Clemenceau). This event marked the opening of the Commune, converting the ill-equipped and ill-led guard into the most powerful armed force in France.

Thiers quickly recognized the enormity of the threat and ordered the regular army to recover the guns. By March 18 some fifteen thousand soldiers and gendarmes, the main brigade of which fell under the command of General Lecomte, descended on Montmartre in a predawn raid, retaking the cannon without resistance.

At this crucial juncture, before Montmartre's citizenry awoke, Lecomte made a singular discovery, an example of almost supernatural stupidity: He had failed to bring with him the horse teams necessary to tow away the guns. And while Lecomte dithered and agonized with his staff over the situation, Montmartre was coming alive. Members of the sleeping guard were flung awake by the news of the government's sortie, and soon, accompanied by a surging canaille, submerged the army regulars, many of whom (green, inexperienced, and unenthusiastic to begin with) held their rifle butts in the air and joined the insurgents.

MacGahan, in Bordeaux most of the time between Bourbaki's internment and the treaty signing in Versailles, was ordered to Paris a few days after the Prussian's triumphal march into the city. He was to report the dissident activities of the National Guard, the capture of the cannon, and the anticipated resistance to the Government's recovery attempts.

Arriving at Montmartre at daybreak that Saturday, March 18, MacGahan saw the barricades being thrown up in the neighborhood

of the Place Pigalle, while the guard and accompanying mob, goaded to
fury by Red agitators, captured General Lecomte in a fierce scuffle and
placed him under arrest. Lecomte and another general, Clement
Thomas, were taken to a nearby garden and executed in a ragged rifle
volley despite the pleadings for mercy by Montmartre's mayor
Clemenceau.

With the failure of Lecomte's mission and the realization that only a
tiny percentage of the guard could be counted on as loyal to the government, Thiers withdrew to Versailles.

The Commune had begun.

3
"I was also a Communard"

MacGahan had achieved some acclaim among his fellow correspondents by being first on the scene at the opening of the Commune, but it
is likely that the dispatches appearing in the *Herald* on the subject are
the work of a more seasoned reporter, perhaps Dr. George Hosmer
himself. MacGahan wrote his daily stint and the "heavy interpreting"
assigned to him resulted in his acquaintance with many key figures of
the Commune: Felix Antoine Philibert Dupanloup, Roman Catholic
bishop of Orleans and member of the National Assembly; Jules Bergeret, commander of the Paris National Guard; Adolphe-Alphonse
Assi, the first chairman of the Commune; and Jaroslaw Dombrowski,
commandant of Paris and among the Commune's ablest and most
magnetic leaders.

His close friendship with Dombrowski, in fact, led MacGahan into
several close brushes with death and, almost as importantly, a series of
columns in the *Herald* which brought his name to the attention of
James Gordon Bennett.

A dapper, thirty-five-year-old Polish nobleman with a massive
forehead and penetrating blue eyes, Dombrowski was largely responsible for whatever fighting trim the Communard forces were to show
in resisting the efforts of the *Versaillais* army to quell the Paris revolt.
In command of the forces on the Parisian Right Bank of the Seine, he
became a symbol of selfless courage at the barricades and a figure of
legendry by the time he died on them.

In a hastily scrawled letter which survives in the MacGahan family
papers, the correspondent wrote in June 1871 of "riding with Dombrowski" and "taking a bullet through my hat which almost knocked
me from my horse." In the same account, written in a looping hand on
a thin sheet of notebook paper, MacGahan mentioned being "laid up

two days by a shell and besides almost shot as a Communist by the Versaillais." The incident was only slightly expanded in a column published in the *Herald* on May 19: "Today, while passing along under the ramparts with Gen. Dombrowski, a shell passed within a few inches of me, and the shock caused a severe pain in my back, and has disabled me, so that I have been unable to write today, and therefore am dictating my letter. This is the second time I have narrowly escaped death with Dombrowski."*

Four days later the *Herald* gave a MacGahan dispatch an impressive three columns on page three with a eye-catching stepladder heading of fourteen lines:

WITH DOMBROWSKI
A Herald Correspondent Making
the Rounds with the In-
surgent General.
Sleeping at Headquarters.
Dombrowski Reveals His Past
Career and Tells How He Is
to Suppress Versaillais.
His Opinion of Cluseret.**
Each House a Fortress and Garden.
Inveterate Hatred Against Thiers.
How Punishment is Served Out
at Headquarters.
The Troops of the Commune.

Dombrowski fell mortally wounded at the barricades on May 23, shot by Thiers's troops under the command of the Comte de Mac-Mahon who had entered Paris two days before at the head of an army of 130,000.

On the evening of Dombrowski's death, as incendiaries burned a

---

*This is the first *Herald* story that can definitely be attributed to MacGahan. While most of the "letters" by correspondents were written in the first person, the absence of bylines together with the proliferation of reporters covering the same events, makes the tracing of authorship a matter of deduction in most instances.

**Gustave Paul Cluseret was military commander of the Commune and Dombrowski's superior officer. It seems likely that MacGahan knew this unfortunate leader. Cluseret had fought with Garibaldi's volunteers in the American Civil War and later in the Fenian insurrection in Ireland. He was hopelessly unfit to organize the military operation of the defense of Paris and was eventually arrested and charged with treason, escaping execution only by the entry of the *Versaillais* troops into the city. He escaped from Paris and returned in 1884, where he served in the Chamber of Deputies.

path through Paris, Communard resistance began its inevitable collapse as *Versaillais* troops took possession of all of central Paris. Savage
reprisals—street bayonetings and executions—were practiced by both
government and Communard soldiery with the *Versaillais* troops merciless in their treatment of any suspected Red.

On May 24, with the resistance at last gasp, MacGahan and another
Herald correspondent, Alvan Southworth, walked from their lodgings
in the Maison Giroux Boulevard to dine with friends on the boulevard
Capucines, a short distance from the Tuileries Palace. Government
gendarmes suddenly accosted the two men and placed them and a
number of others under arrest, marching them rudely through the
streets to the Place Vendôme where the Versaillais had their military
headquarters under the command of General Felix Douay.

MacGahan managed to get word of his and his friends' ominous
predicament to the American minister to France, Elihu B. Washburne.
This gentleman, who had witnessed several pitiless executions and
outright murders on the streets, left an account of the incident:

> Late in the evening, MacGahan got word to me of what had
> befallen his party. I lost no time in going to their relief. I
> found them packed in with the multitude in a dark court
> lighted by a single lantern . . . . Both the ladies and gen-
> tlemen exhibited the utmost *sang froid*. MacGahan was
> without his hat, having been marched off so suddenly that
> he was not able to get it. I at once addressed myself to
> General Douay who, upon my statement, immediately or-
> dered the release of the whole party.

It was a serious and close brush for the *Herald* special and his friends,
for during these dying days of the Commune, the insurgents executed
more than sixty hostages (including the archbishop of Paris) and the
government troops killed a large number of suspected Reds, spies,
renegade guardsmen, and collaborators.

In the mopping-up operation between MacGahan's release and the
end of the Commune on May 28, the Marquis Gaston de Gallifet, cavalry hero of Sedan, established a policy of ferocity toward the Communards which included execution out-of-hand of any prisoner with
the slightest suspicious manner or possession (such as a watch, which
Gallifet felt indicated the owner was probably a Communard "official"). While the guard and the mob responded to such acts with equal
savagery, MacGahan could not avoid, he said, sympathy for the
"Communists." In his post-Commune personal correspondence, he

expressed pride that "the bitterest letters against the Thiers government are *mine*," and he was convinced, with the absolute certainty of a youthful novice at his craft that "the Communists never committed such outrages until at last driven to it."

> Who commenced shooting prisoners and then kept it up in spite of threats and remonstrances? These men [the Communards] had the lives of the people of Paris at their mercy. They might have blown Paris to the skies if they had wished. They held Darboy [archbishop of Paris] and hundreds of others in their power, and Thiers, knowing all this, kept shooting them as fast as he caught them, because he was right and they were the *canaille*.

Now, too, he set forth his personal journalistic credo:

> I have made up my mind to tell the truth as a journalist no matter how much it may seem against religion or order; and I will not excuse a Catholic for being a brute, like Gallifet, much less than a violent, uneducated infidel like Bergeret. I never allow my education or prejudice to blind my eyes to the truth, and I'll tell it if they shoot me for it.

MacGahan was working in an era of peculiarly personal journalism, but for a barely tested reporter, thrust into a story that might daunt any blooded veteran, he had developed (or discovered) a tendency, which would remain a hallmark of his work throughout his hectic career: to become vehemently partisan in his reportage. Although the *Herald* used but a fraction of the dispatches he wrote—and no doubt judiciously edited those—he took pride in bitterly denouncing the Thiers government and siding with the underdog Communards. In his letters home, at least, he could rationalize the atrocities of the anti-government forces and say, "I will venture of assert that History will one day prove that Thiers and his government have killed ten innocent people (who had nothing to do with the Commune) for every one killed by Raoul Rigault [the debauched and bloodthirsty Commune police chief and terrorist whom Minister Elihu Washburne termed "one of the most hideous figures in all history"]." And MacGahan stated sententiously, "Here is Thiers' system of putting down a revolution: Smith burns my house and for revenge, I kill Jones, Brown, Green, and their families. To tell the truth, however, it is in perfect consistence with French logic, and when this is said, all is said."

Of his personal attitude toward this baptism of fire in the profession of war correspondence, he wrote, "All I have to say is that I changed my politics at just 6:30 of the Sunday the *Versaillais* troops entered Paris. . . . Although you knew I was a French Republican, you did not know, perhaps, that I was also a Communard."

And he would write, in defense of this position: "The Commune is vanquished but its leaders are victorious for they have made Thiers repent his brutality. Frenchmen may at least learn that it is cheaper to convince the adversary than to crush him, and that 'Blessed are the merciful for they shall obtain mercy.' "

In a short time, MacGahan, tested now in the rigors of the "campaign," would find his proclivity for strenuous, emotional, partisan newspaper correspondence, tested to its limit.

IV
Varvara

1
"One of the ladies had very beautiful eyes."

In the MacGahan family papers can be found a delicious legend. It is that James Gordon Bennett, the eccentric owner of the New York *Herald*, originally intended sending Januarius MacGahan to Africa to locate Dr. David Livingstone and that only because of some obscure vagary was MacGahan prevented from going and Henry Morton Stanley selected for the assignment.

Here is a marvelous proposition, so fine one hesitates to consult the records which disprove it. But it was in October 1869, many months before MacGahan began his association with the *Herald*, that the immortal meeting between Bennett and Stanley took place in Paris, an interview which led to Stanley's circuitous journey to Zanzibar and on into the bush in search of the great Scotsman. Stanley arrived on the island off East Africa in January 1871, at just about the time MacGahan was joining Bourbaki's ill-fated army in the Vosges mountain region of France.

The first news of Stanley's search appeared in the *Herald* on September 29, 1871; the historic meeting with Livingstone occurred on November 3 at Ujiji on the shores of Lake Tanganyika. At about this time, MacGahan was in Yalta meeting the young Russian lady who would become his wife.

There *is* a cryptic line in a MacGahan notebook which states that after the fall of the Paris Commune, he went to the island of Jersey to see Bergeret "and wrote up his escape, then to London again to see about going to look up Livingstone." It appears that the unpredictable Bennett had a notion of sending his young special to Africa, perhaps to continue the Livingstone story that had won the *Herald* such public acclamation. It is also possible that Bennett sounded out MacGahan about undertaking another African expedition, to search for Sir Samuel Baker, the explorer employed in the Sudan by the Khedive Ismail, who was then making a dangerous voyage up the Nile and who had disappeared from human contact. It is significant that the man finally selected for this assignment was MacGahan's old friend from Commune days, Alvan Southworth, who arrived in Khartoum in January 1872, to begin his search for Baker.

But, while there was never a danger that the words "Dr. Livingstone, I presume?" might not have been uttered, it is also clear that the *Herald* proprietors thought highly of MacGahan's performance in France and rewarded him for it. In the period between the fall of 1871 and the spring of 1873, he was given a roving commission which took him to some of the great cities of Europe, and two important news assignments which any veteran correspondent would have considered plums.

With a salary advance in his pocket and letters of credit and introduction from Bennett, MacGahan traveled from London to his old stamping grounds in Brussels, Cologne, and Dresden; then to Lemberg, Vienna, Budapest, and down the Danube. His precise reporting duties are obscure. "Took train to Giurgevo for Budapest," he wrote in a fragment of a letter which survives from this period, "stayed in Bucharest six weeks, then traveled to Jassy and Odessa."

By the time he arrived in the Russian port on the Black Sea and presented his letters to Governor-General Kotzebue, it was November 1871, and he did have a definite assignment. He was to "observe" and write on Czar Alexander II and the Russian royal family and court, who were then in residence at Yalta on the Crimean coast, having escaped the harsh winter and arctic latitudes of that "Venice of the North" (also called the "Babylon of the Snows"), St. Petersburg.

All along the Crimean coast between Sebastopol and Yalta were scattered the handsome imperial villas and those of the Russian aristocracy, nestled between the cliffs and the sea, in natural seclusion. The czars maintained the Crimean peninsula as an unspoiled wilderness, and the only modes of transportation from the port of Sebastopol to the harbor at Yalta were horses and horse-drawn carriages. The climate was mild year-round, and on the southern peninsula, a veritable carpet of wildflowers lay in gorgeous profusion: wisteria, violets, lilacs, white acacias, and huge blood-red roses; fruit trees, shrubs, and vines forested the region, and Crimean grapes and wild strawberries were particular delicacies.

Yalta, as MacGahan described it, was "a quiet, dreamy, charming spot. Just the sort of place to while away a life and doze through the long sunshiney days like a lizard." Because of the terminal illness of the empress, there was no social life in the imperial suite and MacGahan's quarters became a favorite center for conversation, military news, and games of chess and euchre. The governor-general's aides hailed the American in their midst as saving them from endless hours of ennui as they awaited the day when they would escort the czar and his family on their return to St. Petersburg.

At one time, MacGahan happily counted among his frequent visitors "two princes, a baron, a count and the son of the Emperor's physician," all of them "jolly good fellows."

Among these acquaintances were many young Russian officers, insatiably curious about the recent war in France. Again and again, MacGahan would encounter and renew his friendship with these stalwarts in places like Khiva, Plevna, the Shipka Pass, San Stefano, and Constantinople.

One horseback excursion into the Yalta countryside that November altered his life. The "two princes," Dolgorouky and Troubetzkoi, and some Russian officer friends provided MacGahan "a spirited cavalry mount" and escorted him along a rocky path to the outskirts of the town to view a great waterfall—"a landmark of Crim Tartary," Mac-Gahan called it. On the path, MacGahan and his companions passed a carriage driven by an erect, aristocratic young man, in which rode two young Russian ladies. The occupants of the carriage were Varvara and Natalia Elaguine and the driver, Natalia's suitor, George Cherniaev, an adjutant in the office of Governor-General Kotzebue in Odessa. As the horsemen rode by, Varvara Elaguine later remembered, two of them lifted their military caps, a third his decidedly civilian one. All smiled and rode on. A few paces farther on, however, Prince Dolgorouky rode back to the carriage to announce proudly to its occupants that he "had hold of a live American" and was out showing him around.

Not more than an hour later the carriage caught up with the horsemen and the Elaguine sisters learned that the "live American" had fallen from his horse and sprained his ankle in a gallop down a rocky defile. Prince Dolgorouky and another officer were in the act of hoisting their embarrassed friend back in the saddle when the Elaguine ladies and their escort offered their carriage to transport the injured man back to Yalta. MacGahan politely declined and rode the eight miles back to Yalta, where he fainted as he was carried to his hotel room.

MacGahan had the good fortune to be in the midst of court physicians who fairly leapt at the chance to meet the American and see him recover from his painful injury, the bruising of some small bones of his foot near the heel. For nearly three weeks he was confined to his room, being permitted to walk cautiously on crutches. He was seldom alone as the crowd of young officers and imperial court idlers, bringing with them champagne, budding theories of battle strategy, and endless questions about the late war in France, made his rooms headquarters for card play and military chatter. He made good use of his time, too, in studying the Russian language and taking advantage of his friends to practice it for hours on end. As his wife would later put it, "He learned to understand them and became adept in the way of separating the plentiful wheat from the heap of chaff the Russian conversation is loaded with."

From his window, he gazed out at the peaceful countryside and noted in his journal, "Just across the little inlet on which the village is built is the palace, its towers and chimneys rising out of the brown woods that cover the mountainside and, dimly defined against the luminous sky, like a castle in the air—the Black Sea shimmering in the mellow musty sunshine."

Varvara Elaguine, seven years later, recalled that first chance encounter with the American, whom she called "the invalid": "At first I was interested, but as time advanced, I forgot about him," she wrote. "Being shortsighted, I did not see him well at our first meeting."

MacGahan, though, had seen her. In his notebook he recounted meeting the Elaguine sisters on the path outside Yalta and their kind offer of their carriage.

"One of the ladies had very beautiful eyes," he wrote.

2
"I wanted to live . . ."

Varvara Nicholavna Elaguine* ("Varia" to her family, "Barbara" in the inevitable Anglicization that followed her meeting MacGahan)

---

*Or, with less of the then-current French influence, Elagin.

was born in 1850 on her family's estate in Tula, district of Kashira, a
hundred miles south of Moscow, the youngest of the seven children of
Nicholas Elaguine. Nicholas had three hundred serfs on his Kashira
estate and some two hundred others on his wife's at Ryazan, a short
distance east of Tula. Eighteen servants cared for the Elaguine
children.

The family had roots in Italy during the time of the Crusades, and
the name is believed to have derived from the town of Elagon. Elagon
was the home of the first of the line, Vincent Elaguine, who
ventured to Russia at the end of the fifteenth century. The family
coat of arms depicted a visor below a five-pointed crown of nobility,
supposed to be indicative of military laurels the family had won in the
Crusades. Military glory clearly did have a role in the family history,
for one Gabriel Elaguine is recorded to have risen to *voevod*—
commander of an army, or military governor—during the time of Ivan
the Terrible. Another Elaguine, John, became a distinguished writer,
historian, and cabinet member in the court of Catherine the Great.

Barbara later wrote of her family, "Names of divers representatives
of the family occur in the annals of Russian history under different
Czars as holders of office or as prominent *boyars*, having certain
districts apportioned to them to rule over or 'to feed upon' in the crude
but candid parlance of the time."

With her mother's death in 1855 Barbara spent her youth under the
influence of two elderly men—her father Nicholas, and a tutor, Julien
Marcelin Dutac, whom she described as "a bourgeois from Lyons" and
who taught her to read and converse in French. (Later, though while
still in her teens, she learned German from a special governess.) After
the family dog—a big Newfoundland named "Boatsman"—her father's
library, a massive room filled with Russian and French classics and
histories, was the joy of Barbara's young life.

A staunch sympathizer with the movement to free the serfs, Nicholas Elaguine, in February 1861 read aloud to the gathering of peasants
on his estate the liberation proclamation of Czar Alexander II. Most of
his serfs chose to remain in his employ, and Nicholas distributed salaries, meager by necessity, to all.

Barbara attended a boarding school, studying at home under the
tutelage of her German governess. She was "brought into society" at
the age of sixteen in Tula, chaperoned by her older sister Natalia. The
Elaguine family made frequent visits to Yasnaya Poliana ("Bright
Meadow"), Count Leo Tolstoy's estate, only six miles southwest of
Tula, and Barbara in later years spoke of being "brought up under

Count Tolstoy's influence" and of having "had the privilege of meeting the originals for Count Vronsky and Anna Karenina." To Barbara, Tolstoy would forever be "the incomparable artist and investigator of the human heart."

Nicholas Elaguine, Barbara would later state, "belonged to that portion of the Russian nobility who scorned the very idea of holding court position," but this did not prevent his association and friendship with members of the imperial suite or in following them by taking his family to the Crimea during the pitiless Russian winter.

Barbara, at the time of her encounter with MacGahan, was a striking twenty-one-year-old with soft blonde hair, melancholy blue eyes, and a perfect oval face. She was a talented, budding writer, an able linguist (she and MacGahan spoke French while he perfected his Russian and she her English), and a strong-willed, practical young woman with a quick and active mind, interested in politics, literature, and history, and devoted to the idea of utter independence for herself. Yet, for all the strength of her character, her quickness to sense a slight, her almost haughty self-assurance, and the exactitude of her sense of her own destiny, there existed in Barbara Elaguine an attractive streak of tempering romanticism. She knew things as they were in fact; but she also dreamed of things as they could be and as they should be.

When she first met Januarius MacGahan on the path to the waterfall outside Yalta in November 1871, Barbara Elaguine's carriage companions—her sister Natalia and Natalia's suitor, George Cherniaev —were the focus of her unhappiness. Natalia, seventeen years her senior, was a widow left with some considerable wealth, and Barbara was not comfortable in the role of her demanding sister's traveling companion. In fact, she and Natalia were at loggerheads. Natalia, Barbara felt certain, "did not really have any character, was malicious by nature and spoiled badly." With the recent death of their father, Barbara found herself beholden to Natalia far more than was comfortable: Natalia held the purse strings, even to Barbara's savings from Nicholas Elaguine's modest estate, and Natalia was socially conscious, vain and proud of her court connections, and was hoping to purchase a summer home in Yalta to be near those in power who vacationed there. Moreover, Barbara was certain that Cherniaev's intentions toward Natalia were more focused on her wealth than on love. He had, she remembered disgustedly, tried to gain *her* favor, too, but turned to Natalia because "in getting me would forever tie himself to a girl without dowry."

Barbara was restless. "I wanted to live, to breathe with my whole

Varvara Elaguine, about 1871. (MacGahan Papers)

MacGahan, about 1872, favoring briefly the "Imperial" chinwhiskers made popular by Napoleon III. (MacGahan Papers)

Patrick Augustus, MacGahan's younger brother. (MacGahan Papers)

MacGahan letter to his brother, dated Feb. 28 [1873] from St. Petersburg. The correspondent was at this point still hoping for official permission to accompany the Russian expedition to Khiva. (MacGahan Papers) soul, but not the life and the air that satisfied our 'circle.' " She had hopes of finding a position as teacher, perhaps in a boarding school in St. Petersburg, but was fearful of the schism such a move would create with Natalia, who opposed any such demeaning work for a person of an Elaguine's social standing, especially when it meant a declaration of independence from her protective older sister. Natalia's sole ambition for Barbara was to see her marry well, thus fulfilling her life as Elaguine women always had.

Even the chance encounter with MacGahan, Barbara was certain, provided Natalia and her eager suitor the raw materials with which they could contrive to see Barbara married. Writing several years later of this, Barbara said of the American that, in her sister's eye, "he was a suitable partner and seemed to be sent from heaven to rescue Natalia from the scandal of my taking a position." But, she added, "Natalia was mistaken. I loved to talk to the American, I had fun with his originality, but I had not in my mind to marry him. I did not feel anything resembling love for him."

3
"I will be the one who will marry you . . ."

By the end of November, the Empress Maria Alexandrovna and her entourage were preparing to leave Yalta to return to St. Petersburg via Odessa, with Governor-General Kotzebue and his aides as escort. Barbara and her sister took passage on the *Mikhail*, which escorted the royal vessel, and on board Barbara discovered the American correspondent, "who jumped about on his crutches in a funny way," surrounded, as usual, by his friends from Kotzebue's staff. Barbara politely inquired about his injury and later in the evening saw MacGahan at the door of the *Mikhail* smoking room, glass and cigar in hand.

"Will you not have a glass of champagne?" he asked her.

She stared at him "reprovingly," as she later recalled the incident, and said, "Is it an American practice to speak to unknown women and offer them champagne?"

MacGahan replied that he did not consider her a stranger since she had offered her carriage to him outside Yalta. Barbara found him charming if perhaps a bit of a savage—as Americans were known to be —and they met on deck the next day and talked at length, MacGahan on his experiences in France in the late war, Barbara on her ambition to teach.

"I did not feel like saying goodbye to him," she later wrote. "I had such a good impression of him from our conversation on the deck."

She granted him permission to call upon her in St. Petersburg but had no genuine intention of seeing him again.

In Odessa, Barbara accompanied her sister and Cherniaev to the opera to see a performance of *Rigoletto*. There she spotted MacGahan in the company of Prince Dolgorouky, and in the two weeks that remained before their departure, the American came to visit again and again. "He sat for hours," she remembered, "sometimes without saying a word, drinking endless cups of tea with a kind of abstracted look at me. I was angry with him for staring at me as though I were a piece of furniture."

MacGahan had a knack for upsetting her, it seems. He once said to Natalia, "Is it not right, Madame, that we would make a pretty couple?" It was a remark that could have derived from Natalia's own coaching. Another time he told Barbara, "It would be better for you to get married than to be a governess," to which she responded icily, "Thank you for the idea, but I prefer to do as I please." MacGahan proposed a wager that Barbara "would be married before two years." She said he would be invited to the wedding if his prophecy came to pass. "That is understood," he ventured, "because I will be the one who will marry you!"

After the departure of the imperial entourage and the Elaguines for St. Petersburg, MacGahan spent another three weeks in Odessa awaiting assignment by the *Herald*. The telegram he received from London could not have pleased him more. He was to proceed to Moscow and St. Petersburg to write an occasional piece on Russian politics and to return to the Crimea in the spring to await the forthcoming visit of General William Tecumseh Sherman, who would be touring the Caucasus and the Russian capital. The general was to begin his nine-month tour in January in Spain and would travel by train, boat, and carriage through the Riviera, Italy, Turkey, Egypt, Russia, France, and England. He was traveling as a private citizen and asked for no formalities. Americans, as well as Europeans, were interested in the redoubtable "Cump" Sherman, America's highest-ranking army officer and her army commander—his celebrated "march to the sea" with sixty thousand men following the burning of Atlanta was but eight years past. And, MacGahan knew, Sherman was an Ohioan (born in Lancaster in 1820) and felt that they would "get on famously."

In St. Petersburg, meanwhile, the inevitable confrontation with Natalia took place as unhappily as Barbara had predicted. She made her intentions known that she would soon depart for St. Petersburg to seek a teaching position, that she could not be dissuaded, and that she intended to live her life by her own design.

On the last day of 1871, Barbara recalled, she was in effect "disinherited and banished from the family and wished a good journey." She had her own savings of some ten thousand rubles (about five thousand dollars), and the next day, the first day of 1872, she wrote, "I was hurrying away on a *troika* to the station of the Moscow-Kurskaia railroad. I was twenty-one years old."

By the end of the month she had taken a position giving lessons in French and Russian to young students at a *pension des demoiselles* in St. Petersburg owned by a Mrs. Risenkampf. Although over a hundred students, whose parents paid from 150 to 400 rubles a year for the instruction, were enrolled, the school struggled along in financial difficulty, principally because of the gambling debts of Mrs. Risenkampf's husband, a colonel in the Imperial Guard.

Barbara's position there thus became as perilous as it was uncomfortable, particularly at night as she shivered in her small room while her employer conserved on fuel.

But there were consolations. Barbara told a small lie to the school proprietor—that she was engaged and that her betrothed would come periodically to visit her—and she mailed a note to MacGahan at the American consulate in the city, letting him know her whereabouts "in case he still wanted to see his friend from Odessa."

"We did not have, of course, any formal betrothal," she wrote some years later, "but he told me openly in Odessa of his desire to marry me. . . . I did not love him, but I felt so gay in his presence, I did not want to lose his companionship."

Nor did she have long to wait to resume it. A few days after she posted her letter, Barbara received word of a visitor waiting to see her in her classroom. She thought at first it was her brother visiting from Kronstadt, but instead she was greeted warmly by the smiling American correspondent. They made arrangements to meet on Thursday evenings. She would help him with his Russian, he with her English. She would assist him in translating documents he needed to read, and they would be together—horseback riding on weekends and enjoying the pancakes at the Restaurant Auguste and each other's company.

MacGahan had fallen in love with her, of this she was certain, and when he formally proposed marriage to her soon after their reunion, she recalled, "I felt so much attachment to him that I consented, saying that I do not love him yet, but if he is willing to wait for a year more, I am pretty sure I would gladly marry him. He agreed gladly and sent me the next day a medallion and an engagement ring. . . . They are the only presents he ever gave to me, save for flowers."

Their relationship swung in a wide arc. At times, MacGahan exas-

perated her with his "advances"—so much so that on one occasion she
angrily returned his medallion and ring, only to take them back when
they next met. But he fascinated her with his "singularity and eccentricity" and his mental powers. "I never had seen anyone with a brain
the equal of his," she would write. In April, when he was to depart for
Sebastopol to join the Sherman party, MacGahan suggested they get
married before he left, but Barbara was hesitant. "I was silly enough to
refuse with the small pretext of my dower not being ready," she recalled regretfully.

She resigned her position with the Risenkampfs after MacGahan
left and lived on her savings while awaiting his return. During Sherman's stay in Russia, MacGahan managed to divide his time between
his *Herald* reportage on the tour and days with Barbara in St. Petersburg, days she remembered as "the happiest and most carefree of my
life." She was assessing MacGahan's true feelings toward her and had
concluded, "I knew I was dearer to him than anything else in the world
and I believed in him unlimitedly, forgave him everything, loved him
the way I never dreamt of loving someone."

Their marriage plans were interrupted in the late summer when the
Herald assigned MacGahan to Geneva to watch and report on the final
weeks of the great international arbitration conference there. He left
Barbara in August, and while she wrote him often and pleaded by telegram to have some news from him, he did not make contact with her
for two months.

Between June and September 1872, there occurred in Geneva a
novelty in international law, by far the most peculiar event ever to
strain relations between the United States and England, and something Gladstone's biographer John Morley described as "the greatest
of all arbitrations, the most notable victory in the nineteenth century
of the noble art of preventive diplomacy."

By popular usage, and because of the dominance in the discussion of
one particular Confederate cruiser, the Geneva conference had become known as the Alabama Claims Arbitration. It all had to do with
indemnification claims filed against England by the United States for
damages inflicted by Confederate raiders harbored in and sailing from
British ports during the Civil War.

MacGahan arrived at the city hall in Geneva, on the Promenade de la
Treille, toward the end of the four-month proceeding, but was able to
witness the finale. In September, the tribunal affirmed England's
responsibility in the claims by unanimous vote, and the total award to

the United States was a spectacular $15,500,000, settled forthwith by the Gladstone government.

Following the conference, MacGahan proceeded to Berlin, then to Cologne, where his younger brother Patrick Augustus ("Gus" to the family, "P.A." by his own preference), coming to Europe at Mac-Gahan's suggestion, had undertaken to study law.

4
"This fatal letter . . ."

In October, at last, Barbara received from MacGahan a long and impassioned letter, postmarked Paris. In it he admitted his unpardonably long silence and offered no excuses, he said, except the naked truth. He had met in Berlin a "sprightly" young American woman, touring Europe with her sister. He was dazzled by her, he confessed, and had acted as the sisters' guide, accompanying them to his familiar haunts on the Rhine and on to Paris. The letter ended with ardent assurances of his love for Barbara, beseeching her not to judge his "weakness" too cruelly nor to reproach him for "treachery" because, he said, there was a vast difference between his love for her and his feelings toward the American which were but "sensual." He avowed his passionate love for Barbara and said he dared not think of her as his future wife after this confession but asked for forgiveness and to "let some time pass after which we can meet again and be happy."

Barbara, years later, recalled the communication from Paris as "this fatal letter" and wrote: "It insulted me, my heart was ready to burst, but I repeated to myself that I was not going to cede my happiness without battle, that I would gather all my strength to regain the love of the man, away from whom my life had lost its sense to me."

Within a few days of MacGahan's letter, Barbara also had a message from Patrick MacGahan in Brussels, saying that he had accompanied Jan to Paris since his brother was ill and recovering very slowly. This news served to cement Barbara's resolution: She would go to Paris and join MacGahan there and nurse him through his illness.

She left St. Petersburg on October 18 for Berlin and took the express train to Paris. At the Hotel Helder she had a messenger take a note to MacGahan's room that she was awaiting him in the lobby. She had determined she would not mention the "fatal letter." ("I could be good actress in difficult situations," she wrote several years later.)

They were reunited, she said, "with sincere rejoicing," although she noted he appeared completely healthy. She asked about the long silence. MacGahan was ill-at-ease but retold the story contained in his letter.

"I do not remember just exactly the way he did it," Barbara recalled in 1878. "I was in a fog. One must have known him the way I know him now to understand that he was capable of making me believe whatever he wished. I loved him more than ever, but I told him only that I was not angry."

In the weeks that followed, MacGahan proudly showed her the Paris he had come to know so well and love so deeply. They spent their days at the Louvre, in long walks, in dining and talking, and their evenings in the solitude of the porch of the rooming house on rue St. Honoré in which Barbara boarded. MacGahan expressed over and over his love for her, his belief they would each be profoundly unhappy in separating forever, his hope she would remain with him in Paris until they could resolve their differences. Barbara in turn spoke of traveling on to Zurich, perhaps to undertake some kind of study at the university there. She reminded MacGahan that his affair with the American girl was proof "that his love for me was a temporary passion."

"I still had the hope of the possibility of happiness with the man I loved most on earth," she wrote. "I loved him more than ever and knew and felt that he loved and respected me."

To conserve her savings, Barbara decided she needed cheaper lodgings if she were to stay in Paris any longer and MacGahan proposed they rent an apartment together as husband and wife "to avoid gossip." Barbara, who said later, "I had so much confidence in him and myself," consented, and they moved to an apartment in the rue Caumartin.

"We had two bedrooms and a parlor," she wrote later, "where we met each evening for work. He wrote his telegrams quickly with pencil and I made a copy of his writings. Time passed imperceptibly."

But the matter of marriage loomed heavily over both of them, and Barbara was worried of meeting friends in Paris and having to explain their "situation." She told MacGahan, "You and I know we could not be reproached for anything, but the world does not."

She prepared to depart for Zurich, but the evening before she was to leave MacGahan reavowed his wish to marry her. Thus, toward the end of November, with MacGahan in Lyons on *Herald* business, she visited an official of the archbishopric of Paris on the possibility of being married in the church. She was advised that since both she and her fiancé were foreigners, they would need be married in either the Russian or American consulate. On November 23, from the parish of rue Madeleine, Barbara was issued a paper explaining that "Mlle. Elaguine, of Russian origin and professing the Greek [Orthodox] faith, wishes to marry an American Catholic," and asking that a "judgment" be made on their case. The paper was apparently to be presented to a consular official as part of the necessary marriage documentation.

But seeing the paper and now confronting the reality of marriage chilled MacGahan and again he faltered, telling Barbara that while he loved her deeply and would "fulfill" his promise to her, "all his soul" rebelled against the "chains" of marriage. He could not, however, face the single alternative Barbara had presented him—losing her.

"We were young," Barbara wrote poignantly in later years. "I was but twenty-two, he was twenty-eight."

When she wrote her favorite sister Marie (known as "Masha") in Moscow that MacGahan had recovered from his illness and that they had been married in a Catholic ceremony, she bent the truth only on the nature of the ceremony. In all likelihood it was a civil one, but it took place, according to the emphatic statement in the memoir Barbara wrote some years later, in Paris on January 22, 1873.

Their life together had a hectic five-and-a-half-year course to run. In that brief span, their times of unalloyed happiness would be measured by the day, the times of doubt and anguish by the week and month—measured precisely by MacGahan's absences from the woman who, without a doubt, he learned to love most desperately, as she learned to love him.

5
"My presence did not disturb him . . ."

In the first week of January 1873, MacGahan met with James Gordon Bennett in the publisher's suite at the Hotel de Grande Bretagne and on January 9 met, at Bennett's bidding, with the *Herald*'s European chief, Dr. George Hosmer. From these meetings, MacGahan learned he would be entrusted with a secret and potentially dangerous assignment: The Russian Army in central Asia had embarked on an expedition to the ancient citadel of Khiva. Because it was a purely military operation, no correspondents, least of all from the West, would be permitted to accompany the march. Bennett, however, wanted a *Herald* man on the spot, and MacGahan, with his knowledge of the Russians and familiarity with their language, received orders to begin preparations to leave Paris for St. Petersburg and, in the spring, to find a way to intersect the Russian column in Turkestan.

During the January 9 meeting with Hosmer, both men learned by telegram from London of the death of Louis-Napoléon, living in exile at Chislehurst. MacGahan took the train to Calais the next day, leaving Barbara with instructions to follow him as quickly as she could, and joined the *Herald*'s London correspondents in covering Napoléon III's funeral on the 15th.

Barbara arrived in London on the 24th and met MacGahan in the rooms he had taken at 19 Woburn Place at a modest thirty shillings a week. They were, MacGahan noted in his intermittent journal, "happy as clams," until Bennett recalled his correspondent to Paris for more strategy meetings on the forthcoming Khivan expedition.

MacGahan fell ill with a cold in the first weeks of February, and while Barbara served dutifully as his nursemaid, she made no secret of her anger at his willingness to spend so much time with the newspaper friends who came to their lodgings to visit. In particular she hated the visits of Alvan Southworth, MacGahan's close friend from the days of the Commune, who came as often as three times a day and, she recalled, "stayed sometimes for hours."

Her exasperation, in truth, was with her husband, not with his friends. "Alone, sometimes, it seemed to me that I pretty nearly hated him," she would write, "but he had just to take my hands, tell me a few insignificant words, look at me with his clever, deep, grey eyes, and my doubts were relieved."

He told her that her very presence with him helped make his work easier, his writing better. "I knew he was not mistaken," she said. "He used to put me near him and write like a machine one page after another, stopping just to kiss me and then again to continue to work. . . . My presence did not disturb him; on the contrary, it calmed him and disposed him to intellectual work."

On February 14, the two left Paris for St. Petersburg. In Vienna, MacGahan sent Barbara on alone while he traveled to Peszt in Hungary, and to Warsaw. On the 22nd he rejoined Barbara in St. Petersburg and took rooms for the two of them at the Hotel Angleterre.

The remainder of the month he would devote to attempting to procure official permission to accompany the Russian army on their expedition in Turkestan. On February 28 he wrote his brother in Brussels asking Patrick to send an enclosed letter to the Russian minister in Washington. ("It is not convenient to send it from St. Petersburg," MacGahan added). The letter, scarcely a model for objective journalists, asked, "Will you kindly obtain my permission to go to Khiva at my expense. You know my friendly sentiments and can be sure I would do nothing disagreeable to your Government. I would be very grateful."

To Patrick, he added: "I am to have an interview with the Grand

Duke Michael on Monday," to make the request to accompany the Khivan column.

But from all quarters, MacGahan and all other correspondents were refused the permission they sought. The commander of the Russian army in Turkestan, General Kauffman, strongly ruled against any such meddling, especially by the foreign press.

As Barbara later wrote, however, "MacGahan was not such a man as would stop once a decision was taken, and he prepared for the expedition, even buying an arsenal of arms and cartridges, and the necessary clothing."

In St. Petersburg, MacGahan had a close friend in the secretary of the American embassy, Eugene Schuyler, a thirty-three-year-old native of Ithaca, New York. While Schuyler was unable to help Mac-Gahan convince Russian authorities to grant permission to join General Kauffman's army, he was anxious to accompany MacGahan on the first leg of his journey into Turkestan.

"From the beginning," Barbara wrote, "I was against MacGahan's decision to go to Central Asia. At first I persuaded him to refuse to go, but he proved to me that to refuse Bennett's demand would end his work for the *Herald*. There would be nothing to live on, other newspapers in England knew him little, it would be hard to find work. How would we live, both of us, without money?"

She had been paying half their living expenses from her dwindling savings. Part of the reason for this, she later admitted forlornly, lay in her "foolish" Russian notion that spending her money "asserted my dignity." The very idea, she said, "of being supported by my husband threw me in a heat of indignation." But her savings were vital to their life in this early stage of their marriage. "He was spending all he earned," (which was then not much more than the five hundred dollars a month salary he received in France when first employed by the *Herald*), she said bleakly, "spending his time with the highest class, the richest people." Moreover, she added, "MacGahan idolized his mother and she lived on the only money this oldest son sent to her." He was also helping his brother, who came to Europe to study law, so he had not anything left from the small salary he was getting from Bennett.

She hated the idea that her husband's career, indeed his life, seemed at the whim and mercy of the *Herald* and its scandalous proprietor. "It seemed that MacGahan's marriage was a signal for James Gordon Bennett," she recorded later. "Bennett never let him dwell anywhere in peace for any length of time after that."

But of her husband, she admitted, "He dreamed constantly how he could distinguish himself and make a name as a correspondent."

Now, at the end of February 1873, while MacGahan saw his constant dream materializing before his eyes in the form of the Khivan expedition, Barbara's dreams were turned inward. "There was no doubt about my pregnancy," she later wrote in both exultation and sorrow. "M.G. was filled with joy, raved all the time about our girl that we expected in November."

She would rest and have her baby at her sister Masha's home in Moscow. Of her husband, she said, "I calmed myself by the idea that he would be among my native Russian army and that seemed to me to be a guarantee that he was out of danger."

V
MacGahan Asiaticus

1
"Where hell is going to break loose"

On April 15, 1873, the New York *Herald* carried a tiny notice in its foreign columns datelined St. Petersburg that stated in its entirety, "An American correspondent and the secretary of the U.S. legation in this city have left St. Petersburg for Khiva."

The correspondent was Januarius Aloysius MacGahan; the secretary, Eugene Schuyler; and Khiva, a place as remote from the ken of the ordinary American as the lost continent of Mu, or the moons of Jupiter.

James Gordon Bennett, Sr., the Banffshire Scotsman who launched the *Herald* in 1835, had spent prodigious sums of money for coverage of the American Civil War, and his son continued the tradition even in times when wars were scarce and those available small and invariably far-flung. Bennett, Jr., had Henry M. Stanley in Abyssinia in 1867–68 with the British expedition against King Theodore; devoted hundreds of column inches of *Herald* space to America's "Little War with the Heathen" in Chosen (Korea) in 1871; saw to it the Modoc War in California, the Carlist War in Spain, and the Ten Years War in Cuba, got extensive coverage; and at about the time of MacGahan's departure for the great void of central Asia, had again sent "Stanley Africanus" on assignment—this time to West Africa for the British campaign against the Ashanti tribesmen of the Gold Coast.

The elder Bennett, it was said, used to measure the success of his penny dreadful four-pager by the number of lumps and welts from canings and horsewhippings visited on him by outraged New Yorkers. The more he disgusted the solid citizenry with his titillating brew of crime, scandal, and society gossip, the more papers he sold. And the more money he earned, the more he funneled back into his newspaper. By 1840, the *Herald* was selling well over 50,000 copies a day, while the nine other "major" New York papers had a combined circulation of less than 37,000.

While the elder Bennett has some claim to the title of "the father of yellow journalism," the American Civil War gave the *Herald* a fair chance at legitimacy, and Bennett established a thoroughness of coverage (seldom fewer than forty correspondents in the field) and an editorial liveliness that was unsurpassed. As Bennett, Sr., proved, war also sold newspapers.

Nor was the message lost on his son. James Gordon Bennett, Jr., took over proprietorship of the paper in 1868 and guided it for more than fifty years (forty of them in self-exile in Paris) with the cool eye of the expert yachtsman, while his personal life wandered rudderless in a mounting sea of opprobrium. He was wholly without discipline his entire life, had few redeeming characteristics, many outrageous eccentricities, and money enough to indulge all his whims and fancies—many of them, but not all, connected with the *Herald*.

He was the Don Juan of the Gilded Age, a notorious profligate and scandalizer who, in 1876, would flee to Europe after a drunken stunt of urinating in the fireplace of his fiancée's home.

But Bennett, Jr., made at least two positive contributions to his time: He introduced polo to America, and he transformed his father's scandal sheet into one of the great newspapers of the world.

He knew talent and recruited it assiduously. Mark Twain wrote for the *Herald* from 1868 until his death, and Walt Whitman and Charles Nordhoff were also regular contributors. Among war correspondents, Bennett employed some of the best in the history of the craft: Henry M. Stanley, J. A. MacGahan, James Creelman, and Richard Harding Davis.

The closest he ever came to uttering a journalistic maxim was his statement, "A great editor is one who knows where hell is going to break loose next and how to get a reporter first on the scene."

Bennett probably saw in the Khivan expedition an opportunity to replay his astonishing success of sending Stanley to darkest Africa to find Livingstone. In his 1962 biography, *The Scandalous Mr. Bennett*, Richard O'Connor writes that Bennett ordered MacGahan's dispatches from central Asia "played up" in the *Herald* "because he sensed the 'American desire for information about distant and little-known regions' and was willing to spend thousands of dollars to satisfy it."

O'Connor also identifies a Bennett characteristic which had drastic potential for mischief in his dealings with the likes of Stanley and Januarius MacGahan. Bennett, his biographer states, "could not suppress less admirable traits in his character and be satisfied with the role of strategist and paymaster. Secretly he wanted to play the dashing correspondent himself; he bitterly envied the men who had the talent and determination of Stanley and MacGahan, but he knew himself well enough to realize that their achievements were beyond him. He could only sponsor them, and sulk in the shadows of their renown."

But for the present, Bennett appeared to be merely acting on his belief that a great editor knows where hell is going to break loose, and it was in this spirit that he sent MacGahan plunging southward into Turkestan, toward the Amu Darya River and the ancient walled citadel of Khiva.

2
"I am for Khiva"

The journey late in March 1873 from Moscow to Saratov, far eastern terminus of the Russian railway system, had its pleasant and instructive moments for the MacGahans and Eugene Schuyler. As the train pushed southeast from Moscow toward the Volga, MacGahan discovered a most unusual carriage passenger in the person of Prince Tchinghiz, lineal descendent of Tchinghiz (Genghis) Khan, and son of the last khan of the Bukeif Horde of the Khirghiz people of central Asia. With Barbara and Schuyler assisting in the translation, MacGahan found the prince's discourse on his country and people, in Russian, utterly fascinating.

MacGahan had planned his journey as meticulously as he could, given the urgency of Bennett's instructions, and had even taken the precaution of consulting with the celebrated eastern traveler Arminius Vambéry in Peszt, Hungary. Vambéry, renowned orientalist and writer, knew the difficulties and dangers of travel in Turkestan, had been among the handful of Europeans to penetrate to Khiva, Bokhara, and Samarkand, and related hair-raising tales of the terrible spectacles to be witnessed in the khanates. During his 1863 journey to Khiva,

Vambéry described seeing bounties paid for the heads of those slain in battle, the awful slave markets of the city, wholesale executions of prisoners, and how several old men, useless as slaves, were thrown to the ground and firmly held while the executioner gouged out their eyes and coolly wiped the dripping blade on the beards of the shrieking victims.

MacGahan also heard again and again the story of the two British officers, Captain Arthur Connolly and Colonel Charles Stoddard, sent to Turkestan on a diplomatic mission in 1843. Both were taken prisoner in Bokhara and flung into a pit to suffer as loathsome a torture as man ever devised. The pit was alive with reptiles and vermin, including a specially bred variety of sheep tick, huge and voracious, which burrowed under the flesh and produced hideous sores and raging fever. After some days of this inconceivable hell, Stoddard and Connolly were removed, watched their graves being dug, then were beheaded by the khan's executioner.

Vambéry's ululations, together with the certainty that correspondents would be prohibited from joining the Russian army marching on Khiva, permitted little room for optimism. Barbara was deeply concerned for her husband's welfare, and Schuyler, who had to leave MacGahan at Fort Perovsky to continue on to Tashkent, expressed his own fears for his American friend.

On March 15, as MacGahan's train rolled southward, the Russian army he was assigned to intercept departed Tashkent for its long march to Khiva. In command of the column of this Russian expedition, the sixth against Khiva since the time of Peter the Great, rode the Governor-General of Turkestan, Konstantin Petrovich Kaufmann, a formidable high-domed little peacock with a well-earned reputation for ruthlessness. Because of the ceremonious etiquette he demanded of his subordinates, Kaufmann had earned for himself the title *Yarim Padishah*—"Half King." He was vain, supremely confident, ambitious, but unshakably loyal to the czar. He would state haughtily, "The peace and tranquility of Russia's neighbors constitute the goals of my labors and of my wars. When I can secure peace, I terminate hostilities."

British soldier-adventurer Fred Burnaby, who visited Khiva after MacGahan's departure, met the Half King and described him in *A Ride to Khiva* as "a very weak as well as a very vain man. . . . He never rode through the streets without a bodyguard of 100 Cossacks, and maintains himself at a distance from the Russians also."

In 1867, at a time when Russia barely had a foothold in central Asia, Kaufmann, then forty-nine, had received the imperial ukase naming him governor-general of Turkestan. In a year's time, planning his campaigns from his headquarters in Tashkent, he shattered the forces of the Ameer of Bokhara and marched through the valley of Zeravshan to Samarkand, annexing that ancient city of Tamerlane's tomb and the entire valley in the name of the czar. Two khanates remained. Khokand was left momentarily alone (its ruler was unpopular, and a revolt would break out there in 1875), and attention turned toward Khiva, 150 miles south of the southern shore of the Aral Sea on the Amu Darya (Oxus) River, a clay-built fortress city in the trackless wilderness of the Turkoman tribes.

Of the turbulent, nomadic Turkomans, numbering some 110,000 in 20,000 *kibitkas* (round, felt tents) scattered across the harsh country between the Caspian Sea and the Amu Darya, MacGahan wrote, "Their marauding propensities furnished the principal pretext for the Russian invasion of Khiva." There were other pretexts as well: the attacks by Khivans on caravans of Russian merchants, and the detention of a number of Russians in the city, said to have been held as slaves, though they were released before the campaign began.

In simple truth, Russia had determined to control all of the trans-Caspian region, including the khanates and the territory of the Turkomans. To do so, a show of force was deemed necessary.

Kaufmann's expedition had been two years in the planning and involved the orchestrated movement of five separate Russian forces: one marching from the Caucasus; a second from Orenburg; a third from Kinderly Bay on the east coast of the Caspian; a fourth, commanded by the Grand Duke Nicholas, from Kazala on the Syr Darya (Jaxartes) River near the northeast coast of the Aral Sea; and a fifth— Kaufmann's—marching north from Tashkent. The Caucasus column suffered terribly in the desert and turned back; those from Orenburg and Kinderly Bay merged at Kungrad, between Khiva and the southern shore of the Aral, took the town without a shot being fired, then continued southward, arriving on the north of Khiva on June 9.

Kauffman's column, MacGahan's objective, had about 2,500 men including 600 Cossacks in 4 *sotnias* (roughly, "squadrons"), 4 pieces of horse artillery, 6 smaller cannon, half a battery of mountain howitzers, 6 mortars, 2 mitrailleuses (Gatling-type machine guns), 1 company of sappers and miners, and a train of 4,000 pack camels.

This then was the situation as MacGahan departed from his wife at Saratov on the Volga on March 27, 1873, and in the company of Eugene Schuyler traveled on to Orenburg, 350 miles east, then south toward the Aral and Kazala, jumping-off place for one of the greatest adventures in the history of war correspondence.

At Orenburg on April 2, MacGahan found time to write his St. Louis friend Walter Blakely a chilling letter. "I am for Khiva," he said, adding, "I feel sometimes as though I am never coming back and there is no telling what may happen. . . . So in case we should never meet again, Goodbye, old boy."

3

"Lost in the desert ocean"

Kazala, an outpost on the Syr Darya River just fifty miles east of the northern shore of the Aral, served as MacGahan's first stopover as he and Schuyler departed Orenburg on April 19. In Kazala, MacGahan hoped to find the column commanded by the Grand Duke Nicholas which would in turn intercept Kaufmann's force for the march against Khiva. By now Kaufmann had been notified of the American news-paperman's desire to join the march, but while amazed at the audacity of the request and doubtless curious to meet this bold foreigner, the governor-general had no intention of granting the request and indeed hoped to thwart MacGahan's ambition.

The journey to Kazala was accomplished by means of a peculiar con-traption called a *tarantass*, resembling an outsized baby carriage with a leather hood and curtain, which MacGahan wrote was "absolutely ne-cessary to protect you from the cutting blasts of the steppe," and large spoked wheels, which could be removed to convert the carriage into a sled. In the compartment of the tarantass was flung a straw mattress upon which the two Americans, wrapped in sheepskins, jackknifed their bodies at night to doze fitfully in the deadly cold—the thermome-ter at times dropping to thirty, even forty, below zero. The tarantass could be pulled by camel or horse, but the pitiable state of the animals available for hire was such that at times a dozen or more scrawny horses, yoked three or four abreast, were necessary to move it.

MacGahan described the four-day journey between Orenburg and Kazala:

> Those broad, level, snowy plains, over which the icy winds
> from northern Siberia come rushing down in furious blasts
> with an uninterrupted sweep of a thousand miles, drive the
> snow about in whirlwinds that go scudding over the plain
> like giant spectres; and short days of sunshine, when the
> glare of the snow dazzles and burns; and long cold nights
> passed in half-frozen, half-somnolent state, with the tired
> beasts trudging wearily forward . . .

James Gordon Bennett, Jr. (O'Connor, *The Scandalous Mr. Bennett*, 1962)

Gen. Kaufmann. (MacGahan, *Campaigning on the Oxus*, 1874)

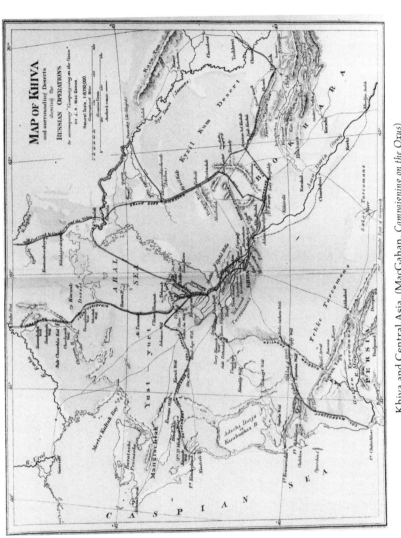

Khiva and Central Asia. (MacGahan, *Campaigning on the Oxus*)

MacGahan and Schuyler made periodic stops at post houses along the route, where for a few rubles they could warm themselves and find a samovar of boiling tea or coffee, a quantity of bread, and occasionally some cold meat.

The Syr Darya MacGahan described as "the most eccentric of rivers, as changeable as the moon . . . a very vagabond of a river, it thinks no more of changing its course, of picking up its bed and walking off eight or ten miles with it, than does one of the Khirghiz who inhabit its banks."

The Russian authorities at Kazala were unusually courteous. Colonel Kozyrev, in command of the fort, proved a genial and hospitable host who talked freely of the progress of the Khiva campaign, as did Admiral Sitnikov of the Aral fleet, a collection of side- and stern-wheel steamers and schooner-rigged barges, which MacGahan saw anchored at the mouth of the Syr.

The next leg of the journey, four more days' travel from Kazala to Perovsky, was a time of "intolerable anxiety and suspense" for MacGahan. He and Schuyler arrived at the fort—"the worst place I was ever in in my life," the correspondent termed it—in the middle of the night and located a five-by-eight-foot room in which to make their pallets. The whereabouts of the grand duke's force and that of General Kaufmann were uppermost in MacGahan's mind, and it was clear to him that if the Russian authorities had their way in delaying him, he would never reach Khiva in time for the battle—if, indeed, a battle were to be fought. "Kaufmann will be in Khiva before I get a foot in the desert," he jotted in his sometime journal.

He must, he determined, push on across the Kyzyl Kum, across the four hundred miles which lay between Perovsky and Khiva. "I had already spent so much of the New York *Herald*'s money," he wrote later, "that I felt morally obliged to push forward, and was very certain that anything less than my entry into Khiva would not be a satisfactory conclusion of my undertaking."

By now he had a solid grasp of the temperament of his employer in Paris.

A few steps remained to be taken. MacGahan's servant-guide, Ak-Mamatov, a Tartar from Orenburg who spoke Russian and all the central Asian dialects, was dispatched to find horses—and made certain to fail. Ak-Mamatov, who, MacGahan later wrote, "proved to be the most worthless, lazy, thieving, contrary old idiot I could possibly have found," simply did not want to cross the desert. A Kara-Kalpak guide named Mustruf was hired, along with a young Khirghiz named Tangerberkhen, to take care of the six horses MacGahan eventually did purchase at prices ranging from $30 to $50 each.

The horses were to carry MacGahan and his guides, the barley fodder for the animals, one hundred pounds of biscuit, sugar, tea, *tursuks* (hogskins) of water, leather buckets for drawing well water, ammunition, weapons, and implements. The decision to travel by horseback instead of by camel had not been taken lightly. Bactrian camels were the reliable beasts of burden and transportation in central Asia, and with them, MacGahan learned, he could take a tent, carpets, camp stool, table, clothing supply, and provisions necessary for a safe and relatively comfortable trek across the desert. "By taking horses," he wrote, "I should, I knew, be deprived of even the comforts of the nomads, but with horses I hoped to make the distance in just half the time and time was with me the great consideration."

Advice from Vambéry, Prince Tchinghiz, and others influenced MacGahan's choice of weaponry. He packed a double-barreled English hunting rifle, a double-barreled shotgun, an eighteen-shot Winchester rifle, three heavy revolvers, one muzzle-loading shotgun, plus assorted sabers and knives. Despite this rather ponderous arsenal, MacGahan insisted that: "Being a man of peace, I went but lightly armed . . . I only encumbered myself with these things in order to be able to discuss with becoming dignity questions relating to the rights of way and of property with inhabitants of the desert, whose opinions on these subjects are sometimes peculiar."

A fair translation of this rodomontade would be that he intended to protect himself against brigands on the road to Khiva.

After finally obtaining permission from district governor Colonel Rodionov to travel to Khiva, MacGahan, on the afternoon of April 30, bid farewell to Schuyler and took the ferryboat across the Syr—a mile wide at Fort Perovsky—to begin the first day of the journey into the Kyzyl Kum. He intended to follow the course of the Yani Darya, a small stream flowing out of the Syr southwesterly to springs at Irkibai, approximately in the middle of the great desert.

Just before debarking from Perovsky, MacGahan learned that Kaufmann had sent a courier to Kazala in response to the correspondent's letter, with a formal invitation, instructions, and even a map to be used in joining the march to Khiva. MacGahan saw through the ruse instantly, observing, "Had I waited for this answer . . . I should have only reached Khiva several days after its fall."

For seventeen days MacGahan was lost to the world, struggling across as trackless and forbidding a place as the jungles of the Matto

Grosso or the polar regions, and beyond the protective limits of the Russians or any westernized people. His life now lay in the hands of the Khirghiz tribes, about whom little was known and that little, ominous. The nomadic Khirghiz, living in their *auls* or villages of movable kibitkas, had a dire reputation. They were bluntly said to be killers and thieves, and it was said that among them murder was not a crime punishable by death but by the mere payment of a fine to the relatives of the victim.

MacGahan found the desert every bit as forbidding as Vambéry and others said it would be, but the Khirghiz people, he wrote, were "slandered by ignorant travelers, do-gooders, and others." The desert was as changeable as the river: His horseback party moved alternately through tangled brush, reeds, low dunes, bare plains, coarse grass and furze, thornbushes, and seamed and cracked flatlands parched by the sun. There were rolling ridges of sand for endless miles, then low mountains, such as those named Buken-Tau, about one thousand feet high and consisting of fragile sandstone which crumbled at the touch.

There were blasts of arctic winds and clouds of whirling dust, and all about him MacGahan felt the presence of death.

"These gentle hills are only sand, and the verdure which clothe them hide horrors as great as those covered by the roses that twine themselves over a sepulcher," he wrote. "Beneath the broad leaves lurk scorpions, tarantulas, immense lizards often five or six feet long, turtles and serpents, and the putrifying bodies of dead camels. Once lost in the desert ocean, without guide or water, you may wander for days, until you and your horse fall exhausted to die of thirst, with the noxious weed for bed, winding sheet and grave."

Even the flowers "shoot up, ripen, die, and rot, in the course of a few days," he noted woefully. "Their verdure consists of but a rank soft weed that breaks out into an eruptive kind of flower, which, dropping off at the slightest touch, emits a most offensive odor." The Kyzyl Kum he characterized as "this plain of charnel house vegetation," and said the single exception to the generally disgusting native flora was a pleasantly fragrant plant trampled under the horses' hooves and upon which the animals liked to graze. MacGahan believed it to be "absinthe," meaning, of course, wormwood, the aromatic herb which is combined with alcohol and other ingredients in making the liqueur absinthe.

Wildlife appeared at times in abundance and variety. Near any reedy pool of water he found ducks to shoot (to the amazement of the Khirghiz, arms-poor and familiar only with the ancient matchlocks of their tribe), golden pheasant, *saigak* (a goatlike variety of desert antelope), lizards, turtles, crows which darted down with raucous squawking, sheep, goats, and camels.

The Ohioan quickly developed an affinity for the Khirghiz people, finding them invariably hospitable, kind, honest, and insatiably curious. Like them he learned to live on milk and mutton, drinking tea stirred with a twig cut from a thornbush, nibbling a small lump of sugar. Occasionally there was a wild duck to roast and a piece of black bread or a Khirghiz dessert called *kishmash* made of raisins, dried apricot, and peaches. He joined the nomads in drinking *airan*, a frothy concoction of camel, sheep, and goat's milk combined and warmed over a fire to a sharp, acrid taste; also *koumiss*, the fermented mare's milk common even among the Gobi Desert tribesmen.

At night in the kibitka, before the fire fueled with the knobby, brittle wood from a low bush called *sax-aul*, MacGahan would delight his hosts by passing out cigars and in return would be treated to the songs of the nomads, accompanied by a small guitarlike instrument shaped like a pear halved lengthwise with a long neck and two gut strings. The singing, he had to admit, was unique: pitched in a shrill, high key and sung in an unnerving nasal whine.

"Why talk of civilizing such people?" he asked in the book he would later write of his Khivan adventure. "What is the good of discussing, as Mr. Vambéry does, the comparative merits of Russian and English civilization for them? The Khirghiz possess to a remarkable degree the qualities of honesty, virtue, and hospitality—virtues which our civilization seems to have a remarkable power of extinguishing among primitive people. I should be very sorry indeed ever to see these simple, happy people innoculated with our civilization and its attendant vices."

Between finding the hospitable Khirghiz auls, MacGahan and his party spent fitful nights on the desert, wrapped in their sheepskins against the biting wind and cold, waking with stiff and sore limbs, and in a drowsy stupor starting a fire for boiling tea and warming a piece of meat for breakfast. The four horsemen wandered helplessly lost at one point in the journey, nearly mad with thirst until finding a pool of tainted water which left their mouths and tongues coated with an evil slime.

At Irkibai, an outpost on the Yani Darya where MacGahan hoped to find word of the whereabouts of Kaufmann or the grand duke, he was welcomed by the Russian commandant who, having no answer on either question, did give MacGahan's party ten bushels of barley for the animals and amazingly entrusted to the American several pieces of mail for the grand duke.

Pushing on southeastward toward the Buken-Tau hills, the days and nights merged into one long, monotonous travail of inching through the desert under a boiling sun, falling exhausted into sheep-skins at night for a few hours of bone-chilling sleep, chewing bits of tasteless mutton and drinking tepid water from the hogskins.

On the morning of May 16, bone-weary and filthy, MacGahan and his guides rode into the camp of Khala-Ata in Bokharan territory.

The Kyzyl Kum now lay behind them.

4
"Americanetz!"

There was a spring of pure sweet water at Khala-Ata and the dis-heartening news that Kaufmann had marched out five days before for the Amu Darya. Colonel Weimarn, commandant of the post, prepared to depart with two companies of infantry, one hundred Cossacks, and two field pieces to join Kaufmann, and MacGahan politely asked to accompany him. Weimarn brusquely refused the request. MacGahan later heard the unpopular colonel referred to as *canaille d'Allemand* [German rabble] and himself said, "I could, in a perfectly cheerful frame of mind, have seen Colonel Weimarn in a considerably hotter place than Khala-Ata." (Weimarn, a few weeks later, was thrown from his horse in the gardens of Khiva and soon died of his injuries.)

Acting on the depressing news that by now Kaufmann camped on the Amu Darya and perhaps had already invested Khiva, MacGahan determined to strike out on his own, without official escort and leav-ing his baggage behind, "and probably with twenty-five Cossacks giv-ing me chase." It was, he knew, a perilous piece of business. He now rode in Turkoman territory, and it was only realistic to fear falling into the hands of these fierce people.

In the Khala-Ata area, the Turkomans fell under the leadership of a famous brigand named Sadyk who, with six hundred horsemen, had already begun snapping at Kaufmann's heels.

"Visions of a picture I had seen in Vambéry's book, with accompany-ing description, began to float in a shadowy way through my imagina-tion," MacGahan wrote, "of a Turkoman emptying human heads out of a sack on the grand square before the Khan's palace at Khi-va . . . of an untold number of human heads piled up in regular heaps like cannon balls. . . ."

But forcing these images aside, he and his three companions de-parted Khala-Ata before dawn on May 24, following Colonel Wei-marn's column unnoticed. After an hour, the American and his entourage angled off from the Khala-Ata contingent and, guided only by the polestar, rode through the darkness in the direction of the Amu Darya. Periodically, climbing a sand hummock, MacGahan could see a scouting party of Cossack horsemen. They were either trailing him or breaking trail for Weimarn's infantrymen and acting as mounted pickets searching for a possible Turkoman ambush.

About thirty miles out of Khala-Ata, MacGahan spotted a glitter of bayonets in the direction of the Amu Darya, and through his glass saw piled forage, baggage, and scurrying men pitching tents. He rode into the camp, Alti-Koudouk (called by the Russians, Fort St. George), and was hospitably welcomed by a Colonel Novomlinsky and his staff. The colonel, through some mysterious desert telegraph, had already heard of the American *molodyetz* (brave fellow) who had crossed the Kyzyl Kum. MacGahan stayed a day in the camp and then took his leave, certain at last that his destination was at hand. (He later learned that he had no sooner left Alti-Koudouk when a Cossack patrol arrived there with an order to disarm and arrest him. The story of the American war correspondent riding in pursuit of Kaufmann's army with a Cossack patrol on his trail created considerable excitement in Turkestan, and Eugene Schuyler heard of it in faraway Tashkent.)

Not many hours out of Alti-Koudouk on May 27, MacGahan and his companions came across the corpses of a number of Turkoman horses killed by Kaufmann's sharpshooters. Most of the animals were tailless since the Turkoman, in the service of the khan, used the tail as a certificate that the animal had fallen in battle and must be paid for. Whether fighting for or against the khan of Khiva, these deadly desert marauders exacted their price.

Dead horses, the ashes of campfires, the tracks of gun limbers, and the occasional wandering camel turned loose by the Russians gave ample evidence that Kaufmann's force was nearby. Then, riding upon a tall dune and looking down, MacGahan sighted the Amu Darya, the ancient river Oxus. "Broad and placid it lay," he wrote, "sweeping far away to the north and south, through the far stretching yellow sand, like a silver zone bordered with green, and sparkling in the morning sunlight like a river of diamonds." He added, "I forgot about Kaufmann, the Turkomans, the object of my expedition, everything, in the one delight of looking on its swiftly rushing waters."

A few hundred yards farther on MacGahan heard what sounded like a clap of thunder rolling up the valley of the Amu Darya toward him. Cannon fire! And from another dune near the riverbank, he spotted the Russian army scattered along the shore for half a mile, firing their twin six-pounders on a Khivan fort on the opposite side. This was a small preliminary battle, at Sheik-Arik, not twenty miles before the walls of Khiva.

He wrote:

> For my own part, I sat on my horse watching the progress
> of events with an interest all-absorbing. There was a sense
> of difficulties overcome and dangers passed, after my thirty
> days' chase, which, with the exciting scene before me, was
> well calculated to put a war correspondent into good humor.
> I could not help thinking how curiously fortune had favored
> me. If I had the selection of the moment when I should ar-
> rive at the army, I could not possibly have chosen a more
> favorable one than the present.

As MacGahan rode into the camp, a Russian officer approached him and called out, "*Vui kto?*" (Who are you?) "*Americanetz,*" MacGahan re-plied. With this the Russian smiled broadly: "You are the man who crossed the Kyzyl Kum alone are you? All right, come along and I will present you to the general."

The general turned out to be not yet Kaufmann but a genial General Golavatchov, whom MacGahan found sitting on a cannon smoking a cigarette. Golavatchov invited the American to breakfast, and the two ate cold boiled beef, chicken, and boxes of sardines, topped off with glasses of vodka, all from a cloth spread on the grassy bank of the Amu Darya as at a Sunday school picnic.

MacGahan presented a sorry spectacle in the midst of the immacu-lately groomed Golavatchov and his officers, "all spruce in their white coats and caps, and gold and silver buttons, as clean and starchy as though they were on parade in Isaac's Square, St. Petersburg." By con-trast, here stood a ragged, dirty beggar in a shaggy reddish beard and tatters, his coat worn through from having slung his rifle across it for hundreds of horse-jolting miles across the desert.

After breakfast, Golavatchov took MacGahan to an audience with the governor-general, object of the extraordinary journey now com-pleted. The correspondent wrote of this first meeting with Konstantin Kaufmann:

> I found him sitting in an open tent, wrapped up in a Bokha-
> ran *khalat*, or gown, taking tea and smoking a cigarette. A
> man between forty-five and fifty [Kaufmann was, in fact,
> fifty-five], bald, and rather small of stature for a Russian,
> blue eyes, moustache, no beard, and a pleasant, kindly ex-
> pression of countenance. He shook hands with me, asked

me to sit down, and then remarked that I appeared to be
something of a *molodyetz* and asked me, with a smile, if I
knew what that meant. . . . He showed no hesitation in
allowing me to accompany the army the rest of the way to
Khiva.

Eugene Schuyler, some years later, wrote of that summer of 1873:

I heard but once from MacGahan during the whole summer, as in some singular way, all our letters which were not
sent by private hands, failed to reach us. I frequently, however, heard of him, his ride across the desert being spoken
of everywhere in Central Asia as by far the most wonderful
thing that had ever been done there, as he went through a
country which was supposed to be hostile, knowing nothing of the roads or of the language.

After meeting with the Grand Duke Nicholas, to whom the correspondent turned over the letters entrusted to him by the post commandant at Irkibai, MacGahan found the tent Kaufmann had ordered
be set up for him, lay down on the rug inside, and, "for the first time in
two months," he said, "slept tranquilly."

VI
The Fall of Khiva

1
"The Khan's guests"

On the warm and bright morning of May 30, 1873, the army of General Konstantin Kaufmann began crossing the Amu Darya at Sheik-Arik on makeshift rafts. Simultaneously from the north, General Verevkin, at the head of the Orenburg detachment, was approaching Khiva combined with the column under Colonel Lamakin which had marched east from Kinderly Bay on the Caspian.

MacGahan crossed the Amu Darya on June 1 with Kaufmann and his staff, having spent the previous day with little to eat but a handful of *djugera* (millet) meal. The Uzbek traders on the west bank of the Amu Darya, however, had opened a bazaar in anticipation of the Russian arrival, and there lay food aplenty for anyone willing to pay the prices thrice normal and willing to haggle over the matter of the Russian paper money which the Khivans at first refused. The small silver coins, ten, fifteen, and twenty kopeks, were readily acceptable, and one could buy flour, chickens, sheep, wheatcakes, rice, sugar, tea, apricots, delicious white mulberries, and Bokharan honey. The Uzbek merchants were a sinister lot: lean, muscular men with long, straggly black beards, a furtive cast of countenance, and dressed in filthy once-white trousers, ugly brown khalats, tall and greasy sheepskin hats.

At this point in the march to Khiva, MacGahan found time to reflect on the manner of the campaign thus far. "To tell the truth," he wrote, "I was considerably surprised at the orderly proceedings of the Russians. I had expected that upon entering Khiva they would sack and burn the place, and slaughter the inhabitants." He pointed out that this was among the principal reasons cited for refusing permission to correspondents to accompany the expedition. "The Russian authorities, it was said, did not want those atrocities reported," he noted.

Kaufmann's system, MacGahan said, seemed generally humane and perhaps unique: Upon reaching the Amu Darya he had issued a proclamation assuring the Khivans that if they would stay quietly in their homes they would not be molested, their property and their women would be safe. Moreover, the Russian commander stated that his soldiers would pay for supplies, food, and forage—but warned that if he had to go into the countryside for these provisions he would take what he needed without reimbursement and his soldiers would burn every abandoned house found.

"I think the world in general has a very imperfect and exaggerated notion of the Russians, and especially of the Russian soldiery," MacGahan wrote at the opening of a long and continuing editorial campaign, at times shrilly unrealistic, in behalf of the Russian army. He continued:

> I remember what my idea of a Russian soldier was, not many years ago. A tall, giant-like fellow, with enormous bristling beard and moustache, fierce eyes, and a terrible aspect, with all the ferocious instincts of a savage, and nothing in common with civilized troops except discipline . . . the Russian soldier is very far indeed from being a savage. He is neither cruel nor bloodthirsty, as far as I have seen, but, on the contrary, rather kind and gentle, when not enraged; and I saw many soldiers do little acts of kindness to the Turkoman children, during the campaign against the Yomuds, which greatly struck me.

Kaufmann's force resumed the march on June 3, leaving Sheik-Arik behind and entering the renowned Khivan gardens on the left bank of the Amu Darya. The landscape changed instantaneously. From the burning sun and sand the army entered a region of lush greenery; fields of golden grain; rows of mulberry, apple, apricot, and cherry trees; and tall, old elms and stately poplars. Here, hidden at times in thick foliage, were farmhouses enclosed by heavy walls fifteen or twenty feet high—Uzbek farms, a very picture of blissful rural life, where the women glanced curiously toward the Russian line of march, then returned to their gardening, weaving, and spinning.

Clearly, however, the countryside was admirably suited for defensive warfare, had the Khivans any sense of warfare. There were bridges which should long ago have been destroyed, walls, hedges, ditches, and dense clumps of trees which would make cavalry action impractical; and every house with its insurmountable wall a potential fortress.

But the Khivans showed no inclination for resistance, and the Russian advance continued unopposed as the soldiers marched warily through fields of wheat, *djugera*, rice, and barley, and along a crude roadway lined with mulberry trees.

Now and again a sign of the enemy would appear for an instant—a horseman scurrying for cover—and Kaufmann threw out a skirmish line when the march had proceeded less than ten miles. Sporadic gunfire broke out as a scattering of Turkoman defenders in the employ of the khan crouched behind a cover of foliage to fire their "falconettes" (as the Russians called the heavy Khivan matchlocks, some of which were mounted on wheels, four or five lashed together and fired in the manner of a mitrailleuse).

As the column approached the fortress called Hazar-Asp, Kaufmann brought his artillery forward, anticipating the need to lay siege to the Khivan outpost. In the lull before the "storming" of the Hazar-Asp, MacGahan heard a voice in English hailing him: "I say, American, don't you want a drink of sherry?" A young officer brandishing a pocket flask rode up. "It is capital sherry; I got it from General Kaufmann himself!" The officer was Prince Eugene of Leuchtenberg, who, as MacGahan recalled him later, was a likable and unpretentious officer almost as popular with the troops as the Grand Duke Nicholas.

The storming of the Hazar-Asp, which all the Russian officers looked toward eagerly as a moment of possible glory in an otherwise uneventful campaign, proved unnecessary. As preparations were made to breech the outer wall of the fort with cannon, two couriers rode up and dismounted from lavishly caparisoned horses, doffing their brocaded hats and announcing that they represented the governor of Hazar-Asp, Said Emir Ul-Umar, an uncle of the khan of Khiva. The governor, his emissaries said, wished to surrender his fortress unconditionally.

Kaufmann accepted this announcement dubiously, and as the Russians marched into the Hazar-Asp, they did so slowly and methodically, prepared for ambuscade. The fortress, forty miles from Khiva, was a rectangular affair covering fully three acres and presenting a majestic appearance from outside its walls and battlements. The town inside the Hazar-Asp walls consisted of five thousand nervous inhabitants, a maze of crooked streets, and the ubiquitous collection of mud huts.

In the courtyard, Kaufmann received the chief dignitaries and *mullahs* (teachers or expounders of Islamic law), and after a long conference, the Russian general took possession of a half dozen outmoded brass cannon and a large quantity of gunpowder.

Thus the Hazar-Asp, a stronger fortress than the city of Khiva, surrendered without a shot being fired.

The Russians broke camp again on June 8 and resumed the march. A day later Kaufmann received a message from the khan of Khiva, humbly offering to surrender and throwing himself on the governor-general's mercy.

Now, with Kaufmann still ten miles distant, the Orenburg and Kinderly Bay expeditions, under the command of Generals Verevkin and Lamakin, arrived before the walls of Khiva on the north. "It is not the least remarkable part of this remarkable campaign," the correspondent wrote in a dispatch to the *Herald*, "that four different columns, starting from as many different points of the compass, more than a thousand miles apart, should, nevertheless, have arrived before Khiva within a day of each other."

(The meticulous timing included arrival of the flotilla under Captain Sitnikov, admiral of the Aral Fleet, sent from Kazala down the Aral to the mouth of the Amu Darya, from which point he ascended the river as far as practicable to "cooperate" with the land forces if his services were needed.)

For MacGahan, thirsting for action, it might have been a better plan had he joined the Orenburg detachment instead of Kaufmann's, for the former was to receive the brunt of what little resistance the Khivans had prepared.

The combined Orenburg and Kinderly Bay column had advanced from the north to within a short distance of the gates of Khiva when there came into the Russian camp deputations of elders and Khivan functionaries promising submission and begging for mercy. Then, on the morning of May 28, the Russians discovered a sizable number of Turkomans assembled in a plain of tall grass and reeds, and the horsemen attacked Verevkin's force on four sides. Before this battle ended in a rout of the ill-armed Turkomans, one Russian officer and eight soldiers were killed, another ten men wounded. Enemy losses were never ascertained, but the number was great and the resistance thereafter greatly enfeebled.

On June 4, Verevkin received an obsequious message from the khan in which the Russian commander was asked, in a masterpiece of naïveté, to "be kind enough to become the Khan's guests in Khiva." The Russian column reached the city's walls on the 9th. Verevkin, during the march, suffered a terrible matchlock ball wound over his eye and relinquished his command to Colonel Saranchov.

Meantime, Kaufmann's army also reached the walls of the city, and hundreds of people flocked to him with peace offerings and rumors that the khan had fled. This rumor was soon substantiated when an official delegation from the city came to surrender Khiva to the Russian conqueror.

Now with Kaufmann about to make a peaceful entry on the south, the northern command under Colonel Saranchov was greatly agitated at this situation. Saranchov was a fiery-tempered man surrounded by "spirited" officers hungry for glory and some reward for their laborious march. Among these impatient officers was a Lieutenant Colonel Skobelev—whom MacGahan referred to at first as "Skobeloff"—who had admirably carried out a number of dangerous scouting missions on the march. This man would loom as an important figure in MacGahan's future career.

Saranchov, although subordinate to Kaufmann, remained for the moment in command of the Orenburg column and decided to make the most of this temporary situation and take Khiva "by storm."

Here now occurred a very peculiar incident. After a short bombardment and the battering down of the Hazavat Gate, Colonel Skobelev, at the head of nearly one thousand men, rushed to the assault under a lively fire from within the city. Skobelev's force streamed through the gate, fanned out, and suffering but minor wounds, stopped only upon reaching the palace of the khan. In less than five minutes within the city, Skobelev's attackers heard band music from the southern side as Kaufmann's army marched in with flying colors to the strains of *Bodji Tsaria Haranyie*, a national Russian air. Upon orders from Saranchov, Skobelev and his men beat a quick retreat through the Hazavat Gate, thereby allowing the governor-general the appropriate honor of a triumphal conqueror's entrance.

From a distance, Khiva seemed to MacGahan apt to live up to its reputation as a fabled, faerie kingdom of surpassing splendor and riches. Despite the ugly, heavy mud wall that surrounded it, there seemed something majestic in the tall battlements, towers and buttresses that gave Khiva a misleading appearance of strength and determination to resist any intruder. Too, over the tops of old elms, the American could see stately minarets, the domes of mosques, and one immense round tower of ancient beauty, the dome of which coruscated as the sun glinted off bits of metal and porcelain.

Once inside, the faerie land vision forlornly evaporated. Khiva, while having a certain mysterious charm, was merely ugly: a place of mud houses and rickety sheds, cemeteries, narrow winding streets, black mud walls. The round tower at least had an aspect of antiquity. It was enormous, fully 30 feet in diameter and 125 feet high, its surface covered with cunningly burnt and cemented tiles—blue, green and lavender—placed in mystical designs. The tiles were etched with verses from the Koran, and from the top of the dome MacGahan heard the shrill, piping voice of the *muezzin* calling the people to prayer.

2
"Zuleika"

More prepossessing than any structure in the city was the palace of the khan, Said Muhamed-Rahim Bogadur, ruler over this great stronghold of Islam, who had now fled ignominiously from his domain. The palace was guarded by two old brass cannon, and MacGahan found it a complex of dark, narrow corridors, a labyrinth of rooms dimly lighted from a skylight hole in the roof, the whole surrounded by a twenty-foot-high wall and shaded by a dense copse of elms. On the north side of the palace rose the square mud tower of the harem; on the south, the grand hall of state and the khan's audience chamber.

After a nap, a meal of wheatcakes and tea, and a visit with the aides of General Verevkin of the northern contingent, MacGahan set out, with Kaufmann's permission, to explore the khan's palace. Most of the rooms showed the marks of hasty abandonment, a motley collection of impedimenta left behind: bedclothes, rugs and cushions, cooking utensils, items of clothing strewn about. The khan's so-called "treasure room" yielded more interest. It was a low-vaulted room with ceiling and walls covered with crudely painted flowers and vines. The khan's throne was a large, square, leather-upholstered chair; his treasure consisted of a few iron chests with heavy locks, one of which was found to contain about thirty pounds of Khivan silver. A saddle, bridle, and harness were found too, studded with strange stones, but MacGahan noted that gemstones of the region were invariably blemished, pale in color, and of little value by Western standards.

Among weapons in the khan's treasure room were splendid old

Khiva and the Hazar-Asp Gate. (MacGahan, *Campaigning on the Oxus*)

View of the Citadel. (MacGahan, *Campaigning on the Oxus*)

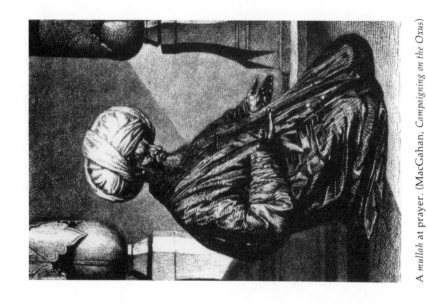

A *mullah* at prayer. (MacGahan, *Campaigning on the Oxus*)

Muhamed Rahim Bogadur, Khan of Khiva. (MacGahan, *Campaigning on the Oxus*)

matchlocks, a beautiful English hunting rifle, Colt revolvers, English sabers, curved Khorassan blades, Persian scimitars with scabbards inlaid with emeralds and turquoise, and suits of armor decorated with raw gold. The khan's library of some three hundred volumes, many written by hand and bound in leather or parchment, included "a history of the world and of Khiva from the beginning of time," according to MacGahan. All these books were confiscated by Kaufmann for the imperial library at St. Petersburg.

The khan's harem held a particular fascination for every officer of Kaufmann's army and most certainly for the American correspondent. Two Russian sentinels had been posted at its entrance, and as MacGahan went to examine it, about 150 women, all crying and wringing their hands, were being escorted from it. The members of this pitiful assemblage ranged from near infants to toothless crones, but some MacGahan considered "pretty" or "sweet." One in particular caught his eye: a calm young woman of about eighteen, with clear, rosy complexion, a broad low forehead, round face, black hair, and large dark eyes. MacGahan thought her "noble in appearance" and probably "sultana" of the harem. She spoke authoritatively to her sisters, calming them, and MacGahan later remembered, "The dark eyes of this woman haunted me after she had disappeared. I could not forget her calm, majestic figure, as she stood in the midst of the enemies of her race and religion, with weeping women and children relying upon her for protection."

MacGahan's gentlemanly version of the "comeliness" of Khivan women was at odds with the facts, at least according to another Western visitor, the British soldier-adventurer Fred Burnaby who traveled to Khiva toward the end of 1875, well over two years after MacGahan had departed there. Burnaby, a six-foot four-inch barrel-chested giant, an officer of the Royal Horse Guards, pioneer balloonist and traveler, conferred with both MacGahan and Eugene Schuyler in St. Petersburg on the best route from Orenburg to the Amu Darya. In his popular book, *A Ride to Khiva*, he wrote of Khivan women in the spirit of examining his favorite steed:

> As a rule, there could not be much said for the beauty of their appearance; indeed, making every allowance for Mr. MacGahan's advocacy of the fair sex of Tartary, I cannot help thinking that the energetic correspondent is either extremely susceptible, or else very easily pleased, as a moon-faced, red-cheeked girl, the acme of perfection from the

Kirghiz point of view, does not quite answer to my ideas of beauty. Most of the women have good eyes and teeth, but the breadth of the face and size of the mouth take off from these advantages.

MacGahan may have been excessively kind in his description of Khivan women—and his history proved the accuracy of Burnaby's guess about his susceptibility—but the "sultana" clearly intrigued him, and he determined to learn more about her for the *Herald* readers, if for nothing else. He knew that she and a small retinue of the khan's harem were permitted to stay within the palace, and despite the fact that he could not expect expressed permission from the Russians to do so, he set out at midnight to explore the palace on his own authority, his only illumination that from a single candle.

The few Russian sentinels easily dodged, MacGahan roamed the palace, crossing large courtyards, passing dimly lighted rooms, testing padlocked doors, climbing stone stairways, and walking stealthily down dark corridors, revolver in one hand, candle in the other.

In one small room with a wet and muddy floor, MacGahan struck a match for extra light and found himself standing on the lip of a well. He dropped a piece of mud into it and estimated its depth at fifty feet.

Nursing his candle end, he came upon another room and saw a strange pile of black earth in one corner. Kneeling at it, he moved the candle closer and picked up a handful of the dirt and sniffed it. Gunpowder! Enough, he wrote anxiously later, to have blown the entire palace to atoms.

The sound of chattering and giggling brought him to another large door, bolted from within. He rapped lightly on it and heard a soft, girlish voice respond questioningly in the Tartar language. *"Aman"* (Peace be with you), MacGahan whispered, using the only expression he knew would be recognized. He was ushered inside and saw eight women, including the sultana, she holding a stone lamp with a flickering flame. He was in the grand court of the harem, a room 150 feet long by 40 wide with a series of high balconies on one side, some large kibitkas on circular platforms of brick arranged on the earthen floor. Of the eight women, three were "repulsive hags, three moderately good looking, middle-aged or young women"; one he described as "very pretty." The sultana, whom the Ohioan called "the hostess," wore a short jacket of green silk, embroidered with gold, a long chemise of red silk fastened at the throat with an emerald and slightly open at the bodice, wide trousers and embroidered boots. She wore no head covering as did the others but had her hair wound in heavy glossy braids. Her jewelry consisted of enormous pendant earrings of pearl and turquoise and heavy bracelets traced with gold.

After MacGahan made the appropriate salaam and was served sweetmeats, apricots, and bread (he was not offered hashish, he said, although the narcotic was in evidence in the harem), he washed his hands in water poured in a bowl from an elegant copper ewer and began trying to converse with "the hostess."

"Fatima?" he asked, pointing to the sultana. She shook her head, then indicated that one of the old women nearby had that name. Pointing to herself, the sultana said softly, "Zuleika." Following this, MacGahan utilized his rudimentary knowledge of the Tartar language to let it be known he was not Russian. After a time he was conducted to the door. Zuleika kissed his hands, and he disappeared down the dark corridor.

Later the same morning, MacGahan learned that all the women in the khan's palace had escaped their captors and had taken refuge with the khan's uncle elsewhere in the city. Kaufmann made no attempt to recapture them.

A few days after entering Khiva, Kaufmann wrote a letter to the khan informing the ruler that if he would surrender he would be treated with all the honors due him; that if he declined to appear, Kaufmann would appoint a new khan to take his place in hearing the terms of capitulation.

As a result of this ultimatum, on June 14 the khan returned to the city, accompanied by a brilliantly dressed entourage of servants, including slaves—one carrying a pitcher of liquid, another a water pipe—on each side of his sumptuously ornamented horse. Kaufmann greeted the Khivan ruler at his tent under the elms of the Russian camp; the khan dismounted, came forward and took off his tall sheepskin hat, bowing low.

Muhamed-Rahim, MacGahan wrote, was a man of about thirty years, with fine, large, slightly oblique eyes, an aquiline nose, thin black beard and moustache and a heavy, sensual mouth. He was a huge and powerful man, fully six feet three inches and weighing between 250 and 300 pounds, dressed in a long brocaded khalat of bright blue silk. With the khan sitting next to the diminutive Kaufmann, MacGahan thought "there never was a more striking example of the superiority of mind over brute force, of modern over ancient modes of warfare." In ages past, the correspondent said, the khan, "with his giant form and stalwart arms might have been a sort of demi-god; he could have put to flight a regiment single-handed, he could probably have been a very Coeur de Lion," but now "the meanest soldier in Kaufmann's army was more than a match for him."

Following a lengthy conference with Kaufmann, the khan promised to preserve order and maintain respect for the "Great White Tsar." Then, after Kaufmann instructed him to form a divan or council of state to discuss raising money for a war indemnity and to free all slaves in the khanate, Muhamed-Rahim was permitted to depart with his retinue.

A few days after the khan's surrender, MacGahan accompanied Lieutenant Serovatsky, astronomer with the Tashkent column, to the palace for an audience with the erstwhile ruler. The khan devoted much time questioning Serovatsky about his instruments—telescope, quadrant, chronometer—but upon completing this inspection, permitted the correspondent an interview.

MacGahan found the khan an affable and courteous host with a quality of self-possession appropriate to his station. Fred Burnaby, who interviewed Muhamed-Rahim two years later, agreed. The khan was not a strong leader, but one who lived simply and indulged himself mainly in keeping a fine harem and stable, leaving affairs of state to his advisers while he wrote endless poetic compositions.

Muhamed-Rahim had never heard of America and expressed amazement that MacGahan was not an Englishman. The correspondent drew a crude map showing the relative positions of France, Germany, England, Russia, India, Khiva, and America, but the information that most fascinated the royal host was learning that the khan of America ruled for only four years and was then replaced by another khan.

The interview went well enough, interrupted every five minutes by a servant bringing into the audience chamber a water pipe from which the khan would take a single puff, then hand it back, the tobacco to be renewed and the pipe returned again. He smoked all day long in this fashion.

Aside from determining that the khan had four wives and one hundred slave women, MacGahan could learn nothing more about the harem, explaining to *Herald* readers that "it is considered extremely unpolite in Central Asia, to make any mention to a man of his wife, or wives."

MacGahan took special interest in the ceremonial religion of Khiva. The city had seventeen mosques and twenty-two *medresses*, where the mullahs spent their time leading holy lives and acquiring religious knowledge. In a small garden stood the most splendid of the mosques, the Palvan-Ata, a structure about sixty feet high and covered with tiles burnt to a brilliant green, the whole surmounted by an enormous gilt ball. Built in 1811, the Palvan-Ata contained the tomb of Palvan, a holy man MacGahan inadvertently referred to as "the patron saint" of Khiva.

Writing with the ugly insensitivity of his time, almost customary among uninvited Western visitors in foreign lands, the correspondent wrote that the mullahs learned the Koran by heart, "without even understanding it, poring over the same theme, to the exclusion of every living human interest," this concentrated study reducing them "to this state of semi-idiocy." MacGahan also observed that "the headgear of these mullahs would be sufficient of itself to numb their brains, and deprive them of the last spark of intelligence." He referred to the pumpkin-sized turban the holy men wore, weighing seven or eight pounds with twenty-five to thirty yards of muslin wound about. This ponderous thing, he remarked disgustedly, "was worn in the hottest of weather."

When not investigating the mosques, MacGahan visited Khivan bazaars like any tourist, enjoying the odors of spice, tobacco, wheat-cakes, and green tea, and sampling such delicacies as the famous variety of Khivan melons and grapes. The bazaar swarmed with exotic peoples: Uzbeks in tall black sheepskin hats and long, filthy khalats, Bokharan merchants, Yomud Turkomans, Persians, Afghans, Kirghiz, and, of course, Russian officers.

The Khivan populace got so used to the Russians in their midst that they regularly sent young children and beggars to Kaufmann's camp, the youngsters selling ice (which melted so quickly the soldiers eventually had to dig a cellar for it), milk, cakes, and fruit.

The Russians built their camp as if they planned to stay permanently—buying cows and sheep and setting up a poultry yard. For the most part, however, life in the camp had begun to pall, the band music wearing thin, the routine and inactivity stifling to the bored young officers and troopers as Kaufmann's long conferences with the Khan continued.

It was this stultifying placidity which made the great open-air banquet, sponsored by the Grand Duke Nicholas Constantinovitch, the more successful. It was held in the camp of the Orenburg detachment adjoining that of Kaufmann's outside the walls of the city. The huge garden forming the encampment was grandly illuminated by improvised Chinese lanterns hanging from the branches of peach and apricot trees; a triumphal arch was fashioned of poplar branches, and carpets were strewn on the ground, banquet tables laid, and band music provided, while flags fluttered in the breeze.

The grand duke made a speech to his troops, and upon its close the vodka flowed, also the champagne. ("You will find champagne among the Russians when you cannot get bread," MacGahan noted wryly.) One particularly potent brew was a Russian punch made from champagne, vodka, apricots, melons, cucumbers, and sugar, which was then ignited and allowed to burn until it boiled. MacGahan, who sampled it, pronounced it "the most diabolical compound I ever tasted, for its every drop is laden with headache for a week and dyspepsia for a fortnight."

Another result of the champagne-vodka punch was the wild and grotesque dancing of the soldiers to flute piping and rhythmic hand-clapping, the songs in Caucasian dialects MacGahan had never heard. At a crescendo in the music, a shout was suddenly raised, and in an instant the grand duke, an innocent handclapping bystander, was seized by his men, disappearing momentarily in the surging throng of soldiers. Then he reappeared, tossed ten feet in the air by soldiers grasping the edges of a huge rug. This act was repeated ten times before the wobbly duke, bellowing laughter, tears rolling down his beet-red face, was lowered to the ground to grope his way back to his seat of honor. (MacGahan later speculated: "Just imagine the Prince of Wales tossed ten feet in the air by the privates of the 'Black Watch'!")

"*Americanetz!*" somebody roared.

MacGahan, standing on the sideline and hugely enjoying the spectacle of the stalwart grand duke cartwheeling in the air, was grabbed up and given the same blanket toss. Half drunk from the evil punch, he could barely withstand the ordeal but managed it manfully and without losing his banquet dinner. When he got both feet on the ground, the grand duke clapped him on the back and guffawed, "The hug of the Russian bear is rough, but it is hearty!"

MacGahan found out later to his delight that the blanket tossing was a mark of particular affection among the Russian troops, and that no officer disliked by his men was favored with it.

That MacGahan had earned the affection of the Russians was avowed by those who remembered, with some awe, his advent among them. One Russian officer present during Kaufmann's march from Tashkent to Khiva, described the American:

> . . . a young man of thirty-five years of age [actually Mac-Gahan had just passed his 29th birthday; that he *looked* thirty-five is, however, indisputable], very good looking and of remarkable constitution. Afterwards we saw he was also very clever. He spoke fluently the French, German and

English languages. . . . He proved his daring and enter-
prising spirit on appearing in our midst during the cannonade at the passage of the Amu Darya . . . it was really only
his American luck that could bring him to us alive and well.

The next time MacGahan would encounter the grand duke the situation would be infinitely more trying: their next war would be serious, bloody business, a conflict of hundreds of thousands, the casualties incalculable.

The correspondent never lost his affection for the Grand Duke Nicholas, brother of the czar, and coming to know him in Khiva in 1873
would prove immeasurably helpful in Bulgaria four years later.

VII

The Cossack Correspondent

1
"A sad tale of blight and ruin"

One tends to visualize readers of the New York *Herald* avidly following MacGahan's adventures in Turkestan: his crossing of the Kyzyl Kum with a Cossack patrol snapping at his heels; his finding Kaufmann's army poised on the banks of the Amu Darya and fighting their first skirmish against the Sheik-Arik fortress; his entrance into the Hazar-Asp, then the legendary citadel of Khiva, flags fluttering and a band playing a grand Russian air; his exploration of the khan's palace, the treasure room, and harem, danger lurking in every dark corner and moonlit room; the midnight tryst with Zuleika, sultana of the khan's harem; poring over a handmade map of the world with the khan of Khiva; the sights, sounds, and odors of the bazaar; the fairyland backdrop of apricot trees, kibitka-dotted plains, and the minarets, mosques, and battlements of the ancient city.

In truth, however, James Gordon Bennett's readers knew little of MacGahan's exploits in Turkestan until the correspondent returned to St. Petersburg in September 1873. There were no telegraph wires in central Asia in 1873, and what few messages he did manage to send out of the desert, via Kaufmann's couriers to the Syr Darya, thence to Orenburg and St. Petersburg, were published months after they were written.

This is not to say that between April and August all was silent on the matter of the correspondent's mission in Turkestan. Bennett was too shrewd a newspaperman not to capitalize on his expensive investment. Throughout the summer months, the *Herald* carried minor notices and editorial page commentary on "The Herald Correspondent," his whereabouts and indeed on some of the news events of the conquest of Khiva. A few of these dispatches indicate that MacGahan managed to send a message to St. Petersburg, others are just as clearly extrapolations on information gleaned from the American consulate in the Russian capital.

Despite MacGahan's continued anonymity in the *Herald* pages, the identity of the daring young "special" was becoming known. Toward the end of July, in fact, MacGahan received from the Russian mail courier a letter written to him in care of the consul in St. Petersburg. The letter invited him to write a paper on the geography of central Asia for the American Geographical Society in New York City.

It would be August 4 before his first full-length dispatch appeared in the paper, published under the heading, "RUSSIAN CONQUEST OF KHANATE." The story mentioned, in the editorial précis, "The Herald correspondent, the only foreigner in General Kaufmann's camp, speaks in terms of praise for the treatment which he received as an American from that distinguished commander and his subalterns."

Kaufmann's treatment of the American indeed had already paid dividends; his treatment of the Yomud Turkomans was yet another matter, and it was this episode, drawing to a close MacGahan's adventure with the Russian army in Turkestan, which prepared him to a degree for what he would experience in the Balkans three years later.

The Turkomans were a nomadic people scattered across the great, sometimes lush, mostly desolate expanse of country between the Amu Darya and the Caspian Sea as far east as Afghanistan, as far south as the Persian border. In the vicinity of Khiva, parts of six separate tribes had settled: the Imrali, Chaudors, Karadashli, Kara Jigeldi, Aleili-Igoklens, and the Yomuds—in all 22,000 kibitkas, or about 110,000 people.

The khan of Khiva had never been successful in subduing these primitive, unruly folk or in exerting any appreciable influence over them. In fact, the reverse was true. The Turkomans allowed the khan his nominal authority as ruler over their neighbors, the Uzbeks, but refused taxation, tribute, or control of any kind themselves. In a fashion, all this worked out, for the khan depended upon them as soldiers, and when not fighting against him, they fought for him, their marauding propensities, as seen, furnishing one of the pretexts for the Russian invasion.

The Turkomans were faithful, in their way, to the khan, and while ignoring his sovereignty, they helped him maintain his rule over others, and it was the Turkomans who offered the only serious resistance to the Russian promenade to Khiva. Significantly, too, when the khan fled his capital, it was among the Turkomans he found refuge.

His fragile alliance with the tribes had a direct bearing on Kaufmann's insistence on immediate payment of an immense war indemnity. The khan politely but firmly refused to be responsible for raising a tribute among the Turkomans, in particular the Yomuds, by far the most numerous of the six tribes in the khanate with eleven thousand kibitkas, or over fifty thousand people.

Kaufmann therefore issued a proclamation ordering the Yomuds to pay thirty thousand rubles (over two hundred thousand dollars) within two weeks. When the Yomud chiefs sent deputations asking for additional time to raise so large a sum, Kaufmann insisted on immediate payment and began preparations to march into Yomud territory.

Kaufmann's own officers criticized this course of action and openly stated that their chief knew very well the Yomuds could not raise the indemnity in so short a time—indeed, perhaps could not raise it at all. There was some speculation, which MacGahan reported with his personal doubt made clear, that the khan had in fact hoodwinked the Russian governor-general, that Kaufmann had become an unwitting tool for the conquest of the Yomuds, a tribe the khan could not control, much less conquer, himself.

MacGahan could not believe Kaufmann foolish enough to be taken in by so transparent a scheme as this and wrote that the governor-general simply did not believe the Yomuds and their protestations. He gave two other reasons for the Russian plan to invade the Yomud lands: Kaufmann wished to conciliate the Uzbek tribes, who would rejoice to see their turbulent neighbors and perennial nemesis conquered, and Kaufmann simply despised the Turkoman people for their independence and defiance of authority—that is, Russian authority. This, MacGahan reasoned, was an unpardonable sin in the eyes of the Russian government, of which Kaufmann was a dedicated agent, and it had thus become necessary to make an example as a warning of the consequences of disobedience to the Russians.

The correspondent did express his feeling that Kaufmann erred in his resolve to march against the Yomuds, writing that of the two peoples, it should have been the Turkomans who were conciliated. They

were, MacGahan said, a better, braver, nobler race, almost free from
"Mohammedhan prejudices," and entirely innocent of the "disgusting
and degrading vices" of the Uzbeks.

But at best, these were postmortem expressions, in keeping with the
propensity of virtually all nineteenth-century war correspondents
(and raised to a sort of art by Archibald Forbes) to restage in hindsight
all military campaigns.

On July 19, five weeks after the surrender of Khiva, MacGahan
joined a force under Major General Golavatchov, composed of eight
companies of infantry, eight *sotnias* of Cossacks, two small cannon,
two mitrailleuses, and a battery of rockets, to advance sixteen miles
north to the Hazavat canal on the edge of Yomud lands. At the canal,
the column camped and waited a day, ostensibly to see if the Yomuds
would come forth and pay the indemnity, but in reality, MacGahan
believed, because Golavatchov did not much relish the expedition and
wished to give the Turkomans a chance to scatter and escape.

Golavatchov's force moved westward from Hazavat on the 21st and
in a few hours' march arrived in the lushly green Yomud lands, a
marshy tract cut by canals, the banks lined with poplars, thick grass
and brush, and here and there deserted farmhouses of mud, clay, and
thatch, fires still smoldering in their hearths and signs, such as a rubble of abandoned belongings, of hasty departure. Cossacks touched
their torches to the thatched roof of every deserted dwelling and they
burned like dry leaves, throwing huge black clouds of greasy smoke
skyward. MacGahan likened the movements of the Cossacks to those
of "spectres, torches in hand, dashing swiftly, leaping ditches and flying over walls like demons, rarely dismounting, applying their torches
to the projecting eaves of thatch, and stacks of unthreshed grain."

Within hours the Cossack incendiaries had set the entire Yomud
countryside to flame. And that first night, a drizzling rain fell which
beat the ashes of the fires and seemed to make them burn the brighter,
driving down the acrid smoke until it hung in the trees in heavy, sullen
masses, darkening the air and forming a lowering backdrop to the
blood-colored fires. "It was a sad, sad sight," MacGahan scribbled in his
notebook, "a terrible spectacle of war at its destructive worst, strangely in keeping with this strange wild land!"

As this scorched earth tactic continued, the Russian force sighted a
great fleeing mass of Yomuds—nearly thirty thousand men, women,
and children, together with their horses, camels, sheep, goats and
cattle—rushing ahead of Golavatchov's force in a ponderous and confused mob. Six *sotnias* of Cossacks were selected to pursue this pa-

Charge of the Cossacks against the Yomuds. (MacGahan, *Campaigning on the Oxus*)

Young Gen. Skobelev. (Nemirovitch-Dantchenko, *Personal Reminiscences*, 1884)

"The Flight"—Yomud tribesmen fleeing the Russian invaders. (MacGahan, *Campaigning on the Oxus*)

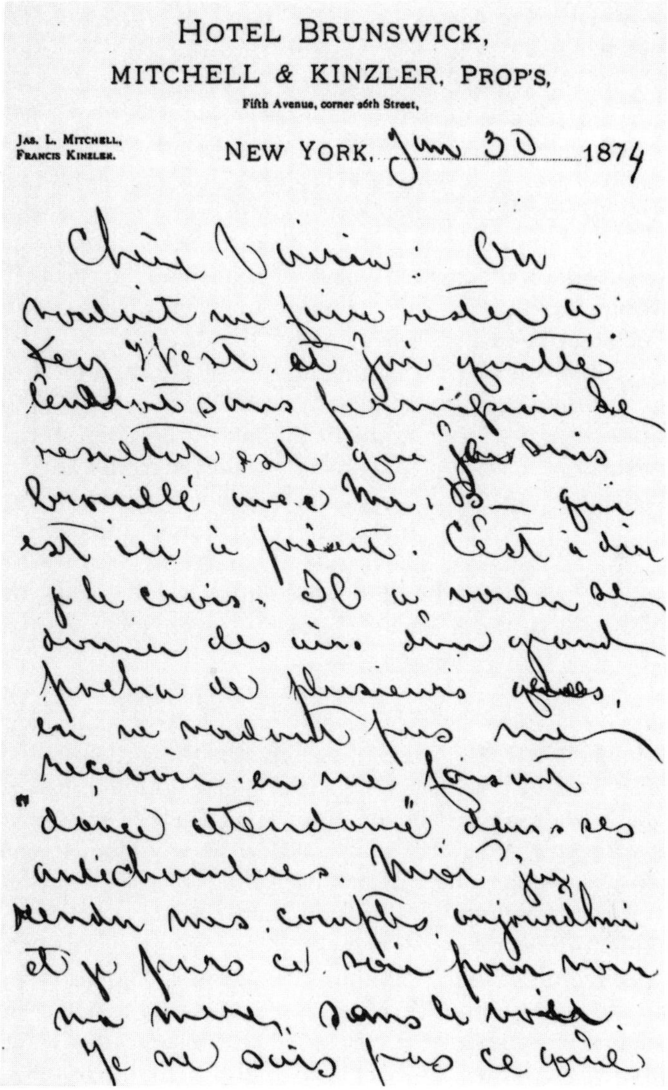

HOTEL BRUNSWICK,
MITCHELL & KINZLER, PROP'S,
Fifth Avenue, corner 26th Street,

JAS. L. MITCHELL,
FRANCIS KINZLER.

NEW YORK, Jan 30 1874

Chère Varia: On voulait me faire rester à Key West, et j'ai quitté l'endroit sans permission. Le résultat est que je suis brouillé avec Mr. B— qui est ici à présent. C'est à dire je le crois. Il a voulu se donner des airs d'un grand pacha de plusieurs queues, en ne voulant pas me recevoir, en me faisant "dance attendance" dans ses antichambres. Moi j'ai rendu mes comptes aujourd'hui et je pars ce soir pour voir ma mère, sans le voir.
Je ne suis pas ce que

Letter in their then-common language, French, to Barbara from MacGahan in New York, Jan. 30, 1874, following his return from Khiva: "They wanted me to stay at Key West and I left the place without permission. The result is that I am crossed up with Mr. B. [Bennett], who is here now. That is to say, I think so. He wanted to give himself the airs of a grand pacha of several queues by not receiving me, by making 'le dance attendance' in his antechambers. As for me, I turned in my accounts today and am leaving this evening to see my mother without seeing him." (MacGahan Papers) thetic swarm, and MacGahan was able to ride in the front of their line toward that scene of wildest disarray, the ground beneath his horse's hooves strewn with their abandoned belongings.

As the Cossacks moved on the fleeing Turkomans, MacGahan caught glimpses of scenes far sadder than the mere burning of Yomud farmhouses. Only a few minutes after the Cossack squadrons charged into the Yomud throng, the American found one tribesman lying on the sand with a bullet through his head; a little farther on a Cossack stretched out on the ground with a hideous saber cut on his face; then two women, with three or four children, sitting on the sand moaning and sobbing piteously and begging for their lives.

MacGahan was shocked at the number of Turkomans he saw lying motionless on the ground, but many, he believed, were feigning death. He found, in a reedy marsh, thirty women and children standing up to their necks in the water, trying to hide in the tall fronds and grass. One Cossack, sighting this huddled mass, deliberately took aim and attempted to fire into their midst. His rifle jammed, and before he could clear it, MacGahan took his life into his hands and rode up, slashing the Cossack across the face with a riding quirt. Miraculously, the horseman wheeled and dug in his spurs, flying off without a backward glance.

In truth, the Cossacks were a murderous lot, giving no quarter and taking no prisoners. MacGahan saw four of them beat a Yomud man to his knees with their sabers, then hack him to death until his body fell to pieces into the nearby marsh. Russian officers did their best to control them, MacGahan believed. At one point in the confused skirmish, he saw Baron Krudener, a young officer he would meet again in the Balkans, punishing one Cossack with the flat of a sword for having tried to kill a helpless Turkoman woman.

Seeing a small band of Cossacks pillaging a group of carts a short distance from the line of march, MacGahan rode over to watch and found a little girl, about three years old, standing beside the bodies of two slain tribesmen, watching the wild Russian horsemen in a bewildered way. The American swept the child onto his horse and found she had an open wound in her foot where apparently she had stepped on a saber. Riding back to the lines with the child, MacGahan made a bed for her under a cart, dressed her wound, gave her some fresh milk, and located her mother—or at least a Turkoman woman—who stoically took charge of the child without a word.

As he returned to the tumult, MacGahan's horse gave a startled, convulsive leap, nearly unseating him. Behind him erupted a shrill, ear-splitting noise followed by a rushing of air. Golavatchov's rocket battery, firing into the Yomud midst, created a pandemonium of terror as the shrieking rockets and clouds of suffocating gunpowder smoke mingled with the sounds of screaming women and children, the hoarse shouts of Cossacks and Yomud fighters, the bleating of animals, the clash of sword on sword, the sharp crackle of rifle fire.

The next day, the 23rd, the march continued. Golavatchov's column burned a path across the Yomud countryside, leaving a strip of scorched earth three miles wide in which nothing remained but heaps of smoldering ashes and the pathetic litter of belongings abandoned by a terror-stricken people. In all, nearly one hundred square miles of Yomud land lay in ruin.

The Turkoman resistance scarcely earned the word, but it did occasionally take a most curious form. When the Russians camped, an assortment of Yomud horsemen, sometimes as many as three hundred, would advance on the encampment, stop a safe distance, and send two or three riders up to within fifty yards of the Cossack sentries to challenge the Russians "to single combat," saluting with their curved sabers, chattering, and laughing.

On one of these medieval occasions, Prince Eugene rode up to MacGahan's tent and asked, "Would you like to take part in a charge? I am going to take a *sotnia* and charge that mass you see away there to the right. Tighten your saddle girth and get ready." MacGahan enthusiastically mounted and joined the royal officer's squadron of one hundred drawn sabers.

"*Gostovo!* [Charge!]," shouted the prince, waving his sword, and in a dense cloud of dust the Cossacks savagely spurred their horses and flew toward the ragged, swaying mass of Turkoman riders some three hundred yards distant.

Were it not for the Yomud's maddening tactics, the charge might have produced some campfire talk that night. But the Turkomans had long practiced evading maneuvers against the khan's periodic, always fruitless forays against them. In a gentle canter, seemingly in no slightest hurry or apprehension, the Yomud riders kept expertly out of range of the furious Cossacks.

In an hour, the frustrated sotnia, with MacGahan and Prince Eugene at its head, rode disconsolately back to bivouac.

Now and then, the skirmishes with Yomud riders proved serious business. On July 27, for example, when the Yomuds and a Russian force clashed in the desert, General Golavatchov himself was wounded and another officer, Colonel Esipov, with whom MacGahan had

shaken hands not an hour before the march out of Khiva, lay dead with
a bullet in his chest, his cross of St. George* spattered with blood.

But for the most part, the Russians advanced unmolested. MacGahan wrote of the rearguard of the daily march reaching camp long
after dark, burdened with the cattle, camels, and sheep captured.
"Their bawling and bleating, filling the whole plain, was mournful
enough in the darkness; while low down on the southern sky could be
seen the glare of the burning, telling a sad tale of blight and ruin."

2
"The best army in the world"

Ultimately, the result of Golavatchov's expedition was the eradica-
tion of the power of the Yomud tribe. Most of their livestock and virtually all their grain and forage had been either captured or burned;
their dwellings were now ashes. Kaufmann invited the Yomuds to return to their ravaged homes and build them again unmolested, but the
tribesmen, their spirit unbroken, refused and did not, in fact, return
from wandering in the desert until the Russians had marched away
from the Amu Darya to Tashkent.

MacGahan learned later that one of their first acts upon returning
was to fall upon the helpless Uzbeks, stealing their cattle, grain, and
forage, and reestablishing their hegemony as before.

At Iliali, on the eastern edge of Yomud country and on Golavatchov's line of march, General Kaufmann issued a further proclamation
addressed to the other Turkoman tribes, informing them he had as-
sessed a war indemnity and threatening them with the same punishment his army had dealt the Yomuds. Delegations of headmen came to
Kaufmann promising to pay and, again, asking for more time. Kaufmann gave fourteen days for the payment of a sum equivalent to about
twenty dollars per kibitka.

Small bits of silver, Turkoman ponies, carpets, ornaments, and jewelry were brought in, but at the end of the two-week deadline only
about half of the indemnity had been paid. Kaufmann at this point
made a seemingly inexplicable turnabout. Making a show of being impressed by the evidence that the tribes intended to pay the full
amount, he extended the deadline a full year.

---

*Purely a military order, the cross of St. George was the most highly prized of all Rus-
sian decorations. Four classes existed, and the name of every knight of the order, together with the date of his knighthood, was inscribed in gold on the white marble columns of the hall of St. George at the Kremlin Palace in Moscow.

In fact, the Russian general was mindful of the necessity of returning to Tashkent by September, for to wait longer would expose his army to the terrible winter of the Kyzyl Kum. Thus, after the Iliali conference, MacGahan joined the Russian march back to Khiva where preparations were made for departure.

On August 23, a treaty was signed by Kaufmann and the khan, sanctioned in St. Petersburg by the czar, the copies written in both Uzbek and Russian. The treaty's eighteen stipulations included a declaration by the khan stating that he was "the humble servant" of the Emperor of All the Russias. More importantly, the document set forth the frontier now under Russian domination, established the exclusive rights of Russian vessels to navigate the Amu Darya, opened all towns and villages of the khanate to Russian commerce, freed Russian merchants from paying all taxes (placing them on the same footing as Khivan merchants in Kazala, Orenburg, and other Caspian ports), emancipated all slaves, and prohibited slavery for all time in the khanate.

The treaty in effect advanced the Russian frontier three hundred miles farther south, annexing eighty thousand square miles of territory and giving the Russians complete possession of the lower Amu Darya. Probably fifty thousand people were added to the population of All the Russias, and the khan of Khiva was reduced to complete vassalage to the czar.

"Of course," MacGahan pontificated for the *Herald*, "the fall of Khiva must exercise a strong moral influence upon all the Mohammedhan populations of Central Asia. Khiva was considered impregnable and inaccessible; it was the last great stronghold of Islamism in Central Asia, after Bokhara had fallen; and its conquest will tend to confirm the belief already widespread in these countries, that the Russians are invincible."

As to the danger now of Russian incursions into India, a British bugbear for over a century, MacGahan explained to his readers two lines of advance the Russians might choose. The first was from the southern shores of the Caspian along the northern border of Persia and Herat and on to the western frontier of Hindustan—in all, one thousand miles. "Whatever the possibilities of an invasion being accomplished by this route," he wrote, "a glance at the map will show that Khiva would not be of the slightest use to any army from a military point of view." The second and more probable line of march, he said, would be from Samarkand across Bokhara to Kerki on the lower Amu Darya, thence up the Amu Darya to Kunduz—the greater part of the distance across desert terrain. But for the possibilities he saw in the Samarkand route, MacGahan stated he did not believe the Russians "had any immediate designs on India." He did admit that the Russians "see that there is a certain amount of territory lying between the English and Russian possessions which must sooner or later fall into the hands of either power. I think they are disposed to seize as much of this territory as they conveniently can; and this comprises their whole policy at present."*

In winding up his dispatches on the Khivan campaign, MacGahan gave considerable space to Colonel "Skobeloff." On the return march from Iliali, Skobelev disguised himself in a Turkoman costume and, accompanied by three Uzbeks, plunged into the desert to map the Yomud lands. He was gone ten days, and all hope had been given up for his safe return when he suddenly appeared in Khiva to hand over to Kaufmann his detailed maps and intelligence.

MacGahan would learn a great deal about this handsome, erratic officer before their friendship ended in Constantinople five years later.

Skobelev was the son of a general, indeed a fourth generation soldier, connected by marriage to one of the oldest princely houses in Russia—brother-in-law of the prince of Leuchtenburg. It was said that after a life of dissipation and extravagance, Skobelev had agreed to marry to get his father to pay his debts, but deserted his betrothed at the church door, volunteering for active service in central Asia. "Personally brave, heroic and magnificent," a contemporary wrote of him, "this Russian officer is as splendid in his vices as in his manly qualities."

Born in St. Petersburg in 1843, Skobelev served with a cavalry regiment in Warsaw in 1863 and saw some action in the suppression of the Polish rebellion and as a spectator in the Danish-German war in 1864. But his true military career began in 1869, when he was twenty-six and journeyed out to Samarkand in command of a Cossack regiment. It was during this service that he became known as an officer who could drive his men relentlessly, demand perfection and yet, at critical times, inspire them to face death willingly at his command. He was a hero to the ranks, it was said, "and they accepted the complaint that he put victory above all else and used men's lives liberally, for they saw that he counted his own life no more valuable than theirs."

Well educated in literature, languages, and military history, he placed great value on his service in Turkestan, remarking that "what

---

*In 1877 the Russians sent a mission to Afghanistan, which was warmly received in the court of Amir Shere Ali, ruler of the country. The British became greatly alarmed at this incursion by the Russians and invaded Afghanistan, fighting a bloody series of battles between 1878 and 1880 against the fierce Afghan tribes.

India is to England and Algeria is to France, Central Asia is to the Russians—a school of arms," and before his service there ended, he would be promoted to major general and given the governorship of Khokand.

As the Russians departed Khiva, Skobelev asked to remain long enough to write the extensive mapping report Kaufmann had requested. He asked MacGahan to remain with him, the two to ride out together to overtake the portion of the Russian army returning to Kazala. MacGahan whiled the time touring the deserted Russian camp and reading old issues of *Revue des Deux Mondes*. After Skobelev completed his work, the two left Khiva together. In two days they overtook the Russian rearguard, riding unmolested through the Uzbek countryside.

Nearly two weeks were occupied ferrying the Russian force to the vessels at the mouth of the Amu Darya. On September 1, MacGahan and his boatload pushed away from the shore of the Amu Darya for the voyage in Admiral Sitnikov's ships on the Aral. In seven days, after camping at night on the shore of the Amu Darya, the correspondent reached the flotilla—two steamers, the *Samarkand* and the *Perovsky*—which soon weighed anchor and departed across the Aral to the Syr Darya under good weather, awnings spread against the sun.

At Kazala once again, MacGahan met a Mr. Kerr who had been sent out by the London *Daily Telegraph* to find Kaufmann's army and report on the march to Khiva. Mr. Kerr was four months too late.

Before leaving Kazala, MacGahan wrote a letter to one of the many Russian officer-friends he had met during the campaign: "I have no words to thank the Russians sufficiently. The time I spent with them will always remain one of the best reminiscences of my life. Your army after the dreadful and unexampled difficulties it had gone through during the terrible campaign, impressed me greatly by its order and excellent discipline. It is the best army in the world."

Then, on September 5, he bought a *tarantass* and set out on the post road for Orenburg.

3
"Sweet, I love you"

There is little likelihood that MacGahan knew anything of his wife's miscarriage during his six-month absence in the deserts of Turkestan. The baby was not due until November, and Barbara, he felt certain, was safe in the tender care of her beloved sister Masha in Moscow. If he received any messages from Barbara from the time he left her at

Saratov on March 27, 1873, until his return in early October of the year, there is no record or mention of them.

Barbara received several long letters from "M.G."—her shorthand nickname for her husband—during his desert campaign, but each arrived six weeks or more after it had been written, and she had no real news of his whereabouts or his safety until, in October, she received a telegram from him from Orenburg. She contacted him there, as he finished some work for the *Herald* and put his notes in order for the book he intended to write on the Khivan adventure.

"He got my letters about my sickness at Orenburg and came to Moscow in big anxiety about me," she wrote. Of their reunion, she added deliriously, "What a happy time we had! It is right that you do not appreciate these moments while they last, but they leave a bright stripe on all your future life. How many plans of future happiness and life together we made!"

After MacGahan had left her at Saratov, she had journeyed to Moscow to rest and enjoy the company and ministrations of her favorite sister. While there, Barbara and Masha learned that their sister Natalia had taken ill and so traveled south to Tula where, to Masha's delight, Barbara and Natalia were reconciled as friends.

Back in Moscow, Barbara became ill herself, experiencing violent abdominal cramps and contractions. In June, she gave birth to a stillborn baby boy.

Many years later she reflected somewhat cryptically on this sorrowful time, writing: "During the days, I was dreaming with open eyes and thinking how good it would be for me and for the others if I would die together with my poor boy. . . . I do not know why it was so hard to lose him. I knew I was not preparing joy for him; the separation from M.G. and the traveling from Paris to Saratov was so hard that it killed him."

She spent the rest of the summer resting, she said, "hardly getting up from the sofa," and she began a "serious study of the English language."

The columns of the New York *Herald* toward the end of 1873 and the beginning of the new year had special meaning to MacGahan. Joining Barbara in Moscow that October and ensconced in a comfortable apartment, he leafed through the back issues his wife had collected for him.

Domestically, the *Herald* seemed almost entirely given over to the Henry Ward Beecher scandal, but there were stories on the growing controversy over a possible third term for President Grant, General

Custer's movements in the Black Hills, the Charley Ross kidnapping, and the illness of the famous Siamese twins, Chang and Eng.

But foreign news really dominated the paper, and MacGahan searched the long inside columns with their interminably stacked headlines for a clue to his next assignment. Bennett, he felt certain, would not let him rest long.

England's Sir Garnet Wolseley was about to depart from the fever hole of Cape Coast Castle to march inland on the Gold Coast to punish the Ashanti; the trial of Marshal Bazaine was commencing in Paris; another of the perpetual Kaffir wars in South Africa had erupted; the mummified corpse of Dr. David Livingstone, who had died the previous June, had reached Zanzibar.

Two long items might have caught MacGahan's attention as he leafed past the unconscionable amount of space Bennett devoted to the various regattas and yachting news around the world. One story from Madrid had to do with some preliminary moves of the Carlist insurrection then gaining some momentum, the second dealt with what the *Herald* was terming "the 'Virginius' Affair," an incident predicted to have the potential of creating war between Spain and America.

MacGahan and Barbara spent a week in St. Petersburg, then a terse wire from Bennett ordered the correspondent to London. In Paris, they took rooms at the Hotel St. Petersburg on rue de Caumartin, and he proceeded on to confer with his employer. Bennett, Barbara recalled later, held a banquet in MacGahan's honor at the Hotel Welder and promised the correspondent that an expensive gold watch was being prepared for him in gratitude for his splendid work in Turkestan. The watch was never delivered, she remembered, and her husband could never quite bring himself to ask about it.

She detested her husband's employer for his "ingratitude" for MacGahan's record in the Franco-Prussian and Khivan campaigns. Bennett, she was certain, manipulated his correspondents like so many marionettes, caring nothing for their sensibilities, health, or welfare. She tried her best that fall and winter of 1873 to talk MacGahan into quitting the paper, but financial problems stood in the way. He was sending money to support his mother in Indiana and contributing what he could to help his brother Patrick's law studies in Brussels.

In late October, Bennett ordered MacGahan to proceed to Nice to join a warship of the American squadron there which was preparing to steam to Key West. The correspondent's assignment was to write on the still-brewing episode involving the American side-wheel steamer *Virginius*, which, running arms and supplies to Cuban insurrectionists, had been captured by a Spanish gunboat on October 31. The *Virginius* crew and passengers, including some Americans and over one hundred *filibusteros* bound to join the island's insurgents, were taken to Santiago de Cuba as prisoners, all charged as "enemies of the state" and all sentenced to death. By early November, more than fifty of the crew and passengers had been executed.

"We were together five weeks after his long absence and now we were to separate again for an unlimited time," Barbara dolefully noted in her memoir. But her husband promised her he would use the trip to America to visit his aging mother, then they would be together for the rest of their lives.

She moved to cheaper quarters in a boarding house on rue de Caumartin, where MacGahan had lived for a time during the Commune, to await his return from America and whatever next lay in store for them.

Adding to the poignancy of their separation was the fact that she was again pregnant. It was imperative, this time, that her husband be with her when the baby came in August.

When MacGahan joined the flagship *Wabash* of the American Mediterranean squadron at Nice, he had already begun work on his book about the Khivan campaign, such a work almost an obligatory exercise for any traveler to remote lands in the Victorian era. And, by the time the squadron made its leisurely way across the Atlantic to anchor in the Florida Keys in January 1874, he had finished the long manuscript.

By then, too, the *Virginius* fuse had sputtered out with the release of all the remaining prisoners by Cuban authorities.

He wrote Barbara from Key West, "God, how I would like to have a letter, even if it were only a line. Sweet, I love you." And, almost as an afterthought, said, "If you have not written me lots and lots every day, or almost every day, I will doubt. I will begin to believe that you are forgetting me, that you are tired of this way of living, that you want no more of me. . . . You *have* written, you have told me that you love me; I know it, I feel it . . . I have confidence."

From Key West, MacGahan proceeded to New York City and wrote his wife on the stationery of the American Geographical Society, of which his friend Alvan Southworth was secretary. He was preparing, he said, to address the Society as he had been asked to do in the letter he received in Khiva.

"They wanted to make me stay in Key West," he told Barbara, "and I left the place without permission. The result is that I am crossed up with Mr. B[ennett] who is here now. He wanted to give himself the airs of a grand pasha of several queues by not receiving me, by making 'le dance attendance' in his antechambers. As for me, I turned in my accounts today and am leaving this evening to see my mother without seeing him." He said he would proceed to Indiana to visit his mother and would be back in New York in three weeks.

He sent Barbara a particularly loving letter on January 28: "I can never describe what a wealth of tenderness I feel for you," he said, proceeding to tell her that Bennett had regained his "good humor" over the sudden departure from Key West, "so that now we are getting along as always . . . he is at present very amiable." He ended this letter by saying, "I love you too much—it is not possible to tell you how I feel about you, but later, Sweet, you will find out."

MacGahan's Khivan dispatches were still a matter of some interest to *Herald* readers. On January 14, for example, the paper carried a report headed "GEOGRAPHICAL WORK OF THE WORLD 1873," which contained the statement that "the letters of Mr. J. A. MacGahan, the Herald correspondent in Central Asia, have furnished valuable and accurate information as to the nature of changes, the most important of which is the addition of the right bank of the Oxus to the Russian dominions."

The New York lecture was held at the Cooper Institute, and the *Herald*, which devoted a great swatch of space to it, described the hall as "well filled." General W. T. Sherman, a special guest of honor, was greeted with applause when he entered, as was the young American correspondent who began his speech with a special tribute to "a soldier whose fame I found had preceded the Russian arms to Khiva." MacGahan proceeded to describe a hot day in June when he and Kaufmann sat on their horses watching the movement of the Tashkent column along the Amu Darya and when the topic of their conversation turned to "Sherman's march from Atlanta to the sea." Little did he dream, MacGahan said, that he would one day soon find "the great American soldier to be an auditor of mine during my recital of the Khivan campaign."

He concluded the introductory remarks by saying, "I need not say how gratified I am to see him here, although I am perfectly aware that in his case, at least, I am carrying coals to Newcastle."

Upon completion of the lecture the correspondent promised the group that when he returned to "the Old World" he would tell General Kaufmann and the Grand Duke Nicholas that "you people have a greater knowledge of Central Asia and the Khivan campaign than any people I have seen since my return from the khanate."

In concluding the meeting, the president of the society asked General Sherman to make a few remarks, and the tough old Union soldier recalled that when he was in Europe two years before, he received a message that a newspaper correspondent, one MacGahan, wanted to join him. Sherman said he felt this "was not welcome news" but that Mr. MacGahan came and "I found him a most agreeable and companionable man." As to the Khivan lecture, Sherman added, "I came to hear my friend MacGahan and I have listened to him with great interest indeed."

The *Herald* reportage on the speech was magnanimous, comparing MacGahan's lecture and "his brilliant letters" to tales of the Orient such as the Arabian Nights and Lalla Rookh, and saying the correspondent "is the first to 'hold up the mirror to nature' and show the people of New York this country of Turkestan and its true and decidedly unpoetic but nonetheless interesting light."

Even the *Herald* editorial page gave the lecture a laconic mention, the lines perhaps written by Bennett's own hand and reflective of his well-known jealousy of the personal triumphs of his correspondents: "Mr. MacGahan read a paper on Khiva, giving an intelligent account of the Khanate and a pleasant recital of some personal adventures."

As a final piece of New York business, MacGahan asked Bennett for a short leave of absence in order to put the manuscript of *Campaigning on the Oxus and the Fall of Khiva* in final order for the publishers. Bennett assented but said bluntly that MacGahan would have to take the leave without remuneration from the *Herald*.

With this unhappy news to carry home to Barbara, he sailed for Europe for the last time on March 5, 1874.

VIII
Riding with Don Carlos

1
"To join the army of the Pretender"

The MacGahans settled in London in the spring of 1874, paying four pounds a week board and lodging for a furnished apartment at 27 Euston Square. While he completed the editorial work on his book, Barbara continued her study of English—which she still "spoke badly," she said—by the difficult route of translating the manuscript into Russian for the *Moskovsk Russkij Vestnik* (Moscow Russian Messenger), the book to run serially simultaneously with its release in England. On May 4, MacGahan signed the contract with Sampson Low, paying a sum of thirty pounds out-of-pocket for the illustrations to accompany it. Harper & Brothers of New York, on June 1, became publishers of the American edition.

The baby was due in August, and Barbara viewed the event as her "coming crisis," worrying over it almost as fixedly as over their financial woes. MacGahan's three-month hiatus from the *Herald* without pay meant they would have to spend the remainder of her skimpy savings. When his brother wrote from Brussels in April to ask for a twenty-pound loan, MacGahan had to turn him down. "I would pawn the watch Bennett is *going* to give me, if I had it," he said.

Among visitors that spring were Henry Morton Stanley, the one-time *Herald* correspondent, now the famous African explorer, and Eugene Schuyler, on leave from his consular post in St. Petersburg.

While waiting for word from the *Herald* for a possible assignment in Spain for the Carlist insurrection, MacGahan tried his hand at writing a play based "on some incidents of the Siege of Paris," but, as Barbara recalled, he eventually "despaired of it and never finished it." He told her he wanted peace and quiet for a time, she wrote, "but Mr. Bennett refused to appoint him resident correspondent anywhere in Europe, wanting him on waiting orders, ready to start at a moment's notice to any place on earth."

Campaigning on the Oxus and the Fall of Khiva appeared in July, and the London *Athenaeum* said of it, "Mr. MacGahan's book is so good that it could afford to have more politics in it. A book more freshly written and with more interesting matter, both general and personal, is seldom to be found." The *Herald* agreed, mentioning the book in the same breath as *Coomassie and Magdala*, Henry M. Stanley's account of his exploits in the Gold Coast and Abyssinian campaigns. "Incomparably the most interesting book of the day is Mr. MacGahan's," the *Herald* proclaimed.

Through the summer and fall, the reviews continued to appear: *The Spectator, The Academy, The Examiner, The Saturday Review*. MacGahan pointed out in a letter to a friend he wrote from Estella in October that the *Saturday Review*, severest of all in its criticism, especially on "matters of style," had said, "there is not a page in the whole book we could wish unwritten." Even the "Thunderer" (the *Times* of London) liked it, he wrote in astonishment.

A month after the book appeared, on August 24, MacGahan received through the Russian legation in Washington the military order of St. Stanislaus "with swords," an honor rarely conferred upon a civilian and certainly never before on an American war correspondent. He received the medal in London: a beautiful gold and crimson enameled Maltese cross with the white eagle of Poland and crossed sabers between the arms of the cross.*

The award came to him, he was certain, through the friendly intervention of General Kaufmann and the Grand Duke Nicholas, and he was greatly moved by their kindness.

On July 7, MacGahan received his awaited orders from the *Herald*.

---

*There were three classes of the order (which was founded in 1765): Knight Grand Cross, Commander, and Companion. It is unclear which was given to MacGahan—his medal has disappeared—but more than likely it was the third.

As the *Herald's* special correspondent with the Carlist forces in the Pyrenees in the summer and winter of 1874, MacGahan proved spectacularly his mastery of his profession. He consistently telegraphed solid copy, an amazing string of beats that included two comprehensive interviews with the pretender, Don Carlos. Just as he had won the trust of the Russians in central Asia, he earned the respect of the Carlists, a group of lost-cause cynics naturally dubious of foreigners, in particular one representing a powerful American newspaper. He witnessed one minor siege in which the Carlist army fled in disarray before the Republican forces. He tramped the battlefield of Estella, near Pamplona in Navarre, a sacred place to the Carlists and scene of their greatest victory. He wore (foolishly, it must be said) the red Carlist *boina* (a muffin-shaped cap or beret) in the presence of the "enemy" and was taken prisoner, having another narrow escape similar to that he experienced during the Commune. He flaunted his pro-Carlist attitude in all his dispatches, going to the extreme of predicting that Don Carlos would march in triumph into Madrid before the summer ended. And he became something of a fixture on the *Herald* editorial page, his name printed in full as "J. A. MacGahan" and not merely as "our special correspondent."

The campaign also revealed a curious rift in MacGahan's thinking. He had found he could support the aims of the Parisian Communards, and he believed that perhaps even rule by the canaille would be better than any form of authoritarianism; yet he slipped comfortably into Carlism and became for a short time an eloquent spokesman for it. Perhaps it was a demonstration of youthful hero worship, for Don Carlos was a most compelling personality; perhaps the strong element of Catholicism in the Carlist philosophy lured him. Whatever the case, he learned a great deal about Carlism in the short time he served as witness to its last stand as a threatening influence in Spain.

The power of Carlism, sustained through two long civil wars, lay not so much in the claims of the pretenders to the throne as in the appeal it made to old national traditions of God, Spain, and king. It was primarily a rural phenomenon, gaining its greatest strength and popularity in the Basque provinces of Navarre and Catalonia, among the peasantry to whom the steadfastness of its religious faith and its championship of a strong regionalist state made the strongest appeal.

The First Carlist War (1833–39) ended in defiant defeat for the followers of Don Carlos I, and Isabella's long reign, fraught with internal disorder and unrest, continued until 1868 when she was forced to abdicate. After an unsuccessful experiment with an imported Italian nobleman, the Spanish Cortés proclaimed the country a republic, and a coalition government was formed in 1874, its initial task to put down the Carlist rising in the northern provinces.

In the summer of 1873, the Carlists captured Estella, hallowed ground for the bloody battle waged there in 1833. Following this, a number of smaller towns fell into their hands. By the end of the year, the Carlists were firmly established in the province and in November, at Montejurra, were able to repulse a Republican attempt to recapture Estella. Don Carlos, the fourth Bourbon pretender of the line, was present on the battlefield.

The Republican army, about 45,000 strong, with eighty pieces of artillery, returned to Estella in June 1874, but in a three-day struggle failed to wrest the "holy city of Carlism" from the insurrectionist force of 16,000. As with the battle of Balaclava in the Crimea twenty years before, the fighting at Estella took place in a sort of natural amphitheater. From nearby plateaus, members of Don Carlos's retinue viewed the battle almost as if it were being staged especially for them. The village of Abarzuza was at the center of the fight that opened on June 25. From the start, the Republicans were defeated by the terrain, their convoys and supplies stuck in passes far behind their lines, their men moving into action half-starved. The Carlists could not be dislodged from their hillside positions, and Republican guns had little effect on them. Ultimately the Republicans lost over one thousand men in the furious struggle (including the capable General Concha, Marquis of Duero) and were finally routed by the Carlist General Mendiri, later created Count of Abarzuza.

Three days after the battle, Don Carlos and his wife Margarite came from Tolosa to honor Estella's defenders. They had been escorted to a nearby village, where two pure white Andalusian horses awaited them. Thus royally mounted, they rode along the Pamplona road to the "holy city." It was the greatest moment of the war for the followers of this handsome young prince, resplendent in his general's uniform, his charming wife dressed in a plain black riding habit, both wearing the scarlet *boina* of Navarre, proudly entering Estella. A solemn Mass was held for those who had died in battle, Margarite visited the wounded, and before leaving the town, Don Carlos reviewed his troops, a force swollen to eighteen thousand men, more than had started the battle, at the foot of Montejurro.

Bennett's cable, which arrived a few days after the Carlist victory at Estella on June 25, specified only that MacGahan would proceed to Biarritz to prepare "to join the Army of the Pretender." He was to

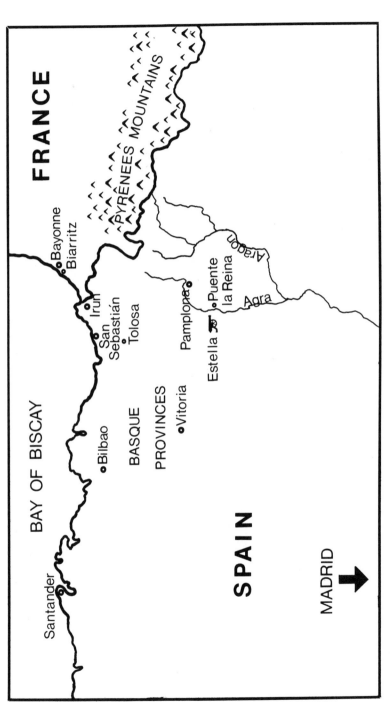

The Basque region of northern Spain, scene of the Second Carlist War fighting. (Map by Kathleen Rogers)

A Carlist cavalry charge. (Forbes, Henty *Battles of the Nineteenth Century*, I)

Estella. (Forbes, Henty, *Battles of the Nineteenth Century*, I)

El General Director Militar de la Frontera

Nº *1296*.

DIOS, PATRIA Y REY

DIRECCION MILITAR
DE LA FRONTERA

NOTA. — Queda sugeto este pase al impuesto que la Real Junta de Navarra y la Diputacion Foral de Guipuzcoa tengan señalado y que deberá satisfacer el portador en el punto fijado por las mismas corporaciones.

Otra.

Concede libre y seguro pasaporte á *Mr. J. A. Mac Gahan, Corresponsal del Herald, Est.* *Unidos* que pasa *al Cuartel Real.*

Las autoridades civiles y militares del tránsito no pondrán impedimento alguno á su marcha, antes bien le facilitarán los auxilios que pueda necesitar en cuanto cumpla con las prescripciones que el estado de guerra haga necesarias.

Frontera de España *16* de *Julio* de *1874*.

Vizconde de Barres

MacGahan's passport permitting him to cross the Spanish frontier. (MacGahan Papers)

MacGahan, about 1873. (MacGahan Papers)

await further instructions on "observing the war on the Republicans and Alphonsists," the latter, supporters of Isabella's son, Alfonso XII. When the instructions came, MacGahan, in Paris, had put the finishing touches on the French edition of *Campaigning on the Oxus* (subsequently published by Hachette of Paris). His Spanish passport in hand, he visited his brother in Brussels, then traveled down to Écouen to visit old haunts before heading for the Spanish frontier. He wrote Barbara, "The farther I get away from you, the more I love you," and gave her instructions to proceed to Rouen, thence to Le Havre or Trouville and take ship passage to Biarritz and await him there.

2
"The battlefield of Estella"

Biarritz, on the Bay of Biscay, where MacGahan proceeded late in June, became home for Barbara, nearing childbirth, and a pied-à-terre for her husband in the first few months of his assignment in Spain. The MacGahan household was established first in a picturesque old hotel, then in a small house in the Villa Laurent. The telegraph office was handy, and Barbara's sister Marie came from Moscow to join her in the difficult weeks ahead. "She was not like Natalia," Barbara wrote in later years in a memoir for her son. "Natalia wrote long letters with many good wishes. Masha spent lots of money from the little she had to come from afar to help me."

At Biarritz, and later in Bayonne, Barbara did the translations of her husband's hastily scrawled dispatches, forwarding them to the telegraph office, keeping the originals to use in the stories she based on them for *Golos* (Voice), the St. Petersburg daily for which she had begun writing as a freelancer.

In mid-July, MacGahan set out for the Spanish frontier to find the Carlist army. For two weeks he dropped from sight as completely as he had in the deserts of the Kyzyl Kum. One thing is certain: The two weeks he had with the Carlists before his first dispatch arrived by courier to Biarritz, committed him irrevocably to Carlism. The victory at Estella mesmerized him. The gaiety and optimism of the ragged Carlist troops, their resolute stand in the path of the juggernaut forces of the Republic, their endearingly pathetic devotion to their leaders, the utter seriousness of their victory-clouded dreams of marching into Madrid, their devout Catholicism, his own warm reception into their camp, and the generosity and attention paid him by their generals and their King—these things moved MacGahan; one might almost say they *enlisted* him.

The correspondent's first duty was to report on the aftermath of the Estella battle of June 25, and his extraordinary dispatch, datelined Biarritz, August 4, 1874, appeared in the *Herald* on the 21st, the longest story in the entire paper and given extra prominence under a typical stack of headings:

ESTELLA
The Significance of the Carlist Victory
The Defeat of Concha's Army, Due Chiefly to
the Starving Condition of the Men.
A Glance at the Battlefield.
Marshal Serrano Will Not Declare in
Favor of Don Alfonso.
Don Carlos, King of Spain.

MacGahan, writing as always anonymously in the first person, exhibited his personal feelings in his lead paragraph, referring to Don Carlos as "the King." Like the most famous of his contemporaries, too, he had no qualm in giving his readers expert generalship on how the battle was lost and won. He dilated, pontificated, extemporized, philosophized, and editorialized.

"I have just returned from Estella," he commenced his stentorian five-column dispatch. "I have seen the Carlist troops, observed their discipline, their organization, their soldier-like appearance; have conversed with Carlist officers, even talked with the King himself." He continued: "I have been over the battlefield of Estella, have seen the spot where Concha fell, the house in which he died, have retraced the movements which led up to the battle, and endeavored to form a calm and impartial opinion, not only on the battle itself but on what it may indicate of the future, and I have come away with the conviction that Don Carlos will be King of Spain before a year."

He declared in elaboration of his conviction that "Don Carlos will march to Madrid when the time comes as easily as the Prussians marched to Paris after the battle of Sedan." And he insisted that the battle of Estella ought to be viewed as "an omen of what may be looked for in the future," something "significant to the Madrid government of its approaching doom as was the battle of Gravelotte to the French and for the same reason."

The seasoned thirty-year-old veteran of Bourbaki's and Kaufmann's armies then examined the battlefield, writing with the unshakable confidence that is the exclusive possession of amateur strategists that the strength of the Carlist position was grossly exaggerated and the difficulties Concha had to contend with were overestimated. Concha's only course of action, MacGahan contended, was for a frontal attack, an attempt to crush the enemy by brute strength and superiority of numbers. (This rudimentary alternative he would describe again, three years distant, this time in a major war.)

The Republican troops, he recounted, were repulsed three times and at last utterly routed by the Carlist defenders. "With a small force of cavalry and artillery," he concluded, "Don Carlos might then and there have marched to Madrid."

From what he learned of Estella, his information gained almost solely from his talks with Carlist officers, MacGahan was able to state unequivocally that "the Carlists are better soldiers, better men." As to the story that Concha's army had been without rations for two days and that the soldiers went into battle starving, he observed: "For such reason can be offered to account for the loss of every battle that has ever been fought. It might just as well be urged that the troops went into battle without cartridges." The battle had been prepared for many months, he reasoned, and it was to be the final blow to Carlism, and now "we find that, after all these months of preparation, the troops had no rations. . . . The truth is, Concha's army ought, with its advantages, to have completely crushed and annihilated the Carlists, and it was routed instead."

He continued: "Indeed, it may well be asked, if the Carlists, without cavalry and without artillery, can whip three times their number of Republicans and Alfonsists, what will they do with artillery?" Since the battle, he stated, the Carlist forces had received from different sources forty-seven pieces of cannon of the best models, of calibers varying from four to twenty pounds. And since Estella, soldiers "are flocking to his standard from all over Spain. Catalonia, Aragon, Castile, all are rising. It is my opinion that within three months Don Carlos, instead of 30,000 will have 100,000 men at his disposal, well armed if not well dressed. Does it not look as though Don Carlos' star were in the ascendent?"

Why this passionate belief in the ascendency of Don Carlos? MacGahan explained it: "The Carlists have a flag, a faith, a belief, and their opponents have not. Call it religion, fanaticism, bigotry, ignorance, what you will; the fact remains the same, that men with positive ideas, men who know just what they want, usually get it and carry the day."

Contributing to the impending Carlist victory, he wrote, was the lack of unity of the Republicans. He found few people who would maintain that the country was in any way Republican, fewer still who had an idea of the meaning of the word. "Who else then, but Don Carlos, the male representative of the old line of kings, the lineal descendent of Ferdinand and Isabella I, can succeed to the vacant Spanish throne? . . . I believe that if a plebiscite were taken today, freely and fairly, Don Carlos would be proclaimed King by an overwhelming majority."

MacGahan's amazing dispatch, so youthfully exuberant—and like so much youthful exuberance, wrongheaded—was read with interest not only by *Herald* readers, but by the *Herald* editor. Bennett printed it—he was not so small-minded as to refuse space to correspondence he personally found repugnant—but he added his own cooling comment in his editorial pages: "While we think our correspondent has exaggerated the significance of the victory to the Carlists, there is no question about the value of his analysis of the situation and his explanation of the reasons upon which Don Carlos bases his faith in ultimate success."

With the Estella postmortem out of his system, MacGahan turned to the only story of significance in the lull between the fighting: twenty-six-year-old Charles Marie de los Dolores Juan Isadore Joseph Francis Quirin Anthony Michael Gabriel Raphael, prince of Bourbon, duke of Madrid, great-grandson of Charles IV, fourth Carlist pretender to the Spanish throne—Don Carlos VII.

3
"The old fashioned hero-king"

Born on March 30, 1848, Don Carlos, the grandson of the first pretender, had been married since 1867 to Princess Marguerite, daughter of the Duke of Parma and niece of the Comte de Chambord. He had a son, Don Jaime, born in 1870, the year he asserted his claim to the throne, two years after Isabella II was driven into French exile. He himself had spent more than a year in the French Pyrenees, where authorities looked the other way while he fomented rebellion.

He had reentered Spain on July 15, 1873, just before his followers captured Estella, a town which, along with Tolusa and Durango, in the Basque provinces, became a favorite residence.

Don Carlos had been present in actions around Estella and near Bilbao during the sieges of early 1874 until these were raised by Generals Concha and Serrano. He was also present at the battle of Abarzuza on June 27 in which Concha received his mortal wound. Twice Don Carlos had lost golden opportunities to assert his strength and, indeed, perhaps to march to Madrid: in 1873 after declaration of the Republic, and in 1874 after the death of General Concha.*

He was a poor leader, a poorer military mind; lacking decision, wavering, apathetic, difficult. He had great charm, a strikingly handsome face and a regal bearing. He loved pomp and ceremony, and he was almost totally amoral. When he became a wanderer in exile, traveling about England, France, Austria, and Italy, he became a magnet for scandal.

Only once, after the accession to the throne of Isabella's son, Alfonso XII, late in 1874, did Don Carlos's army check the liberal forces again. This time, in Lacar, in Navarre, he surprised and made prisoners of half a brigade of Alfonsist troops with guns and colors, almost under the eye of the new king and his headquarters staff. This became the last Carlist success. The tide of war set in favor of Alfonso almost from the moment he was proclaimed king; the star of the pretender, from that moment, began to wane. Alfonsist armies swept the Carlists out of central Spain and Catalonia in 1875 and ultimately forced Don Carlos and his faithful to retreat and surrender to French frontier authorities in March 1876.

MacGahan's interviews with the engaging young Bourbon prince provided some exclusive material for the *Herald* in August 1874 and answers to several ringing questions of the day, among them the matter of the execution by a Carlist firing squad of the correspondent for the *Koelnische Zeitung* (Cologne Gazette), a certain "Captain Schmidt."

The first interview with the Pretender appeared in the *Herald* on August 10, on page five, under the dateline, "Special Dispatch by Cable to the Herald, Elorrio, August 4." The twelve-line heading ran:

DON CARLOS
Herald Special Interview With the
Uncrowned Monarch of Spain.
A Graceful Compliment to the Impartial
American Press.
"The Absurd Stories of Carlist Atrocities"
Captain Schmidt's Execution—Prominent

---

*Even in 1885, upon the death of Alfonso, Don Carlos failed to profit in the discontent, nor did he following the Spanish-American War of 1898 in which Spain lost her two remaining colonies in the New World, Cuba and Puerto Rico. To his death in 1909, he remained "the Pretender."

Causes and Unavailing Regrets.
Why Germany Will Not Intervene.
What Spain Needs—Tranquility, Enlighten-
ment and Progress Guided by Religion.
"Touching Cuba"

After being received "in a very friendly manner," to the royal presence, MacGahan quoted Don Carlos as saying: "We are pleased at having a representative of such an impartial journal as the Herald near us.
In fact we are always glad at seeing a newspaper correspondent willing
to tell the truth. Our cause is so good that it does not fear the
daylight."

MacGahan expressed the hope that he "would not meet the fate of
Captain Schmidt, the Austrian correspondent," and was assured,
"There is no danger. Schmidt was arrested under most suspicious circumstances, tried by court martial, found guilty and executed as a spy.
Nevertheless, I regret very much that my order to spare his life arrived
too late." The pretender said he did not fear German intervention as a
result of the Schmidt case: "Spaniards strongly dislike interference in
their home affairs. Foreign intervention would result in our favor.
Spain would have then only one army, and Don Carlos would be its
chief."

The Bourbon prince expressed his aims upon being "restored to his
rightful place as King": "I desire to give the country a necessary repose,
which it has never enjoyed since the time of Charles V. I desire to
restore Spain to something of its ancient grandeur. That is my only
task."

Touching on the sore subject of Cuba and the insurrection there
that came to be known as the "Ten Years' War," Don Carlos told Mac-
Gahan, "I would offer a free pardon, an amnesty. My government
would be devoted to the interests of the island. I am opposed to slavery, and would abolish the system with all speed."

MacGahan ended the dispatch with this observation: "Don Carlos is
very sanguine of his succession to the throne of Spain, his present
prospects giving him good reason thereof."

On Bennett's editorial page of the August 10 Herald appeared this
comment:

> Our correspondent has been, in his time, in warmer places
> than most men care to go in their cooler moments; but he
> has never been in any that seemed less promising for com-
> fort and safe issue than the country within the Carlist lines,

just on the heels of such an event as the execution of the correspondent of the Cologne Gazette, for that occurrence seems to be the fault of a mot d'ordre and the beginning of a resentful war on the press.

MacGahan returned to Biarritz, only a few miles across the French frontier, a few days after his Don Carlos dispatch had been cabled to New York. His timing, Barbara recalled, was uncanny.

"I woke up at dawn on August 13, with pain," she wrote in her still-halting English, "and at 3 p.m. my dear Paul was born. At four came M.G., who did not know of the situation, and stayed for two weeks. He seemed to be very glad of the birth of the child, but a son took us unawares: I do not know why, but we waited for a girl, and prepared her the name of Mary."

Still under a local physician's care and with Marie staying on, Barbara fell ill seven days after her son was born. She was terrified she had contracted puerperal fever, the dreaded, often fatal, childbirth infection. "I had to stay three weeks in bed," she recalled, "and had to take a nurse for the child, as I did not hope anymore that the milk would come back."

During her illness, she and MacGahan debated on their son's name, while Marie made arrangements for the baptism. Finally they agreed on Paul "as the most convenient name both in Russian and English," she said. When her husband and sister returned from the baptism, Barbara later recalled, "M.G. told me that our son was inscribed in the records of Biarritz, the legitimate son of J.A. MacGahan and Barbara Elaguine."

MacGahan crossed and recrossed the Spanish border in pursuit of his *Herald* assignment, and with Marie returning to Moscow as soon as Barbara had recovered from her illness, MacGahan moved Barbara and Paul to a small house in Bayonne, where Barbara hired as wet nurse for the baby a young woman from Dax named Justine. "At the start, she was ugly, awkward and rude," Barbara noted ruefully years later, "but soon she grew prettier, and her sarcastic brain made me laugh. She had a wonderful milk and her natural cheerfulness acted well on the child."

Barbara passed the time during her husband's absences reading, laughing at Justine's stories, hovering over the baby, and receiving MacGahan's couriers. In a short time she was able to resume her writing for *Golos*, sending daily translations of the Carlist dispatches.

The day after Paul's birth and before the move to Bayonne, MacGahan cabled a last dispatch under the dateline Biarritz to the London bureau of the *Herald*. It was a pretentious manifesto from Don Carlos, without comment from the correspondent, which ran under the heading, TO THE CHRISTIAN POWERS, and said, in part: "I have formed an army with the elements which the abnegation and enthusiasm of a great nation have furnished me. I have vanquished the enemy wherever he has offered combat when I have not offered it myself." What followed this was a simple lie: "My vanguard is at the gates of Madrid, and the hour is at hand when I shall have completely annihilated the army of the Republic with which it has vainly attempted to oppress the progress of our victories."

MacGahan's second and final interview with Don Carlos carried the dateline Lequeitio, August 20, and ran in the *Herald* on September 11. In it the Cuban question was paramount, most likely the result of a cable from Bennett to dig deeper into this question since the island, but ninety miles from the Florida Keys, had closer-to-home consequences.

The interview began with Don Carlos asking a question. What, he inquired of the correspondent, were the *Herald's* views on the Cuban issue? "The question was a somewhat embarrassing one," MacGahan admitted, "and I had to confess that the Herald entertained very strong opinions on the subject of Cuba. He then asked me if it represented the opinions of a large class of the American people, and here again I had to confess that on this subject, as upon every other, the Herald represented the majority of the America people."

Having set forth this astonishing statement, his story continued: "Seeing my embarrassment, Don Carlos remarked, with a smile, 'Well, whatever be our respective opinions on this subject, I hope it need not lead to any want of cordiality between the Herald and myself.' " The correspondent assured "his Majesty" that once he had carried out the reforms in Cuba he had previously named—abolition of slavery and the establishment of an honest government which would leave American citizens unmolested in "peaceable vocations of agriculture and commerce"—the *Herald* would "be appeased."

MacGahan described Don Carlos's appearance: black hair, brown eyes, slightly aquiline nose, and black beard covering his lower face.

> He is very handsome. The ladies may be interested to know that he will be the handsomest sovereign in Europe. He has an active, powerful frame, and stands six feet three in his boots. Young and brave, fighting an unequal fight against fearful odds, holding with his handful of men the armies of Madrid at defiance and rapidly preparing to take the offensive, fighting for what he considered his rights . . . he is, every inch, the old fashioned hero-king.

No hired court sycophant could have improved on MacGahan's work, and judging from Don Carlos's handling of MacGahan's questions, the pretender had a mastery, if not of war, of press relations.

4
"Great indignity"

In what MacGahan apparently considered a mere lull in the fighting before Don Carlos marched to the gates of Madrid, there was little to do except cable an occasional "color" story to his newspaper while waiting for the big news to break. Thus, on August 27, datelined from Estella, he wrote of riding through the Basque countryside, the beauty of the provinces, of seeing Carlist soldiers, the sandals they wore of hempen rope soles, their motley attire, their cartridge boxes and Remington rifles. In September, he found a village in the valley of the Bidassoa, about ten miles from the sea and two from the French frontier, in which 113 Carlist sympathizers turned out about three hundred artillery shells a day, working at a wage of one franc per day plus rations.

Occasionally he found a meal to his liking and duly reported on it. He was also dutiful in recording the reactions of the peasantry upon their seeing Don Carlos for the first time, splendidly mounted, riding through a village: "Viva el Rey!" they shouted, "Viva Carlos!"

In late October, MacGahan established his headquarters at Hendaye, a frontier town on the narrow Bidassoa river. He learned from the Carlist camp that there would soon be some serious action in the vicinity of Irún, on the Spanish side of the river and less than a half mile from the wineskin maker's cottage in which he had hired a room.

The action at Irún, fought in the third week of October, was an obscure clash of Carlist and Republican troops which MacGahan insisted on calling a "siege." And, since there had been no serious fighting since Estella, Irún gained a certain stature in the dispatches he wrote on it and its aftermath. His account of the "battle" there ran nearly a full page in the *Herald* of November 5.

Starting leisurely, MacGahan admitted a certain precariousness of his own position, writing that "a more intimate acquaintance with the Republicans was undesirable, more especially as I wore my boina with the insignia of Carlos VII." Of the pretender's presence at the "siege," MacGahan noted his manner of walking, comparing the Bourbon prince to "an alligator, inasmuch as he is very awkward upon land and has a more ungraceful gait. On horseback, however, he is perfectly at home." Don Carlos wore the *boina* with a gold tassel, a red scarf tied around his waist, and rode a spotless white charger. Most often he was surrounded by "a bevy of beautifully dressed ladies, chatting and laughing in the gayest manner."

Of the battle itself, MacGahan had to admit, "The Carlists have been signally defeated. Instead of taking Irun they have lost the entire country around that place. . . . The siege of Irun was a mistake."

However, his last dispatch from Irún, appearing on November 13, contained a message of optimism:

> A heavy snow fell which covered the mountains around Irun has increased the sinister aspect of the spectacle which the scene of the recent battle presents . . . the Spanish Republican troops are actively pursuing the retreating Carlists. As they advance they still burn the houses of Carlist sympathizers. Three hundred have already been destroyed. . . . the Carlists are not discouraged. . . . The Royalists mean to fight again.

Directly below MacGahan's November 13 story ran an item in neat juxtaposition, datelined London, which said: "The Standard's telegram from Paris says the impression here, in circles favorable to Don Carlos, is that his cause is utterly ruined and his situation hopeless."

MacGahan must have realized the truth of this although he never admitted it in print. His defense of the Carlists and their cause was unwavering. "It is my firm conviction," he wrote from Hendaye, "founded upon what I have seen since I have been with the Carlists, that they have been far more sinned against than sinning."

Through the fall of the year, despite the transparent hopelessness of the Carlist cause, and what must have been a dwindling public interest in the static "war" in Spain, Bennett kept his correspondent on the job, and MacGahan continued to send to Barbara in Bayonne dispatches for the *Herald*. Typical of them was a piece dated September 24 from a place named Puente la Reina in which MacGahan spoke of the "wonderful rapidity of movement of which the Carlists have shown themselves capable—a rapidity which I do not think has ever been equalled, even by the armies of Napoleon and Wellington."

In this story he wrote of the Carlist soldiery:

> One is lost in admiration of these soldiers, and I do not think any general, no matter to what soldiers accustomed, can see these fellows on the march, with their long, swinging stride, and iron sinews and joyous shout, without a feeling

of exultation in them and a desire to lead them into battle. They remind me more of the soldiers Michigan, Wisconsin, Illinois and Indiana sent out during our own war than any troops I have seen in Europe. The truth is, the world does not understand or appreciate the valor of these men.

Occasionally, as in the Puente la Reina dispatch, he questioned the capabilities of the Carlist military commanders, commenting on their "very decided want of the power of combining and executing a plan." On both sides, he noted "a lack of generalship," something he found remarkable "considering the education and experience of the Generals engaged."

Their new quarters in Bayonne were to have made it easier for MacGahan to visit his family and to send his cables and correspondence; but although he managed to make his way back to their apartment, near Bayonne's church of St. Etienne, now and then, Barbara described her existence as "living like a hermit all winter and spring, waiting for M.G. to return."

She wrote her correspondence for *Golos*, read all her husband's dispatches, visited the telegraph and post offices daily, collected his newspapers and carefully scanned all issues of the *Herald* for his work, took Paul and Justine on outings, and corresponded with Marie in Moscow.

MacGahan, when delayed in returning to Bayonne, wrote Barbara faithfully. On October 11, for example, he wrote from Estella during a lengthy absence, "You must not worry. We are expecting a battle soon and then I will arrive immediately and there will probably be nothing more here during this season." He added, "Is the little one doing well? He is beginning to possess my heart." Eleven days later he sent another message: "It is possible that I can come soon; I am terribly bored here. A thousand caresses." And, in response to Barbara's sending him a tracing of Paul's hand: "The little one's signature pleased me greatly. Only you would have such ideas."

And on October 27, still holed up in Estella awaiting some momentous decision from Don Carlos, MacGahan wrote his wife a playful and revealing letter which demonstrated as much as anything he ever wrote his genuine feelings toward her:

It is all right that there is a woman who must be 45 or 50 who makes eyes at me and even squeezes my hand effusively, but she does not tempt me. In the past I would have seized a similar opportunity to amuse myself in passing;

now I rather avoid it. I have become delicate, it seems. When
one is accustomed to Chateau Lafitte of the finest vintage,
it is difficult to accustom oneself to the taste of very ordinary wine.

He added,

If I could spend the day with you once a week even, I would
not be bored as I am. . . . How I love you! How I love
you! . . . How I would like to see the little one. . . . I have
reflected several times of the possibility of bringing you
both to Tulosa but it does not now appear possible. . . . I
suppose there is a young man in the house who is paying
court to you. Tell me about it.

Copies of the *Herald* arrived for MacGahan at the Bayonne post office from London daily. Each was many days old, but Barbara read the
foreign columns avidly for news of her husband and general developments in Spain for her *Golos* work. The execution of Captain Schmidt
of the Cologne *Gazette*, covered at length, proved to her that foreign
newspapermen might not be safe in either Carlist or Republican
camps.

An October 20 item she spotted seemed to prove this beyond doubt.
The item stated that Cecil Buckland, correspondent of the New York
Times, en route to the Carlist headquarters with Francis Jerrard, a representative of the "English Carlist Committee," had been "assassinated." Jerrard also was believed dead. The story said the American
legation in Paris had received no official confirmation, but the two
men were alleged to have been shot by "Spanish Republicans."

This unsettling news paled, however, when on November 28 she
opened the issue of the *Herald* dated November 23 to read it over her
morning coffee. She ran quickly over the foreign news, stopping
abruptly at a tiny item with a London dateline:

Intelligence has been received from Spain, but it is not as
yet deemed reliable, which reports Mr. MacGahan, the special correspondent of the Herald, as having been captured
this afternoon on the Spanish side of the Santiago ferry by a
republican officer, who refused to give an explanation of his
action in making the arrest. The Report states that Mr.
MacGahan was marched off to Fontarabia, at the mouth of
the Bidassoa, on the dividing line between France and
Spain.

The implication seemed clear that MacGahan would be treated as a spy. "I knew how prompt justice could be by the half wild Spanish Republicans," she said. She left the baby in the nurse's care and flew off to the office of the American consul at Bayonne. There she was informed that the consul had already departed for the Alfonsist headquarters across the frontier and that MacGahan and the New York *Times* correspondent Buckland had both been taken prisoner. A clerk in the consulate gave Barbara the chilling news that "the Consul hopes to reach there in time to prevent the execution of both Americans."

Left with no alternative but to return home to await news of the consul's mission, Barbara walked the short distance to her apartment house and there found her husband, playing on the floor with their son!

"He explained he did not telegraph me about his adventure because he did not want to disturb me and hoped the news would not reach me," she recorded many years later. "I could not scold him, I was so glad to see him safe."

Following the brief speculative announcement of the 23rd, the *Herald*, next day, carried this editorial page notice: "The Spanish news is interesting today . . . and one of the most painful reports is that of the arrest of the special correspondent of the Herald and his imprisonment by the republicans. No cause for this arbitrary act is given, but it is no doubt utterly unjustifiable, and, if the unconfirmed rumor is true, we trust soon to hear of his liberation by the Madrid authorities."

On the 26th, the story began to flesh out. A column datelined Hendaye informed *Herald* readers that MacGahan and Buckland were indeed under arrest by Republican authorities at Fontarabia and that Buckland had already been released. MacGahan, the story related, "is still in custody, but steps have been taken for his release." Both men were arrested while crossing the Santiago river, "notwithstanding they had passports," and the story went on to say, "the correspondents were subjected to great indignity. In Fontarabia they were confined in a privy for three hours and then removed to a cell swarming with vermin."

2
"All my own fault"

The November 26 account said MacGahan had been detained by the mayor of Fontarabia. The mayor, the *Herald* stated, "has begun a civil action after Buckland's release for using threatening language against

Mr. MacGahan, but it is supposed that the complaint will not be pressed."

Editorially, the *Herald* took the obligatory position that "a gross outrage has been committed in Spain on the correspondents of the Herald and Times, who were arrested in defiance of their passports and afterwards subjected to revolting indignities."

The next day, a story out of London ran: "At last account, Mr. MacGahan . . . was still imprisoned at San Sebastian. No further information has been received concerning his case. It is thought that the Carlists have cut the telegraph wires communicating with the town."

MacGahan, comfortably back in Bayonne, celebrating Christmas with wife and son, read his own account of the capture which appeared in the *Herald* in a four-column display in the issue of December 20 with the heading:

CROSSING THE SPANISH 'LINES'
How American Correspondent Got
into Trouble.

The story began:

> It was all my own fault. I ought to have known better. To go into Irun, booted and spurred, wearing a Carlist boina, was simply a tempting of the devil in the shape of an ignorant Chief of Police, arbitrary and brutal as the police always are the world over. Imagine, if possible, the besotted ignorance of a man holding an important official position who has never heard of the New York Herald or the Times and never reads any paper but a small weekly appearing in his own little village . . .

It was beyond comprehension to MacGahan that a police chief of a flyspeck on the map of Spain would not be conversant with the two daily New York newspapers and instead was content to read his small Spanish-language village weekly. But as astonishing as this revelation appears to have been to him, more surprises were in store.

He and Buckland, he wrote, had been captured as spies and thrown into a six-by-twelve-foot dungeon—in fact, a privy. "A dog kennel or pigsty would have been sweet and wholesome beside it," MacGahan said. The two men quickly determined that the pile of rotting straw on the floor was, to quote MacGahan's wonderful circumlocution, "already inhabited to its fullest capacity by a numerous and powerful coterie of animated beings who immediately proceeded in the most hospitable manner to invite us to supper." (The lice must have given MacGahan a momentary reflection, once again, of the horrors of the infamous pit at Bokhara.)

After a few hours the two correspondents were removed from the privy by the military commandant of the Irún district who treated his prisoners well, offering them cigars, wine, and coffee. The American consul at Bayonne, meanwhile, had been informed of their arrest. This mysterious message, MacGahan said, "came from a beautiful creature, daughter of the proprietor of my hotel in Hendaye," who, with her father, were Carlist sympathizers.

The guards assigned to MacGahan and Buckland were given to believe that the two prisoners were under sentence of death when ordered to march them out for transfer to San Sebastian. But in that town, both were released without explanation, and both returned to Hendaye through the Carlist lines. One final indignity was visited on them: Before reaching the safety of the town, they were accosted on the road by robbers who took their watches and wallets containing a combined total of three hundred francs (about sixty dollars).

The *Herald* editorial on their release ran on November 29:

> Happily we are able to chronicle the release from a Spanish prison of our correspondent, Mr. MacGahan, who, as previously reported, was taken by Spanish soldiery at Fontarabia, and, though released by them, was substantially thrown into prison by a super-serviceable flunky at Santander.

The editorial went on to pay a super-serviceable tribute to the *Herald* correspondent:

> MacGahan has, in the service of this journal, passed through more than the usual perils that beset the steps of a correspondent in their general difficulties and often dangerous attendance on great enterprise, but has always come handsomely through at last, and the star of his good fortune is evidently not dimmed yet.

The war obviously did not end as MacGahan had predicted; the Carlists never, in fact, moved on Madrid in anything but rhetoric. The monarchy, restored under Alfonso XII, provided the most stable government Spain had enjoyed in over forty years. Upon his death in 1909, Don Carlos VII was succeeded as pretender by his only son, Don Jaime, duke of Madrid, whose death without issue in 1931 threw the succession in turmoil. Carlos VII's brother, Don Alfonso, finally wore the mantle for a time, but with his death in 1936 the Carlist line became extinct.

After the end of the Second Carlist War, Carlism remained strong only in Navarre. It sided with the army in the 1936 Spanish Civil War and helped mobilize Navarre in the nationalist cause. In 1937 the remnants of the Carlist *causa* were merged by Generalissimo Franco into the Falange Española Tradicionalista.

The same issue of the *Herald* in which Barbara MacGahan first saw the rumor story of her husband's capture by the Republicans ran yet another brief item which, unknown then to either of them, gave a clue to MacGahan's next—and last—assignment for James Gordon Bennett: "In view of the Arctic expedition about to be fitted out by the British government, Lady Franklin has renewed her offer of a reward of $10,000 for the recovery of official records of Sir John Franklin's expedition."

IX

Under the
Northern Lights

1

"The Commodore informed me"

He roamed the Bayonne apartment, which Barbara called their "hermitage," with the caged-cat restlessness of one who suddenly finds time to waste after years with no time to call his own. Justine, the homely peasant woman from Dax, scurried about with young Paul, relieving his parents of hour-to-hour care and giving the MacGahans time together. Barbara, always disquieted from not knowing her husband's whereabouts or well-being, was in a rare state of contentment, channeling her free time into her writing without the stress of waiting for a knock on the door.

That winter of 1874–75 produced certain changes in MacGahan— or at least threw them into focus. He was six months past his thirtieth birthday, yet he looked fifteen or perhaps twenty years older. There is a telling photograph of him, taken in a London studio within days of the departure of the *Pandora* for arctic waters. It is of a handsome, sturdy man, seemingly close to fifty years of age. The face is squarish and well-formed, with a high forehead, the head bald on its crown with a few fugitive hairs brushed across it while the longer hair of the sides is newly clipped and brushed back. The brows grow close together at the juncture of a perfectly shaped nose, and the eyes are magnetic, light of pupil, calm and steady in their gaze past the shoulder of the studio photographer. There is a hint of crow's-feet at their outer edge, but the eyes are wide awake and resolute with none of the hooded indolence often affected by men of action. The man's mouth is lightly set, the form of it hidden beneath a downward-brushed moustache blending with a bristly beard which thins out toward the temples. If there is a weakness of the chin, the beard hides it.

It is not only the baldness which ages MacGahan in the photograph, there is also a maturity in the grim determination of the face which also seems older than a mere thirty and a half years. It is the face of a man who has seen a great deal more horror and unhappiness than a man of his years should have seen.

In the six months of freedom before him, between his return to Bayonne from Spain in the last month of 1874 and his departure before the mast in June 1875, inactivity quickly palled for him. He read carefully of the dismal end of the Carlist campaign and had his daily dispatches to write. He gave some thought to the book the publishers Sampson, Low suggested he write on his experiences with Don Carlos's camp. He studied the *Herald* columns, especially the foreign news. Silence and solitude, Barbara later wrote in her personal memoir of those days, weighed heavily upon him and "presented such a crushing effect on his mind that his thoughts seemed chained."

He could not bear to write, she said, at his desk in a fixed place. He had developed the war correspondent's knack of writing under trying conditions and tried to simulate them even in the Bayonne apartment. He sought, Barbara wrote, "turmoil in order to produce his daily stint," and "whatever serious reflection his work required, he chose the most inconvenient place to do it in." She recalled:

> He would come into the room where there was the most noise and conversation, undisturbed even at children's play, he would take the nearest table and place it near a window overlooking the street, then would begin covering one sheet of paper after another with incredible speed. He would stop and spend five or ten minutes watching the scenes in the street, and so went on writing again. He frequently got up and played with the children [presumably Paul and a neighbor's child], made fun of the cat, and then, whistling some merry tune from a French opera, he would sit down to work again and the writing would go on— fluently and with great rapidity—seldom crossing a word out.

He had learned Spanish in his months with the Carlists and now worked steadily on his Russian, especially the conversational language. Barbara's patient tutelage, together with what he had learned during the Khivan campaign, brought him fluency in the difficult tongue long before it would become a priceless asset to him. Already proficient in French, he conversed with Barbara in that language until 1876 when, during the siege of Plevna, she spent six months in concentrated study and mastered spoken English.

Money and career problems plagued both of them. Barbara found it inconceivable that he would spend much more time in Bennett's employ, yet the regular salary was necessary to support them and their child. MacGahan, over and over, spoke of "a literary career of some sort," yet he wondered if the ordinary writer's life would ever really suffice. There could be no return to pedestrian things. He had come too far, gone too far, to retrogress. He was yet a young man, his life lay before him, and there seemed ample time before retiring to be a writer and a family man.

He stood now on the brink of fame, he felt certain, and he was feverish to pursue some great destiny.

The spring of 1875 produced the only extended period of introspection for MacGahan in his five years service with the *Herald*, but Barbara's is the only record we have of these months, and there can be no certainty that she accurately reflected her husband's attitude. Indeed, there are some clues that the contrary was true.

Whatever renown MacGahan had achieved was the product of his association with the *Herald*, not vice versa. This he knew and admitted; Barbara did not. The sense of his letters prior to 1875 and even after he left the newspaper indicate that MacGahan was satisfied with Bennett's "treatment" of him; Barbara was forever outraged by what she considered Bennett's record of slights and lack of appreciation.

The truth appears to be that MacGahan was reasonably content with the rewards of the career thrust upon him through his good fortune to have been in France in wartime, a career any of his contemporaries could envy. The rewards of salary, public renown, and the trust placed in him by the *Herald* proprietor to handle a difficult assignment— these seemed to MacGahan commensurate with his accomplishments for the paper and its owner.

Barbara's discontent, given fuller expression in hindsight many years after her husband's death, was based on a different set of values and priorities. She needed MacGahan as husband and father; the frenetic life of the special correspondent would never fit such a need, and it was James Gordon Bennett who kept her from realizing her dream. She thought her husband's misadventures in Spain—his imprisonment, in particular—"would disaccustom him to risk his life," but, she said, "I was badly mistaken." Hers, more than anything else, was a reflection of "what might have been" had she been able to alter the events that followed the respite in Bayonne in 1875.

On March 26, MacGahan recorded in his occasional diary that he met with Bennett at the Café Voisin in the Voltaire Hotel in Paris and that the "Commodore," a nickname based on Bennett's yachting mania, "informed me I am to go with Arctic expedition."

But it was not until June that MacGahan received details of his assignment, meeting Bennett again in the Paris offices of the *Herald*. During this brief meeting, the correspondent learned he would join the ship's company of the *Pandora*, under command of Captain Alan Young, leaving England on June 26 for Greenland. Bennett explained that he, Lady Jane Franklin, Captain Young, and Lieutenant Innes Lillingston, second in command of the *Pandora*, were sponsoring the voyage and that its purpose was twofold: to search for the Northwest Passage—that tantalizing dream of passage between the Atlantic and Pacific oceans through the arctic ice that had haunted navigators since the time of John Cabot in the sixteenth century—and to search for traces of the lost Franklin Expedition.

It appears, given the secrecy surrounding the expedition, that MacGahan's duties were to chronicle the voyage, perhaps to write of it upon his return. Bennett, knowing of the fine critical reception accorded his correspondent's first book, may have hoped a new book would immortalize the *Herald*'s role in the history of the Franklin expedition's mysteries.

MacGahan made a show of discussing the matter with Barbara. "In reality," she recorded, "he put the question in such a way that I had to confess it was impossible not to go. Our funds were low as usual, my sickness in Biarritz costly and the expenses in Bayonne not small. If M.G. refused to join the *Pandora*, he would be finished with Bennett."

They took a hotel room in Paris for Paul and Justine and spent five days in London before MacGahan's departure. Barbara needed to return to Russia, there to settle accounts and gain new assignments with the various newspapers and journals for which she now served as translator and sometime correspondent. MacGahan managed to scrape up one hundred pounds for her trip, and on June 20, the two parted.

She took Paul and Justine with her. The railway schedule permitted her to stop over in Warsaw to visit her sister Natalia, now married to George Cherniaev, who held an important governmental post in the Polish capital. In Moscow, she spent some time with her younger sister Marie and stayed at the summer resort of Bogorodsk near Moscow. It would be October before she heard from her husband.

"The more I lived with him, the more I loved and understood him," she wrote in later years. "I forgave all. . . . I asked the mercy of God to return M.G. safe to me so that we could provide for the future of our child."

2

"Is not the arctic before us?"

Pandora's voyage was shrouded in secrecy.* MacGahan, though a bona fide passenger "having the honor to represent Mr. Bennett of the *Herald*," found even Captain Young reticent about the details of the journey north. Bennett introduced MacGahan to the forty-eight-year-old merchant naval officer in London. Young, a remote, gray-eyed man with an encyclopedic knowledge of the polar regions, had taken part as navigator in the Franklin Search Expedition under Captain Leopold McClintock on the *Fox* in 1857–59 and had returned to the north a year later with the North Atlantic Telegraph Expedition. He was a favorite in the Victorian court, where his friends called him "Alleno." In two years he would become Captain Sir Alan William Young, knight commander of Bath.

Captain Young did give MacGahan some pointers on what to read in the nearly three weeks before *Pandora* would weigh anchor, and in that time the correspondent undertook to find out as much as he could about the Northwest Passage and the man credited, by dying in its vicinity, with discovering it.

Sir John Franklin, one of those charters-of-the-unknown that England produced in such abundance in the nineteenth century, had entered the Royal Navy in 1800 at the age of fourteen and had served with Nelson at Copenhagen and Trafalgar before making his name as an arctic explorer. In 1818 he had his first arctic experience as second

---

*The first published notice describing its purpose did not appear until October 23 when Rear Admiral George H. Richards gave the details in a letter to the *Times* of London. By then, the *Pandora* had returned to England from Arctic waters.

in command of the *Trent*, which spent several months off Spitsbergen after an abortive attempt to reach the pole. In 1819–22 and again in 1825–27 he commanded overland expeditions across the Canadian Barrens.

On May 19, 1845, after an eighteen-year absence from the northlands, Sir John sailed from England with two bark-rigged vessels, *Erebus* and *Terror*, to attempt the Northwest Passage. On July 25, at the entrance of Lancaster Sound, the opening to the west on the northern edge of giant Baffin Island (and the true entrance to the Northwest Passage), Sir John's black-hulled, white-masted, and yellow-decked ships were last sighted.

The white fastness of the Canadian Arctic Archipelago swallowed them up, and it would be fourteen years before the fate of Franklin and his 126 officers and men was revealed to the world.

It was expected that the Franklin expedition might spend two or even three winters in the Arctic, and thus it was 1848 before the first search parties, inspired by an admiralty reward of £ 20,000 for any ship bringing aid to what was then called the "lost" expedition, set out to learn his whereabouts.

The years passed with no substantial news. Lady Franklin steadfastly refused to give up hope that her husband and at least a few of his men had miraculously survived, perhaps living with arctic Eskimos and awaiting rescue, and in 1857 she purchased a 177-ton schooner, the *Fox*, and enlisted the aid of an experienced arctic sailor to undertake a search expedition.

Twenty-seven months later—fourteen years, four months, and a day after Sir John Franklin's ships had set sail—Captain Leopold McClintock brought back the tragic details of the fate of *Erebus* and *Terror*.

The story McClintock had been able to piece together, from written records of the Franklin party, from the testimony of Eskimos on Boothia Peninsula, and from the mute final evidence of human bones and abandoned equipment on King William Island, told a melancholy tale of unimagined suffering.

Erebus and *Terror*, the latter commanded by Captain Francis R. M. Crozier, made significant progress at the outset. Franklin's vessels had sailed up Wellington Channel at 77° north latitude, found no open sea, and circumnavigated Cornwallis Island to winter quarters at Beechey Island at the westward terminus of Lancaster Sound. In the spring of 1846 the ships labored southward down Peel Sound and Franklin Strait to the open water between Boothia Peninsula and Victoria Is-

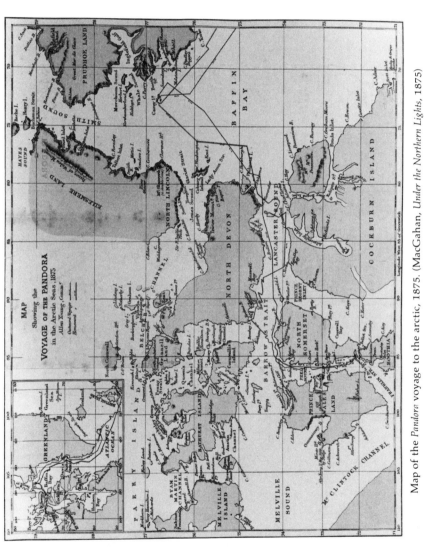

Map of the *Pandora* voyage to the arctic, 1875. (MacGahan, *Under the Northern Lights*, 1875)

The *Pandora* in Greenland waters. (MacGahan, *Under the Northern Lights*)

Northumberland House. (MacGahan, *Under the Northern Lights*)

MacGahan, about 1876. (MacGahan Papers)

land. But ice moving down the then-unnamed (later McClintock) channel, locked the ships in a vise in sight of Cape Felix on the northern tip of King William Island.

As yet, there was no great concern. The ships were provisioned for three years' subsistence, and Sir John and his officers had plenty of work to occupy them and even a twelve hundred-volume library on the *Terror* for the anticipated long winter months.

By the spring of 1847, after two winters in the Arctic, twenty-four officers and men had died and were buried by raking shallow graves in the ironlike ice and topsoil. On June 11, 1847, Sir John Franklin succumbed to some unknown ailment, perhaps to simple exposure, and was buried on the ironically named "Victory Point" on King William.

The one hundred or so survivors of the expedition, now under the command of Captain Crozier, spent another winter locked in the ice of McClintock Channel, then on April 22, 1848, *Erebus* and *Terror* were abandoned and the party moved overland hoping to find relief among the Eskimos of Boothia Peninsula. McClintock found records at Point Victory which established that Franklin's ships had been deserted after having been beset by ice since September 1846. These records, signed by F. R. M. Crozier and dated April 25, 1848, were the last definite trace of the expedition, but McClintock's thorough investigation revealed that in all likelihood the survivors had died, one by one, in the months to come. Most had died on the west side of King William, some venturing as far south as Simpson Strait which separates King William from the mainland, and some even to the northern shore of Adelaide Peninsula, northernmost mainland point of Canada.

Although the fate of the expedition was now sealed by McClintock's findings in 1859, Lady Franklin continued her work in her husband's memory by urging and financing searches for Sir John's lost logs and records. As late as 1870, twenty-three years after her husband's death, she visited America and journeyed to MacGahan's home state of Ohio, where, in Cincinnati, she spoke to Charles Francis Hall, the eccentric amateur explorer, who had made a near religion of searching for traces of the Franklin party.

The *Pandora* expedition of 1875 was one of over forty similarly inspired search parties which hoped to find new evidence or traces of Franklin's records.

Just before leaving London for Plymouth, where he would board the *Pandora*, MacGahan received an accounting from his publishers Sampson, Low and royalties of about £80 for *Campaigning on the Oxus*. Low expressed interest in a book on MacGahan's experiences in the Carlist campaign and on the *Pandora* voyage as well.

The ship, with Captain Young, Lieutenant Lillingston, and a crew of thirty-one officers and men, sailed at dawn on June 27 from Cowes, touching at Plymouth, where MacGahan boarded. The 570-ton *Pandora*, powered by sail and a single screw, had been built at Pembroke in 1861, commissioned in the Royal Navy in 1863, and spent four years patrolling the African coast. Now, with arctic seas facing her, she had undergone refitting by Messrs. Day and Summers of Southampton and was ready for the rigors of the far north. Her hull of American elm was four and a half inches thick, her stem covered with solid-plate iron. Bark-rigged—originally built as a gunboat and bomb ketch—she was 150 feet long with a beam of 20 feet, drawing 12 feet of water, and powered by 80-horsepower engines. She carried, in addition to her crew, provisions for eighteen months and fuel in the form of 150 tons of coal.

The opening lines of the daily diary MacGahan compiled during the voyage reveal a romantic notion of the rigors of arctic exploration facing any vessel venturing into the far north:

> We are leaving the homes of men, the swarming cities, the careworn, anxious faces of the toiling multitudes, the smoky, poisoned atmosphere, the fetters of civilization— for a world of pure air and savage freedom, for the frozen regions around the Pole; the home of the reindeer and the walrus, the haunts of the white bear, the land of the Midnight Sun. . . .
>
> Is not the Arctic before us in all its glory? Are not the icebergs awaiting us with all their weird phantasmagoria of shape and colour, the cold green water dashing around their feet, gurgling through caverns it has itself worn deep into their icy hearts?

He wrote of mountains to be scaled, continents to be explored on which no mortal foot had ever trod, cozy little bays and inlets landlocked and hidden by towering mountains, quiet little rivers "whose waters have never been rippled by prow of boat or canoe, teeming with such delicious trout and salmon as Isaac Walton never dreamed of," grassy glades with musk ox and reindeer grazing.

In reality, while the voyage of the *Pandora* would not be without interest ("remarkable only for its dash and rapidity" the much-subdued correspondent would later admit), and the Arctic a land of haunting beauty at times, few of MacGahan's effusions were more than that. The *Pandora*, her deck a bedlam of boxes, barrels, and coal—everywhere coal and soot—was no yacht on a pleasant jaunt. Her prow was designed for butting through pack ice, her destination a forbidding land fraught with danger to man and vessel. There were no mountains to scale, no continents to explore, no hidden rivers, and certainly no reindeer and musk ox at the latitudes Captain Young intended to cross.

MacGahan's cabin opened into the mess room below the maindeck, a tiny cubicle loaded with books, guns, oilskins, arctic boots, chamois-lined foul-weather gear, and furs. As the ship made her way toward the southern coast of Greenland, the correspondent made acquaintance with the ship's officers: Lieutenant George Pirie, navigator, on loan from the Admiralty; Lieutenant Beynen of the Dutch Royal Navy—a seasoned arctic hand nicknamed "Tromp" after the old Dutch admiral who once sailed up the Thames with a broom lashed to the masthead as a sign he intended to sweep it clean; and Dr. Horner, the young ship's surgeon. Another civilian on board was Mr. DeWilde, a noted pen-and-ink artist.

Pandora departed Portsmouth for the northwest on June 27 with the expectation of reaching Disko Island, on the midwestern coast of Greenland, in twenty days. But unpredictably rough seas and a gale encountered in mid-Atlantic doubled that time. On July 28, Cape Farewell on the southern tip of Greenland was sighted, surrounded by floating ice—Spitsbergen ice, it was called, which had broken off that great pack west of the Norwegian island to float down the east coast of Greenland.

MacGahan waxed especially poetic over this first major ice sighting: ". . . old castles with broken, ruined towers, battlements and loopholes . . . castellated fortresses; cathedrals, with the fantastic gothic carving and delicate tracery, never equalled in beautiful irregularity of design by anything carved by man . . . huge mushrooms, ice foliage, breadfruit trees, swans with long slender necks, dragons, lions, eagles."

Coming along smoothly under reefed topsails at about five knots, *Pandora* plunged slowly through the floats with battering ram force, making her way around south Greenland, past Cape Desolation, where the first seals were spied "like plum puddings floating in the water," he wrote. A few were shot and hooked aboard, their livers considered a special delicacy.

Captain Young decided to make his first anchorage at Ivigtut, a tiny Danish settlement on the west Greenland coast, lying at the mouth of Arsuk Fjord, a narrow, crooked inlet penetrating nearly fifty miles toward the great Greenland icecap. The village, a collection of fifteen or twenty wooden huts scattered over a rocky slope, was an important anchorage in the cryolite trade.* Already at anchor were the brigantine *Traveller*, bound from Peterhead to Cape Farewell to obtain a cryolite cargo, and *Fox*, McClintock's (and Captain Young's) old ship, now also in the mineral trade.

As the first order of business, the *Pandora* officers paid a brief visit to a Swedish physician named Arctander and were served mugs of "banko," a warmed mixture of sherry and some unidentifiable ingredients.

MacGahan found west Greenland a place of surpassing beauty with its high, rugged mountains rising abruptly out of the water in lowering perpendicular masses, some as high as three thousand feet. "Over these the sun and atmosphere combine to produce the most fantastic effects of color," he wrote. "A thick veil of mist gathers over them, as if to drape and hide their savage nakedness—a kind of spider-web, of gigantic proportions, that catches the sunlight and holds it prisoner in the meshes of a fairy net."

The rugged coast was periodically broken by deep narrow fjords extending from five to seventy miles inland; these teemed with the salmon and trout of MacGahan's poetic imagining, their banks and mountain valleys alive with partridge and ptarmigan. Once, during the voyage up the coast, three kayaks approached the *Pandora* and were hoisted aboard, boat and all, the Davis Strait Eskimos having with them fifteen beautiful trout and a half dozen smoked salmon which they eagerly traded for sea biscuit and tobacco.

At latitude 66°12′, the *Pandora* scraped against reefs, giving the ship's company a scare but doing no serious damage. It was the first of their arctic discoveries, and "Pandora Reefs" entered the cartographer's lexicon for the first time. In the early morning hours of August 5 the ship passed the Arctic Circle and two days later, forty days out of Portsmouth, dropped anchor in the little bay of Godhavn on the westerly coast of Disko Island.

3
"Thus saith the Lord, Consider your ways"

Godhavn was little different from any other Greenland coastal village, though larger. Half-wooden, half-earthen huts clutched the sides of rocky slopes. The village now was enjoying its few short weeks of

---

*Cryolite, sodium-aluminum fluoride, a white mineral used in electrolytic production of aluminum, was found in abundance on the Greenland coast.

summer, but except for sparse grass growing valiantly among the out-
croppings of lavalike rock, there were few other signs of vegetation
save for a variety of moss and a tiny yellow flower which grew in
abundance.

Mr. Elberg, Danish governor of Disko, and his wife, an Inuit woman,
called on the *Pandora* and delivered the latest news. The Royal Navy's
Alert and *Discovery* had proceeded on their voyage north ten days before, and *Valorous* had sailed for England at about the same time. The
latter news disappointed *Pandora's* crew since Captain Young had
hoped to intercept the *Valorous* at Disko and transfer mail to her. Now
the letters would have to go to Denmark by Danish merchant ship,
then to England via Copenhagen.

MacGahan meanwhile, as appears to have been his habit, was studying the local scenery. "This is the country of Mrs. Bloomer," he observed in his diary. "The women all wear trowsers, and would scoff at
the idea of anything else as absurd and probably indecent." He noted
that the women's apparel consisted of seal-skin trousers, hairy side
out, extending down to the knee, where they were tied with garters.
The boots were worn with red and white cloth stockings.

The *Herald's* amateur anthropologist had a chance for a closer study
of the lady folk of Disko when the *Pandora* followed local custom and
gave a ball a few hours after dropping anchor. The dance was held with
great success in a carpenter's shop, cleaned out and spruced up for the
occasion, a sign over the door proclaiming "Musi chal dor E ope Nat 8
clock," an Inuit attempt at written English translating to "Music Hall
door open at 8 o'clock." The shop, with one window, accommodated,
in relays, the nearly fifty people who showed up to dance—officers and
bluejackets from the *Pandora* and the civilians of Disko merging in
waltzes, polkas, cotillions, all accompanied with homemade music on a
strange variety of instruments.

"I am ready to aver," MacGahan declared, "that I never enjoyed a
dance more in my life."

He found, as was also his custom, one particular partner who gave
him no end of diary-jottings. Demonstrating that knack which Fred
Burnaby noted of MacGahan's Khivan experiences, of finding female
pulchritude in the strangest corners of the earth, the correspondent's
partner he described as "a demure little beauty, with dark, slightly
almond-shaped eyes, a skin as brown as that of the nut-brown maid
herself, the reddest, ripest lips, and the daintiest little feet that ever
were seen."

Like all young Disko Inuit women, she wore her hair "in a queer
little topknot" tied with a red ribbon (denoting a maiden; married

women wore blue, widows black, and "those of neither maid, wife nor widow, restricted to green, or to a simple handkerchief tied around the head"). And since she was short of stature, her topknot barely reached the level of MacGahan's chin. He said in a hilarious recollection, "I must have looked as though I had an enormous imperial [the pointed-beard made popular by Napoléon III], with a girl suspended to it by a red ribbon."

His dancing partner was graceful in the extreme, and MacGahan ventured to say that "a greater pleasure even than to encircle her slender waist or to gaze into her dark eyes, was to watch her little red-booted feet as they skimmed over the ground like the wings of a sea-bird over the waves—a pleasure quite lost when you dance with a girl who wears petticoats."

After a day at Disko, the *Pandora* sailed up the Waigat Strait, which separates the island from the mainland. The purpose of this venture was to coal the ship at the villages of Yuyarusuk and Kidliset. The coal seams in the cliffs surrounding these villages were particularly rich and were tapped by the simple expedient of cutting away the soap-stone and loose earth that covered them, then prying the coal loose with crowbars from the crevices. The great black boulders were then transported (often by merely rolling them down) to the water's edge. An occasional cry of "Heads!" meant that a particularly large chunk, often half a ton or more, was being launched down the hillside, people scattering in all directions out of its erratic path. Once *Pandora*'s waiting boats were filled to the gunwales with sacked coal, they were towed by the steam launch to the ship.

In a few days a full forty tons of raw seam coal had been hoisted on board the *Pandora*, the ship loaded from jibboom to taffrail. A heavy fog created moisture on the shrouds and rigging of the ship, hanging in festoons and trickling down in streams to drop on the deck and mix with the coal dust. The ship, MacGahan observed graphically, was "drunk with coal—she greedily gorged herself until she rolled and staggered deep down in the water, groaning and protesting against being disturbed until she had digested her gluttonous meal."

Pandora's mascots, a pig named "Mr. Hogan" and a nondescript dog, were black with soot, he wrote, and the ship's crew glared at each other like Negro minstrels.

The coaling monotony was at last broken when Captain Young announced that the ship would hold a party for the villagers. This time, MacGahan's observations were of his "pain and grief" at the conduct of the ship's company. He wrote that "no sooner had they discovered that the girls were pretty" than *Pandora*'s sailors "commenced making the most violent love to these girls with a cynicism worthy of Don Juan himself."

MacGahan's pain and grief over this situation, while well intentioned, was overwrought. Sailors, he ought to have known, were not noted for the permanence of their far-flung relationships nor for the sincerity of their "protestations of attachment." On a nineteenth-century sail-and-steam brig, with a dog and a pig for companionship, it is small wonder their lovemaking was perfervid.

That MacGahan felt a strong attachment for the Inuits of Disko Island is undeniable. He learned with increasing wonderment of their adaptation to their hostile land, of their ability to find food, fire, light, clothing, arms, and implements in a single animal—the seal—as did the American Indian in the buffalo (though in an environment less unrelentingly hostile to humankind), and of their apparently enduring light-heartedness and gaiety.

In the weekly handwritten paper, inevitably called *Pandora's Box*, established aboard ship that month of the Disko anchorage, MacGahan wrote a series of popular articles on the Inuit women of Disko. In one of the pieces he said, "The dear girls! We shall never see them again, but we shall not soon forget their mirth and smiling faces that made the dreary desolation around them bloom as with roses."

Upon completion of the coaling operation, *Pandora* took leave of the island, returning down Waigat Strait to follow the Greenland coast northward, with good breezes from the southwest and southeast.

On the next leg of the voyage, up the Greenland coast to Upernivik, MacGahan tried to learn the Inuit tongue from Joseph Ebering, "Eskimo Joe," the hunter, interpreter, and able-bodied seaman of the *Pandora* crew who had wide experience working with exploration parties. Ebering had wintered several times with the *Polaris*, commanded by Captain Charles F. Hall, the Cincinnati mystic and amateur arctic explorer who died, quite mysteriously, far north of Kane Basin in 1871. But the Inuit language defied even MacGahan's linguistic talent, and he pronounced his effort with Eskimo Joe "an ignominious failure."

Pandora reached the coastal jumping-off village of Upernivik on the morning of August 13, transferring mail to a visiting small boat but not dropping anchor. This was the last Danish station the ship would touch until the return voyage.

The ship now entered Melville Bay, the northeast corner of Baffin Bay, and waters much dreaded by whalers and arctic sailors. It was a region of unpredictable ice and ceaseless noise, as well as a dangerous sea for navigation, as great groaning ice floes found a temporary home there after breaking off in more northern latitudes.

But *Pandora*'s captain and crew found the days of August 15 to 16 almost supernaturally beautiful, the bay fairly clear of impediment ice and the sea glassy smooth. Sighting a polar bear, crew members were permitted to lower a boat to kill the great beast, yet another welcome change from the salt meat, seal, and fish diet.

The thermometer registered thirty-two degrees off Cape York, the northwest extremity of Melville Bay, but the ice became more frequent, and the ship soon found herself wallowing through the loose, rotten floes called "pash ice," while the fat burgomaster gulls ("pollumawks" in sailor lingo) were now seen in squawking abundance.

Captain Young set *Pandora*'s course for Lancaster Sound, a name of magic to arctic men since it was believed (correctly) to form the only practicable entrance to and through that enormous exploded jigsaw puzzle of inlets, islands, sounds, bays, straits, channels, and capes that form the northernmost extremity of the American continent.

One detour had to be taken before entering Lancaster Sound, however, and that a one hundred-mile jump northward to Cape York, between the Greenland coast and Ellesmere Island, to the Cary Islands, a group of specks on the arctic chart. Captain Young hoped to pick up some dispatches left there by the *Alert* and *Discovery* expedition.

Pandora reached the Carys on the evening of August 19. At daybreak, a shore party found the cairn there empty. They did find a half-pint of rum which had undergone eight successive freezings and thawings (having been left there in 1867) and which was now, MacGahan declared, "as rich and mellow as old Rhine."

The Cary Islands detour was a waste of coal, but it did prove to be the highest latitude, 76°, reached by the *Pandora* and the only time her crew would see the midnight sun.

On the morning of the 20th, the ship arrived at the eastern opening of Lancaster Sound and found, off Cape Warrender on the southeastern coast of Devon Island, a heavy fog and the edge of an extensive icepack—both unusual for the month of August. Still, *Pandora* groped her way into the Sound, moving slowly westward through the ice and fog so close to the magnetic pole that the ship's compass was rendered useless. Early on the 24th she arrived opposite Prince Regent Inlet, then moved on through Barrow Strait to Beechey Island, where the anchor was dropped and a party went ashore to see the place where Sir John Franklin had passed his first winter after leaving England.

Beechey Island, MacGahan wrote, was "a sad, silent and lonely place." As the starting point for any Franklin Expedition search party, at one time or another as many as ten ships lay at anchor in her little bay. And everywhere lay traces of them. On the southern beach of the island a large boat had been dragged high on the rocky coast, her tall single mast still pointing at the sky. Two smaller boats were nearby, as well as a house, a fireplace of stone, a blacksmith's forge, a huge cairn built of empty meat tins, a group of graves, and boxes and barrels and trash in profusion.

"Northumberland House," the single real landmark on Beechey Island, had been built by Sir Edward Belcher in 1854. Around this rather stately dwelling, the ground was strewn with forty-pound tins of pemmican and smaller tins of other preserved meat, rolls of heavy blue cloth, hundreds of pairs of woollen mittens and socks, rolls of white flannel materials, bales of blankets, clothing—all in confusion, as if dropped by fleeing refugees ahead of some nameless horror.

Northumberland House had suffered considerable damage too, evidently by polar bears, for huge clawmarks were found everywhere. Barrels of salt meat had been gnawed and clawed open, holes were punched in pemmican tins; flour, sugar, beef, and preserved milk had been partially consumed by this strange banqueting bear orgy. Only a few barrels of meat, put up in solid iron-hooped casks, had proven too strong for their claws and fangs.

The little masted boat, the *Mary*, proved in good condition, her sails stowed beneath her deck, dry and preserved, along with a quantity of oakum (a caulking material), and only slightly rusted carpenter's tools.

Near the house were two sad monuments: a stone marker commemorating Lieutenant Bellot, the young French naval officer of the Belcher expedition who lost his life in the search for Franklin, and, lying at its foot, on a stone platform, a marble slab in memory of Sir John Franklin, both memorials set up by Leopold McClintock on the *Fox* expedition of 1857, the stones provided by Lady Franklin.

Three miles from Northumberland House, near the head of the bay where *Pandora* lay at anchor, were the graves of three of the crew of *Erebus* and *Terror*, standing in a row and marked with simple two-inch-thick oaken headboards on which were cut their names and those of their ships, their ages, and dates of death. Two of them contained scriptural lines: "Choose ye this day whom ye will serve," and "Thus saith the Lord, Consider your ways."

MacGahan wrote: "Such texts are not ordinarily chosen for inscriptions on gravestones, and they seem to hide some mysterious meaning as sinister as that of the graves themselves."

After a day of contemplative wandering about Beechey Island, Captain Young was ready to steam for Peel Sound, a southward stretch of unknown water separating Prince of Wales Land from Somerset Island. No ship was known to have penetrated Peel Sound to its extremity, where it emptied into McClintock Channel at the north of King William Island—*Pandora*'s ultimate destination. McClintock had attempted it with the *Fox* but was stopped almost at its entrance by a wall of ice. Some felt Sir John's *Erebus* and *Terror* had traveled the length of it to reach what was destined to be their graves on King William Island.

4
"Only an accidental atom"

When raising anchor, *Pandora*'s crew set up what was known as a "capstan song," the long stream of verses flowing in a monotonous chant as the men heaved on the capstan, bringing the anchor chain rumbling up through the hawsepipe. One of the ship's petty officers, an old whaler, set the cadence and was soon joined by twenty other voices. MacGahan was entranced by the capstan song and wrote down a typical verse in the dialect in which it was sung:

> Oh, Shanadoa, I longs to hear you.
> (Chorus) Ha! Ha! the rolling water.
> Oh, Shanadoa, I longs to hear you.
> (Chorus) Ho! Ho! the cold, pale water.

Lines were continually added, the next verse being "Oh, Shanadoa, I've seen your daughter," then "Oh, Shanadoa, I loves your daughter," then "When I return, I'll wed your daughter," then, "For seven years I've woo'd your daughter," then "Oh, Shanadoa, where *is* your daughter," and finally, "Oh, Shanadoa, beneath the water," and "Oh, Shanadoa, there lies your daughter."

At 9 A.M. on August 27, *Pandora* reached the entrance to Peel Strait, just twenty-four hours after departing Beechey Island. As far as the eye could see, packed ice blocked the way, and a dejected Captain Young ordered his crew over the side to take on water while they awaited a change in the weather. The ice seemed movable, and after the water casks were filled, the ship nosed her way southward into the Sound. MacGahan wrote of this careful picking southward between Somerset and Prince of Wales Land:

> There is something unaccountably oppressive in this Arctic
> universe. The immensity of these regions, their dreariness,
> their silent immobility that appears like the stillness of the

grave, have a strangely depressing effect. They weigh upon the mind, and bear it down like some fearful incubus, like that half-waking, half-dreaming, indistinct consciousness of weight upon the chest felt in the oppression of nightmare.

Man's anthropomorphism, he felt, received its critical test in this silent, overpowering land, and he wrote of this in an excellent philosophical passage in the book he would write on the *Pandora* expedition, based on his daily journal:

> We have hitherto been accustomed to look upon the world as made for our particular convenience and use. The Earth brings forth its fruits for us and teems with plenty; the flowers bloom for us; the sun rises and sets for us; it rains, because rain is necessary to our well-being. The moon revolves around the Earth only because we need a moon; the stars adorn the sky for us to look at; the Earth, the World, the Universe, in short, is made for us and our wants. But here is a world uninhabited and uninhabitable by man—a world that can never have been made for him; that has been created without the slightest regard for his wants and necessities—a world that will not afford him sustenance for a day. Nature, wrapped up in her own silent, desolate, mysterious sorrow, ignores his existence; she is indifferent whether he lives or dies; she will let him perish without offering him a berry or a root.

The result of this hauteur, this clear sign that planet Earth contained unmistakable evidence of nature's obliviousness to man and his needs, MacGahan said, "is stupefaction; a vague, oppressive feeling of blank terror. You begin to feel that instead of the world being created for you, you are only an accidental atom, an insect, upon it, and that it is a wonder you have not perished long ago."

The *Pandora* inched southward down Peel Strait, past the point where Sir Leopold McClintock had to turn back. The ice appeared to be thinning, giving Captain Young hope that the Sound might be navigable all the way to Bellot Strait, that tiny belt of water which separated Somerset Island from the Boothia Peninsula. If so, *Pandora* would approach King William Island, which lay to the south, "the goal of all our hopes," in MacGahan's words.

As the ship's navigator announced to the captain that the ship had now reached the farthest point attained by Ross and McClintock in their 1849 expedition, Young ordered the ship hove to. With Mac-Gahan, Young set off to the shore of Somerset Island to search for the cairn the famous explorers had left there. This five-foot-high heap of stones was soon located and, stuck in a chink of rock, a tin tube, placed there by Captain Ross twenty-eight years before, was removed. In the tube, sealed with red lead, they found a quarter sheet of foolscap dated June 7, 1849. The message, signed by "Jas. C. Ross, Captain," said that the Franklin search party of *Enterprise* and *Investigator*, having wintered at "Port Leopold" had formed a depot of provisions for the use of Sir John Franklin's party, sufficient for six months sustenance.

The *Pandora* now approached Bellot Strait, to within a day's run to King William Island, 170 miles southward, with no ice in sight. Hopes held high until the ship sighted La Roquette Island and ice again appeared, followed by a sharp dip in the thermometer. Bellot Strait, now only ten miles distant, was seen through Captain Young's glass as clearly locked in ice. From the topsail yards and fore crosstrees, *Pandora*'s crew kept watch, hoping to catch a glimpse of open water to the south—but to no avail. The pack ice varied in thickness from five to thirty feet, the heavy floes jammed together in jagged, murderous heaps with sharp serrated edges like a monster saw, with craggy hillocks and hummocks bristling with spikes, cones and peaks—all hard as granite, all capable of holing a ship or locking one in any icy vise.

The situation was infuriating. The *Pandora* had traveled 8,000 miles to come within 120 miles of her goal, the northern shore of bleak and tragic King William Island, and now further progress was thwarted by the very ice barricade that had proven to be Sir John Franklin's own fatal nemesis.

All eyes strained southward toward that melancholy spot where Sir John's ships had been abandoned twenty-seven years past. Nothing could be done. The immense plain of ice was moving with agonizing noise, and *Pandora* clearly lay in danger of being locked in its death grip.

After three days in the La Roquette Island vicinity, within the maddening vision of Bellot Strait, Captain Young ordered *Pandora*'s navigator to set course for the return up Peel Sound.

By September 10 the ship once again dropped anchor off the Cary Islands, and by October 16 had tied up at Spithead in England after an uneventful return down the Greenland coast and across the North Atlantic.

In a letter to James Gordon Bennett, dated November 3, 1875, from Portsmouth, Admiral Sir Leopold McClintock wrote: "Young's attempt to accomplish the Northwest Passage was as bold and skilful a one as was ever made. . . . Although baffled in the main objects of his voyage, other important and useful work remained for him to do and well he has done it."

And, in a letter to Bennett from Captain Alan Young, dated October 26, from St. James Street, London, the *Pandora* commander wrote: "Your representative, Mr. MacGahan, who accompanied me, was of the greatest assistance to us."

MacGahan was reunited with Barbara and Paul at the Hotel de la Grande Bretagne in Paris. He soon reported to Bennett, and from the evidence had an unhappy conversation with the *Herald* proprietor. Bennett, probably coldly furious at his correspondent's ingratitude for the important assignments given him, for the limitless trust afforded him, and for the growing renown the *Herald* had created for him, was apparently unmoved by MacGahan's pleas to be permitted to settle permanently in Paris—his and Barbara's first choice—or anywhere else.

The best MacGahan could do, again, was to obtain permission from Bennett for a three-month leave of absence, without pay, to write his book. But Barbara was impressed by her husband's resolve. He appeared to have decided at last, Bennett take the hindmost, he would settle down.

"He wanted me to start to buy furniture and to rent a separate unfurnished apartment," she recalled. "I told him that with our wandering life the furniture could be a bother but he said he would not go far away any more, he would get busy with his book, take a position afterwards in a big town and we would move to America."

They rented a small flat on boulevard Clichy in Paris, near the Parc Monceau, spending nearly four thousand francs (about two hundred dollars) furnishing it. There, with Justine caring for fourteen-month-old Paul ("very much like his father, not only in the face but also by disposition," Barbara said), MacGahan turned his attention to his book on the *Pandora* voyage, a light-hearted travelogue he titled *Under the Northern Lights.*

With his burgeoning reputation as a special correspondent of rare talent and intrepidity, and with his *Campaigning on the Oxus* enjoying great critical if somewhat less monetary success, Barbara wrote that her husband "felt he had achieved enough to do without the slavery of Mr. Bennett."

Although MacGahan's role in it was now ended, the *Pandora* once again would make an attempt at the Northwest Passage, but with even less satisfactory results. With a crew of thirty-three (seventeen of them from the first voyage), she made her second run between May 31 and November 3, 1876. Dogged by adverse winds, mountainous seas, fog and storms, plus a fire that destroyed the harbor stores at God-havn, the *Pandora* by late July was at one point locked in the grip of ice so inextricably that explosives had to be used to relieve the pressures on her hull. Her captain brought her limping home to Portsmouth at last but with nothing but frustration to report.

In the spring of 1876, MacGahan watched the darkening horizon to the east, the reports of risings in the Turkish provinces of Serbia and Bulgaria, the rumors of awful events taking place in the villages of the Balkans.

Part II

X

Bloody Batak

1
"I have had the best of luck"

In the Paris apartment he had furnished for Barbara and Paul, Mac-
Gahan worked furiously to meet his publisher's deadline for his narrative of the *Pandora* expedition. He welcomed the interruption of a meeting with Captain Frederick Gustavus Burnaby of the Royal Horse
Guards, whom MacGahan had met briefly in Spain. The commander
of the "Blues" would soon depart for Khiva, and MacGahan advised
him on the importance of acquiring a knowledge of the Tartar language and of traveling unencumbered by excess baggage or precon-
ceived ideas.*

In the first week of December, the correspondent received at his
Paris quarters a long letter from one of Bennett's secretaries in New
York. Bennett, the secretary wrote, proposed to refit his personal
yacht, *Dauntless*, for arctic waters, lengthening her and furnishing her
with steam engines capable of delivering ten to twelve knots speed

---

*Although MacGahan would not meet him again, Burnaby later joined Gen. Valen-
tine Baker at Adrianople in 1877, ostensibly as an observer in the Russo-Turkish War.
But inevitably he found himself under fire, and at Tashkesan in December of the year,
he actually commanded the Fifth Turkish Brigade. Burnaby was killed in battle at Abu
Klea in the Sudan in 1885.

without sail. The fifty thousand-dollar refitting complete, Bennett intended sending *Dauntless* to "the Polar regions" under the command of "a dashing young fellow," Lieutenant George Washington De Long of the U.S. Navy. The secretary said the *Herald* proprietor wanted MacGahan to join the expedition "in such a manner as to allow you an equal share of the glory without weakening the unit of command or lessening the discipline of the force or exposing the expedition to the clashing or jarring of interests and ambitions."

In a reference to some previous and probably unsettling "orders," the letter ended:

> You can remain in Europe for the present, writing your book, and you may consider the previous orders by telegraph as hereby rescinded. Good use can be made of your time by the diligent study of Arctic explorations and all matters connected therewith that may prepare you for the intended voyage. . . . In conclusion all I have to say is 'gird up your loins' for the fight. If you succeed you will eclipse Stanley, Livingstone and any former explorers whether African or Polar.

Other events would intercede, however, and MacGahan would be girding up his loins for a far different fight not long after this message was received.

In a letter to his mother in Huntington, Indiana, written at the end of 1875 in a curious backhanded penmanship which nearly defies deciphering, MacGahan said that he had just completed his *Pandora* narrative. He admitted, in a clear reflection of Barbara's objections to the crushing pace of Bennett's persistent "orders," that he would like to be "independent of the *Herald* so I can do a good deal of my work at home." He continued:

> I am in excellent health as I have, in fact, always been. But when I came back in the Pandora I was strong as an ox owing to the amount of hard work I did in working the ship, and I think I would have been a match for any of our Huntington boys. . . . I became quite a sailor and used to run up the rigging to the very top of the masts like any other.

As to his work and his association with Bennett's newspaper, MacGahan said his main problem was being away from his wife so frequently. Otherwise he considered himself fortunate:

The truth is that I have had the best of luck and the best kind of work on the paper. The Khivan expedition, in spite of the hardships a part of the time, was very good for my health. I was a year in Spain and during the whole of the time I was riding about through the mountains on horseback. . . . Everything considered, I would have no reason to complain of the Herald if I could get home oftener. But we can't have everything at once and I must be contented with good health, good pay, pretty easy work and a little glory. Everything considered, I think it is better than if I had stayed in Huntington or St. Louis and if I succeed, I will be able to have many things and be home besides, a part of the time.

At the end of January 1876, MacGahan signed his book contract with London publishers Marston, Low, Warren and Searle and turned the *Under the Northern Lights* manuscript over to them.

The book appeared in April, and the notice it received in the *Saturday Review* in late May was typical of the lukewarm reception awaiting it from reviewers jaded by the avalanche of exploration journals, in particular those which were accounts, essentially, of failure. The *Saturday Review* writer damned the book with the faintest of praise, noting that MacGahan devoted most of his space to ruminations on arctic exploration in general rather than the specifics of the *Pandora* voyage. These ruminations, the reviewer said, "are collected in the volume with which we have now to deal, and of which, from a literary point of view, there is not much more to be said. It is augmented by several chapters made up of tolerably pertinent information extracted from other books."

In America, by the time *Under the Northern Lights* saw print, plans were blossoming for the centennial celebration, and MacGahan thought he might ask the *Herald* to let him return for a while, perhaps to write on some aspect of the observances. There did not, after all, seem to be much happening in Europe.

But in fact, terrible things were happening in obscure places on the eastern side of the continent. In a region south of the mighty Danube, in the foothills of the Stara Planina—that 370-mile-long weal of mountains called the Balkans—in a land ruled by the Ottoman Empire since 1396, the Bulgarian people were rising against their oppressors, and these insurrections were being answered with savage reprisals.

The year 1876 saw publication of Mark Twain's *Tom Sawyer* and Leo Tolstoy's *Anna Karenina*.

It was the year in which Alexander Graham Bell spilled battery acid on his clothes and called to his assistant over his "telephone" invention, "Watson, come here, I want you."

It was the year in which 264 troopers of the Seventh U.S. Cavalry Regiment, commanded by Lieutenant Colonel George Armstrong Custer, spilled their blood and left their bones above the Little Big Horn River in Montana.

It was the year in which, in Philadelphia, President Grant officially opened the U.S. Centennial Exposition at Fairmont Park.

And, while America celebrated the centennial or its independence, Bulgaria had now begun its fight.

2
"Dark rumors have been whispered"

The uprising in Bulgaria, as well as earlier ones in Bosnia, Herzegovina, Serbia, and Montenegro, had its origins in the corruption of Turkish rule and its feudal system of tithes, taxes, and usury. In simplest terms, Bulgar peasants had reached a point where they could no longer earn a living from the land or from their few hand-manufacturing enterprises. In such Balkan mountain villages as Batak, Panagyurishte, and Perustitsa, where the soil was rocky and fallow and where villagers made a heavy woolen cloth called *aba* and an ornamental braid, *gaiten*, the Turks' unrelenting burdensome taxes were as keenly felt and as passionately hated as those on once-prosperous farms.

But the rebellion was doomed from the outset. It lacked the support of a large cross section of the Bulgarian people and the coordination of the several noncontiguous regions supposed to participate in it. It lacked professional officers with military training. It lacked weaponry. (Homemade cannon fashioned from cherry trees were commonplace, bound with metal hoops and lined with copper from the pipes of vats for the distillation of rose oil.) Even gunpowder had to be purchased in small amounts from the Albanian and Turkish black markets.

Plans for the rising were betrayed by a wealthy farmer of a town near Tatar Bazardzhik who collaborated with the Turks. Thus, while rebel leaders sewed their shabby woolen uniforms, fashioned black thongs for their footwrappers, and designed their black fur hats with peacock feathers and lion emblems; while wives and children busied themselves making green and red silk banners proclaiming "Freedom or Death" on a design depicting a lion trampling the crescent; while bandages were rolled, biscuits and medicinal ointments prepared— while all this was taking place, the failure of the revolution was foreordained.

Turkish response to this feeble insurrection was what MacGahan termed "Government by *yatagan*," a reference to the curved, double-edged saber employed by the Turkish soldier, regular and mercenary alike.

On April 26, 1876, a band of brigands in the employ of the Turks entered the town of Klissura, where they had been promised the blood of the *giaour* (infidel) and booty. Over two hundred men and women were slaughtered there, along with their children. On the same day, a mob of these mercenaries, called *bashi-bazouks*, surrounded the village of Perustitsa and hacked down its inhabitants with yataghans. On May 2, village leaders were shooting their own wives and children and anyone else who asked to die, then themselves, to thwart the horror of mutilation and torture by these hired butchers.

On April 30, bashi-bazouks and Turkish irregulars under the command of one Achmet Aga attacked the mountain town of Batak. Those villagers who had not fled into the hills were promised mercy if they would surrender. The offer was foolishly accepted, but the result was three days of undiluted horror which left Batak a rubble and a charnel house and gave the obscure town a certain bloody immortality.

Inevitably, when news of these atrocities leaked to western Europe, great ramifications were in store. England's stance on the matter slavishly followed the country's Ottoman policy, formulated by Lord Palmerston in the 1830s and postulated on an independent, vigorous Ottoman Empire as a buffer against Russian and French ambitions in the Near East. The Turks were to be bolstered to protect the liberties of Europe and to secure the British position in India. The Crimean War had been fought to keep Russia from the Dardanelles, Constantinople, and the Mediterranean, and MacGahan well knew about Russian ambitions in central Asia to obtain a doorway southward.

The Bulgarian "troubles" were viewed by the Disraeli ministry as simply an explosive Christian-Moslem controversy in which the integrity of the Porte* must be maintained, by whatever means, to prevent the Russian bear from loping across southeastern Europe.

Thus, as news of the "Bulgarian horrors" began to seep out of the

---

*"The Porte" and "the Sublime Porte" were official shorthand for the Ottoman government in Constantinople.

Balkans, the British foreign secretary, Lord Derby, would complain of the "weakness and apathy of the Porte in dealing with the insurrection," and England's envoy to Constantinople, Sir Henry Elliot, madly pursuing his government's policies, encouraged the Turks to crush the rising "at all costs."

Within Bulgaria, the first man to report the atrocities was Stanislav Dospevski, who compiled data of the murderous attack on Tatar Bazardzhik and reported it to Naiden Gerov, the Russian vice-consul at Philippopolis on April 27. Dospevski (a noted artist who was to die in prison in 1877) sent dispatches to several Russian newspapers—*Golos*, *Moskovskie Vedomosti*, *Sankt-Petersburgskie Vedomosti*, and *Novoe Vremya*. Another Bulgar, Georgi Hadzhitilev, vicar of Tatar Bazardzhik, also compiled information for the western press, and Archimandrite (later Archbishop) Metody Koussevich risked his life to take data to Constantinople, there to hand it personally to Dr. George Washburne and Dr. Albert Long, two American administrators of Roberts College, and to Edwin Pears, the resident correspondent for the London *Daily News* and a well-known barrister.

While the first vague reports of the faltering insurrection and the Turks' savage response appeared in the London *Spectator* on June 3, Edwin Pears's three "telegrams" in the *Daily News* on June 8, 23, and 30 marked the actual beginning of Western knowledge of the Bulgarian rising. Pears's June 23 dispatch, in particular, caused an awakening. "Dark rumors have been whispered about Constantinople during the last month of horrible atrocities committed in Bulgaria," he began, and gave a reasonably full account of the Turkish reprisals, reporting that "reliable estimates of men, women, and children massacred ranged from 18,000 to 30,000 with upwards of a hundred villages wiped out."

"I have hitherto refrained from mentioning these rumors," Pears wrote, "or from stating what I have heard, but they are now gradually assuming definiteness and consistency, and cruelties are being revealed which place those committed in Herzegovina and Bosnia altogether in the background."

As the weeks passed and evidence continued to mount of the truth of the "dark rumors," Prime Minister Benjamin Disraeli became more recklessly dogmatic under increasing pressure from Liberal questioners in the Commons. "I doubt," he said flippantly at one point, "that torture has been practised on a grand scale among an oriental people who seldom, I believe, resort to torture but generally terminate their connexion with culprits in a more expeditious manner."

Punch would later print a cartoon showing the prime minister sitting placidly in the foreground reading a book and saying, "Bulgarian atrocities! I can't find them in the 'Official Reports'!!" while in the background, Britannica points to a scene of rapine and murder. And in Paris, *Le Charivari*, in August, ran a cartoon depicting a hideous bashibazouk in the act of hacking a child with uplifted yataghan, another child lying dead on the ground beneath him, while in the distance a lance was being driven through the breast of a Bulgar peasant. In this shocking scene a figure representing Europe looked on quite calmly with a pair of spectacles in hand. Beneath the picture were the words, *"Chère Madame, il serait grand temps de mettre enfin vos lunettes* (My dear Madam, it is really high time for you to put on your glasses)."

Details of the events in Bulgaria, as they unfolded in the daily press, were the subject of incessant railway-carriage and breakfast-table chatter. The centerpiece of this sudden fixation on the Balkans was, of course, the "horrors," and these exemplified by the fiendish bashibazouks, soon spoken of everywhere in hushed tones. Even Queen Victoria described them in her diary, basing her information on what her ministers told her and what she saw in newspaper drawings. She said they were "horribly cruel mutilators, with narrow faces, pointed beards, no uniform and knives stuck about in their belts."

An undisciplined rabble originally organized as irregular infantry, thirty thousand bashi-bazouks were employed by the Turks in the Crimean War. When the war ended, each regiment was marched to its homeland—many were from Circassia in the Caucasus region of southeastern Europe—and there dismissed, each man given the arms he carried and an English sovereign.

William V. Herbert, a young Englishman who served in the Turkish army during the siege of Plevna, called the bashi-bazouks "a ridiculous newspaper bogey," saying he never heard the term uttered in Turkey. Herbert did explain the meaning of the word, however: *Bashi* was derived from *bash* meaning "head" and indicated possession thereof (as in *binbashi*—a man with one thousand heads, i.e., a regimental major). *Bashi-bazouk,* Herbert said, meant "mad-headed."*

---

*In Turkish, the word is *bashi-bozuq* and indicated one whose head was turned or broken, later taking on the meaning of a "leaderless" or "unattached" person, and still later indicating any Muslim subject not in the armed forces—a civilian. The term gradually came to mean any irregular volunteers of cavalry or infantry attached to the Turkish army but under independent command and providing their own weapons and horses. Large numbers of *bashi-bazouks*, gathered from many of the provinces of the Ottoman Empire, fought against Napoleon in Egypt, in the Crimean and Russo-Turkish wars. Turkey abandoned their use after 1878.

Once the "rumors" from the Balkans reached a certain fever pitch in the English press, the Porte denounced the Constantinople-based correspondence as a "monstrous exaggeration." Between the individual pronouncements of her ministers, the English government would officially admit only that the published reports were without "official confirmation." A certain portion of the press continued to say the disclosures of Turkish atrocities in the Balkans were "sensationalism" and "unworthy of notice."

3
"I fear I am no longer impartial"

It was in this climate of confusion that MacGahan journeyed to Bulgaria. The evidence seems to point to this chronology: He first tried to interest the *Herald* in sending him to eastern Europe and failed. Barbara MacGahan noted in her journal of this period that Bennett "was not interested in the heavy expenses that would be incurred in couriers, horses, baggage, etc. and believed that the 'little war' would soon be over in any event." Her husband "severed his connection with the *Herald*," she wrote, and next made contact with the *Times* of London but was again turned away*: "John McDonald regretted he had no suitable mission to offer," Barbara noted, "saying it would be unusual to engage one 'who had won such honourable distinction on another paper.' " Finally, MacGahan turned to the London *Daily News*, the great Liberal daily founded by Charles Dickens in 1846. Its manager, John Robinson, took an interest in sending the American directly to the Balkans and engaged him, Barbara MacGahan recalled, with a salary of three thousand dollars (afterward increased to ten thousand dollars in gold and ample allowances, an extraordinary salary for the day), ordering MacGahan to Constantinople in late June 1876 to confer with Edwin Pears.

Once he arrived in the Ottoman capital, events moved quickly. The atrocity stories and the evidence backing them up were mounting, and the *Daily News* manager telegraphed MacGahan to proceed. Meanwhile, the U.S. consul in Constantinople, Eugene Schuyler, MacGahan's old friend from Turkestan days, had also been assigned to investigate the rumors, as had Walter Baring, secretary of the British embassy in the capital.

The three men arrived in Philippopolis on July 23 to commence their

---

*According to the history of the newspaper covering the years 1841–84, the *Times* declined MacGahan's services because "of his reputation for sensational proclivities."

NEUTRALITY UNDER DIFFICULTIES.

Dizzy. "BULGARIAN ATROCITIES! I CAN'T FIND THEM IN THE 'OFFICIAL REPORTS'!!!"

THE STATUS QUO.

Turky. "WILL YOU NOT STILL BEFRIEND ME?"

Britannia. "BEFRIEND YOU!—NOT WITH YOUR HANDS OF THAT COLOUR!"

Typical of the *Punch* cartoons of 1876 are these depicting Prime Minister Disraeli trying to ignore the "dark rumors" of Turkish atrocities in Bulgaria while Britannia, presumably reflecting common British sentiment, grows more impatient and anti-Turkish.

Bashi-Bazouk: an unknown artist's interpretation. (Furneaux, *The Breakfast War*, 1958)

The burning and sack of Batak; a group of Bashi-Bazouks. (Forbes, Henty, *Battles of the Nineteenth Century*, I)

Copy.

July 3rd 1876.

Dear Mr. McGahan,

It is understood that you leave to-day as a special correspondent of the Daily News with the Turkish army. If you cannot absolutely join that army, get as near it as you can and keep us informed of its doings.

We will pay you Twenty pounds per week and actual travelling expenses, the arrangement to be terminable

Daily News editor John Robinson's letter to MacGahan directing the correspondent to Constantinople as special correspondent "with the Turkish Army." (MacGahan Papers)

work, and three days later MacGahan wrote his first angry dispatch, to be carried by hired courier to Edwin Pears in Constantinople, then by telegraph to the *Daily News*.

He wrote,

> I fear I am no longer impartial, and I am certainly no longer cool. There are certain things that cannot be investigated in a judicial frame of mind. . . . There are things too horrible to allow anything like calm inquiry; things the vileness of which the eye refuses to look upon, and which the mind refuses to contemplate. . . .
>
> I have already investigated enough to feel convinced that, except from a purely statistical point of view, further investigation would be unnecessary. . . . The atrocities admitted on all hands by those friendly to the Turks, and by the Turks themselves, are enough, and more than enough. I do not care to go on heaping up the mournful count. When you are met in the outset of your investigation with the admission that 60 or 70 villages have been burned, that some 15,000 people have been slaughtered, of whom a large part were women and children, you begin to feel that it is useless to go any further. When, in addition, you have the horrid details of the vilest outrages committed upon women; the hacking to pieces of helpless children and spitting them upon bayonets; and when you have these details repeated to you by the hundred, not by Bulgarians, but by the different consuls at Philippopolis, and the German officials on the railway, as well as Greeks, Armenians, priests, missionaries, and even Turks themselves, you begin to feel that further investigation is superfluous.

In that first dispatch, as well as in subsequent ones when the information was at hand, MacGahan named the guilty. He named one Chefket Pasha "who burned the village of Bazardjik and slaughtered nearly all its inhabitants under more than usually revolting circumstances," and who was promoted for his work to a "high position in the Palace of the Sultan at Constantinople." He named Achmet Aga, a captain of a company of bashi-bazouks, "who likewise distinguished himself by his ferocity." This Achmet Aga, MacGahan wrote, wanted to burn Philippopolis but was withheld from doing so by a higher authority. It was this man who burned Batak, who "is a low, ignorant brute who can neither read nor write, and yet who has been promoted to the rank of Pasha, and with that exquisite mockery of European demands for justice, for which the Oriental mind is so distinguished,

who has been named a member of the commission appointed to prose-
cute and punish the *bashi-bazouks*."

Traveling on nearly impassable roads, on horseback, in bone-jolting
carriages, or on foot, MacGahan and Schuyler journeyed together,
often spending fifteen hours a day moving from village to village, wilt-
ing under a broiling August sun.

After a time, MacGahan's reportage transmuted from angry disclosure to Hyde Park peroration to sad prognostication to Russophilic
warmongering—a brew the *Daily News* readers found intoxicating,
judging from the paper's skyrocketing circulation during the summer
of 1876.

At Panagyurishte, twenty miles from Tatar Bazardzhik, MacGahan
wrote:

> These Turks have no pity, no compassion, no bowels. They
> have not even the generosity, the pity of wild beasts. Even a
> tiger will not slay the young of its own species. But these
> Turks, these strong, bearded men, picked infants up out of
> their cradles with their bayonets, tossed them in the air,
> caught them again and flung them at the heads of their
> shrieking mothers. They carried little babes about the
> streets on the points of their bayonets.

But in Batak, he found even these outrages could be surpassed; that,
indeed, there was no limit to the savagery one human could inflict on
another.

4

"I have supped full of horrors"

It was at Tatar Bazardzhik, toward the end of July and several days
after MacGahan and Eugene Schuyler paired off to begin their investigations, that the two men learned of Batak, a town lying thirty miles
to the south and spoken of in horror everywhere. Three months ago,
three-quarters of Batak's inhabitants, the tales ran, had been murdered after peaceably surrendering to a Turkish commander, Achmet
Aga, and his mixed band of bashi-bazouks and Turkish village volunteers. Hundreds of Batak's people had been burned alive in a church,
the testimony continued, and there were mass beheadings, impalings,
torture, the ravishing of women and girls.

At Pestera, MacGahan and Schuyler had some momentary difficulty with Turkish authorities who were offended when their offer to send along an official with the American investigators was politely but firmly refused. As a result of this *lèse-majesté*, the villagers of Pestera were ordered to tell the Americans that no horses would be available to them. The villagers mocked the orders of the *mudir* (provincial governor), so anxious were they to have the Americans visit Batak, and horses and saddles were provided, and the procession began on August 1. Some sixty women and children followed the Turkish rural police, or *zaptiehs*, the dragoman (guide-translator), and the Americans. Many of the followers from Batak village grabbed the reins of Mac-Gahan's and Schuyler's horses and sobbed their mournful tales of lost families and burned-out homes. MacGahan understood much of what was said to him, finding the Bulgarian language so like Russian that he said he could easily "have fancied myself amongst the peasants of the Volga."

For three hours the climb was steadily upward away from Tatar Bazardzhik, the trail at times narrowing and further slowing progress. The Rhodope range, the southern sweep of the Balkans, was covered with brush, trees, and flowers in gorgeous profusion, but the furnace blast of the August sun was enervating, even to the two Americans, proud of their ability to withstand the debilitating heat and sudden temperature changes of central Asia.

Emerging at last through a thick copse of woods at the top of their mountain pathway, MacGahan, Schuyler, and their guides and entourage stood above a magnificent green valley, a thick carpet of grazing land spread out below them, bisected by a blue mountain stream on the banks of which stood great sawmills. All was silent. The mill wheels were still, and MacGahan noted that these rich, grassy slopes, which ought to have been covered with grazing sheep and cattle, were as void of habitation as a graveyard. The mountains seemed to girdle the valley, and the pasture land, some eight or ten miles in diameter, was, upon closer inspection, traversed in all directions by ravines and hollows. In the bottom of one of the hollows the Americans could make out the dim outlines of a number of small buildings. This was the village of Batak.

Descending to the valley floor, the hillsides were now seen covered with golden fields of wheat and rye and corn, the corn so ripe the heavy ears had broken down their stalks and lay flat on the ground. Approaching the village, MacGahan saw the scurrying of wild dogs, careening through the fields to some hidden cache, digging furiously, and running back again to their lair. They passed the debris of once-

sturdy walls and several untended gardens, and as the party neared
the town, the Americans felt an almost palpable sense of impending
horror.

MacGahan's horse stumbled. Dismounting, he picked up a human
skull, dry and picked clean, gnaw marks on the white bone. A bit
farther on he saw another skull and part of a human skeleton. Moving
closer to the outskirts of Batak, the fields seemed as a giant ossuary:
Human bones, skulls, and skeletons, partly articulated, lay everywhere, and more frequently now, half-dried, putrid flesh still clung to
them, giving rise to an unutterable stench. On a little plateau outside
Batak where the ground was nearly level, MacGahan and Schuyler
drew rein suddenly. Directly in front of them lay a heap of skulls, inter-
mingled with bones from all parts of the human body; a few skeletons,
the bones articulated except for the missing skulls; and a heap of
rotting clothing, human hair, and gaseous flesh from which rose a
miasma so thickly foul it nearly knocked the riders from their horses.
From this charnel heap a scattering of wild dogs snarled, worrying the
bones still carrying leathery strips of flesh.

In his dispatch for the *Daily News*, MacGahan wrote:

> I could distinguish one slight skeletal form still enclosed in a
> chemise, the skull wrapped with a colored handkerchief,
> and the bony ankles encased in the embroidered footless
> stockings worn by Bulgarian girls. The ground was strewn
> with bones in every direction, where the dogs had carried
> them off to gnaw them at their leisure. At the distance of a
> hundred yards beneath us lay the town. As seen from our
> standpoint, it reminded one of the ruins of Herculaneum or
> Pompeii.

Except for the murmuring and sobbing of the retinue behind them,
the party stood before the hideous cairn of bones in silence. From
Batak, they could hear yet another sound: a low, plaintive wailing, like
an ancient funereal keening. Not long after, MacGahan learned the
origin of this sound. The cairn of bones, he had already noticed, contained remnants only of women's clothing, the human hair on the
grinning skulls was invariably long. The skulls were all separated from
the rest of the bones; the skeletons were all headless. These were the
remains of women and girls, all of them beheaded. The keening was a
chorus of sorrow from the survivors in the town.

Batak was a ruin and a rubble, a place of shattered walls, heaps of
stone, shells, and hulls of houses, and here and there an old woman

sitting on a pile of debris, wringing her hands and moaning. "There were few tears in this universal mourning," MacGahan wrote. "It was dry, hard and despairing. The fountain of tears had been dried up weeks before."

Batak had been a town of nine hundred houses and some eight thousand or nine thousand people, the Bulgarians adhering to the patriarchal traditions in which fathers and mothers, married sons, and their children and grandchildren lived under the same roof. MacGahan felt moved to admit that far from being the "mere savages" of his and the popular mind in England, the Bulgarians were an industrious, honest, civilized, and peaceful people. Most Bulgarian villages had a school supported by a voluntary tax, and he said, "there is scarcely a Bulgarian child who cannot read and write. . . . Do the people who speak of the Bulgarians as savages happen to be aware of these facts?"

As he and Schuyler continued their tour of the ravaged town, many of the remaining villagers emerged, joining with those who had followed from Pestera, forming a procession of four to five hundred people, mostly women and children. Descending into the principal street of Batak, the Americans noted heaps of ashes by the roadside and could distinguish a great number of calcined bones—apparently the result of a futile attempt to cremate a few of the dead. A bit farther on they found a skeleton of a young girl partly covered with the debris of a fallen wall, the skull marked with a long saber crevice, and a rich mass of yard-long brown hair still clinging to the naked bone. Nearby, a woman, dryly sobbing, sat on a doorstep rocking to and fro, her fingers twisting and tearing at her hair. In her lap lay three tiny human skulls.

At one house, a villager pointed out to MacGahan the place where his blind brother had been burnt alive, his charred bones left on the hard, earthen floor; close by lay the skeletons of two children, lying side by side and partly covered with stones, their skulls cracked with fearful saber cuts. The tales of bashi-bazouk treatment of babies and children was so indescribably savage as to defy belief: children spitted on bayonets, babies carried about the streets on the points of bayonets, pregnant women ripped open.

"The reason is simple," MacGahan explained to his horrified *Daily News* readers: "When a Mahometan has killed a certain number of infidels, he is sure of Paradise, no matter what his sins may be. Mahomet probably intended that only armed men should count, but the ordinary Mussulman takes the precept in broader acceptation."

They continued their walk through the town. The schoolhouse and church stood opposite one another on the side of the roadway, the ground near the buildings carpeted with human bones, articles of clothing, and bits of flesh and the air tainted with the revoltingly sweet ordor of putridity. The school had once been a fine and large building capable of accommodating two hundred students or more. Beneath the stone rubble now were the bones and ashes of two hundred women and children who sought refuge there and who were burned alive within its walls.

Entering the churchyard, MacGahan and Schuyler were struck with an odor so overpoweringly hideous that only by taking a handful of tobacco and holding it to their noses could they proceed. The church was small, surrounded by a low stone wall, the area in the churchyard no more than fifty yards wide by seventy-five yards long. All about were heaps of rock and rubbish, in some places piled as high as five or six feet above street level. On closer inspection this wall was seen to be an immense heap of corpses covered with a thin layer of stone and gravel.

"The harvests are rotting in the fields," MacGahan summed up in his description of this searing scene, "and the reapers are rotting here in the churchyard."

They witnessed more. The church of Batak, aside from the blackened woodwork, appeared nearly unharmed, a low building with a tile roof supported by heavy irregular arches scarcely tall enough for a man to stand under. Inside lay another mass of corpses, sending the investigators fleeing to the street, sick and faint.*

In some cases, shallow graves had been scratched in the ground for burial of relatives, but for the most part the Batak victims were left to the gnawings of the dogs, or to rot in the summer sun. The surviving villagers, weak and starving, were without spades to dig graves, without implements to harvest their grain, without strength to do either in any event, wrung dry with misery and hopelessness.

MacGahan was satisfied that the wholesale slaughter at Batak was not, in fact, the sole work of bashi-bazouks, but of Turks of neighboring villages as well, all led by Achmet Aga.

> The village of Batak was comparatively rich and prosperous; it had excited the envy and jealousy of its Turkish neighbors, and the opportunities for plunder offered a tempta-

---

*Eugene Schuyler later wrote that about one thousand villagers had rushed to their church when the bashi-bazouks entered Batak and were able to resist for a time attempts to burn the building. Soon, however, Schuyler said, "the assailants mounted the roof, tore off the tiles and threw inside lighted rags and pieces of wood dipped in oil. The door was at last forced and the massacre completed."

tion to the Turks which, combined with their religious fanaticism and the pretext of an insurrection in another part of the country, was more than they could resist. The man Achmet Aga, who commanded the slaughter, has not been punished and will not be, but, on the contrary, he has been promoted to the rank of Yuz-bashi, and decorated.

Before departing from Batak, MacGahan asked about the heap of skulls and bones encountered on the little plateau upon first arriving in the outskirts of the town. These, he was told, were the bones of about two hundred young girls who had first been captured and reserved "for a fate worse than death." They had been kept alive until the last day of the massacre—a rampage that took several days—"and had been subjected to every brutality their captors were capable of. Then, when the town had been pillaged and burnt, when all their friends had been slaughtered, these poor young things. . . . were taken, in the broad light of day, beneath the smiling canopy of heaven, coolly beheaded, then thrown in a heap there, and left to rot."

At Tatar Bazardzhik on the evening of August 2, 1876, MacGahan completed his long, emotion-laden dispatch to the *Daily News*, an angrily scrawled document filled with anguish and outrage and paragraphs of such unrelieved horror that they have a shuddering impact on the reader over a century after their composition.

"Since my letter of yesterday," he began, "I have supped full of horrors." He then leveled his weaponry, in best *Daily News* liberal tradition, at the Tory government of England:

> And yet Sir Henry Elliot, and Mr. Disraeli will keep prating to us about exaggeration, forsooth! The crimes that were committed here are beyond the reach of exaggeration. There were stories related to us that are maddening in their atrocity, that cause the heart to swell in a burst of impotent rage that can only find vent in pitying, useless tears. . . . If I tell what I have seen and heard it is because I want the people of England to understand what these Turks are, and if we are to go on bolstering up this tottering despotism; if we are to go on carrying this loathesome, vice-stricken leper about on our shoulders, let us do it with open eyes and a knowledge of the facts; let us see the hideous thing we are carrying.

And he had a special message from Batak for the prime minister, always a special *Daily News* target:

Mr. Disraeli was right when he wittily remarked that the
Turks usually terminated their connection with people who
fell into their hands in a more expeditious manner than by
imprisoning them. And so they do. Mr. Disraeli was right.
At the time he made that very witty remark, these young
girls had been lying there many days.

5

"You shall see the soldiers of the Czar here"

In his final dispatch to the *Daily News*, dated August 22 from Bucharest, MacGahan said, "It is useless to go on reporting these harrowing
stories to infinitude." He felt that England's most radical response to
the proof of the atrocities would be a barely perceptible shift in her
stance with Turkey, perhaps a diplomatic reprimand and a public re-
nouncing of Turkish "excesses." He warned those statesman who
would protect the status quo, "You must find another solution to the
Eastern Question,* or another solution will find you. It will not last, or
civilization is a delusion, justice a mockery, and Christianity a farce
and a failure."

He knew too, however, that with Russia there would be a wholly
different response. Russo-Turkish rivalry had a long history, and
from the sixteenth century, wars had been fought between the two
empires time and again over territory in the Crimean Peninsula, the
Sea of Azov, Moldavia, Wallachia, Bessarabia, Bosnia, and Serbia. And
now, very likely, over Bulgaria.

Russia's response, he felt, would be based on more than her "Christian outrage, her humanitarian instinct to provide succor to the Bulgar
peasant." It was believed that Russia had lent moral, perhaps material,
support to the anti-Turkish risings in Herzegovina and Bosnia the year
before and that Russia instigated the joining of Serbia and Montenegro
in the rebellion. Imperial Russia was known to be incessantly searching
for a motive to plunge southward, to find a means to dominate the Balkans, to gain control of the Dardanelles and the Bosporus, and thereby
to gain access to the Mediterranean and world trade routes.

---

*The term "Eastern Question" often appeared in newspaper headlines in MacGahan's
time, as in stories dealing with the Congress of Paris, which followed the Crimean War
(1854–56), the headlines often stating simply, "More on the Eastern Question." The
term historically concerned the problem of the fate of European territories controlled by
the Ottoman Empire, in particular those of the Balkan Peninsula.

And no country had a more sustained belief in the imminent collapse of the Ottoman Empire than Russia. Czar Nicholas I, in a historic colloquy with the British ambassador in St. Petersburg in 1853, declared at the outset of the Crimean War that he desired to come to an understanding with England over the fate of Turkey. Of that country, the czar said, "We have on our hands a sick man . . . a very sick man."

To MacGahan, the Bulgarian atrocities spelled the doom of the sick man of Europe, an empire which had spread in a vast polyglot dominion from the Adriatic to the Persian Gulf, from the Black Sea through Syria and Palestine to Arabia. He was not concerned that the czar's ultimate intent might be to use the Bulgarian tragedy to go to war with the Porte. Neither was he persuaded by Schuyler's argument that the atrocities in the Balkans were not, after all, unprecedented. Schuyler, while not the eyewitness of the Khivan campaign that MacGahan could claim, knew from his own investigations of the Cossack treatment of the Turkomans that the Russians practiced cruelties as deliberate and merciless in central Asia as had the bashi-bazouks at Batak.

MacGahan disagreed. He saw the cruelties of the Khivan campaign as a natural, even if not civilized, outcome of legitimate warfare. Moreover, he felt the Russians demonstrated a quality of mercy and kindness in central Asia after their aims were carried out. Neither case applied in Bulgaria. There was no war, only a pathetic "rising" among a primitively armed handful of peasants. And he saw no instances of mercy.

At the Brofft Hotel in Bucharest, he finished his last dispatch for the *Daily News*, taking special pains to lay blame at the feet of Disraeli and the English ambassador at Constantinople, Sir Henry Elliot, for misleading the British public on the gravity of the Bulgarian situation. He wrote of Schuyler's plan to bring about appointment of a commission that would be empowered to protect the Bulgarian peasantry from further outrages, rebuild the devastated villages, indemnify the survivors of the atrocities for their losses at the expense of the Porte, try to punish the bashi-bazouk leaders, and execute by hanging the destroyer of Batak Achmet Aga, as well as Chefket Pasha, Tassum Bey, and other leaders of the destruction of Perustitza, Klissura, and the other of the sundered Balkan hamlets.

"Will Mr. Schuyler succeed in having these measures carried out?" MacGahan asked. "I do not think it. The comfortable old gentlemen who are directing the destinies of Europe are too well fed to care for these wretched women and children."

Thus he completed his "investigation" of the Bulgarian horrors,

drinking chilled glasses of pilsner and slivovitz in the comforts of the
Brofft Hotel in Bucharest, his companions more often than not the
Russian army officers who made the hotel a sort of informal head-
quarters.

Before he left the stricken villages of the Rhodope, when taking
leave of Schuyler, their dragoman and friends, MacGahan said on
more than one occasion to the surviving peasants and their leaders, "In
less than a year you shall see the soldiers of the Czar here."

XI
The Triumvirate

1
"Dreadful excitement and indignation"

The final long dispatch complete, MacGahan sent it by courier directly to the telegraph office in Bucharest. This was a modification of the system he had established with Edwin Pears in Constantinople at the beginning of the investigation. When he was in the Bulgarian villages, MacGahan's handwritten pages were stuffed into a courier's pouch and delivered personally to Pears. Sir Edwin, when he published his memoirs in 1916, admitted that the system he had devised disintegrated with MacGahan's first dispatch out of Philippopolis. That story, he wrote, detailed events "so horrible that I recognized at once that it would not be transmitted by the Turkish authorities in Constantinople. I therefore sent it by letter to be despatched from Bucharest."

Subsequent stories, giving more than ample confirmation to the "dark rumors" Pears had written of in his *Daily News* cable of June 23, were even less likely to pass Turkish authorities, and Bucharest thus became the cablehead for MacGahan's copy.

Those reports from Philippopolis, Batak, Panagyurishte, Pestera, and Tatar Bazardzhik "struck the British public like a thunderbolt," Pears said, and in the *Daily News*, months later, it was stated, extravagantly, that the effect of the American's work on England "was to create in a few weeks a complete and utter reversal of a policy which had been traditional of all English statesmen and of the overwhelming majority of the English people for generations." MacGahan, the editorial continued, pierced the philosophy of the English support for Turkey with his pen, and "there was scarcely a town throughout the whole country in which enthusiastic meetings were not held; and in each of these, the resolution condemnatory of Turkish rule was followed by another resolution returning thanks to MacGahan for having helped expose the horrors."

Even the New York *Herald*, though not through James Gordon Bennett, came forth to congratulate MacGahan on his work in Bulgaria. The message came from Julius Chambers, a friend of the correspondent's and one of Bennett's chief editors (until being lured away a few years later by Joseph Pulitzer's New York *World*). From the *Herald's* London offices at 46 Fleet Street, Chambers wrote on August 25, 1876:

> I have asked whether 'he' [Bennett] wants any atrocities or anything else in your line—I await the answer with breathless anxiety, it is needless to say. The Herald is doing nothing about the war. The Daily News people are very much delighted over your success in Bulgaria. Mr. Robinson said to me that you 'had done grandly.' Keep it up, old man, from a news point of view you have struck a bonanza. Instead of Kinglake's picture of 'two monks in Palestine quarreling over a key and a silver star,'* the people of London now see a new legend looming over their breakfast tables, taking the form of 'Turkish Atrocities in Bulgaria.' Russia looks as if preparing for a new crusade. Therefore, I say to you, keep it up and you will probably be the means of stirring up a war beside which the Crimean unpleasantness will be mere child's play.

Chambers went on to say,

> You have a great chance and I know that you are fully equal to any emergency. God knows the corpses of those poor dead girls cry out for revenge and nobody except the Rus-

---

*The reference is to historian A. W. Kinglake's analysis of the origin of the Crimean War in his multivolumed *The Invasion of the Crimea*, a new edition of which appeared in 1876.

sians seem likely to give the civilized world this justice, so I say let the Big Bear go in. I enclose your last article in the DN. It has created a profound sensation.

The effect of MacGahan's dispatches even reached the queen, who noted in her diary on August 23 that the "recent news was causing a dreadful excitement and indignation in England, or indeed in Great Britain." Victoria was at first appalled at the atrocity stories in the *Daily News*, but in a short time, when she espied Mr. Gladstone entering the arena against the Turks, her attitude underwent a change. "Hearing as we all do the undercurrents," she wrote on September 28 to Disraeli, "and knowing as we do that Russia instigated the insurrection, and caused the cruelty of the Turks . . . the world ought to know that on their shoulders and not on ours rests the blood of the murdered Bulgarians."

Disraeli, meanwhile, drifted in his own reactions. He initially dismissed the news as "coffee house babble," and wrote of the "atrocities" in quotation marks. But as the mournful reports accumulated and the governments's sangfroid crumbled, even Disraeli (who accepted a peerage on August 11 as Lord Beaconsfield) condemned in his private correspondence England's envoy to Constantinople Sir Henry Elliot's "lamentable want of energy and efficiency of information" which had placed the government in an embarrassing plight. Moreover, he realized that the news of the events in the Bulgarian villages had "completely destroyed sympathy with Turkey."

Ultimately, Sir Henry Elliot conveyed a denunciation, in the name of the queen, of the Turkish massacres in the Balkans, calling for justice on the perpetrators of the savagery, and for reparations to be made to the survivors.

Newspapers, journals, and privately issued screeds vied for the public's attention in the meantime, and the reaction to the revelations of MacGahan's correspondence was by no means uniform. The *Manchester Guardian* referred to the American's dispatches as "horrible and repulsive" but said that it was "incumbent upon Englishmen to read them in order that they may rightly understand what their duty is in the matter." In the *Times* of London on September 12, the Earl of Derby, foreign secretary, referred to MacGahan's "skillful and artistic narratives" with obvious bitterness. The *Saturday Review*, in its issue of September 16, contended that MacGahan had deliberately set out to project his own sense of indignation, and that this clearly "infringed the conventions of higher journalism."

And, in a tongue-in-cheek statement in the *Spectator*, under the heading "A Gentlemanly View of the Eastern Question," an anonymous correspondent wrote:

> The gentlemanly politicians have heard that the man who first unveiled the conduct of our Turkish allies is either an Irishman or an American by birth and that he does not write in the superfine style. It follows that he is, in gentlemanly eyes, 'a damned Yankee newspaper fellow' and I assure you you must be cautious in adopting his statements.

MacGahan's "pictorial style" bothered several critics. Edmund Ollier, later a historian of the Russo-Turkish War, said:

> The letters of Mr. MacGahan and the reports of Mr. Schuyler were valuable contributions toward a knowledge of this dismal series of transactions; but they were too obviously written with a strong bias against the Turks to be entirely satisfactory guides, taken by themselves. What those gentlemen saw with their own eyes they doubtless reported with accuracy, though the highly pictorial style of Mr. MacGahan stood a little in the way of the reader's calm appreciation of the facts.

MacGahan's *Daily News* dispatches were collected in a pamphlet, issued in the summer of 1876 by the London firm of Bradbury, Agnew & Co., under the title *The Turkish Atrocities in Bulgaria*. This cheap, paper-covered booklet had as its subtitle, "Letters of the Special Commissioner of the 'Daily News,' J. A. MacGahan, Esq., With an Introduction and Mr. Schuyler's Preliminary Report." Its sales were brisk upon issuance but were soon to be overshadowed by a new assessment of the situation by one who was clearly influenced by the American's work.

William Ewart Gladstone, according to Archibald Forbes, MacGahan's great friend and *Daily News* colleague, was "stirred . . . into a convulsive paroxysm of burning revolt against the barbarities" MacGahan's dispatches described. Said Forbes of his friend's Balkan reports:

> They moved England to its very depths, and men traveling in railway carriages were to be noticed with flushed faces and moistened eyes as they read them. Lord Beaconsfield tried to whistle down the wind the awful significance of the

disclosures made in those wonderful letters. The master of sneers jibed at as 'coffee-house babble' the revelations that were making the nations to throb with indignant passion.

Doubtlessly, Forbes's bombastic prose cannot be taken as a flawless interpretation of reactions, but there was an element of truth in what he wrote. Gladstone, the Liberal leader who had retired from politics only the year before, had followed the Bulgarian situation closely from the first hints and "dark rumors." He had resigned as leader of the Liberal party in 1875 because, he said, he "deeply desired an interval between Parliament and the grave." But now, approaching seventy years of age and devoting his time to chopping down trees at his park in Hawarden, he found he had a fight left in him.

Walter Baring, the member of the embassy staff in Constantinople who was sent out at the same time as MacGahan and Schuyler to investigate the alleged atrocities, made a preliminary report on his findings on August 11. The report, which confirmed the extent of the bloodshed, was not actually published until September 19, but Gladstone knew of, or anticipated, its conclusions, and in a four-day period while lying propped up in bed suffering from lumbago, he wrote in white heat one of the most famous political pamphlets of all time, a masterpiece of invective, *The Bulgarian Horrors and the Question of the East*.

Not only did the pamphlet anticipate Baring's conclusions, it was clearly dependent in its factual matter on the *Daily News* stories of MacGahan and on Schuyler's "Preliminary Report" published in the *Atrocities* booklet of but a few weeks before. As one historian has put it, the *Bulgarian Horrors* "was less a case of Gladstone's exciting popular passion than of popular passion exciting Gladstone."

Barbara MacGahan in later years wrote that while Gladstone did not know her husband as author of the *Daily News* dispatches from the Balkan villages, the prime minister did credit them, though not their author, in a note to Edwin Pears in Constantinople. Whatever the case, Gladstone's tract practically erased memory of MacGahan's collection of dispatches. Published on September 6 (a copy delivered forthwith to Lord Beaconsfield), the *Bulgarian Horrors* sold an astounding 40,000 copies in its first week, 200,000 by the end of the month, and continued to sell well throughout the weeks and months to come. It would ultimately net its author twelve thousand pounds. The newspaper comment it generated buried the notices of one of Beaconsfield's last campaigns, to have Victoria proclaimed empress of India, and its publication was followed by huge rallies at Blackheath, St. James Hall, Piccadilly, and elsewhere.

In his opening to the tract, Gladstone gave a measure of credit to the *Daily News*: "The first alarm respecting the Bulgarian outrages was, I believe, that sounded by the Daily News on the 23rd of June," he wrote, saying that the service rendered by the paper through its foreign correspondence, "has been the most weighty, I may say, the most splendid."

The critical portion of Gladstone's inspired screed was this statement:

> Let the Turks now carry away their abuses in the only possible way, namely by carrying off themselves. Their Zaptiehs and their Mudirs, their Bimbashis and their Yuzbashis, their Kaimakams and their Pashas, one and all, bag and baggage shall, I hope, clear out from the province they have desolated and profaned. . . . There is not a criminal in an European goal, there is not a cannibal in the South Sea Islands whose indignation would not arise and overboil at the recital of that which has been done.

Gladstone immediately collected a number of influential supporters to his stand on the Bulgarian issue, the number including John Thaddeus Delane, editor of the *Times*; James Anthony Froude (later editor of *Fraser's Magazine*); Edward Augustus Freeman, the Oxford scholar, historian, and *Saturday Review* contributor; Poet Laureate Alfred Tennyson; Thomas Carlyle; Charles Darwin; John Ruskin; and the duke of Argyll.

The "Grand Old Man" and the Liberals won a resounding victory in the spring of 1880, Gladstone returning to the prime ministry. Disraeli's cause, damaged by his failure to act swiftly and resolutely after the atrocities were confirmed, was further weakened in foreign affairs by costly military reverses in Afghanistan (1878) and in Zululand (1879).

Diplomatic pressures meanwhile were pushing ahead. In Constantinople, Sultan Abdul-Aziz was deposed and replaced by Murad V, shortly after declared insane and replaced by Abdul Hamid II. A constitution containing many reforms was suspended as one of Abdul Hamid's first acts, and the Porte's attitude toward foreign interferences solidified. A Conference of Six Powers was called for November 20 in the Ottoman capital with France, Germany, Austria, Italy, Russia, and

England sending delegates. The purpose of the conference was to establish certain protocols, extend the shaky armistice between Turkey and the revolutionary parties of warring Bosnia, Herzegovina, Serbia, and Montenegro, but the conference broke up, with no progress made, on January 18, 1877.

2
". . . to cross the Turkish frontier"

Up to the opening of the grandly named Six Power Conference, MacGahan remained in Bucharest, writing a daily stint for the *Daily News* of Russian activities in the Rumanian capital. Barbara, Paul, and Justine remained in Paris.

In an October 5 letter, MacGahan's publisher, E. Marston of Sampson, Low, wrote him: "You are making so much stir in the world with your 'atrocities' as Byron with his poems when he woke up one morning and found himself 'famous.' Surely your hair must be turning white at the horrors you have witnessed."

Marston proposed a book—"not a partisan book, our friends of the Daily News have worked that oracle dry"—on what MacGahan had witnessed in Bulgaria. "But whatever is done," the publisher stressed, "it must be done quickly. This public is as fickle as it is frail, and will rush after any new sensation for a time, but will leave a good book to perish as coldbloodedly as any Bashi-Bazouks, if it doesn't happen to be about something the world is talking of at the moment. Witness 'Northern Lights'." Marston also proposed that MacGahan consider collaborating with Eugene Schuyler on the book.

But nothing came of this project: Greater events were unfolding, and MacGahan had no time for further book writing.

In November, upon instructions from John Robinson, MacGahan proceeded from Bucharest to Constantinople, there to join Edwin Pears in the observation of the Six Powers Conference. Other correspondents in the capital, who all met periodically in a private room at a hotel called Missere's on the Grande rue de Pera, included three notables representing the pro-Turkish *Daily Telegraph*: George Augustus Sala, one of the most popular journalists of the day who sent his paper lively dispatches filled with social commentary and humor; Campbell Clarke, Paris correspondent-in-chief; and Drew Gay, a younger lion of Fleet Street. The *Morning Post* and the *Standard* were ably represented

by Sir George Thomas and Francis Scudamore; and the youngest of
the group was a superb sketch artist, Melton Prior, of the *Illustrated
London News*.

Bucharest remained MacGahan's pied-à-terre. He felt certain Russia would go to war against the Turks in the spring but was determined to have his family in close proximity, at least in the lull before
the storm. Thus, in November, he cabled Barbara to come ahead to
Bucharest with Paul, there to await word from him.

But Barbara had her own ideas, and after sending Justine back to
Dax, embarked at Varna, on the Black Sea coast, for Constantinople
on a half-steam, half-sail Greek tramp whose captain assured her that
the voyage would take four, no more than five, days. Barbara recalled
the nightmarish journey decades later, still with a shudder. There
were sixteen male passengers on board, no other women, and no one
who spoke any language save Rumanian or Greek. The passage took
over a week in unmercifully bad weather—high greasy-looking seas, a
buffeting gale—which combined with a diet of salt pork and canned
stringy beef that drove her time and again to the rail. Paul suffered
only a bit less.

Arriving at last in the capital, she and her son took rooms at Pera,
north of the inlet on the Bosporus known as the Golden Horn, which
the sultans had reserved for foreigners and their embassies. In the
freezing weather, the Pera Hotel management moved tall, portable
urns, higher than a man's head, into the rooms. These contained a
smoldering layer of charcoal which gave off a suffocating gaseous
smoke and forced the hotel occupants to throw open windows to rid
the rooms of the fumes, welcoming in the cold air in the process.

For Barbara, the misery of the voyage and the discomfort of the
hotel were bearable, but her husband's absences were not. She was at
wit's end, and the five days she spent in Constantinople proved to be
no reunion with MacGahan. "We still loved one another," she wrote in
later years, "but M. G. seemed to belong to the Bulgars who came by
deputations to thank him for his defense of them and for the good
change in public opinion he created, thanks to his frank correspondence. The Bulgars, dinners and different celebrations took all his
leisure."

When MacGahan's work at the conference ended, he personally
took charge of moving his family back to Bucharest, installing them in
the Hotel de Francis there. He received new orders from the *Daily News*
in February to travel to St. Petersburg to observe the Russian preparations for war. He could not take Barbara or his son with him.

The spring of 1877 brought the last attempt by Russia to reach an accord with the Sublime Porte. A protocol was drawn, calling on Turkey to immediately implement promises made to the Christian subjects of her empire and to carry out certain administrative reforms already agreed upon. The Turks rejected the protocol on April 9 on the grounds that the supervision Russia stipulated was unacceptable. To a certain degree, Abdul Hamid's obduracy was based on his belief that England would never permit the Russians to wage a war that would reach Constantinople, and in this he was partially correct. Upon announcement of hostilities later in the month, England declared her neutrality subject to certain "vital interests" being protected: the maintenance of free communication with the East through the Suez Canal, the exclusion of Egypt from the sphere of military operations, and the recognition by Russia of the inviolability of Constantinople, along with the navigation of the Dardanelles.

Russia's foreign minister, Prince Alexandr Gorchakov, assented on all points.

In St. Petersburg, on April 24, the Turkish chargé d'affaires, Tavfek Bey, received a note from Prince Gorchakov which announced that "his Majesty, my august master, sees himself compelled, to his regret, to have recourse to force of arms. Be therefore so kind as to inform your Government that from today, Russia considers herself in a state of war with the Porte."

Simultaneously, the czar's manifesto was issued, couched in that tone of chivalric self-sacrifice and lofty altruism which nations attribute to themselves while denying to others: "Profoundly convinced of the justice of our cause and help of the Most High," the document read, "we make known to our faithful subjects that . . . in now invoking the blessings of God upon our valiant armies, we give the order to cross the Turkish frontier."

At Jassy (Iaşi), in Moldavia, at about the same time, the Grand Duke Nicholas issued a proclamation to the Rumanians, announcing the passage of the Russian armies across the Pruth River that morning, and calling for the cooperation of the Rumanian people.

In Jassy, MacGahan stayed with the Russian army for their advance to the Danube. Barbara and Paul remained in Bucharest during this spring commencement of the war except for one brief, nearly disastrous occasion: Just before the Russian crossing of the Pruth, he arranged to meet his wife and son in the Moldavian capital. Barbara arrived in Jassy on April 15, took a room at a cheap hotel and waited. On the 20th she received a telegram from her husband in Kischenev that he had fallen from a horse in St. Petersburg and reinjured his ankle and would be delayed in meeting her. Barbara soon ran out of money. Desperate and as a last resort, she sold her gold watch for thirty francs to feed Paul and herself, and to send a telegram to her husband requesting money. Finally, MacGahan arrived, limping but happy, to spend a few days with his family before returning to Russian army headquarters. The fracture would plague him throughout the coming year.

Before rejoining the Russian advance in the north, MacGahan hired a house in the Strada Verdi of Bucharest for his wife and son. He arranged for Barbara to meet his courier regularly for the *Daily News* dispatches to be telegraphed from Bucharest, and Barbara made arrangements to rewrite her husband's correspondence for *Golos*, as she had done during the Carlist campaign.

On April 26, MacGahan returned to Kischenev and there reported on the review of the troops by the czar, Alexander II:

> The spot was well chosen, on a gentle undulating hillside, which enabled the spectators to see the whole army at once, as the lines rose behind each other higher and higher up the slope.
>
> It was a beautiful sunny morning and the bright colours of the uniforms, the glitter of bayonets flashing in the sunshine, and the broad blaze of light reflected from a long line of polished field-pieces. There was something strangely impressive and awful in this prolonged silence and immobility. The crowds looking upon the serried lines so silent and motionless became themselves silent, and gazed with wonder and awe.

And so it began, with elegantly phrased diplomatic manifestos, the sun glinting off bayonets and cannon, serried and silent lines of men in review. Thus began a war that would last forty-five weeks and spill the blood of hundreds of thousands of Turks, Russians, Bulgarians, and Rumanians, throwing on center stage of the world, through the dispatches of the war correspondents, places like Shipka Pass and Plevna, and people like Skobelev and Osman Pasha—and Januarius MacGahan.

3
"We never had a difference"

In the months that followed the czar's grandiloquent declaration of war, MacGahan's circle of friends, colleagues, and confidantes broad-ened as never before. These included a tough, resourceful, grimly capable Russian general named Joseph Gourko; a young American army lieutenant, Francis Vinton Greene, observing the war as military attaché to the U.S. legation in St. Petersburg; a humanitarian woman, the Viscountess Strangford (moved by MacGahan's dispatches to come from her comfortable home in England to the squalor and misery of Tatar Bazardzhik with food, medical supplies, and a zealousness to help the downtrodden);* and correspondents such as Frederic Villiers of the London *Weekly Graphic* and Francis "Frank" Millet of the New York *Herald.*

More significantly, the story of Januarius MacGahan in the Russo-Turkish War is the story of a memorable triumvirate: the thirty-three-year-old American; the dashing Russian officer, Michael Skobelev, now a general; and the war-wise Scotsman Archibald Forbes, chief correspondent of the *Daily News.*

As the Russian army massed in the countryside of the Danubian provinces of Moldavia and Bessarabia, Forbes and Skobelev emerged as MacGahan's staunchest and most influential friends. Their paths did not merely cross and recross, they united into an almost seamless relationship for a period of one year and forty-seven days. War, often a thin mortar for the purpose, cemented this alliance firmly, leaving each man marked by it to the end of his days. And, because of its endurance and the mark it left, both of the other members of the triumvirate warrant closer scrutiny.

Forbes, in later days, would write: "There is nothing in my experience that tries the temper like war correspondence; nor any pursuit so prone to engender jealousy and ill-feeling among the men engaged in it." Forbes's pronouncement is significant—he was a man of the loftiest self-esteem, inclined to ill-tempered outbursts, especially on the perceived incompetence of others—and it is something of a testimonial to MacGahan's calm and even temperament that the two of them, from the start, struck off a working relationship and a personal friendship that endured in the face of great adversity.

In a gracious phrase, William Howard Russell, the immortal "special" of the London *Times,* dubbed Forbes "the incomparable Archibald," and there is ample evidence that Russell's remark was more than a felicitous choice of words.

---

*Lady Strangford was the wife of the seventh viscount Strangford of Ireland, philologist-ethnologist, who died in 1869. After her husband's death, she devoted herself to nursing and humanitarian causes. She died in 1887 of a cerebral hemorrhage on board a ship bound for Port Said.

Born in 1838 in Morayshire, Scotland, where his father served as a Presbyterian minister, Forbes led a frenetic life that had the hallmarks of a Victorian novel by Ouida or G. A. Henty. In 1859, after a brief time at the University of Aberdeen, he inherited twenty-five hundred pounds and went to Canada, settling for a time in Quebec until, legend has it, an unhappy love affair ruined him financially. The story goes that he shipped as a sailor to Liverpool with eight shillings in his pocket and in London enlisted in the Royal Dragoons. This act, he said, was inspired after hearing a lecture by William Howard Russell on the charge of the Light Brigade at Balaclava. Invalided out of the army because of ill health after five years' service, Forbes launched his own weekly newspaper, the short-lived *London Scotsman*, and began writing professionally, actually publishing a novel on the Indian Mutiny which eventually led to his first "commission" as a war correspondent.

In 1870, the *Morning Advertiser*, searching for a capable writer to send a few "letters" from France on the progress of the war going on there with the Prussians, gave Forbes a position. Advanced thirty pounds for a kit and expenses, he bought a knapsack, provisions, and notebooks and took the mail train to Dover.

From the start, Forbes compiled an amazing record from a commingling of luck, hard work, physical fortitude, cunning, and a then unheard-of brand of news intuition. His baptism of fire came at the battle of Saarbrücken on August 2, 1870, which he wrote up brilliantly. He also sent out stirring letters on the bloodbath engagements of the French and Prussians at Courcelles, Vionville, and Gravelotte. On September 12, overhearing a remark about fighting going on in the valley of the Meuse, Forbes reached the scene in time to see the last of a series of cavalry charges by the French Chasseurs d'Afrique. That same day, he met MacGahan's friend, the American general Philip Sheridan, and noted how Sheridan watched the repulse of the cuirassiers as they charged headlong down the slope of Illy, and how he snapped his glass shut and said quietly, "It's all over for the French now."

The next day, the Scotsman saw Bismarck gather his blue military cloak about him, mount a powerful bay horse and gallop off across country. Instinctively, Forbes followed until he came upon an open carriage containing four French officers. The face of one of the officers Forbes instantly recognized—"impassive and sphinxlike as ever, but with its lines drawn and deepened as if by some spasm." This was Louis Napoléon, emperor of the French. Forbes and Jacob de Liefde, a Dutch journalist, were the only civilians to witness the surrender of Napoleon.

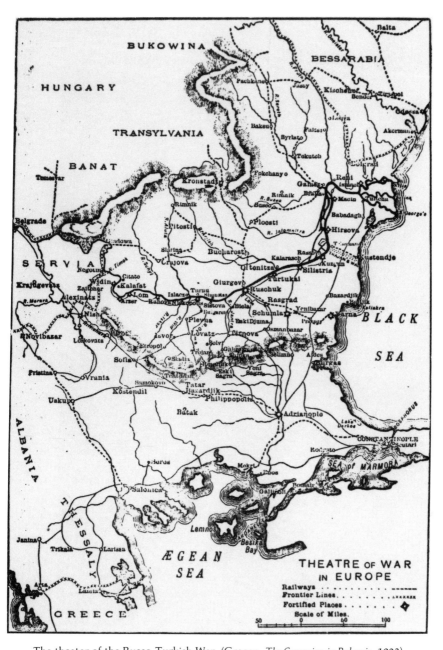

The theater of the Russo-Turkish War. (Greene, *The Campaign in Bulgaria*, 1903)

Frederic Villiers.
(Bullard, *Famous War Correspondents*)

Archibald Forbes
(Bullard, *Famous War Correspondents*)

Forbes also became the only civilian spectator of the fight at Mézières-les-Metz, but suffered a wound in the leg which turned gangrenous. A battlefield surgeon drained the pus from the wound and burned away the dead tissue with acids, but Forbes had to return to England for more intensive and sophisticated treatment lest the leg be amputated. He returned to Paris, now representing the *Daily News*, in time to witness the Prussians' triumphal march into the city on March 1, 1871. William Howard Russell, also a witness, left by chartered train for Calais to personally deliver his dispatch to the *Times* offices. For years afterward a story circulated that Forbes, disguised as a fireman, had stolen a ride on Russell's private train.

Less apocryphal and an example of Forbes's methods was his notable beat on the bombardment of St. Denis. A few days before this cannonade, Forbes simply asked the crown prince of Saxony for a description of what would take place, wrote it up at length and sent it to the *Daily News* by courier to be set in type. The moment the bombardment commenced, the correspondent sent a two-word cable to his editor: "Go ahead."

After the Franco-Prussian War, Forbes spent eight months in the Tirhoot district of Bengal, reporting on the famine there, and came home invalided from sunstroke. In 1873, he joined the forces of Prince Alfonso from Madrid to Navarre in pursuit of the Carlists, and in 1876, reported the Serbian war against Turkey.

He was a tall, tweedy Scotsman with a briar pipe clenched in his teeth, a tam-o'-shanter on his head—an utterly fearless, arrogant, resourceful, and somewhat forbidding man. As a reporter he was unexcelled; as a writer he was florid, contumacious, and verbose—but somehow readable, and at times, even endearing.

Although their paths came close to crossing in France during the Commune and again in Spain, MacGahan and Forbes met for the first time in the railway station at Jassy, the ancient town near the Pruth River in Moldavia, early in April 1877. Both correspondents were en route to Kischenev, headquarters in Bessarabia of the Russian army commanded by the czar's brother, the Grand Duke Nicholas, and had made arrangements through the *Daily News* office in London to meet and lay plans for the coming campaign.

Forbes, later recalling the meeting, described his American partner as "limping up to shake hands" and said MacGahan was "a shortish,*

---

*Walter Blakely, on the other hand, gives MacGahan's height as about five feet ten inches, not "shortish" by any standard, certainly not in 1876.

thick-set man, with calm eyes, short, dense beard, and singularly small hands and feet, pleasant voice, his ankle set in a plaster of Paris cast."

In the MacGahan family archives is a fragment of a letter to Barbara MacGahan in which Forbes wrote that the manager of the *Daily News* was troubled that Forbes and MacGahan might not "hit it off." Forbes claimed he had a "dormant commission of sorts" which, if he needed to cite it, would put him in charge of the team. "So far as I am concerned," he told Barbara, "I am sure MacGahan went to his grave without the knowledge that, in the last resort, I was his master. We never had a trouble. Often we differed. Then we argued the matter out, and the man whom the other convinced, loyally gave in."

Mutual admiration had something to do with the warm friendship that developed from this first meeting. MacGahan, although he would leave no record of his impressions of Forbes (nor, indeed, of any of his other colleagues, and, sadly, of few others) could not have been unaware of his partner's record of achievement. Forbes, who left a considerable body of autobiographical writing, admired MacGahan's work in Khiva, Spain, the Arctic, and Bulgaria, and recognized in his younger comrade a man capable of the fortitude and initiative required to put into effect the Forbesian maxim cited earlier: "The paramount duty of the war correspondent is to transmit important information without delay, to the abandonment or postponement of every other consideration."

To Forbes, indeed, can go considerable credit for interpreting the correspondent's duty along the lines of being *first* with the news—not the most comprehensive, nor the most literary, nor necessarily most accurate, but *first*. He demonstrated his zeal for being first (and whenever possible, *only*), time and again, and he inculcated MacGahan with the spirit of it.

Looking back on it, Forbes later declared that the Russo-Turkish War signaled a new era in war correspondence. Writing of the "pooled news" arrangement the *Daily News* and New York *Herald* were to experiment with in 1877–78, Forbes wrote that "the journalism of both worlds made up its mind to put forth its full strength when, in the spring of 1877, the Russian hosts destined for the invasion of Turkey were slowly massing in the squalid villages of Bessarabia." He emphasized that the telegraph—the means of "annihilating distance," as William Howard Russell had written of it from the Crimea two decades before—was the key: "There had been a thorough awakening as to the advantages of copious telegraphy in war correspondence, and it was now for the first time thoroughly realized that strategic organization for the rapid transmission of intelligence was a thing sedulously to study."

An organizational master, Forbes explained his tentative system to MacGahan. He was dubious of the chances of their dispatches being transmitted uncensored from Bucharest and, in the early days of April, set up an alternate "pony express" courier route of eighty miles across the Carpathian Mountains to Kronstadt, in the Austrian province of Transylvania. If this circuitous, strenuous, and complex string of couriers proved faulty (as it did), they would fall back on gambling on the good nature of the Russian censor. In this event, they would use a system of couriers along thirty-mile intervals from Bucharest to the front.

As it turned out, both Forbes and MacGahan, apparently distrustful of this courier system to and from Bucharest, at least for their most critical dispatches, taxed their energies and luck throughout the war to take long rides through the battle zone to the Rumanian capital with their accounts of such actions as the fighting at Shipka Pass in August 1877.

Hewing to the dictum of George W. Smalley and John T. Delane to "telegraph freely," both correspondents were to make liberal and expensive use of the Bucharest telegraph office. Forbes recalled the rate then was about thirty-five cents a word and that he himself sent several stories running in excess of eight thousand words. MacGahan frequently sent stories out which cost the *Daily News* management two thousand dollars and more.

Just as the courier route to Kronstadt was not to prove workable, Forbes's organizational skills reached another, smaller impasse when he attempted to outfit his lamed American colleague with saddle horses, a wagon and team stored with supplies, and even a "trusty coachman" for MacGahan to use in traveling down the banks of the Danube. Although this was a kind of comfort Forbes would deny himself, lame or not, he wanted to ensure his American colleague's recovery from his ankle injury, but the scheme simply would not work. Forbes later admitted that MacGahan abandoned the coaches, coachman, and supplies once the Danube was crossed by the Russian army. He recorded that MacGahan didn't see his transportation and driver again until after the fall of Plevna, then used it for two days and lost it again.

"MacGahan's coachman was a sort of standing joke amongst the correspondents," Forbes wrote, describing the driver as "a forlorn wandering Jew, ever in vain searching for his meteoric master." Periodically, Forbes said, "poor Isaac" would turn up somewhere behind the lines, following MacGahan's phantom trail, always asking the same melancholy question, "Have you seen my master?" followed by a request for a little money to keep himself and his horses alive. "For aught I know," Forbes wrote years later, "Isaac and the wagon may be hunting Bulgaria to this day."

Forbes admired what he called the "spunk" of his *Daily News* partner. "MacGahan never had any clothes save what he stood up in and a clean shirt or two in his saddlebags," he would recall. "He 'took his chances' as to food. Wherever there was a Bulgarian hut or a Russian regiment, he was all right for food, such as it was, and when he could get nothing to eat he went without with a light heart."

And so the two *Daily News* men prepared for whatever eventualities the war might bring. They arranged their kits, got their credentials in order (a sort of passport, this document carried a photograph of the bearer together with a description of his authority to accompany the Russian army, and the signature of the issuing officer), pulled on their armbands bearing the word "Correspondent" in Russian letters surmounted by an identification number, and made ready for the "opening of the ball."

4
". . . the conqueror of Khokand"

In a May 20 dispatch, MacGahan told of meeting General Michael Skobelev on the railway carriage between Ploeşti and Kischenev. Both had been observers of the little naval exploit on the Danube involving some Russian steam launches against Turkish monitors. "The last time I saw him," the correspondent wrote, "we were both standing on the banks of the Oxus [Amu Darya], in the Khanate of Khiva. He was starting on his way to Tashkent; I on my return to St. Petersburg, in a boat which was to float me down to the mouth of the Oxus into the Aral Sea, where I was to find a Russian steamer."

MacGahan had avidly followed Skobelev's career in the Russian newspapers and described the young general as "tall, handsome, with a lithe, slender, active figure, clear blue eyes, and a large, prominent, but straight, well-shaped nose, the kind of nose it is said Napoleon used to look for among his officers when he wished to find a general. . . . It was the famous General Skobelev, the conqueror of Khokand."

Skobelev, who was destined to become the most magnetic personality of the nineteenth-century Russian army, had by 1876 risen to a major general's rank after distinguishing himself in central Asia, a part of the campaign being the march on Khiva of MacGahan's experience. In the press he was continually confused with his father, Dmitri, also a general in the Army of the Danube, in command of an independent division of Cossacks who had made a famous march to Galatz to protect a bridgehead on the day of the czar's declaration of war.

Skobelev the Younger, as the *Daily News* correspondents often distinguished him, now had a divisional command of his own but was subject to flights of eccentricity and independence of mind that infuriated his superior officers, in particular those much older. He had a predilection for wearing white in battle, his white uniform "flashing like the plume of Henry of Navarre," as one writer put it; he rode a white stallion and was often accompanied by an orderly carrying an immense white banner bearing the letters "MS" in the center. (His white uniform and horse won for him the nickname, in the Turkish army, of "White Pasha" or "White Devil.") When questioned about his uniform, horse, and flag, he liked to answer, cryptically, "We must all be prepared for death, and go to meet it as we are when going to take Holy Communion."

In private, he was mentally and physically a man of protean character, an unfathomable mixture of nobility and meanness, manliness and childishness: bold, imperious, inspired, querulous, morose, sanguine, and despondent. Physically he oscillated between great vigor and outright nervous prostration. His men worshiped him, though he was known as a strict disciplinarian, demanding work and exercise behind the lines and the utmost in battle. In turn, he cared for his soldiers in ways no other Russian commander would have dreamed: Skobelev once spent fifteen thousand rubles of his own money to charter a steamer to take some hundreds of his troops, sick and wounded, across the Black Sea to the Russian port of Odessa. And he frequently bought vegetables and other food to supplement the meager soup and black bread diet of his men.

Of brilliant intellect, he was a linguist and voracious reader, and as George Curzon would write of him in a book on Russia and Turkestan: "In many ways his character was typical of the Russian nation, in its state of development then—one foot planted in a barbarian past, the other advancing into a new world of ideas and action."

But as keen an observer as Francis Vinton Greene, the American army lieutenant attached to the U.S. legation in St. Petersburg, was unimpressed with Skobelev's flamboyance, describing him as

> perpetually riding at break-neck speed over some ditch or fence, leaving half his staff and orderlies sprawling in it. He

never lost an opportunity of *displaying* courage. He went into battle in his cleanest uniform and fresh underclothing, covered with perfume, and wearing a diamond-hilted sword, in order, he said, that he might die with his best clothes on. For a time he wore, with evident affectation, a coat in which he had been wounded, and which had a conspicuous patch on the shoulder.

Greene said Skobelev, at the beginning of the war, had made up his mind firmly that he would never come out of it alive.

Skobelev completely captivated the ordinarily hard-to-please Archibald Forbes, who eventually concluded that the Russian was one of the two or three greatest battlefield generals he had ever witnessed in action. But early in the war, Forbes's impressions were based more on seeing the young general in action at the Brofft Hotel in Bucharest, just before the crossing of the Danube. Forbes knew of Skobelev's attainments—"He had carried a flying reconnaissance from Khokand over the Pamir Steppe, round Lake Victoria, and right into the flanks of the Hindoo Kush,"—and of his erudition and opinions:

> He quoted Balzac, Herbert Spencer, Hamley's *Operations of War*, and the School for Scandal; he had no belief in the first favorite for the approaching Derby; he thought Madame Chaumont very *chic*, and considered our household cavalry rather underhorsed; he imparted the information that the upper fords of the Oxus were dangerous because of quicksand; and he gave it as his opinion, after deliberate consideration, that you could get as good a *supreme de volaille* at the Cafe Royal in Regent Street as either at Bignon's or the Cafe Anglais.

To Forbes, one of the most memorable events of the war occurred when he joined MacGahan and Skobelev at the Brofft: the three men drank icy flagons of pilsner and sang songs to Skobelev's accompaniment on the pianoforte—songs in French, German, Russian, Kirghiz, Italian, and English, winding up the evening with "Auld Lang Syne," which Forbes sang in "impeccable burr," Skobelev and MacGahan in impeccable English.

One other correspondent in frequent company with Forbes and MacGahan was Frederick Villiers, war artist for the London *Weekly Graphic*, whose job was to make detailed sketches to be sent by courier and mail to his paper, there to be refined for engraving, and to send written dispatches to accompany them. The war declaration had been issued on Villiers's twenty-fifth birthday, and he had already become known as a seasoned, dependable "campaigner," having gone out to Serbia in the little war regarded as the first act of the drama about to unfold on the Danube. The greatest blow to the Serbian effort against the Turks had been the fall of Alexinatz on October 31, 1876, and Forbes and Villiers were the last civilians out of the town, dodging Turkish outposts by taking a mule path through the forest skirting the main road, then joining the retreating Serbian army at Deligrad, where the final battle of the war was fought.

MacGahan and Villiers met for the first time at the Viscountess Strangford's hospital at Tatar Bazardzhik in the winter of 1876–77. Like Forbes, the *Graphic* correspondent was familiar with MacGahan's exploits and grew to have great admiration for the American's efforts in Bulgaria in reporting the atrocities and the war.

On March 17, at a time when it remained uncertain whether the war might be averted by diplomatic means, MacGahan wrote his mother a long letter from St. Petersburg, the first, apparently, he had found time to write in nearly a year. The letter is especially interesting in what it reveals of MacGahan's own attitude toward his accomplishments in Bulgaria, in his plans for the future and his off-again, on-again relationship with James Gordon Bennett and the New York *Herald*. Yet another remarkable feature of the letter is the absence of references to his wife and son.

"The fact is that I have been in such a mess with the Turks, the Bulgarians, and the English government, that I have been neglecting my own affairs," he began.

> I have become rather famous since last summer, and have had more to do with the Eastern Question—if you know what that is—than ever I thought possible. I can safely say that I have done more to smash up the Turkish empire than anybody else—except the Turks themselves. Besides this I have fought several pitched battles with the English government, and the English embassy at Constantinople. And come off victorious each time. . . . You never thought I was such a desperate character, did you?

Clearly, even considering the innocence of private braggadocio to his mother, MacGahan was believing to a strong degree what the *Daily News* was telling him of the impact of his work. He continued, "I don't expect to be here much longer; it begins to look as though the Russians are not going to make war after all. They are going to patch up a peace which may last a few months; and then the whole dread business will begin over again."

He said he intended to return to England to "write another book" (presumably the Bulgarian book Sampson, Low had proposed), and then return to America for a series of lectures.

From this letter it appears MacGahan had never made a formal split with the *Herald*, and the letter indicates that James Gordon Bennett regretted not sponsoring MacGahan's investigation into the Bulgarian massacres.

"I don't know whether I am still on the Herald or not," he said, proceeding: "I had a very polite telegram from Bennett asking me if I was still going on with him or whether I had taken a permanent position with the Daily News. And asking me what I would like to do! A rather unusual proceeding with him."

He said he had been offered, but did not wish, a permanent assignment with the *Daily News*, but wished he could work for both papers in the event of war in order to double his salary.

"I have not been ill a day since I was in America," he ended, and whether expressly for his mother's comfort or as a true declaration of his feeling, he added, "I am tired enough of this kind of life, and would like to quit it and go home for good."

As it would turn out, the war did come, the *Daily News* and New York *Herald* worked out a cooperative pooled news arrangement on coverage of the war, and shortly after his encouraging health report to his mother, MacGahan broke his weakened ankle.

For a believer in omens, even his last statement home had ominous overtones.

XII

Guns Across the Danube

1
"Iron compliments"

British army officer William Francis Butler, a literary and historical-minded veteran of colonial wars in Burma, India, Canada, and the African Gold Coast, wrote for a London magazine in the midst of the Russo-Turkish War: "In no war of this century or in the last, since Frederick deliberately overran and annexed Silesia, has Europe witnessed a war so thoroughly undertaken for conquest as this one which we are now beholding. The invasion of Spain by Napoleon was not nearly so aggressive in its character."

Butler reflected one segment of the British point of view on the Russian invasion; another segment, such as that of the *Daily News* and of liberal opinion, put the conflict virtually in the framework of a holy war, the march of a Christian army against a barbarous, heathen empire.

Whether a crusade or a war of geopolitical gain, it was to be a major war of enormous significance in changing the map of Europe. Its forty-five-week course ran in three general phases: (1) the concentration of Russian forces in Rumania, the crossing of the Danube, and the establishment of the army on the river's southern bank; (2) the operations in forcing the passes of the Balkans and in the siege of Plevna; (3) and the final passage of the Balkans and the march to Constantinople.

In Rumania—"friendly" territory since that country's declaration of independence from Turkey—the Russians mobilized 275,000 men of all arms, 850 fieldpieces, and 400 siege guns, while another 70,000 men invaded Turkey's Caucasian provinces. Initially, the Russian command expected an easy victory—the chimerical "promenade" of a perceived strong army against a perceived weak one—over the ill-assorted and scattered forces of the Turks, believed to number about 135,000 men and 450 guns in Europe and a similar number in Asia.

Commanding the Russian armies in Europe was the Grand Duke Nicholas, brother of Czar Alexander II and inspector-general of cavalry and engineers. At the age of forty-six, he was a tall, robust, popular leader and a dedicated, if not brilliant, soldier.

The Turkish sirdar (commander in chief) was Abdul Kerim Pasha, old and indecisive, whose training had been completed forty years before in a Viennese military academy. He had served with some distinction in the Crimea and in the suppression of revolutionary risings in Armenia and Bulgaria. To his credit, he had an intense distrust for irregular troops such as those from Circassia and for the plundering rabble known as *bashi-bazouks*.

There was a great disparity in the training and ability of the opposing armies. A glimpse of the Turkish side was provided by Drew Gay, correspondent of the London *Daily Telegraph*, who served throughout the war with the Turks. When the call to arms was issued in Constantinople, Gay said, the conscripts were herded into the streets, drilled night and day, and inculcated with the fervor, but not the skill, to fight the hated *Muscovs*.

To make up for a deficiency in cavalry, the Ottoman government employed thousands of "irregulars" from all over the empire who flocked to the capital for reasons ranging from religious fervor to promises of booty, and who supplied their own horses while being issued arms and ammunition. They were, by and large, an insubordinate and unruly lot, more marauder and pillager than soldier, completely unpredictable in battle and, as the shrewd young American officer, Francis V. Greene said, "of little military use whatever."

The Russian common soldier was the product of a stiffly regimented military system. On attaining the age of twenty, every able-bodied male commoner had his name placed in a village urn to be drawn for military service. When his name was selected, he had a minimum of six years' active service facing him. At the end of that time, with no war at hand, he returned home on a sort of permanent furlough for the remaining years of his military obligation, liable to be recalled at any time to rejoin his regiment. At the age of thirty-five, his service obligation ended.

Greene described the average specimen of a Russian soldier as sallow in complexion and lank of figure with straight yellow hair, a heavy expression of face, wearing high boots in all seasons, his dark cloth trousers tucked inside them, his bright red shirt gathered at the waist by a wide belt. He wore a slouch cap with a peaked visor and a greasy sheepskin pelisse and was sustained by a diet of cabbage and onions, mutton or beef, a gruel of unbolted buckwheat called kasha, and black bread. His favorite drink was kvas, a sour and nonintoxicating brew of flour, leavening, and water.

The Russian soldier carried a heavy knapsack and rifle, ninety rounds of ammunition, and a short sword girt around his waist in addition to his bayonet. His feet were swathed in strips of linen cloth instead of stockings.

In small arms, the Turks held a decided disadvantage, being equipped with the Winchester, a repeating rifle of small charge and short range. The Russians had the Peabody-Martini, a .45-caliber breechloader made in Rhode Island and the English-made Snyder. But in artillery, the Krupp steel cannon of the Turks was far superior to the old, bronze siege train of the Russians.

MacGahan passed through a violent snowstorm between Moscow and the Rumanian frontier but found Kischenev in good weather that April 17, the peach and plum trees in bloom, Chinese lanterns and street decorations everywhere, and tall standards bearing flags and streamers with the letter *A* for Alexander sewn on them in bright colors.

The Russian invasion of the Danube opened with an exchange of "iron compliments" at Braila on Thursday, May 3. In this preliminary, the Russians opened fire with two fieldpieces, and the Turks replied with heavier guns from five monitors on the river, aiming not only at the Russian batteries but on the town itself, possibly mistaking the Russian consulate there for the headquarters of the invading army. Frederick Villiers of the *Weekly Graphic* witnessed the opening shot of the war and claimed it came from a Turkish monitor, the shell rising out of the Danube, piercing the mud wall of a house in Braila and landing, unexploded, nose first in the backyard soil.

Ranging from Russian headquarters in Kischenev up and down the river where the crossing preparations were to commence, MacGahan wrote admiringly of the Russians' "energetic and rapid march," which he said enabled them to win the first two moves of the war: first, in preventing the destruction of the railway bridge near Galatz by "a wonderful march," and secondly, in "throwing forward a sufficient number of troops to prevent the occupation of Rumania by the

Turks." Characterizing the Turkish army south of the Danube as "supinely inactive," MacGahan remarked that the Russians had occupied Rumania virtually without firing a shot.

On the last day of May, ending the first month of the war, Mac-Gahan telegraphed a lengthy story on a naval engagement off Ploeşti, the bulk of his information deriving from interviews with two Russian officers involved in the fight. He wrote:

> Two steam launches were, with a handful of men, steamed boldly into the midst of the Turkish flotilla, placed two torpedos under one of the monitors, and succeeded in blowing it up and completely destroying it. The engines of the launches were so constructed as to make very little noise, and when they were slowed down all the sound they made was a low dull kind of throbbing noise that was almost drowned by the continual croaking of the frogs which are very large and very numerous along the marshes of the Danube.

Each of the steam launches was equipped with two rude torpedos in an odd configuration: strapped to the end of a long spar projecting from the bow, which could be maneuvered under the hull of an enemy vessel. In the case of the Ploeşti incident of May 31, MacGahan wrote: "This is the first instance, I believe, in which a vessel has been destroyed in time of war by an enemy's torpedos, and the ease with which this was accomplished makes it a most important event in naval history."*

2
". . . this pretense of secrecy"

When the czar left St. Petersburg for the war zone on June 2, Mac-Gahan located in the town of Giurgevo, on the river south from Bucharest, and there took a room in a small, attractive hotel. From his window he could see boulevards with graveled walks and benches, a

---

*An earlier, perhaps the earliest, instance occurred during the American Civil War when, on December 12, 1862, the armored river gunboat *Cairo* was sunk in the Yazoo River by a "torpedo" made of a large demijohn placed in a wooden box and anchored in the Yazoo channel, exploding by means of a friction fuse. The nineteenth century "torpedo" of MacGahan's dispatch was more a semistationary mine, while the modern concept of "torpedo," a self-propelled submarine projectile loaded with explosives, was not used successfully in warfare until the Russo-Japanese War of 1904–1905.

The Grand Duke Nicholas.
(*Illustrated London News*, May 23, 1877)

Gen. Joseph Gourko.
(Hozier, *The Russo-Turkish War*)

small quay in which six small boats bobbed at their moorings, and beyond the quay the mile-wide Danube itself, rolling its swift, muddy waters along. South across the river, he wrote, he could see "the tall, slender minarets of Rustchuk, which glisten and burn in the sunshine in a wonderful way; and behind the town the green hills of Bulgaria, covered with orchards, vineyards, pasture-fields, and clumps of trees, among which may be seen here and there long lines and hillocks of fresh earth, the newly-constructed earthworks and defences of the Turks."

He wrote of the "thousands of white specks, that look about the size of eggs, that come out bright in the sunlight, and disappear when a cloud darkens the landscape." These, seen through field glasses, were in reality the tents of the Turkish army "which may be seen here and there all over the slopes hidden among the gardens and trees, and may be counted by the hundreds and by the thousands."

The people of Giurgevo had fled soon after the war began, leaving stranded a pathetic traveling circus, which MacGahan patronized two nights in a row. The tiny crowd of perhaps two dozen people watched two clowns, two riding girls, a contortionist, a performing horse, and a gymnast. "The laugh of the clown was a hollow one," MacGahan observed, "the old stale jokes were thrown off in a sad, depressed voice which was anything but laughable."

Of more interest was the occupation of the town by a large number of Kuban Cossacks under the command of the senior General Skobelev, with Skobelev the Younger serving as his father's chief of staff. MacGahan and Forbes were able to visit frequently with the Skobelevs, learning much about the plans for the crossing, and eating huge and satisfying meals in the shade of an apple tree near the generals' headquarters. The favorite pièce de résistance of Skobelev's cook was a meat and vegetable kabob roasted over an open fire.

From the Skobelevs, MacGahan learned a great deal about the Cossacks he had known in his rides with them against the Turkomans. There were, he found, several tribes of Cossacks: those of the river Don, alone liable for general military service anywhere; the Kuban Cossacks and Cossacks of the Terek, furnishing detachments for the czar's Imperial Guard; and the Astrakhan, Orenburg, Ural, and Siberian Cossacks, available only in time of war.

Divided into *polks* (roughly equivalent to a regiment), which in turn were divided into *sotnias* (usually four to six to a *polk*), these peasant soldiers were dressed in tunics, loose baggy trousers, cloaks, and sheepskin hats. Variously armed, they commonly carried pikes, Circassian-made sabers and *shaskas*—curved, guardless swords—

along with their rifles, and wore the *tcherkeska*, a long coat, the breasts of which carried rows of cartridge receptacles. With this, their horse, blanket, wooden saddletree, rug, shabrack, forage rope, and similar gear, the Cossacks were a mobile, fearful force when disciplined and strongly led.

"The Russians have at last begun to cross the Danube," MacGahan wrote on June 22 from his position on the north side of the river from Sistova. The Russian plan of action, he explained, was to make a number of feints at crossing, causing the Turks to divide their forces to cover the whole line of the Danube, thereby rendering it weak at every point.

General Zimmermann, chief of the Russian XIV Corps, held command of the left wing of the Army of the South, and to him was committed the duty of making the first crossing into enemy territory on pontoon bridges constructed by Russian sappers. The grand duke had set June 23 for the passage, but rains had brought the river up to a danger point, and the orders were redrawn. Even so, about six thousand Russian troops crossed on the morning of the 22nd with four pieces of artillery, opposite Sistova on ground so marshy the guns could not be drawn into action. Turkish resistance was slight, and Russian losses were given officially as three officers and forty-one men killed and about one hundred wounded. The Turks were said to have suffered much heavier casualties. By midmorning, MacGahan reported, the people of the village of Biela, several miles south of the river, could hear the boom of artillery and crackle of musketry, evidence that the passage had been accomplished.

In all, the Army of the South consisted of 180 battalions of infantry, 200 squadrons of cavalry, and 800 guns—about 180,000 men in all, of which about 100,000 crossed at Sistova.

On the 26th, the right wing of the invading force sent a pontoon detachment over the Danube from Simnitza under the command of the generals Skobelev, who drove out the small force of Turks posted there. Young Skobelev urged his father to swim the whole Cossack force across the river, but the old general refused, whereupon the Younger swam the river accompanied by a Kirghiz servant and three orderlies. The orderlies and their horses drowned.

The problems Archibald Forbes anticipated in using the telegraph office at Bucharest were realized from the beginning, although there would be a softening of restrictions later on. MacGahan complained about censorship as early as June 24, two days after the Danube crossing began, writing in a dispatch doubtlessly delivered to the *Daily News* by post: "It is difficult for an ordinary mortal to understand why this pretense of secrecy should be kept up any longer by the Russian head-quarters. It is a great annoyance to correspondents not to be allowed to telegraph anything, even of the most harmless character, relating to the Army, and it certainly makes not the slightest difference to the Turk."

He wrote of the success of the Russian crossing but buried this real news in an editorializing indictment that is the hallmark of unbylined foreign correspondence of the day. "Owing to the obstinate stupidity of the Rumanian telegraph officials," he wrote, "no one was allowed to telegraph even to announce a Russian victory, simply because they had received a general order forbidding the transmission of anything about the movements of troops."

Had MacGahan campaigned with the Turks, he would have discovered their very simple system of dealing with correspondents' telegraph copy: If it reflected favorably on the Turkish effort, it was cleared; if critical in any way, it was prohibited.

On horseback or by hired coach, he roamed from village to village on the Bulgarian side of the river, looking for anything remotely resembling news that would feed the insatiable appetite of the *Daily News* management (and presumably the paper's readership) for "intelligence" from the war zone. At Matchin he wrote of discovering an old house with a room filled halfway to the ceiling with tobacco, old, musty, and partly rotten, which the Russian troops carried off by the armload, like hay. In Turna Magurelle, he witnessed an even stranger spectacle, seeing "the red flame of burning houses on the opposite shore of Nikopolis" and "what at first appeared to be a monster comet with its head on the horizon, and its tail reaching to the zenith, extending across the sky in a broad, flashing white light." This phenomenon was caused by a huge arc light employed by the Russians to light the opposite shore and reveal the Turkish positions there for the artillery batteries protecting the Danube passage.

In the mud-walled village of Gorni Studen, MacGahan found the new headquarters of the Army of the South a strange compound of squalor and splendor. The town was without sanitation and its stench overpowering, but neat tents and white pavilions had mushroomed overnight, along with the colorful marquees of the Grand Duke and other high-ranking officers and nobility. These luminaries passed to and fro through the foul mud past rotting carcasses of dray animals, their resplendent uniforms contrasting splashes of color with the filth and squalor all about. Valets and cooks, English grooms and high-stepping horses, and coachmen with peacock-feathered hats were in abundance. It was here, after all, that the czar himself had made headquarters, in a Bulgar hut with a mud floor, taking his meals under a huge fluttering marquee with his officers.

Now that the passage of the Danube had been completed, the first Turkish line of defense had been breached with only feeble resistance and low casualties. Between Constantinople and the Russians, who now camped just below the fever-ridden marshes of the Danube, lay the main Turkish army and the mountain barrier of the Balkan range. Another Russian army under the command of the Grand Duke Michael had already invaded Ottoman territory in the Caucasus.

The Army of the South had next to force the lock of the Balkans— this at a natural door across the range lying fifty miles directly below the czar's Gorni Studen headquarters at a place called Shipka Pass.

3
"Deep in a gorge of the Balkans . . ."

For three weeks after crossing the Danube, the Russians encountered no serious obstacle to their move southward. Biela, a town on the Yantra River commanding an important juncture of roads to the southeast, was seized on July 7, and two brigades of cavalry under the command of General Joseph Gourko took the old Bulgarian capital of Tirnovo with only feeble firing from the Turks. The next day, the Grand Duke entered the ancient town, and Gourko, commanding an advance guard of cavalry, infantry, and artillery, set out southwestward toward Shipka Pass.

From Simnitza on July 5, MacGahan wrote: "The army is moving steadily across the river without intermission. Horses, ambulances, fourgons, caissons, infantry, baggage wagons, are pouring down across the flats day and night, raising clouds of dust and making Simnitza scarcely habitable."

And from Sistova, the Danubian town on the south bank directly across from the main Russian passage, he likened the activity to "a military promenade rather than a forced march," and described the people who came out to meet the Russians, offering bread and salt, fruit, and bouquets. Arches had been erected, he wrote, covered with leaves and flowers, and there were processions headed by chanting priests and singing peasants. Old bells that had lain hidden in the basements of mountain monasteries for centuries were hoisted up and beaten with wooden mallets to the accompaniment of chanted prayers in the old Slavic tongue. In Tirnovo, MacGahan watched the Grand Duke Nicholas assisting in religious ceremonies, people singing in the streets, Turks fleeing from their villages ahead of the advancing Russians, and Bulgarian villagers ransacking houses and helping themselves to whatever was abandoned.

Gourko's force had plunged across the Danube on June 23 in the vanguard of the army and, learning that the Turks had strongly garrisoned the Shipka Pass, received orders to penetrate this cordon defense of the Balkans. His command consisted of five thousand infantry, two thousand *tirailleurs* (sharpshooters), one thousand dragoons, five hundred hussars, twenty-five hundred Don Cossacks, two hundred Kuban Cossacks, and half a squadron of the czar's Imperial Guard—in all about eleven thousand men with eighteen fieldpieces and fourteen mountain guns.

The sternly efficient Gourko not only penetrated the Turkish defense but led his force through the smaller and undefended Khainkoi Pass to the east of Shipka, ultimately forcing the retreat of the Shipka defenders. Meanwhile, his patrols raided to within ninety miles of Adrianople, destroying railway and telegraph lines. In all, Gourko's work in the Shipka Pass formed one of the few brilliant episodes for the Russian army command in the entire war.

Iosif Vladimirovich Gourko, forty-nine years old at the time his name became familiar to readers of the *Daily News* and New York *Herald*, was, as Francis V. Greene wrote, "the least popular of the Russian generals." Brusque of manner and harsh with his men, indifferent to the needs of the common soldier, Gourko made up for these deficiencies with his exercise of a high order of military acumen. He had foresight, imagination, a driving energy, and a resoluteness of purpose that were uncommon characteristics in the Russian army of his day.

Gourko was a sort of minor Wellington or Pershing in his relationship with the common soldier. As Lieutenant Greene wrote, comparing him to the other prominent generals of the campaign, "The men worshipped Skobelev as a legendary hero; they loved Radetsky [commander of the VIII Corps of the Army of the South] as a kind-hearted father, but they never developed any personal affection for Gourko."

Nor did they for Wellington or Pershing, but like the Iron Duke and Black Jack, Gourko won battles.

The Balkans rise steeply from three thousand to five thousand feet on the western shore of the Black Sea to the south of Varna and run westward, broadly speaking, parallel to the Danube, until they terminate toward the south of Sofia at their highest point, about nine thousand feet. They are chalk and limestone formations, broken through in many places by masses of volcanic rock. The Bulgarian plains which lay ahead of Gourko's advancing force, at the northern foothills of the range, are covered for an immense distance with underbrush and oak forests.

Fifty years before, the Prussian field marshal Count von Moltke, who had served the Turkish sultan as a military adviser in the 1830s, said that in all wars against the Turks, the Porte should limit itself to concentration of its forces at the foot of the Balkans. There, he said, the true defense of Turkey should commence. As for any invading force, von Moltke described six routes leading southward from the Danube and converging upon Adrianople, but his choice of the best passage to force was the one from Sistova, then to Tirnovo and Shipka Pass, over the Balkans to Kazanlik.

Now, one great difficulty had already been removed by the Russians: the occupation of Tirnovo.

Arriving in Tirnovo the day after Gourko left it to push on south to the Shipka Pass, MacGahan wrote: "I do not know how many troops there are before us, nor what force is destined for the defense of Constantinople, but unless they impede the march of this army more than hitherto it will be in sight of Saint Sophia within a month."

Riding on to find Gourko's column, MacGahan took a route across gently rolling hills, separated by brooks and streams of pure cold water; fields covered with corn, wheat, barley, and dotted with copses of elm and oak and patches of green grass where sheep grazed. There were huts congregated in tiny villages, and occasionally on the outskirts of these hamlets he spotted men reaping and gathering grain and women threshing it—life moving on, serenely innocent of the great events of war that were now intervening.

Gourko's army reached Shipka Pass toward the close of the day on July 12, the roadway becoming so treacherous that the march was halted, not to resume before daybreak. The road, actually only a mountain path, so narrowed in places that two of the mountain guns rolled down the hillside to the bottom of the valley and had to be laboriously hoisted up again with makeshift block and tackle. The steep and narrow pass permitted one gun and team at a time, the men marching in single file.

MacGahan caught the rear echelon of Gourko's column on the 15th and wrote a brilliant long dispatch from the mountain town of Parovci to describe the Shipka crossing:

> Deep in a gorge of the Balkans, in a dark, narrow little dell, whose sides are so steep that the dozen houses which make

up the village seem to be holding on with hooks and claws to keep from slipping down into the deep ravine beneath them. . . . It is night and a thick veil of darkness covers mountains, trees, rocks, and forests. Almost perfect silence reigns, and the occasional cry of some bird, startled in its slumbers, echoes fearfully distinct and alarming. Other sounds may be heard if one listens closely: an occasional hum of voices, the impatient stamp of a horse's hoof, the rattle of harness. The fact is, that just beneath the little house where I have found refuge, stands a battery of artillery . . . and three or four miles further down the dark, crooked, rocky little hollow, lies an army sleeping on its arms, without fire or supper, waiting the first ray of daylight to resume its march.

      . . . We are in one of the most difficult defiles of the Balkans, at the entrance to a pass which the Turks have left unguarded, a pass which we hope to get through early in the morning, and this is the reason for our secrecy and silence, the absence of camp fires and supper, and the usual sights and sounds of a bivouac.

Russian advance scouts had found that, while the Turks were posted at the exit of the pass, no entrenchments had been dug, and acting on this intelligence, Gourko resumed the march at six, soon reaching the valley floor where the Turkish camp was pitched. At the sight of the Cossacks in the vanguard of the line of march, the motley assortment of Turkish soldiers in advance posts flew at a gallop toward Kazanlik. As the Russian infantry, *tirailleurs*, and artillery descended, the Turkish camp panicked and fled, leaving behind all their provisions and gear.

While Gourko's force penetrated Shipka Pass, the Turkish commander at the town of Vidin, far to the west, gathered his army of forty thousand choice troops and began a long march to the Vid River, which falls away southward out of the Danube just west of Nicopolis. This commander, Osman Pasha, had as his objective the fortress town of Plevna, a distance of 115 miles, which he and his troops covered in just six days.

MacGahan's ill fortune with horses continued to plague him. Nursing his fractured ankle and riding gingerly along the narrow Shipka trail, he suffered a severe fall, wrenching the leg once again. One British army officer, Henry Brackenbury, attached to Gourko's force as observer (and serving also as correspondent for the London *Times*), said MacGahan reached the village of Hainkoi a day after it was taken "in such a plight that nothing but the indomitable resolution of a brave man would have caused him to follow the advance to Kazanlik two days after the march of the force. To the great regret of all who knew him, MacGahan was laid up during the whole of our stay at Kazanlik, and no other correspondent crossed the Balkans until some days after General Gourko's capture of the Shipka Pass."

Kazanlik, which lay on the southward exit of Shipka, was captured by Gourko on July 19, and from the town MacGahan managed to write a long, descriptive dispatch to be carried by courier back to Tirnovo, then on to Bucharest. As in so much of his work, MacGahan brought the reader with him to observe the events at hand. The dispatch ran, in part:

> We are 200 Cossacks drawn up on this ridge. . . . The first streak of day is just growing visible in the east, and a long flash of rosy light is climbing slowly up the sky. Before and beneath us is a dark narrow gorge, still a pool of blackness, into which we slowly descend. . . . We eat a piece of hard bread and whatever bits of cold meat we have left about us, make shift to smoke a cigarette, wrap our blankets about us, and lie down on the ground for a sleep, expecting to hear the alarm sounded at any moment.

The fight was sudden and decisive. MacGahan observed that "for two hundred Cossacks to attack two companies of infantry would be the height of absurdity in any other country in the world but Turkey. Here, however, it seems the most natural thing to do imaginable, and we accordingly began to advance, firing. . . . The Turks were, as usual, completely taken by surprise."

The securing of Shipka Pass with so little resistance amazed all the correspondents, the Russian and Turkish high commands, and the British government. As MacGahan put it: "With this force (11,000 men), half of which are raw recruits not yet four months under arms, and one-fourth more (the Cossacks) irregulars, the Russians made and secured the passage of the Balkans, one of the most formidable bulwarks ever raised by nature for the defense of a country. And they did it with the loss of six men wounded."

At about this point in the successful Russian advance, there occurred in the pro-Turkish press and among foreign officers serving in the Turkish forces, rising speculation of atrocities committed by Bulgarian troops attached to the Russian force, and by the Cossacks, in reprisal of the Turkish horrors of '76. In a two-volume "Narrative of Personal Experiences," the result of serving as a lieutenant general in the Ottoman army in the Balkans in 1877, the British army officer Valentine Baker wrote: "Whilst at Haim-Boghaz we heard that on our road to Shipka we should pass by some villages where fearful atrocities had been committed by the Bulgarians and Cossacks upon a large number of Musselman women and children who had taken refuge there during the advance of Gourko's army through the Balkans. Their bones, to the number of 120 persons, were said to still be lying unburied." Baker admitted he could not personally confirm this story, but gave it his mark of approval in any event.

MacGahan, the authority on atrocities, added his assessment of these rumors:

> I should like to observe that there were no houses burnt here, that there were no Turks murdered, that no Turkish women were outraged, that no Turk was roasted alive, and that no Turkish children were spitted on bayonets and carried about the streets. Let it be further remembered that many of the Turks living here now were engaged in the massacres of last year, and we have the measure of difference between the Turk and Bulgarian.

With the village of Kazanlik now in Russian hands, Gourko resolved to complete the success of the day by occupying the village of Shipka, center of the trade in attar of roses, situated at a height of two thousand feet on the southern slope of the Balkans. By three o'clock in the afternoon of July 19, the Russians occupied the outskirts of the town and had closed the mouth of the pass against the Turks.

In the days to follow the securing of Shipka, Gourko's Cossacks proceeded to raid the valleys to the south, giving rise to increasingly widespread tales of Cossack brutalities and Bulgarian reprisals against the innocent Turkish villagers along the Tunja river.

In eight days' time from leaving Tirnovo, sixteen from the Danube, Gourko had gained possession of three key passes of the Balkans— Hainkoi, Travna, and Shipka—covering a length of thirty miles; he had dispersed various Turkish detachments numbering ten thousand men, had captured eleven guns and a large quantity of ammunition, clothing, and provisions, and had disarmed the civilian Turkish populace—all with a loss of less than five hundred casualties, killed and wounded.

In addition, yet another passage across the Danube had been secured through the capture of Nicopolis by General Krudener in a single assault on July 16. Thus, in the first four weeks of the war, Russian successes were uninterrupted. It appeared that MacGahan's prophecy would be realized that the czar's army would be viewing the dome of Santa Sophia in Constantinople in a month's time.

4

". . . the sheets fell from his pen"

The result of Gourko's successes and the seeming imminence of the Russian march on Constantinople created an international panic. The Muhammadan population of towns on the Russian line of march south as far as Adrianople, fled toward the Turkish capital; the sultan wavered between fleeing with his cabinet to Brusa in Asia Minor and remaining in his palace. Decisions were made for him. He was overthrown along with his cabinet, and the commander in chief, Kerim Pasha, dismissed and banished, along with the war minister, to one of the islands in the Aegean. Mehemet Ali Pasha was recalled from Montenegro and made commander in chief, and Suleiman Pasha was appointed to command the Turkish army between Adrianople and the Balkans.

In Constantinople, Gourko's force was reported to be sixty thousand strong instead of about eleven thousand, and the scare had effectively cleared a path from the southern slopes of the Balkans to Adrianople, a path Suleiman Pasha's army hoped to block, just as he hoped to retake Shipka Pass, and would ultimately expend twenty thousand men in the futile attempt to do so.

There were upwards of seventy newspaper correspondents attached to the Russian army, and all of them believed, after Gourko's exploit, that nothing could stop the Russian steamroller. So too, as the news dispatches appeared and as the reports of other observers poured in, did the British government. With Gourko's army bringing the southern escarpment of the Balkans into Russian hands, and with the road apparently open southward to the Ottoman capital, Lord Beaconsfield ordered Her Majesty's fleet to Besika Bay at the mouth of the Dardanelles as a "precautionary measure."

Archibald Forbes, with characteristic bombast, called Gourko's passage of the Balkans "an event in European history of an actual, and still more of a contingent, importance scarcely second to any occurrence of the century," and maintained the unprecedented passage "is the strangest testimony at once to his soldierhood and to the comparative

ease with which a Russian army might actually have reached Adrianople, if only moderate support had been accorded to the daring leader."

Forbes and MacGahan could easily agree on Gourko's successes, but
on another matter, the recurring theme of the atrocities, they were to
strongly dissent, and both their opinions saw print.

MacGahan, on the day of the closing of Shipka Pass, wrote of an
attack at Gabrovo, a town on the northern slope of the Balkans closest
to Shipka. There, after the Turks raised a white flag, Gourko sent
forward an officer under a flag of truce. The Turks, MacGahan wrote,
seized the officer and murdered him, then opened fire on the Russians.
"The next day," he concluded his story, "when the Russians entered
the fort, they found the body of the bearer of the flag, decapitated and
horribly mutilated, together with the bodies of other Russian soldiers
who had been captured."

Forbes, on the other hand, felt that the plight of the Bulgarian peasant had been overstated, and made a startling statement, published
not in the *Daily News* but in a magazine article:

> I know that the Russian peasant soldier who crossed the
> Danube as the "deliverer" of the Bulgarian from "oppres-
> sion," feels with a stolid bewildered envy that, to use a slang
> phrase, he would be glad indeed "to have half his com-
> plaint.". . .
>
> The Bulgarians begged arms of the Russians, and receiv-
> ing them, hot with the fell memories of last year, and con-
> scious that Russians were with them and for them, they fell
> on the Turks with the most ruthless reprisals. . . . All the
> Turks are reported as having done on their reoccupation of
> the districts, is on credible evidence not one whit more bar-
> barous than was the conduct of the Bulgarians towards the
> Turks when Gourko's star was in the ascendant.

Forbes suggested that while "it can be the task surely of no decent
man to be the apologist of the Turkish wild beast who ravaged and rav-
ished in those fell days" of Tatar Bazardzhik and Batak the year before,
the Turkish government might have been ignorant of the "North Balkan conspiracy."

In the *Daily News*, MacGahan's reaction to Forbes's claim and all others of a similar nature was one of disdain: "It has been said and reiter-
ated a thousand times that the Bulgarians are just as bad as the Turks,"
he wrote. "I make the assertion, and I make it without fear of contra-
diction, that on this side of the Balkans, and in the valley of the Tundja,
the Bulgarians did not commit any of the acts I have enumerated—and

they have done nothing to justify the assertion that they are as bad as the Turks."

The key to the controversy, MacGahan insisted, was the difference between actually seeing the atrocities alleged to have occurred and merely hearing of them. "I have not seen a single correspondent or other disinterested person, who said he saw any such acts committed by Bulgarians," he stated, and he permitted himself a small but acute thrust at his colleague Forbes: "I have hitherto only discussed what occurred within the sphere of my observation."

As for the atrocities of the Turks against their captured enemy prisoners, MacGahan was not alone in citing cases. Lieutenant Colonel Brackenbury, a veteran of the Indian Mutiny and Ashanti War of 1873 (and later Sir Henry Brackenbury, G.C.B., K.C.S.I.) and military correspondent of the *Times*, wrote his paper on August 7 that the Turks defiled every Russian soldier who fell into their hands. He said he saw bodies beheaded and sexually mutilated, and bodies with feet, hands, ears, noses, and sexual organs severed.

Although there was to be little respite for MacGahan between the capture and securing of Shipka Pass and the opening of the operations at Plevna, Bucharest remained the focal point for any time away from the front. MacGahan left no memoir of Bucharest in those days nor more than a passing reference to the city in his work, but Archibald Forbes, in later years, came to reflect on the great city and wrote one of his prose poems on it:

> And that capital—the Paris of the East—was throbbing in a delirium of wild pleasure, accentuated by the clank of martial accouterments, the clatter of sword scabbards on the parquet floors of the restaurants, and the steady tramp of the cohorts which poured through her seething streets. Bucharest was a ballroom wherein Mars, Venus and Bacchus were dancing the cancan in a frantic orgy. Princes, grand dukes, countesses without their counts, *ci-devant* operatic ladies, whose troupe had despersed itself in favor of more probable engagements that did not strain the voice, diplomats, aides-de-camp, Polish Jews, maquereaux [procurers, brothel keepers], and war correspondents belonging to every European nation, jostled one another politely in the broad staircase of the Hotel Brofft.

And Forbes, who left the most comprehensive (and thoroughly uncritical) memoir on MacGahan of any of the American's colleagues and friends, said with ardor that "in the Russian army in those Bulgarian days, it was next best to being MacGahan himself to be MacGahan's friend."

The Ohioan, Forbes and others claimed, had a facility for friendship, a natural modesty (the latter certainly not so muted in print as in person, it would appear), an undoubted prowess as a writer and reporter, the high esteem and confidence of the principal Russian commanders, and a gregariousness and humor considered typically American (or "Irish-American," as he was often identified). He attracted attention, and all who knew him well enough to write about him later (Forbes, Villiers, Frank Millet, and Brackenbury among them) seemed impressed with him as a man and as an exemplar of his profession.

Forbes, who in retirement wrote often of his colleague and of those infrequent hours of relaxation in Bucharest, was a tough customer—a scowling, puzzling, complex man given to long and soporific flights of melodramatic prose mingled with passages of stunning insight and clarity. He was blunt and rude, temperamental, egotistical; he missed no opportunity to lecture military commanders in print if he felt them generally ignorant or particularly mistaken—conditions he found countless times. His writings were forever blessed with that corruscating veracity that hindsight affords. Yet he could be frothily romantic, humorous, sensitive and generous, and while he cultivated few friendships, he was an unwavering, lifelong friend to those few. And in MacGahan, Forbes seemed to see something quite special, focusing on it often in his latter days when, retired from "campaigning," he wrote appealing autobiographical books and articles and spun tales in the London military clubs.

Forbes wrote, for example: "When traveling in Bulgaria with MacGahan in war time, we would occasionally enter some village which he had previously visited during the investigation into the atrocities. It was touching to see how the people thronged about him, fondly treating him as their liberator and kissing his hands with a devotion that was thoroughly sincere."

The time spent in the comfort and color of the Hotel Brofft was forever fleeting. It seemed only to serve as a place to prepare, on a moment's notice, for the next battle, to partially rejuvenate tired muscles and brain cells, to replace days of death and devastation with moments of life and gaiety, and in MacGahan's case, some moments, not many, with his wife and son.

In May, at about the time the Russians began their advance on the Danube, Barbara and Paul were staying at "a good hotel," the Hugues, in Bucharest, waiting for MacGahan to join them after recovering in

Kischenev from his ankle fracture. At the Hugues and later in an apartment she rented from a "Mme. Moscou," a Rumanian woman who became a friend and confidante, Barbara worked on translation for *Golos* and other Russian papers of her husband's dispatches from the front, delivered to her by couriers every four or five days.

She saw him fleetingly, a day or two at a time, then he would depart and be absent for weeks at a time. Even when reunited with her he worked incessantly, and she recalled in later years, "He composed easily and rapidly in a clear flowing backhand, using square paper, and the sheets fell from his pen and fluttered on the floor like leaves from Valambrosa."

At the front, or on the march, she said, or in cold weather when his ink froze and he used a pencil, he could write with facility, anywhere and at any time. His capacity for continuous labor, even when suffering with the pain of his broken leg, or with the species of "Danube fever" that occasionally brought him to bed, was, she said, "astonishing."

And now, in the third week of July 1877, another battle was in the making—a battle which put the Turks back in the war, which slowed the Russian advance to a standstill, which taxed the best efforts of every man in the field, Russian, Turk, soldier, general, and correspondent; a battle which claimed the blood and lives of tens of thousands.

It would unfold at a town named Plevna.

XIII
Promenade to Plevna

1
"Beware of Plevna!"

William V. Herbert, the young German-born Englishman who served in the Turkish army in Bulgaria, wrote that Alexander II jokingly consulted a gypsy before the war and asked of its possible outcome. According to Herbert, the seer warned the czar: "Beware of Plevna!" Although probably an apocryphal tale, the old Thracian settlement and Turkish trade center near the Vid river below Nicopolis earned some attention and concern early in the war.

General Baron Krudener's IX Corps on the right wing of the advancing Russian army, took Nicopolis on July 16, and the next day, while en route to "neutralize" the Turkish forces at Widdin commanded by Osman Pasha, sighted the vanguard of Osman's army marching from the west on the road to Plevna. Neither Krudener nor the grand duke's headquarters at Tirnovo attached much significance to this development, the latter sending a laconic order to "occupy Plevna as promptly as possible."

Two critical factors now intervened in the conduct of the war: the nature of the Turkish commander now at Plevna, and the nature of the town and its defenses.

Mushir Ghazi Osman Nuri Pasha, born in Tokat, Asia Minor, in 1832, was a tall, solidly built man, delicate of health but an active, highly intelligent, self-denying, and above all, patient and resolute professional soldier. He had fought in the Crimea, in Eupatoria in 1855, served in the Syrian rebellion, in Crete, Yemen, and Serbia. *Mushir* denoted his rank, that of field marshal; *Ghazi* was an honorary title that soon would be bestowed upon him by the sultan. It means "Victorious."

In 1877, Plevna had a population of seventeen thousand, of whom ten thousand were Bulgars. Drew Gay of the *Daily Telegraph* described the town as "one of the most labyrinth-like in the world. It is pleasantly situated between a huge marsh and an odorous ditch, called by courtesy the river Vid. Its streets are paved on the principle of one huge boulder to three great holes. It boasts a mosque, a huge Christian church, a prison, and a khan." And Frederick Villiers of the *Weekly Graphic*, standing on a high vantage point known as Radischevo Ridge, wrote: "The red tiles of the houses and the metal-topped minarets of its white mosques were easily discernible nestling behind the formidable works of the Moslems, which bristled from every mound."

Plevna was a natural fortress, standing in the hollow of a valley surrounded by hills and rugged ravines. The Turks had worked in a frenzy to erect breastworks and rifle pits, bastions, lines of defense, one within the other, and redoubts* such as that on Grivitza Ridge, key to the entire position on the north, and the Krishin redoubt on the south. Both of these commanded the countryside for a range of three thousand yards on all sides.

While MacGahan rode with Gourko's column to the south, the Russians made their first test of Osman Pasha's defenses at Plevna. Command of this probe was confided by Baron Krudener to a Lieutenant General Schilder-Schulder, whose first mistake was a classic one: attacking in two columns too far separated to afford one another either communication or support. There were other miscalculations as well: The Russians had no clear idea of Osman's strength and were sending only 7,500 men under Schilder-Schulder against a force later reckoned at about 20,000 manning the Plevna defenses; and there was overconfidence in the effect of the artillery on the Turkish entrenchments.

On July 19, Russian cannon lobbed shells all afternoon toward the front of the Turkish position. The next morning, Schilder-Schulder's force made its advance as far as Bukova on the northern outskirts of the town and managed to capture three lines of trenches in the vicinity of Janik Bair. But the thick screens of musketry fire, the showers of ball and shell that erupted from the Bukova and Janik Bair redoubts

---

*A self-enclosed defensive work protecting a strategic point.

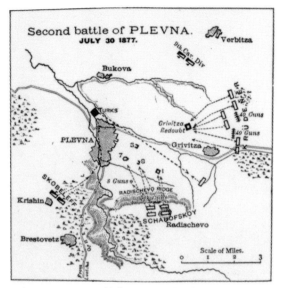

Plevna, positions of July 30, 1877. (Forbes, Henty, *Battles of the Nineteenth Century*, I)

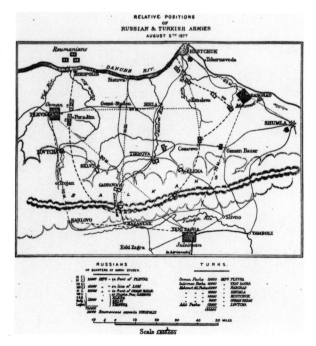

Plevna, positions of August 5, 1877. (Greene, *The Campaign in Bulgaria*)

A view of Plevna after the Russian occupation. (Hozier, *The Russo-Turkish War*)

Turkish troops at Plevna, awaiting battle. (*The Graphic War Number*, Sept. 29, 1877)

The battle of Plevna, July 30, 1877.
(Hozier, *The Russo-Turkish War*)

Turkish attack in the Shipka Pass.
(Hozier, *The Russo-Turkish War*)

Osman Pasha.
(Hozier, *The Russo-Turkish War*)

HIS MAJESTY ALEXANDER II., EMPEROR OF RUSSIA.

Czar Alexander II.
(*Illustrated London News*, May 23, 1877)

The Russo-Turkish War of 1877—"The War in the East," as English newspapers called it—generated a phenomenal interest in England, almost as much as the Crimean War of 1856-58. Typical of the lavish coverage was the work of such one-shilling illustrated papers as *The Graphic*.

and from Osman's entrenchments on the north and east of Plevna, sent the Russian flanks backward in retreat. The Russian casualties were 2,771 men and 71 officers; the Turks were believed to have lost about 2,000 men in all.

News of the events of July 20 quickly reached the headquarters of the grand duke at Tirnovo. There, while a great celebration continued over the passage of the Balkans by General Gourko, the grand duke grasped the gravity of the situation. There would be no question from now on of the importance of Plevna and the extraordinary defenses the Turks had erected and which they strengthened every day.

Of that first sortie by the Russians, a historian of the war, Henry M. Hozier, asserted that "the march upon Plevna was arranged more like a promenade than a military movement from which any serious consequences might be suspected."

The promenade illusion now had vanished, and ten days from the first, the Russians launched a second assault, an event witnessed by Forbes and Villiers from the vantage point of Radischevo Ridge. In the interim, the Turks had added to their fortifications around Grivitza and Bukova and to the east of the town. Baron Krudener had reconnoitered the ground but was reluctant to take the responsibility for another assault, given the strength of the defenses and the reinforcements known to be pouring into Plevna from Lovtcha on the south. His negative report to the Grand Duke, however, fell on deaf ears, and a sharp order was issued from Tirnovo: attack.

Krudener led a force on July 30 totaling thirty-six battalions of infantry, thirty squadrons of cavalry—close to thirty thousand men in all—and 176 guns: nine- and four-pounders, horse and mountain cannon. On the move at seven through a dense morning fog that shrouded Plevna and hid the lay of the land, the day long battle ended in a thorough Russian failure, a sad tapestry of interwoven mistakes, miscalculations, and sheer ignorance.

Three principal errors cost the Russians 7,300 officers and men— 2,400 of the total killed outright and left on the battlefield: The columns in attack were again not in supporting distance; the timing of the assaults, such as the critical one against the Grivitza redoubt, was ill-organized; and close formations were maintained long after the troops came under fire, accounting in large measure for the enormous casualties, over 25 percent of all the Russian troops in the field.

The single redeeming feature of the July 30 bloodbath was the conduct of General Michael Skobelev on the left flank of the attacking force. Even Francis Vinton Greene, not given to idle praise, said of Skobelev's command: "It was hotly engaged during the whole day, and, although small in numbers, was handled with such skill as to establish beyond doubt the military genius of this brilliant young general."

Skobelev advanced through the mist to the village of Krishin and, with two *sotnias* of Kuban Cossacks and four pieces of artillery, arrived to within six hundred yards of the southern outskirts of Plevna. At a critical moment his Cossacks opened fire and diverted about four thousand Turkish infantrymen from Krudener's attack. He also posted his *sotnias* in such a manner as to keep the Turks from occupying a key hill from which they would have been able to enfilade the entire line of the Russian right wing, commanded by Lieutenant General Prince Shakofskoi. Skobelev lost 50 percent of his force in the day's battle, had one horse killed and another wounded, and when the time came for him to retreat to Krishin, he coolly alighted from his third mount of the day, shot his sword into its scabbard, and marched along with the rearguard.

Even in retreat, the Turkish shells whistled through the Russian lines, the men falling in the undergrowth or fleeing through the stubble and maize fields. As night came on and streams of wounded found their way over the ridges, a baleful sort of night animal swarmed over the battlefield—the bashi-bazouk. Lingering on the ridges until the moon rose, the Russian staff could hear below them on the still night air the sharp cries of pain, the entreaties for mercy, the hoarse yells and grunts of the blood-and-booty crazed bashis. Indeed, throughout the battle, the Turks took no prisoners and gave no quarter. The wounded were executed in their bloody wrappings, the soldiers who surrendered were killed where they stood. From one end of the battlefield to the other, from the vineyards, maize fields, hillocks and ridges, trenches and earthworks, came the shrieks of those being hacked to death by the masters of the yataghan.

Osman Pasha's losses were estimated at between five and six thousand—at the most, fifteen percent of his force.

Of all the lessons of Plevna II, one seems to rise as a portent of the future, a lesson unlearned as late as World War I: that artillery is of little purpose in dislodging troops from deep or well-constructed entrenchments. MacGahan could have spoken to this point, as could have Forbes: General Concha in the battle of Abarzuza had shelled the Carlist trenches for three days with eighty cannon at a distance of less than a mile. He inflicted a loss of only eighty men killed and wounded.

His greatest story of the war in his saddlebags, Archibald Forbes felt certain he would encounter trouble from the Russian censors at Bucharest. What he had described, after all, was a serious setback for the grandly named Army of the South. He had been an entire day in the saddle, his head rang and throbbed with the awful noise of the cannon, he was filthy and hungry, yet he rode out to the north for the Danube. From Giurgevo he traveled by rail to Bucharest and then, still without rest, rode across the Rumanian frontier to the nearest telegraph office in Transylvania.

His story, appearing in the *Daily News* on August 3, had the Forbes touch—flamboyant, dramatic, portentous.

> How bright seemed the Russian military future this week! Gourko stretching out his arm almost within clutching distance of Adrianople; the Czarevitch waiting but the word from Tirnova to cast a girdle of stalwart soldiers and solid earthworks around Rustchuk. Schahofskoy and Krudener, in the full expectation of wiping out the slur of Schilder's failure at Plevna. . . . then, lo! the scene changes; the sunshine is overcast by black clouds; the advantages of the Russians crumble like burnt-out tinder.

2
"Imbecile neglect"

During the time of the first two assaults on Plevna, MacGahan remained with Gourko's column in the Balkan passes, which, by the end of July, amounted to sixteen thousand men standing against the whole of the newly formed army of Suleiman Pasha, numbering at least fifty thousand. With the fighting in Plevna, Gourko had no hopes of reinforcements and had orders to retreat slowly and come to rest on the northern slopes of the entrance to Shipka Pass.

MacGahan reported that despite the necessity of moving back in the face of overwhelming odds, Gourko's was an admirably conducted operation. The retreat, beginning on the morning of August 1, through the Dalbouka Pass, was led by a detachment of Cossacks, the cavalry covering the rear. The worst part of it all, the correspondent said, was the terrible suffering of the wounded, jolted in the agony of their wounds in wagons and gun limbers, unsheltered from the sun. A great many of the wounded died, and many healthy men succumbed to sunstroke and withered from the sheer fatigue of the dolorous retreat.

What MacGahan could not know was that, after the August 1 retreat, Suleiman would continue his move forward and keep up his harassment of Gourko with more or less energy for the next four months. In so doing he would sacrifice the better part of the army he had brought north from Montenegro.

The Grand Duke Nicholas devoted the month of August to conferences with his staff to prepare for a new attack on Plevna, one which, it was hoped, would erase the memory of the debacles of July and make possible resumption of the advance on Adrianople. The *Daily News*, meanwhile, was filled with assessments of the Russian defeat of July 30. Forbes's dispatch filled several columns, and when he returned from Shipka, MacGahan contributed a quite extraordinary one.

MacGahan's leisurely dispatch, datelined "Headquarters, Army Before Plevna, August 19" and running under the heading, "The Russian Mistakes," totaled well over eight thousand words, but there were yet more remarkable features. There was a brutal cogency in its appraisal of the Russian conduct of the Plevna assaults, a relentless bill of particulars against the Russian generals—naming the "guilty" and those responsible for specific blunders. No high Russian commander, no matter how sacrosanct his reputation, fell entirely free of MacGahan's microscopy, not even Gourko or Todleben, the great engineer-hero of Sebastopol.

And perhaps the most remarkable fact of all was that the author of this extraordinary dissertation was not present when the events he examined took place.

He viewed the failure to take Plevna as the result of two distinct "blunders," the first of which was Gourko's overextension of his small force; the second, the failure to occupy Plevna and Loftcha immediately after the Danube crossing. "The imbecility displayed in this by educated military men is of that kind which simply surpasses belief and defies explanation," he stated.

As the most culpable for the failures, MacGahan pointed to two men: General Baron Krudener, commanding the IX Corps on the right flank of the July 30 assault, and General Levitsky, assistant chief of staff to the grand duke. Krudener failed to seize Plevna as ordered, MacGahan said, and Levitsky, the man "whose business it was to see that the grand duke's orders were executed," failed to execute those orders. For the latter, the American had a withering observation, stating that Levitsky, among the youngest generals of the army, had won his special place "on account of the talent he displayed in the peace manoeuvres at St. Petersburg." MacGahan continued: "Here, on the level plains about the capital, where every inch of ground and every road was known to him, where the fighting was done with blank cartridges, and where there were neither killed nor wounded, General Levitsky succeeded in handling an army corps very well. . . . Fighting a real war and handling an army of two hundred thousand men is, however, a different kind of thing."

And so the grueling indictment continued, recounting instances of "gross and culpable carelessness and stupidity," "recklessness and incapacity"; of commanders "proverbially careless, neglectful, and indifferent"; of Krudener, who "hesitated and vacillated," who was "wavering, undecided, irritable and excited," who "threw his army blindly against the Turkish entrenchments, like a mad bull going at a stone wall, with no other idea of taking it but the employment of pure brute force in the undirected if sublime bravery of the Russian soldier." Indeed, MacGahan wrote, "If battles were to be fought in this way there would be no need of officers; the soldiers might do all, and the generals had better return at once to the cafes of St. Petersburg and Moscow."

The Russian engineers, headed by the redoubtable General Eduard Ivanovich Todleben, hero of the defenses of Sebastopol in the Crimean War, had the reputation as the best in all Europe. "If this be true," the correspondent wrote, "all I can say is that the engineer service had better do something to justify its reputation. I never in my life saw roads and bridges in the condition in which they are used by the Russian army. Even the Carlists did better than this."

He issued a blanket indictment of the "sixty or seventy generals of brigade, division, and corps command" of which, he said, "there is not yet one who has given any proof of extraordinary talent, who has risen enough above the level of mediocrity to attract attention."

Of the July 30 battle, he wrote:

> The fact is that the battle of Plevna is as disgraceful for the Russian generals as it is glorious for the Russian soldiers. The soldiers knew their duty, and did it. It was the Russian generals who neither knew nor did theirs. The fearful losses sustained show how well the Russian soldier did his part. . . . The Prussian loss at Gravelotte, the bloodiest battle of the Franco-Prussian war, did not exceed eight percent, and if we wish to find a parallel for the Russian losses at Plevna, we must look at some of the hard fought battles of the American Civil War, Shiloh, Antietam, the Wilderness, with this difference: that the American troops who fought these battles were veterans, while the greater part of the Russians at Plevna had never been under fire before.

He saw some hope for the new commander of the Russian forces at Plevna, General Zotov, who replaced Baron Krudener. Zotov, he said, "owes his present position to neither protection nor favor. He has won it solely by his sword, and something may, therefore, I think be hoped for him. He appears to be a man of resolution and energy, and it is he who will command the next attack on Plevna, which we are expecting daily."

He dismissed out of hand the Turkish "want of military knowledge, the utter lack of good officers, of discipline, of military skill," but of the Turkish common soldier, MacGahan had the greatest admiration:

> Put a Turk in a ditch, given him a gun, a sackful of car-
> tridges, a loaf of bread and a jug of water, and he will remain
> there a week or a month under the most dreadful artillery
> fire that can be directed against him, without flinching. He
> can only be dislodged by the bayonet, and with the rapidity
> of fire of modern arms it is very difficult to reach him with
> the bayonet, as the Russians found to their cost at Plevna.

As to the likely outcome of the "final battle for Plevna," MacGahan was certain of a Russian victory, providing "the minimum of skill is displayed by the Russian generals," but, he added, "if they conduct the attack with the sort of imbecile neglect which allowed the Turks to get possession of Plevna—with the hesitation, want of decision, careless-ness, and disorder which marked Krudener's attack, then I should say the Russians are sure to be beaten."

Everything considered, he added, "I must say I think the result not doubtful. The Russian generals will display at least a minimum of mil-itary skill, and they will inflict a crushing defeat upon the Turks."

Before the coming September storm, that which would become known as "The Great Assault," MacGahan had an opportunity to see in action once again one of the few Russian generals in which he had total confidence, the one general, indeed, who may have been the source of much of MacGahan's enviably intimate knowledge of the Russian high command.

In his bruising August 19 dispatch, MacGahan wrote:

> General Skobelev, who is the most brilliant of the younger
> men, and who gives more promise for the future than any I
> have yet seen, is still too young for the command of more
> than a division, unless he should have some extraordinary
> chance of distinguishing himself, and the headquarters
> staff should meet with another reverse which would neces-
> sitate their taking the best man they can find without re-
> gard to age or rank.

Such an opportunity soon arose, at Lovtcha, a village of key strategic importance to the south of Plevna.

3
"It will be a miracle"

MacGahan's excoriating attack on the conduct of Plevna II, relayed to London by mail rather than by Bucharest telegraph office, was probably read to Czar Alexander II and his advisers, and it is a tribute to the czar's forebearance that the American was not escorted out of the Russian camp under armed guard. There were censorship problems early in the war, which both Forbes and MacGahan described at length in the *Daily News*, but these seemed to clear up quickly after the czar arrived at the front from St. Petersburg.

Colonel F. A. Wellesley, the British military attaché in the Russian capital, told of Alexander's attitude toward the press, using as his example the siege of Plevna. The czar gathered about him every evening his top military advisers and had the European press reports read aloud. Many of them, Wellesley recalled, were embarrassing in what they said about the conduct of the campaign against the Turks and about Russia's motives in the war in general. But no matter how infuriated his advisers became, the czar took the news with aplomb, even bowing to the military attaché of the country whose newspapers were being read.

The correspondents could get away with their stock-in-trade—opinion—but the Russians could be quixotic when it came to matters they interpreted as aiding the enemy. Frederick Boyle, correspondent for the London *Standard*, was actually expelled from the Russian camp for publishing information on troop movements considered "sensitive." Archibald Forbes thought the incident amusing, knowing Boyle wrote the questioned dispatch in "letter" form, not for the telegraph, and that by the time it appeared in the *Standard* it was hopelessly stale.

MacGahan's popularity in the Russian camp was not diminished by his flaying of their generals. He remained "that American who crossed the Kyzil Kum," the *molodyetz* who won the confidence even of Konstantin Kaufmann, who witnessed the fall of Khiva and the subjugation of the Turkoman tribes. Here was a handsome, outgoing, hardworking young man who could clasp the Grand Duke Nicholas in an American handshake, chat with Prince Shakofskoi, Baron Krudener, and generals Skobelev and Gourko. Small wonder he was looked upon with awe by the Russian peasant soldier standing with him in the soup line, as well as by the Russian officers who vied for his company. He spoke Russian, and it was known he had married a Russian woman from an influential family close to the royal court; he was a Russophile and a Turkophobe, his dispatches made this clear no matter how critical they were of the conduct of the battle at hand. And MacGahan, who was not so ingenuous as to suppose the Russian motives in the war were those solely of a Christian crusade, felt passionately that in Russia lay the only hope for the Bulgarian to have a measure of freedom and protection of livelihood, family, and life.

In the press camp near Plevna, the expelled *Standard* correspondent Frederick Boyle reported that "dawn was heralded by MacGahan's cheerful song, which scarcely ceased throughout the day and chases us to our beds at night." The American's apparently endless string of popular songs was also remembered by Forbes, Villiers of the *Graphic*, and Frank Millet of the New York *Herald*. Boyle continued:

> Solomon's ditties were a thousand and five, but no man hath numbered MacGahan's. . . . Nothing quenches the harmonious flow of our comrade. He lies, when discovered by daylight, rolled in his greatcoat and rugs singing; he rises presently, and, midst a philosophical discourse with D.,* he sings: each gulp of tea is alternated with a stanza, and he rolls his early cigarette with a chorus. Skobeleff declares with comic rage that MacGahan has learned nothing since they rode together through the Khivan desert except some new song hits more abominably stupid than his old assortment.

Behind the lines, MacGahan had, in addition to a sense of humor, and a good, or at least memorable, singing voice, a quality of panache that his comrades remembered. Forbes, for example, said:

> On one occasion, before Plevna, MacGahan's imperturbable coolness stood him in good stead in the matter of "proviand." He, his comrade Millet, and Prince Shakofskoi, were eating together under the shade of a tree within range of the Turkish fire. There was about food enough for one, and all were hungry. A shell burst among the branches of the tree, and Millet and Shakofskoi left off eating. Then came a

---

*Boyle's recollections contain references to several persons identified by initial only. "D." probably denotes H. Dobson, correspondent of the *Times* of London.

splattering of bullets that brought the leaves down about their ears. Millet and Shakofskoi hurriedly jumped up and sought a safer place. MacGahan sat still and serenely finished his victuals.

While the Russians made plans for their renewed assault on Plevna, Skobelev was ordered to make an extensive reconnaissance of Lovtcha, the town twenty miles directly south of Plevna, believed to be strongly garrisoned, and known to be strategically important for its proximity to Plevna and for its position on the road leading to Gabrovo and Shipka Pass.

MacGahan accompanied the expedition when Skobelev departed the grand duke's headquarters at Tirnovo on August 3 with five battalions of infantry, his own brigade of cavalry, and two batteries of horse artillery. Arriving on the heights a mile from Lovtcha on the 6th, Skobelev's force immediately opened fire with sixteen pieces of artillery, the infantrymen pushing forward so rapidly that MacGahan believed the young general might attack, contravening his orders merely to reconnoiter the area. On the heights, however, the Russians sighted fifteen to twenty thousand Turkish troops camped in and about the town and the strong interlaced trenches crisscrossing the low hills that surrounded it.

Skobelev resolved to "feel" the enemy with his artillery, MacGahan reported, and ordered a cannonade toward the trenches which was answered with a "lively fire" from the other side. "Several shells fell near the Russian guns," MacGahan wrote, "but as the ground was very soft—we were planted in a vineyard—they rarely exploded, and when they did explode they only threw up the earth a little, doing no harm."

Skobelev pushed forward with his infantry through a thickly wooded area in front of a hillock sewn with Turkish entrenchments from which poured a fierce hail of bullets. To MacGahan's amazement, the Russians appeared to be headed up the hill, seeking cover behind the bushes and hollows of the lower extremity of it, while the Turkish musketry grew in intensity until it seemed a continuous, deafening roll rather than the intermittent whip-snapping sound of the isolated sharpshooter finding a target.

MacGahan wrote:

It was evident from this fire that the Turks were three times as numerous as the Russians. An assault under such circumstances would be madness, and I was beginning to

wonder if Skobelev could really be madman enough to attempt it. Suddenly I saw a small party of horsemen dashing
down the road within full view of the Turks, and within
easy range of their fire, and perceived in a moment Skobelev. He was mounted on a white horse, and wore a white
coat, offering a splendid target for sharpshooters. As I afterwards learned, he, like myself, began to perceive that the
attack was growing far too serious, in spite of his orders,
and was now going forward to stop it.

In the withering fire, Skobelev's white Arabian was struck by a bullet and the general's escort of six Cossacks quickly reduced to
three—two wounded, one killed. Mounting a sorrel, Skobelev reached
the foot of the hill shouting and gesticulating while his trumpeter
sounded retreat. The skirmishers withdrew slowly, and MacGahan
again saw the general and his horse go down:

It is impossible for him to go on this way long without getting killed. He is fairly under the Turkish entrenchments,
and within easy range of the Turkish fire, which is growing
stronger and stronger. They are evidently getting reinforcements from the other side, where they are only threatened with cavalry. The roar is continuous, and rolls up and
down the hollow like one continuous crash of thunder, only
broken by heavier booming of artillery. The bullets must be
falling about there like hail. It will be a miracle if Skobelev
comes out of it alive.

MacGahan's theatrical present-tense dispatch then described Skobelev, astride a fresh horse, emerging from the smoke and dust like a
wraith coming down the road at a trot. He had not been scratched. The
reconnaissance had ended and the troops retired. The Russians had
lost five killed and twenty wounded—"rather heavy for a mere reconnaissance," MacGahan observed, but noted further, "Had the troops
not been stopped in time, they would simply have been annihilated, as
several battalions and regiments were at Plevna."

Skobelev retired about two miles from Lovtcha, camped, and made
his report. "I do not know what was its nature," MacGahan wrote,
"but it is very evident no attack can be made on Lovtcha until the Russians are ready for an attack on Plevna likewise; and no attack can be
made on Plevna until the arrival of more troops from Russia."

Upon returning to their camp, MacGahan found the Kirghiz orderly
Skobelev had brought with him from Turkestan sitting on the ground
crying over the general's white Khokandian stallion. The orderly,

himself slightly wounded, had had to kill the animal, and while not paying the slightest attention to his wound, cried spasmodically over the dead horse, which he had skinned.

In completing his dispatch on the day's events, MacGahan wrote: "This reconnaissance has been the most thorough and best conducted in the war. Had there been such a one pushed against Plevna before the battle the result would undoubtedly have been different." He added that Skobelev had now been assigned to protecting the Russian left flank from any surprise on the Lovtcha side during the forthcoming assault.

4
"Into the Valley of Death"

The scandal-mongering Irish-American editor and literary dabbler Frank Harris claimed to have made his way to Bulgaria at about the time of the respite after the July 30 assault on Plevna, specifically to meet Skobelev. Harris wrote in his pornographic autobiography, *My Life and Loves*, a half-century afterward, of his determination to meet "the conqueror of Turkestan." He first wrote to the young general in both English and French, brashly asking for an interview "to allow me to see him at work and to chronicle his doings against the Turks for some American journals." Then, after receiving no response, Harris says he proceeded to Moscow in the spring of 1877, only to learn that Skobelev was "at the front." Harris claims then to have proceeded on to the Danube, locating the general at Plevna.

It is conceivable, at least, that Harris actually met the young Russian general, whether at Plevna or later. The journalist said he was attracted to Skobelev's "contempt of convention," adding, "there was something ingenuous, young in him, which made him accept my enthusiastic admiration, my hero-worship, if you will, without afterthought."*

He described Skobelev as "above middle height, broad and strong" and gave this typically unfettered word portrait:

> The lower face was concealed by a thick wavy moustache, beard and whiskers all coquettishly brushed away from the center; the forehead was both broad and high, the nose

---

*Harris (1856–1931) was about twenty-one at the time of this alleged encounter. He claimed to be at Skobelev's heels during the siege of Plevna and would later say that Skobelev and Field Marshal Sir Frederick S. Roberts (earl of Kandahar, Pretoria, and Waterford) were the greatest generals he had ever met.

thick and of Jewish type, the eyes grey and keen; nothing
remarkable in the face; the impetuosity of his character
showed itself in quick abrupt movements; he always appeared ready to strike; yet underneath there was much
kindness in him and a fund of good humor.

Skobelev fortunately did not live to read this caricature.

Toward the end of August, MacGahan returned to the vicinity of
Shipka Pass to report that "the fight is still raging here with unabated
fury. The arrival of Radetsky with reinforcements saved the situation
for the moment and drove back the Turks, who were on the point of
seizing the Pass; but the Russian position is still most critical."

An unexpected development in the Russian plans for a renewed assault on Plevna took place on August 31 when Osman Pasha, until
now the defender, decided to conduct a raid against the Russian lines
at Pelisat, southeast of Plevna beyond the Radischevo Ridge, moving
out of Plevna at daybreak in the van of twenty thousand troops. Mac-
Gahan, a lucky eyewitness of the battle, described it at length from the
village of Poradim, just east of Osman's position. He said that the attack came so unexpectedly that, because of their certainty that the
Russian offensive against Plevna was still some days distant, most of
the correspondents had departed the vicinity and that he was about to
do the same.

"I had saddled my horse to follow their example," he wrote, "when,
about eight o'clock my ear caught a dull, scarcely audible thumping
that sounded more like a horse stamping at flies than the booming of
artillery. Artillery it proved to be nevertheless, for in a few minutes it
grew louder and clearer; and looking toward the line of low hills in the
direction of Plevna, some four miles distant, we saw several columns
of white smoke rising behind them."

Riding toward the cannon thunder, MacGahan in the level plain between Pelisat and Poradim, met throngs of Bulgarian refugees and
passed their carts, wagons, and small herds of livestock. Soon he came
upon the ambulance wagons, already bringing back the Russian
wounded, and saw clouds of smoke rising in white balls that rolled up
the slopes of the vineyard-covered hills. The ceaseless rattle of small-
arms fire and the roar of the big guns proved that the action was no
small skirmish.

From the vantage point of a high hill, joining a small knot of Russian
cavalrymen, MacGahan saw drawn across the horizon a black streak
like an inked line. It was the Turkish advance formation moving down
the slope of a hill in front of Pelisat. He wrote later that day:

My own position, with a handful of cavalry behind the hill, now became rather disagreeable. . . . In less than five minutes the Turks began to descend the hill in our direction, not with a rush, but leisurely, and without firing, neither in masses nor lines, but scattered and diffused. They came down about half way in this manner, the Russian artillery tearing up the groups among them all the time in the most savage manner.

He noted the change in the Russian cannonade, rolling now along the hillcrest in his direction, the Turks descending the hill dropping in large clots on the grassy slopes. Those who reached the bottom disappeared from view for a moment, while the Russian trenches facing the Turks erupted in flame and smoke, a storm of ball and shell that lasted almost twenty minutes. The Turks withdrew, reformed, and in the correspondent's words, "dived down into the Valley of Death to struggle there amid smoke and fire, a death struggle of giants; for there is nothing to choose between Russian and Turk on the score of bravery."

The Turks were again repulsed, the little slopes in front of the Russian trenches covered with dead and dying. Incredibly, they reformed and charged again—and again—at the Russian strong-point, repeatedly turned back with heavy losses.

Finally they withdrew, sullenly firing and carrying off their dead and wounded, still tracked by a murderous Russian fire and by six companies of infantry in full bayonet pursuit.

Osman Pasha and his chief lieutenant, Tewfik Bey, both in the thick of the battle, got their stragglers back behind the Plevna fortifications before nightfall, but could not rest. Lovtcha was again under heavy Russian attack.

In company with several other foreign officers, Lieutenant Francis V. Greene had departed Russian headquarters at Gorni Studen on the evening of August 31 to ride toward Plevna, where the great battle was reported in progress. Greene left a vivid account of his first meeting with MacGahan:

About midnight we had stopped at the bank of a little stream and lain down for a few hours' sleep. At daylight, just as we were waking up, a rough, shaggy pony, carrying a man wrapped in a large ulster and wearing the correspondent's badge on his arm, came ambling along the road and stopped to speak to us. It was MacGahan who had passed the previous day watching the battle in which Osman attacked the Russians on the east of Plevna. He had written his dispatches during the early part of the night, taken a few hours' sleep, and started off at two o'clock in the morning to carry the dispatches forty-five miles to the Danube, where he had a courier awaiting to carry them to Bucharest.

Riding over the battlefield the next day, MacGahan wrote of the Russian sanitary corps assembling the dead for burial, the corpses lying in neat rows, Russian and Turk side by side.

The purpose of Osman's sortie was never clear. It had been too strong for reconnaissance yet too weak for serious attack. Greene wrote that "whatever its object, it accomplished nothing beyond the loss of 1,000 Russians and 3,000 Turks. The Russians continued undisturbed their preparations for their assault on Plevna, first to gain possession of Lovtcha, then to close in around the town with 100,000 men and attack it on the north, east and south."

Lovtcha, twenty miles south of Plevna, was considered to be the extended left flank of the Russian forces before Plevna and therefore a place of extreme strategic importance. Command of the force sent to Lovtcha on September 1 was entrusted to Major General Prince Imeretinsky, with Skobelev commanding the advance detachment of infantry, Cossacks, and artillerymen.

At 2 P.M. on the 1st, this force drove the Turks from the ridge east of the town. The next morning, Skobelev opened fire with the eight guns he had with him, compelling the Turks to further evacuate the ridge on the south. The result of Skobelev's work was to enable General Imeretinsky, arriving with the main Russian force on the evening of September 2, to have possession of the dominating ridge east of the town, and to have his epaulements (breastworks to protect the gun crews from enemy small-arms fire) ready for his fifty-six heavy guns.

An eight-hour cannonade on September 3 was followed by a frontal assault by a large force commanded by Skobelev, with the result that the Turkish line of defense crumbled and fell by three o'clock that afternoon. The Turks evacuated their trenches as the Russians advanced until nothing remained but a huge redoubt, a last bastion before the town proper. Skobelev's detachment surrounded it on three sides and carried it after a nightmarish hand-to-hand combat in which its defenders were killed to a man, the bodies of the dead gorging the redoubt in a mass six feet deep.

Russian losses were 1,477 men and 39 officers; the Turks suffering terribly: upwards of 5,200 casualties, including 3,000 who fled after the fall of Lovtcha and were cut down by Cossacks on the road toward Mikren, to the southwest.

In his "Order of the Day" before the September 3 assault, Skobelev had written: "I direct the soldiers to the fact that in a bold attack the losses are minimized and that a retreat, especially a disorderly retreat, results in considerable losses and disgrace." In his gospel of the offensive, Skobelev never wavered; in battle he was the most sanguine and self-disciplined of men, ready for death, fatefully certain it would come before the war would end.

And neither would he overlook a breach of discipline, even in a friend and a civilian friend at that. This is attested to by Skobelev's biographer, V. I. Nemirovitch-Dantchenko. "In questions bearing on the army or action he would admit of no excuse and showed no mercy. MacGahan, with whom he was on very good terms, once offered a suggestion during action. 'Silence! Leave me at once!' Skobelev shouted."

Skobelev's commander at Lovtcha, Prince Imeretinsky, wrote graciously in his official report that "the reputation which this brilliant General has acquired by his military talents and bravery is known by the whole army, and it is sufficient for me to say that it is principally to him that I owe the success that has been obtained at Lovtcha." Even the czar read this gallant encomium, and in a dinner party at imperial headquarters the emperor hailed Skobelev as the "Hero of Lovtcha."

Archibald Forbes had the honor of informing Skobelev the Elder of the exploits of his son, and Forbes never forgot the moment, recalling the old general tearfully climbing down from his saddle to embrace the bearer of the news.

Now, a day after the capture of Lovtcha, Prince Charles of Rumania was named to command the Great Assault.

The attack would take place on September 11, the czar's name day.

XIV
The Great Assault

1
"A steady wave of flame"

That fall of 1877, Plevna was thrust for the first and only time into international prominence. The newspapers of the world, through the work of the correspondents in the war zone, brought the obscure north Bulgarian town into the public's consciousness.

Now, in the early days of September, massing on the east of the town was a Russian army of ninety thousand men and 364 cannon. Toward the front of Plevna and to the north, center, and south, the Turks had stationed about 56,000 men with perhaps 80 pieces of artillery, another 2,500 cavalrymen, and 1,500 bashi-bazouk irregulars.

Osman Pasha had not followed a systematic plan of erecting fortifications around the town. He nonetheless had worked diligently, confining his efforts to the hills nearest Plevna on the north and east, where the Russians threatened him with their greatest numbers. By September 1, these defensive works consisted of eighteen redoubts and complex trench systems northwest, east, and southwest of the town.

It was generally agreed that the keys to the Turkish positions were those of the Grivitza defenses on the north, the Krishin on the south.

The Russian troops were issued three days' rations of two pounds of cooked meat and four pounds of biscuit. Leaving their knapsacks and

shelter tents in bivouac, they moved into position, some carrying fas-
cines (long bundles of sticks used in building earthworks and gun batteries) and gabions (wicker baskets filled with earth and rock for shor-
ing up defenses), others carrying hewn logs for siege gun platforms.
All batteries were in place by midnight of the 6th.

At six o'clock on the morning of September 7, the first shot of an
eight-gun Russian battery opened a four-day bombardment of the
Turkish trench network. Almost without abatement the deafening
roar and concussion of the Russian pieces continued, sending an estimated sixty thousand shells singing and hissing into the Plevna
stronghold. Only a violent thunderstorm on the afternoon of the 10th
brought a brief respite from the ear-splitting noise, the acrid stench,
and black-powder filth of the guns, and that lull came only after the
rain turned the ground into a pasty mud, making it impossible for ammunition to be brought forward from the artillery parks.

Archibald Forbes now took his position on Radischevo Ridge to observe the attack on the eastern center of Plevna, and MacGahan had
moved on the 7th toward Prince Imeretinsky's and Skobelev's force on
the south of Plevna. There, in a vineyard, MacGahan jotted in his
notebook:

> We threw ourselves down under the shade of the trees to
> lunch with the aid of some delicious grapes just ripe, and
> watched the battle from this point. . . . the view from
> here is exceedingly fine. Down in what seemed a narrow
> valley or gorge, we could perceive the town of Plevna, with
> its masses of green foliage, and from which rose the slender
> spires of two or three minarets. On the mountain behind
> Plevna, some distance above the town, we could distinguish
> two redoubts on the other side of the Lovtcha Road, from
> which rose two columns of smoke.

What MacGahan was about to witness was the initial probe of the
Krishin defensive works by Skobelev. Imeretinsky had taken a position about two miles to the south of the Krishin position, and an advance guard under Skobelev moved toward the redoubt. On the afternoon of the 8th, Skobelev, following a rain of shells from his batteries,
moved forth with a force of infantry and drove the Turks out of the
wooded area on two knolls in front of him, a very warm skirmish that
lasted until 5 P.M. Skobelev was now only about fifteen hundred yards
south of Plevna, quickly coming under a withering fusillade from Krishin that drove him back.

MacGahan wrote:

> The sun is hot, and a veil of smoke hangs over hill, valley,
> and mountain, which often makes it difficult to distinguish
> with certainty anything but a sudden flash of fire and a
> huge ball of white smoke that rises from each discharge of
> the line described by the Russian and Rumanian positions
> around Plevna. Columns of white smoke were rising to the
> sky, and the sharp whiplike cracks of these field pieces were
> mingling angrily with the dull heavy roar of the siege guns
> in the big battery above.

MacGahan had climbed a tree to get a better view when a Cossack
rode up with the news that "there was something more interesting on
our left, that the Russians were advancing there, with 'hurrahs.' "
What the correspondent saw turned out to be Skobelev's and Imeretinsky's troops moving loosely, cavalry ahead, toward the Krishin redoubt. He watched twenty minutes:

> Then from the whole side of the mountain began to be
> heard the rattle of small-arms, which grew heavier and
> heavier, and the mountain and trees were soon covered
> with clouds of thin blue smoke.
>   The Russians pushed down steadily nevertheless in loose
> order, firing as they came; but as they neared the foot of the
> slope the Turkish fire became terrible. From the parapets of
> the redoubts poured forth a steady wave of flame, and the
> redoubt itself was soon hidden in the thick fog of smoke
> that rose over it. The roar of this tremendous fire was
> simply fearful. . . .
>   At the time the Russians were advancing down the hill,
> the whole valley was filled with smoke. The town of Plevna,
> as well as the Turkish redoubts, and even part of the wood
> where the Russians were, had become invisible. The sun
> was now just setting behind a mass of clouds, but it was
> seen for a few minutes like a fiery bloodshot eye, which
> tinged the smoke hanging over everything with the color of
> blood. Then it suddenly disappeared behind the mountain,
> and darkness settled over the scene.

Skobelev lost nine hundred men in the attack of September 8. At
5 P.M. on the 9th he was counterattacked, the Turks again driving him
back, and coming within sixty yards of his line before they retired
under a hail of Russian bullets.

Prince Imeretinsky had the general command of all troops on the Russian left flank at this juncture, and Skobelev, although of the same rank—major general—was junior by date of rank. A curious event of the night of September 9–10, however, changed this picture. General Zotov, chief of staff in the Russian headquarters before Plevna, sent a message to Imeretinsky, dividing his troops into two independent commands. Skobelev, the message said, would attack "according to instructions already given him," and Imeretinsky would support Skobelev in any attack. The orders effectively gave Skobelev the entire control over left flank operations and virtually relieved Imeretinsky of his command.

Meanwhile, MacGahan completed his day's work:

> The greater part of this telegram was written here in the fields by the light of a spluttering candle blown about by the wind. All around us we see the flickering of lights and camp fires in the distance, and every now and then flashes of fire in the direction of the battery of Russian siege guns or the Turkish redoubts at Grivitza, followed by a dull booming like thunder, showing that here neither Turk nor Russian is asleep.

2
"To simple slaughter"

The day of the Great Assault dawned in lowering skies and amidst sheets of rain sweeping down the valley in front of the targeted town and the Russian army massed to its east; lightning flashes illuminated the vast amphitheater of the valley with a weird glare, trees were swept about in demoniacal fury, and in all this, the sporadic firing of cannon and crackling of musketry continued. Soldiers around their soggy encampments stirred embers of fires of burning tree roots, warming numbed limbs and drying their heavy greatcoats. Prudence might have indicated a delay of the attack, but it was the czar's name day, a good omen not to be missed. Sappers had been working for days to erect a platform on a slope out of the line of fire behind Radischevo Ridge from which the czar and his Imperial Highness the Grand Duke Nicholas and their staffs, fifty men in all, could watch the battle. One half of the platform was in the open with a rail around it, the other half covered with an enormous marquee under which a large table was laid with white damask and spread with the choicest food and wine. Even on the morning of the battle, the commissariat brought in cold mut-

Gen. Skobelev, MacGahan's friend and confidante.
(Nemirovitch-Dantchenko, *Personal Reminiscences*)

Skobelev in retreat.
(Forbes, Henty, *Battles of the Nineteenth Century*, I)

Russian repulse during the Great Assault.
(*Graphic War Number*, Sept. 29, 1877)

Rumanian troops in the Great Assault, capturing the Grivitza Redoubt. (*Graphic War Number*, Sept. 29, 1877)

The Turks in the last sortie from Plevna. (Forbes, Henty, *Battles of the Nineteenth Century*, I)

Osman Pasha at Plevna. (Forbes, Henty, *Battles of the Nineteenth Century*, I)

ton, eggs, and a great brass samovar five feet high and holding sixty gallons of tea for the grand duke's staff officers.

The attack was scheduled to commence in the afternoon at three after a sporadic cannonade that began at eight that morning. The fog began to rise at about noon; the rain abated, and the sun emerged almost on cue to permit the battle to begin. At three, on schedule, the main offensive against the Grivitza redoubt commenced with four columns moving forward in a terrible rain of fire that was sustained until 7:30 that evening. The result was a repulse for the Russians, the losses amounting to over 1,300 out of the 25,000 men in action.

At daylight on the 10th, Skobelev's force rushed forward to seize a knoll on the southeast of Krishin, then dug in with their copper soup dishes, bayonets, and naked hands (entrenching spades were in short supply everywhere) while their commander brought his thirty-two artillery pieces forward. The position secure for the night, Skobelev conferred with his chief of staff, Captain Alexei Kuropatkin,* on the operations facing them next day.

At ten o'clock the next morning, Skobelev's force, aided by Prince Imeretinsky's, again took the offensive, moved out of their hasty entrenchments, and pushed forward to yet another knoll, driving the wedge deeper toward Plevna. By early afternoon, the Russians were advancing through Turkish trenches in ferocious hand-to-hand combat—a madhouse of stabbing bayonets, hacking yataghans, and clubbing rifle butts; growls and shrieks and hoarse curses; gouts of blood spattering frantic, grimy faces, greatcoats, and trousers; the stink of gunpowder exploded in close quarters; and the nauseating coppery-sharp odor of fresh blood.

By 4:30, Skobelev had lost three thousand men, one-quarter of his force, but aided by Imeretinsky, he now occupied a line of trenches and small redoubts just southwest of Plevna with the enemy dug in six hundred yards in front of him. His men exhausted and ammunition running short, the indefatigable young Russian commander paced through his lines, supervising Cossacks bringing crates of bullets up from the rear, setting his men to work digging trenches, bringing his nine-pounders forward. Then he sent word by courier to the rear that his position was not tenable without reinforcements, but that he would hold on as long as he could.

MacGahan, positioned on a high point near the Lovtcha road be-

---

*The same Kuropatkin who commanded the Russian armies in Manchuria in 1904 in the Russo-Japanese War.

tween Radischevo and Brestovitz, found himself with a splendid view, despite the remnants of fog and cannon smoke, of the attack on the redoubts between Plevna and Radischevo Ridge. The opening of his long and memorable dispatch on the action before him is interesting in its conceit—a common one among the Correspondents (with a capital C in their dispatches)—that only they were actually privileged to "see a battle." Rarely, if ever, has a war correspondent seen a battle in the way MacGahan described—that is, more than "an occasional scene or episode." Even William Howard Russell, positioned with Lord Raglan on the heights above Balaclava, looking down on the North Valley as if in a theater box, could not see all of the battle before him. That he saw the charges of the Heavy and Light Brigades and described them magnificently is undeniable. But did he see more than "scenes" and "episodes"? He could not, no more than could Lord Cardigan who led the Light Brigade to immortal disaster, or the Russian gunners at the east end of the Valley of Death, or Lord Raglan himself through his glass on the ridge above. Any sizable battle is simply beyond the senses of single human beings, perhaps least of all war correspondents. They, in fact, actively seek the "scenes" and "episodes" that will satisfy their readers' appetites for varnished, colorful war reportage, and not the grand strategy and tactics which would bore average readers but which historians must ponder after the battle is over.

MacGahan began his dispatch:

> It has been said that nobody ever saw a battle. The soldier is too much excited with the passions of the fight as well as enveloped in smoke to see far around him. The general is too far away from the actual conflict, too much busied with the news arriving from different parts of the field, and with giving orders, to see the battle, although he knows it better than anyone. It is only the Correspondent who is daring enough to take and hold a good position who really sees a battle.

What MacGahan saw, looking toward the crest of Radischevo Ridge, were the Russian guns at work, figures flitting around them dimly seen through the smoke and strangely magnified by the fog "until the gunners appeared like giants, the guns themselves, enlarged and distorted by the same medium, appeared like huge uncouth monsters, from whose throats at every instant leaped forth globes of flame."

In front of a redoubt down the valley toward Plevna he saw "a mass of Russian soldiers rise up in a field of Indian corn, and push forward with a shout. The Turkish fire just then seemed to have been dominated, nearly silenced, by the terrible storm of shot and shell poured in by the Russians."

But, from the parapet of the Turkish defenses, no sooner had the shout of the charging Russians died away, than MacGahan saw "a stream of fire that swayed backwards and forwards, while the smoke rose over the redoubt in one heavy white mass. One continuous crash filled the air with bullets . . . it did not seem possible for even a rabbit to escape."

Then, in a particularly memorable passage, he wrote,

> Into this storm of bullets plunged the Russians, with a shout as though of joy, and then disappeared into a little hollow, and for the moment were lost to view. Then they emerged again, disappeared in the low ground at the foot of the glacis [the area around a redoubt, usually of loose earth and rock, that slopes downward, requiring that it be scaled to reach the redoubt walls] rushing onward as though the bullets were but paper pellets; but, alas! sadly diminished in number. Would it be possible for them to reach the parapet? Was it possible for flesh and blood to break that circle of fire? To me it seemed utterly out of the question. Did but one bullet in ten find its billet, not one of these gallant fellows would return through the cornfield. While waiting to see them emerge from this little hollow, my excitement was so great, my hand trembled so, that I could not hold the fieldglass to my eyes, and for the moment was obliged to trust my naked vision. They were evidently very near the redoubt. A rush might do it. Victory was almost within their grasp.

But the desperately needed reinforcements were not forthcoming. MacGahan concluded then:

> My heart sunk within me, for I saw that all this bravery, all this loss of life would be useless. . . . not a man was sent to help them. They were left to die overwhelmed, broken, vanquished. It was sublime, and it was pitiful. I see a few of them struggle up the glacis one by one. They drop. They are not followed, and here they come again, a confused mass of human beings rushing madly back across that cornfield, less than half of those who went forward. . . . I could have cried for pity, for I knew that most of them went uselessly to simple slaughter.

September 11 was truly a day of surpassing horror; a day of bullets flying in torrents and clouds, as if by the tens of thousands they were launched at once by a monster catapult. It was a day of grenades exploding into splinters of sharp, burning edges which ripped and tore the flesh; of shrapnel shells bursting in the air with the sound of a snapping of some gigantic cord by invisible hands. Blood that day virtually flowed in streams, the boots of Turk and Russian steeped in it. On that day, entire hillsides were strewn with hideously maimed and limbless corpses; the glacis of redoubts were strewn with bodies and splashed with blood, and inside their walls the dead and dying were piled four and six deep. It was a day of struggles of the wounded and their cries of agony drowned by the incessant thunder of cannon and rifle fire like strings of popping firecrackers: a day of bullets, bayonets, and blood.

And by the night of this day of horror, on the slopes and hills in front of Plevna and in vineyards and cornfields, redoubts, earthworks, and trenches, fifteen thousand Russians and Rumanians lay dead, carrion for wolves and ravens, while with the sun's setting came the first bite of coming winter.

3
"It is the will of God"

Now, after forty hours of fog and intermittent rain, the 12th dawned with clarity, and at six the Turks opened fire with artillery on Skobelev's precariously held position in the Krishin area; the big guns quickly followed by the first rattle of small-arms fire of the day. Not long after this, a long line of Turkish infantry from the Krishin redoubt advanced to within three hundred yards of Skobelev's lightly entrenched force before being driven back. Another attack followed at 8:00, yet another at 10:30, and now, after thirty hours' incessant battle, Skobelev's men began to falter, his position becoming desperate. General Zotov had notified Skobelev by courier message that reinforcements were impossible and that he was to hold out to the last extremity, then retreat.

Osman, in the meantime, had begun to mass his troops at Krishin specifically to drive Skobelev out, twelve thousand men coming to the south of the Plevna for this purpose. Between 2:00 and 2:30, this force began its fourth assault on the Russians, approaching to within four hundred yards before Skobelev's orchestrated volley firing halted them, then drove them backward once again.

Skobelev received thirteen hundred men in reinforcements in the afternoon, but by then the Turks began their fifth assault, advancing in the face of a murderous sheet of fire from the Russian line. In minutes, worn and discouraged after thirty-six hours in the lines, it was now the Russians who fell back, retreating in small weary groups toward the rear.

MacGahan, seemingly everywhere at once, watched the retreat of Skobelev's men and, in a long and subsequently famous dispatch datelined "Left Wing, Lovtcha Road, September 12," gave a vivid account of the young general's role in the battle:

> Skobelev is the only general who places himself near enough to feel the pulse of a battle. The advancing column was indistinctly seen, a dark mass in the fog and smoke. Feeling as it were, every throb of the battle, he saw this line begin to waver and hesitate. Upon the instant he hurled forward a rival regiment to support, and again watched the result. This new force carried the mass farther on with its momentum, but the Turkish redoubt flamed and smoked, and poured forth such a torrent of bullets that the line was again shaken. Skobelev stood in this shower of balls unhurt. All his escort were killed or wounded. . . . now only two battalions of sharpshooters left, the best in his detachment. Putting himself at the head of these, he dashed forward on horseback.

The next long paragraph of MacGahan's dispatch was widely quoted:

> He picked up the stragglers; he reached the wavering, fluctuating mass, and gave it the inspiration of his own courage and instruction. He picked the whole mass up and carried it forward with a rush and a cheer. The whole redoubt was a mass of flame and smoke, from which screams, shouts, and cries of agony and defiance arose, with the deep-mouthed bellowing of the cannon, and above all the steady, awful crash of that deadly rifle fire. Skobelev's sword was cut in two in the middle. Then, a moment later, when just on the point of leaping the ditch, horse and man rolled together on the ground, the horse dead or wounded, the rider untouched. Skobelev sprang to his feet with a shout, then with a formidable, savage yell the whole mass of men streamed over the ditch, over the scarp and counter-scarp,

over the parapet,* and swept into the redoubt like a hurri-
cane. Their bayonets made short work of the Turks still
remaining. Then a joyous cheer told that the redoubt was
captured, and that at last one of the defenses of Plevna was
in the hands of the Russians.

The victory, as has been seen, was short lived: "Skobelev had the
redoubt," MacGahan wrote, "the question now was how to hold it."
And the answer was that he could not. Massing his forces against Skobelev, Osman drove the Russians back. MacGahan wrote that "one
bastion was held till the last by a young officer, whose name I regret I
have forgotten, with a handful of men. They refused to fly, and were
slaughtered to the last man."

The officer whose name MacGahan forgot was a Major Gortalov,
and the manner of his death was so nightmarish that it is clear the
correspondent did not witness it. Those who did had it etched permanently on their brains.

Gortalov had remained behind after Skobelev's men had retired, and
was standing calmly on the rampart of the redoubt when a wave of
Turkish infantry closed around him. Gortalov lowered his sword to
them and stood with his arms folded on his breast as he was literally
lifted in the air on the Turks' bayonets. Not far off, some of Skobelev's
rearguard could see him writhing and struggling on the cold steel and
how, at last, he was thrown down as the Turkish force moved forward, his bloody corpse trampled beneath them.

After the retreat from Krishin and shortly after Gortalov's appalling death, MacGahan met Skobelev in the rear encampment and
wrote of him:

> He was in a fearful state of excitement and fury. His uni-
> form was covered with mud and filth; his sword broken; his
> Cross of St. George twisted round on his shoulder; his face
> black with powder and smoke; his eyes haggard and blood-
> shot, and his voice quite gone. He spoke in a hoarse
> whisper. I never before saw such a picture of battle as he
> presented. I saw him again in his tent at night. He was quite
> calm and collected. He said, "I have done my best; I could do
> no more. My detachment is half destroyed; my regiments
> do not exist; I have no officers left; they send me no rein-

---

*The scarp is the inner slope or wall of a ditch surrounding a redoubt; the counter-scarp
the outer wall. A parapet is the highest point of the wall of a defensive fortification.

forcements, and I have lost three guns." They were three of the four guns which he placed in the redoubt upon taking it, only one of which his retreating troops had been able to carry off. "Why did they refuse you reinforcements?" I asked. "Who was to blame?" "I blame nobody," he replied. "It is the will of God."

Skobelev had covered his retreat with twenty-four artillery pieces and had carried off his wounded, leaving the dead on the field. He had lost eight thousand men and 160 officers of the eighteen thousand men in his force, "a carnage rarely witnessed during even the wars of the French empire," as another correspondent wrote. Most of the correspondents, upon learning of Skobelev's heroic defense of the redoubt, placed the blame upon the higher Russian command for permitting the gains—won at such an extreme cost of life—to be thrown away. Five thousand of his men had been lost in the five Turkish onslaughts against him, and it was unimaginable that ground won so dearly would be lost for want of reinforcements.

Francis V. Greene, a severe critic of the Russian conduct of the siege of Plevna, provided a balanced picture of Skobelev's abilities. Greene said the young general held his men well in hand, sent a portion of them in reasonably open order, and at the critical moment, when the line began to waver but before the attack had failed, sent in his reserves and went in himself with the last of them. He held on to the last extremity according to his orders; he withdrew against overwhelming numbers and without reinforcements, under cover of artillery. Greene said Skobelev's "extremely reckless courage, while it compels that personal admiration which such qualities always command, is of course open to serious criticism when it is remembered that he was the commanding general on all that part of the line." Greene did say that "there is no doubt that without the aid which this display of daring gave to his men, the position would not have been carried or held as it was."

Skobelev's own viewpoint on what others considered to be "personal heroics" was summed up in a statement MacGahan quoted:

> "A soldier *may* be a coward, a subaltern may be excused for possessing the instinct for self-preservation; but the cowardice in a commanding officer, from a captain upwards, is indefensible. A coward general is in my opinion a contradiction in terms; and the fewer such contradictions in terms we tolerate the better. I don't expect everyone to be madly brave, that he should be roused to enthusiasm at the sound

of musketry. That is stupid. I only want everyone to do his duty in action."

MacGahan, Forbes, Villiers, and the other correspondents present left the battlefield around Plevna in the afternoon of September 13 to write their dispatches summing up the Great Assault. That it had failed disastrously was undeniable. Russian and Rumanian losses reached more than eighteen thousand of the sixty thousand infantry actually brought into action. Turkish losses were also heavy, probably as high as fifteen thousand.

In a period of three months, the Russians had crossed the Danube, taken the fortress at Nicopolis and secured Shipka Pass—all this, and above all the failures at Plevna, had cost fifty thousand men, a third of the original Army of the South, and the march to Constantinople remained virtually at its first step.

Now the czar ordered the assault abandoned. Plevna's investment and systematic siege operations were placed under the command of General Todleben, the town to be starved into submission.

During the week of the Great Assault, the *Daily News* brought out an "Extra War Edition" each evening, and detailed maps of Bulgaria and plans of Plevna were on sale in bookstalls and newsstands all over London. Returning war correspondents were in special demand as lecturers. To have been at Plevna was a passport to certain, if ephemeral, fame. The Canterbury Theatre of Varieties in London presented a scene depicting "The Gallant Defense of Plevna," and at Madame Tussaud's, the wax figure of Osman Pasha was added to the "Chamber of Historic Personages."

The six days of constant exposure in the rain and fog of the battle zone had worn Archibald Forbes down, and he finally left the battlefield with a raging "Danubian fever." After a time in a Bucharest hospital, he returned to England.

As for MacGahan, Forbes reported that his American comrade "was still limping, looking thin and tired, and wearing the sheepskin coat of a Bulgarian peasant."

4
"Their minds have rusted"

"I had become very much excited for the fate of M.G.," Barbara MacGahan wrote in her private memoir many years after those turbulent days on the Danube. She and Paul, staying in an apartment in a

private home in Bucharest during the battle of Plevna, waited apprehensively for MacGahan to make one of his brief, sporadic visits from
the front. She recalled:

> On September 22 he came safely to me, but had to leave
> again on the fourth. Never before did his attachment to me
> and Paul show itself so much as in these troublesome times.
> Not paying attention to his weariness, the bad roads, and
> the value of time to him, he came every two or three weeks
> for a few days. . . . His foot had been hurt when he
> crossed the Balkans during the night with the army . . .
> this adventure gave him intermittent fever. He came a sick
> man, stayed three weeks in bed, and worried that Plevna
> might fall before he could return.

The MacGahan apartment in Bucharest was known to all the correspondent's news colleagues as well as to his friends among the Russian officer corps. "They came often to see him and stayed for hours,"
Barbara said somewhat exasperatedly. She said her husband and Paul
played together for hours, MacGahan reading to his son from Victor
Hugo's *La Légende des siècles*, putting his sheepskin coat on inside out to
resemble a bear, dragging Paul around the rooms on a makeshift sled
made from a pillow or rug, building houses out of boxes, putting a
variety of clothes on the house cat, teaching Paul his ABCs.

During Christmas week of 1877, MacGahan spent one hundred
francs for a giant tree and decorations and for food for a party with
their landlady, her daughters, and a few Russian officers. Between
Christmas and the New Year, Barbara remembered wistfully, she and
her husband and son, together with some friends, took sleigh rides in
the evenings. "We talked nonsense, laughed like crazy, galloping
through the streets, and at the end, stopped at midnight at a confectionary shop to eat pastry while M.G. added to it a bottle of wine."

Then, as she sadly and suddenly noted in her journal, "M.G. left on
January 9, 1878, behind the army."

With Forbes now back in England, MacGahan occupied his time assessing and reassessing the Great Assault and the Russian "situation."
In one dispatch, for example, he concluded that "the Turks are better
soldiers individually than the Russians. Of that, after seeing not a few
battles, I stand assured." He continued:

> The strategy of both, perhaps, is equally bad; but as regards
> both major and minor tactics the Turks are simply immea-

surably superior. The Turks are better armed than the Russians, both in great and small arms. The Turks have engineers who can design admirable defensive positions. The Russian engineers seem incapable of repairing a hole in a bridge. The Turks seem as well provisioned as the Russians. The Turks are flushed with success. The Russians are depressed by failure after failure. . . . There is no braver man alive than the Russian soldier, but a brave soldier cannot continually face more than the fair chances of war.

From Bucharest on October 15, while resting and convalescing at the apartment with his wife and son, MacGahan wrote a leisurely essay-length dispatch, containing in addition to notes on the weather and a capsule summary of the deadlock below the Danube, a devastating glimpse of card-playing Russian generals. This article would be quoted again and again by historians of the war and of the Russian army.

"The rain has been pouring down for a week—steadily, persistently, obstinately, with scarcely a respite," he began his five thousand-word piece, moving then to his summary of the recent campaign: "For be it remembered that the only real conquests, the passage of the Danube and the capture of Nikopolis, were made with a loss of less than three thousand; and we have absolutely nothing to show in exchange for the rest of this immense loss of 47,000 men."

The blame (distributed with that species of hindsight that was as much a feature of the correspondents' profession as their armbands and notepads) for "one-third of the army lost and nothing to show for it but three defeats," MacGahan placed on General Ievitsky, assistant chief of the general staff of the Grand Duke Nicholas. He sarcastically referred to Ievitsky as "the Moltke of Russia" but failed to explain how this man would have to shoulder more blame than his immediate superior, General Nepokoitchitsky, chief of staff, or than the grand duke himself.

The correspondent wrote bitterly of "the madness of attacking trenches defended by breech-loaders by assault," saying "the Russian generals have at last learned it at an expense of 15,000 men." Then, in a remarkable display of newspaper generalship, MacGahan dilated on methods that might be employed in capturing Plevna. What he described were precisely the kind of "madness" methods of assault on trenches, earthworks, and redoubts he had flung in the face of the headquarters staff.

In my opinion there are, besides the plan of a siege and starvation, two ways of taking such a place as Plevna. The first is the plan of an assault, made with about three times as many men as the Russians had in the last affair, that is about 120,000, and handled in the manner of Skobelev by hurling them against the positions, brigade after brigade, until by mere force of momentum and bravery they sweep everything before them like the waves of a rapidly rising sea. The loss to be incurred in such a plan is fearful, but the loss of the enemy would be greater still.

The other plan, MacGahan admitted, would be slower, perhaps less sure, but would require a smaller force for its execution. This was to advance to Plevna by means of "flying saps"—narrow, shallow trenches rapidly dug under cover of night and, no doubt, under heavy rifle fire. The trouble with this plan, he said, was that in the Russian army there were only about five hundred shovels to a division, or about one for every twenty men, "and this in a war against the Turks, which the whole military history of the Russians might have been taught was destined from the first to become a war of sieges, a kind of war in which the shovel plays no less important role than the rifle!"

Turning now to the Russian generals, MacGahan's observations form one of the most devastating and often quoted indictments of an army's high command written in the nineteenth century:

In the first place, all those high in command are very old men. They are men who studied the military art forty and even fifty years ago, since which time the science of war has undergone most important changes and developments—a revolution, in short. In addition to this, they are men who, for the most part, never look in a book, and who rarely read a newspaper, and appear to be utterly oblivious of the march of progress and of science, especially in the military art. Their whole lives may be said to have been passed in one occupation; their whole minds, whatever they had, concentrated on one object, and that one of the most trivial to which the human mind can descend—card-playing. They have done nothing else, thought of nothing else, for years. Their minds have rusted until they are as dull, as heavy, and as incapable of receiving new impressions as the veriest clod-hopper. Called from their card-tables by the trumpet of war, they rise, rub their eyes, look round them completely bewildered, and are as thoroughly out of the current of modern war as if they had been asleep for forty years. Not even Rip van Winkle, with his rusty gun dropping to pieces after his long sleep, was more bewildered and lost than the majority of these poor old generals, suddenly thrown into the campaign at the heads of their brigades, divisions, and corps.

As to why the czar did not recognize these awful truths, the correspondent ventured to guess that the old dotards were not sent back to their card tables because of the czar's sensitivity to the tradition that no high officer or faithful public servant could be removed or "disgraced" except in the most egregious circumstances of betrayal or gross criminality. Thus, MacGahan said, "the Government assumed the responsibility for all their stupidity, perversity, and dishonesty."

In the spring of 1878, the *Daily News* brought out a three-volume collection of *The War Correspondence of the "Daily News": 1877.* The volumes stated on their title pages, "Including the Letters of Mr. Archibald Forbes, Mr. J.A. MacGahan and Many Other Special Correspondents in Europe and Asia." In reviewing the volumes in *Macmillan's Magazine* in March of that year, the British army officer William F. Butler remarked on MacGahan's memorable word portrait of the Rip van Winkles:

> Those who had the good fortune to accompany Mr. Mac-Gahan through his adventurous 'Campaigning on the Oxus and the Fall of Khiva,' will not need to be told that the courage and determination which carried him four years ago across the blinding desert of the Kizil Kum and made him a sharer in all the hardships and glories of the Khivan campaign, have again been conspicuously manifest in Bulgaria and Roumelia.* Nor will his power of description and keen insight into the errors of the Russian generals and the corruptions of commissariat officials be subject of surprise to those who know how long and varied has been his experience of men and things in the great Republic of the West, as well as the great Despotism of the East. Indeed his remarks upon Russian generals are so plain spoken, that one if forced to conclude that he must have enjoyed the protection of some one in command in the Russian army; otherwise it is difficult to account for so keen and trenchant a pen being allowed to continue unchecked its career of criticism.

---

*Roumelia was a geographic division of the Ottoman Empire in the Balkan Peninsula which included southern Bulgaria.

But MacGahan explained on November 20, while with Gourko's headquarters at Dolna Dubnik on the west of Plevna, that no such protection was necessary:

> The Daily News correspondents have probably been most severe of all in their criticisms on the arrangements of the campaign; those criticisms have been reproduced in the Russian papers, and yet the writers are welcome everywhere in the army, because, whether rightly or wrongly, the Russians believe the criticisms to be fair and honest. When I saw the Grand Duke he immediately gave me permission to go everywhere around the positions. He said in English, smiling, "Oh, it is all right; you can go where you please," and with a large sign of the cross made in the air at me, "God be with you."

Skobelev too, in the meantime, had left the front for Bucharest, there to pull himself together after the Great Assault and to restore his shattered nerves. His friend and future biographer, Nemirovitch-Dantchenko, wrote that the young general told him, after the failure of September 11–12:

> Until the third battle of Plevna, I was young; but I have come out of it an old man. Not, of course, physically nor intellectually. I feel as though years had elapsed between Lovtcha and our defeat. It is a nightmare which may lead me to commit suicide. The recollection of that slaughter-house is a sort of Nemesis, only more revengeful than the classical. I will tell you honestly, I sought death there. If I did not find it, it was no fault of mine.

In Bucharest, however, Skobelev could not rest. He took his books along, and those who saw him in the Brofft and the Hugo restaurant, found him drinking his wine with his friends—MacGahan among them—and receiving perfumed billets-doux from "the lionesses" of the Rumanian capital.

5
"When the guns ceased firing"

The investment and starvation of Plevna continued, and MacGahan wrote on November 4: "The belief here that Plevna cannot hold more than a few days longer is very strong. No supplies have reached the

place for more than a month, and it is invested by a circle of earthworks manned by troops that are growing stronger every day with the
arrival of troops from Russia."

On the 10th, Skobelev won a minor but morale-building victory in
taking the Brestovitz redoubt in the vineyards east of Krishin with
small losses, and on the 13th, the grand duke sent a letter to Osman
Pasha informing the Turkish commander that he was completely surrounded and begging him, in the name of humanity, to surrender.
Osman's dignified reply came the next day through the lines, delivered
under a flag of truce: "I recognize the motives of humanity which have
prompted the invitation addressed to me; but I do not consider that I
have yet exhausted all the means of resistance which my situation
commands me to employ."

On the 20th, from Gourko's headquarters at Dolna Dubnik, ath-
wart the road to Sofia, MacGahan wrote, "The siege of Plevna has
become a kind of monster picnic." He continued:

> Everywhere officers may be seen at the dinner hour seated
> at their tables dining in the open air in preference to their
> tents, so warm and soft are the days. All around the posi-
> tions, where the soldiers are cooking their dinners or lying
> lazily stretched on the ground, basking in the warm sun-
> shine, rise thin columns of light blue smoke, that hangs
> over the country in a fine luminous haze, turning these lazy
> afternoons into a glorious Indian summer. The low hills,
> covered with furze and brushwood, are brown with the lus-
> trous golden tint so beautiful in a woman's eye and hair.
> The fields of Indian corn, of a pale dull straw yellow, with
> the light spring green of the little valleys where the grass is
> springing up again, as it always does in Bulgaria in the
> autumn.

As 1877 trudged to a close, Todleben was named to command all the
Russian troops assembled at Plevna, with Prince Imeretinsky his chief
of staff. Skobelev was raised to a lieutenant generalcy and placed in
divisional command. Gourko's cavalry on the west of the city prevented convoys from revictualing the Turks or reinforcements in men
and matériel from entering the town. Of this latter situation, Mac-
Gahan noted, "Here General Gourko is watching Osman Ghazi with
the Guard, ready to fall upon him at the first indication of an attempt
to get out. On the 'Wooded Hill' overlooking Plevna stand Osman
Ghazi and Skobelev face to face with caution and respect, like two

athletes who have already tried to fall, and are waiting for breath and an opportunity to begin again."

In mid-November, several Turkish prisoners were sent into Plevna by the Russians with copies of the *Daily News* and London *Times*, which contained details of the total defeat of the Turkish armies in Armenia and the fall of Kars. This old fortified mountain town had been destroyed by Tamerlane in the fourteenth century and was now occupied for the third time in the nineteenth century by the Russians.* The papers also carried the news that Shipka Pass was blocked with snow and that no aid would be forthcoming from Turkish forces in the south. Osman sent a message through the lines thanking his enemy for the papers, saying they would help pass the long winter evenings! The Russians next erected huge placards and even one illuminated sign carrying messages in misspelled and ungrammatical Turkish to the effect that Kars had fallen, Plevna was surrounded, and that further resistance was futile.

MacGahan, who had a strong claim to Plevna as "his" story, saw it through to the end. He had been on the Danube at the beginning of the river passage and in Shipka Pass with Gourko, observed the Great Assault, and telegraphed thousands of words and mailed thousands more to his paper. His final chapter on Plevna, a dispatch of five thousand words, was telegraphed from Bucharest on the night of Monday, December 10, and was as vivid and complete an account of Osman's last stand and surrender as would be written.

The Russians knew as early as the 7th that the Turks planned a sortie, and every preparation was made to "receive" it: the trenches manned to full complement, all troops alerted, posts doubled and trebled, and ammunition and rations issued. Saturday and Sunday passed, and while nothing unusual seemed to be occurring within Plevna or its defenses, the sky darkened at noon on Sunday, snow began to fall steadily, and the wind came up suddenly, creating violently cold blasts along the lines. MacGahan made his way to Skobelev's headquarters near Lovtcha. A spy had just reported to Skobelev that Osman had issued three days' rations to his troops, 150 cartridges, a new pair of sandals for each man, and a small portion of gun oil. Other intelligence reported a great many mysterious lights moving inside the town, that Osman was abandoning the Krishin re-

---

*Another example of the *Daily News*'s unprecedented coverage of the war is the fact that it had the sole English correspondent, a Mr. V. Julius, present with the Russians at the fall of Kars that November.

doubts, and that his forces werè gathering near the Vid bridge on the northwest side of Plevna.

Skobelev moved to Krishin from his position behind the redoubts and took over the now abandoned area in which so much Russian and Turkish blood had been spilled. As the night wore on, the snow ceased and ominous clouds scudded across the sky, followed by a hissing downpour of sleety rain. The Russians in their trenches huddled in their greatcoats, blowing clouds of vapor.

Dawn came on almost reluctantly, muddy clouds hiding the sun and portending more snow, wind, and cold. At that first light there came a sudden boom of guns, thirty or forty in unison, and a rattle of rifle fire in the direction of the Vid river on the west. MacGahan awoke and rode off toward the river and the Sofia road, and in thirty minutes came in sight of "a terrible and sublime spectacle."

Osman had concentrated the greater part of his army across the Vid, passing across two bridges and taking three batteries of artillery, bullock carts, and several hundred carriages loaded with ammunition and provisions. He had moved his force and their guns and train across the river before daybreak. The Turks, using their wagons and draft animals as cover, were facing a terrible enfilading fire from the Berden breechloaders of the Sibrersky (Siberian) regiment; then, as their protecting cover of cattle was killed or frightened off, Osman's troops dashed forward with a blood-curdling yell upon the Russian sharpshooters.

MacGahan described the action:

> They swept over them like a tornado, poured into the battery, bayoneted the artillerymen, officers and men, who with desperate heroism, stood to their pieces to nearly a man, and seized the whole battery. The Sibrersky Regiment had been overthrown and nearly annihilated. The Turks had broken the first circle that held them in. Had they gone on they would have found two more; but they did not have time to go on.

The Russians rallied in an instant, and the first brigade of Russian grenadiers flung themselves on the Turks in a furious onslaught—one of the hand-to-hand episodes so appalling that few correspondents could find adequate language to describe it. This face-to-face, bayonet-to-bayonet fight lasted several minutes as the Turks clung to their captured guns with dogged determination. "They seemed to have forgotten in the fury of battle that they had come out to escape from

Plevna, and not to take and hold a battery," MacGahan observed. Nearly all the Turks in the battery were killed, those who fled joining others in flanking trenches, and retreating to the Vid banks under a hail of bullets.

Despite the violent repulse of the Turkish attack, the battle continued unrelentingly for four hours. MacGahan recorded: "We could hardly yet realize that it was to be the last fight we should ever see around Plevna, and that when the guns ceased firing it was the last time we should ever hear them here."

At about noon on December 10, the firing began to diminish noticeably, then it stopped still, the smoke lifted, and a weird silence fell over the battlefield—"a silence that will not be broken here for many a long year, perhaps never again, by the sounds of battle," the correspondent stated.

A half hour later, a white surrender flag was seen waving from the Turkish lines, and an officer came riding toward the Russians over the bridge with the flag in hand. Skobelev, MacGahan, and a group of officers and correspondents gathered near the Sofia road, mounted, and rode toward the bridge, arriving to within seventy-five yards of the Turkish lines before dismounting. Two more horsemen approached from the west carrying white banners. One had a brief conversation with Skobelev's interpreter, then turned and galloped back.

Osman Ghazi, it was whispered, was coming out.

As they waited, MacGahan looked around him at the grim relics of the last battle—a horse snorting blood and struggling to die; an ox "silently bleeding to death . . . his great, round, patient eyes looking mournfully at us"; another horse lying dead in his yoke as he had fallen; a wounded Turk under a wagon, and nearby, four others, lying, gazing up at the sky, not one uttering a sound. "They lay there and bore their suffering with a calm stolid fortitude which brought tears to my eyes," MacGahan wrote.

"There he is! He is coming!" shouted the Russians as MacGahan rode forward for a better view. He saw two horsemen approaching with a truce flag, the bearer of which appeared to be a common soldier in a dirty brown cloak. The other man wore a clean blue coat and bright red fez and had a youngish, round, rosy face with clear blue eyes that stared straight ahead. This was Tewfik Pasha, Osman's chief of staff, who informed Skobelev that his commander was wounded. MacGahan scribbled the conversation on his notepad:

"Not severely, we hope," Skobelev replied.

"I do not know," Tewfik answered, pausing between each word.

"Where is His Excellency?"

"There," said Tewfik, pointing toward a small house overlooking the road beyond the Vid bridge.

There followed some moments of silence on Tewfik's part; he remained impassive, examining Skobelev and his officers silently and at embarrassing length.

Skobelev blurted out, "Is there anybody you would like to see?"—(pause)—"With whom did you wish to speak?"—(pause)—"Is there anything? . . ."—(pause)—"What the devil is the matter with this man? Why don't you speak?" he stammered, glancing at MacGahan.

Finally, calmer, the young general said to Tewfik Pasha, "General Ganetsky is in command here. He will be here presently, in case you should like to speak to him." Tewfik nodded. An officer spoke up: "Osman Pasha has made a most brilliant and glorious defense. We esteem highly his soldierly character." Tewfik gazed ahead, giving no sign he had heard or understood. Another officer said, "We look upon him as a very great general." This elicited no response, and finally all conversational ploys were abandoned.

A general from the czar's staff arrived at last and determined that Tewfik apparently had no powers to negotiate the surrender and that Osman, lying wounded, wished to do so himself. Ganetsky, the general in command of the corps of grenadiers, arrived long minutes later, and finally the Russians began crossing the Vid bridge toward Osman's hut.

MacGahan, riding through the melancholy flotsam of wagons, dead horses and bullocks, overturned carts, and corpses, spied one young Turk lying wounded who had lain himself carefully down, his cloak about him, and put his rifle and knapsack under his head. "He evidently takes pride in his gun, for it is very bright and clean, and he has put it away carefully under him, so that it may not be taken away," MacGahan wrote. "He did not think to part with it so soon. He is scarcely seventeen, and the doctor who has dressed his wounds says he will not live till night."

Ganetsky and a small group of officers entered the house where Osman lay and in a conference that lasted only minutes reached the terms of capitulation. It was now about two o'clock. MacGahan wrote: "So Osman Ghazi, the Victorious, surrendered unconditionally the gallant army with which he had held this now famous stronghold for so long, with which he upset the whole Russian plan of campaign, and with which he defeated, in three pitched battles, Russia's finest armies."

Now, riding back toward Plevna, MacGahan observed the proprieties of war as Osman's carriage, escorted by fifty Cossacks, met that of the Grand Duke Nicholas, who had come out to meet the Plevna defender. The two commanders gazed at one another for some seconds, then the grand duke stretched out his hand and shook that of Osman heartily, saying: "I compliment you on your defense of Plevna. It is one of the most splendid military feats in history." The Turk smiled sadly, rose painfully to his feet with the help of his surgeon (his wound was in his lower left leg and foot) to acknowledge the graciousness of his captor, then reseated himself while the Russian officers about his carriage raised a shout—"Bravo! Bravo!"

MacGahan described Osman Pasha:

> He wore a loose blue cloak, with no apparent mark on it to designate his rank, and a red fez. He is a large, strongly built man, the lower part of whose face is covered with a short black beard, without a streak of gray. He has a large Roman nose, and black eyes. The face is a strong face, with energy and determination stamped on every feature—yet a tired, wan face, also, with lines on it that hardly were graven so deep, I fancy, five months ago; and with a sad, enduring thoughtful look out of the black eyes.

Skobelev commented on Osman's strangely magnetic countenance: "It is the face of a great military chieftain. I am glad to have seen him. Osman Ghazi he is, and Osman the Victorious he will remain, in spite of his surrender."

MacGahan was not quite willing to extend military immortality to Osman, yet he was appreciative of the Turk's extraordinary fortitude and leadership genius:

> There may be exaggeration in the Russian estimates of Osman Pasha. History will judge. . . . But it must be remembered that Osman Pasha cannot be judged on ordinary military rules for the reason that he had not a regular army; technically speaking, not an army at all, but a mob of armed men, with scarcely any organization, with no discipline, save the natural and passive obedience of the Turkish peasant, and only such military education and experience as were gained in trenches and on the battlefield. This is the highest form of generalship, to accomplish mighty results with means which most military men would have regarded as hopelessly inadequate. . . . He has borne the weight of

this stupendous defense on his own shoulders, a very Titan, defying, with his untrained and scanty levies, the serried legions of one of the greatest military powers of Europe.

Those serried legions were now ready to resume the march Osman Ghazi had halted for six bloody, interminable months.

XV
On to Constantinople!

1
"I have been pursued by a fatality"

The czar and Osman Pasha spent the night of December 10 inside Plevna, the two meeting the next day over fine imperial cuisine prepared by Czar Alexander's chef. As he entered the czar's quarters, Osman removed his sword and offered it to his conqueror, but Alexander, in a courtly gesture, declined it. The two held a quiet conversation during the meal, after which Plevna's defender was made ready for his journey to Kharkov in the Ukraine, his designated place of internment.

On the 15th the czar left Bulgaria for Bucharest, and on that day snow began to fall, not to cease for seven full days. After that week, the country was buried under a shroud of snow and ice three feet thick; the temperature plummeted to twenty below zero degrees Fahrenheit in some places, and the Russians suffered as many as 150 cases of frostbite a day.

Riding along the Lovtcha road, MacGahan and Skobelev found Tewfik Pasha wandering about unescorted and invited him to dine. The three passed the two redoubts taken by Skobelev in September, now silent and deserted, across the labyrinth of trenches in the vineyard region between Plevna and Brestovitz. Off to the left lay the Radischevo Ridge, to the right, Krishin—names now written in blood.

In Skobelev's hut, a thawing fire awaited them, with glasses of vodka and red wine and bowls of steaming soup. Tewfik, normally diffident and somber-faced, brightened as the young Russian general, ever the most gallant of hosts, proposed a toast to the health of Osman Ghazi and the valiant defenders of Plevna.

While MacGahan had written of the surrender in one of the finest dispatches of the war, it was left to Frank Millet, representing the New York *Herald* in the *Herald-Daily News* pool, to write the final appalling chapter on Plevna.

Millet rode into the town on December 17 from Gourko's headquarters at Dolna Dubnik. The only living thing he passed on the road was a stray dog "which slunk away to his horrible meal among the shallow graves in front of the redoubts on the hills." Inside Plevna, what Millet saw he could liken only to the awful visions of Dante: human beings lying supine in the streets, stretching their arms heavenward for food and water and relief from pain; people dragging the living from grotesque piles of corpses; dimly lighted rooms sheltering the wounded in a malodorous atmosphere of disease and putrefaction, the air in makeshift hospitals so tainted with the stench of undressed and mortifying wounds, blood, and corrupted flesh that "pestilence could almost be seen stalking the town"; peasant carts carrying off bodies for burial in shallow ditches; and Bulgarians aiding Russian soldiers dragging bodies down stairs by the legs, the heads bumping step to step with sickening thumps until all were removed and flung on ox carts, arms and legs dangling overside, these tumbrils jostling over pot-holed roads, an occasional corpse jolted into the mud, sinking beneath as the wheels rolled over it.

Not all the horrors were within Plevna. Millet found fifteen thousand Turkish prisoners bivouacked on the plain near the Vid bridge, fighting each other for a scrap of bread, freezing in the open air. In the valley of the Vid were thousands of unburied corpses being torn by dogs and birds.

"Plevna is one vast charnel-house, surpassing in horror anything that can be imagined," Millet wrote.

Frederic Villiers of the *Weekly Graphic* followed the forlorn march of the prisoners from Plevna to Bucharest, describing them as "a ghastly line of living phantoms trudging wearily forward" while carrion crows, dogs, and even pigs waited for them to drop dead in their tracks. In villages along the way, the lazarettos built by the Russians reeked with the effluvium of frostbitten, gangrenous flesh.

Villiers sketched them: footsore, fatigued, cadaverous men with ice-

Constantinople and the Golden Horn in the 1870s.
(Hozier, *The Russo-Turkish War*)

The house at San Stefano in which the treaty was signed.
(Forbes, Henty, *Battles of the Nineteenth Century*, I)

The Grand Duke announces the treaty signing to his officers at San Stefano. (Forbes, Henty, *Battles of the Nineteenth Century*, I)

War correspondents of the Russo-Turkish War gathered for a studio photograph, probably Constantinople, early 1878. MacGahan is seated, second from right. (MacGahan Papers)

laden beards, some shuffling along on their heels, their toes having sloughed off in the merciless frost, many half-naked in rotting rags, their limbs showing great pale patches where the frost had bitten deeply. Traveling by sleigh through Rumania with Colonel Humphrey Sandwith, Villiers saw Turkish soldiers lying face up in the snow, the flakes settling on their opened eyeballs while hundreds of crows wheeled in the sky and village dogs and pigs worried and quarreled over the corpses along the death trail.

Colonel Sandwith, a British medical officer, sniffed the taint of disease in the air and said to his companion: "For our lives, Villiers, we must get to windward of these poor fellows."

MacGahan began to suffer the effects of the arduous campaign now as the deadly Balkan winter set in. A recurring fever took him out of action for a day or two at a time, and his broken ankle, which had never been permitted to heal, caused him increasing pain afoot or even on horseback, at times swelling to the point that he could remove his boot only with the most excruciating exertion.

Frank Millet wrote John Robinson, manager of the *Daily News*, that during the great assault and surrender of Plevna, he often wrote MacGahan's dispatches from dictation when the American was too ill to write them himself. Millet later wrote that "MacGahan was so badly injured by a horse that he was never afterwards able to walk or ride without great pain."

And, in an apologetic letter to Robinson written after the fall of Plevna, MacGahan said: "I who have been lucky all my life, who never undertook anything without succeeding in it, have failed most miserably during this campaign. I have been pursued by a fatality, an evil genius, or something of the most persistent and exasperating kind."

He gave, as extenuating circumstances, loss of horses, stupidity of servants, "even to the obstinate perversity of inanimate objects," and gave an account of trying to get his dispatch on Osman's surrender to the telegraph office:

> Upon arriving at Sistova my driver, a man who had shown himself to be most docile hitherto, suddenly let the devil put it into his head to stop and feed his horses before crossing the Simnitza, although it was only another half hour further and end of his journey. After an altercation with him, I mounted my riding horse to ride across when he seized my reins and would not let me go until I paid him. . . . I tried to make my horse break loose from him but he held on, then I struck and beat him over the head and still he

held on til I spurred my horse against a wall and dragged him off and rode over him finally and galloped off to the bridge.

After he telegraphed his long surrender dispatch on December 10, MacGahan stayed in Bucharest, where Barbara had arrived once the fall of Plevna seemed imminent. He took to bed with his "Danubian fever" and swollen ankle but rose with enthusiasm in time for a New Year's dance being held in the city by the Russians celebrating Osman's surrender as much as the advent of 1878. Barbara MacGahan wrote decades later, "Maybe our young enjoyment of life was all the keener spurred on as it was by the sense of ever-present danger, by the signs of intense suffering and death that had hemmed us all in since early summer."

2
"There is no happiness without alloy"

Archibald Forbes, in a lecture before the Royal United Service Institution on November 30, had predicted that if Plevna fell before Christmas and weather conditions favored, there would be "no serious obstacle to prevent the Russians from crossing the Balkans immediately afterwards by Shipka Pass." This opinion was echoed by MacGahan in January when he wrote the *Daily News* as though the campaign were over, naming its heroes as Gourko, Radetsky, and Skobelev and adding, "I doubt whether there is any Turkish force between them and Constantinople sufficient to arrest them should they choose to celebrate a religious service in the capital."

Early in January, Gourko made a reconnaissance of the Turkish fortifications around Sofia, the city known as such a stronghold of the Ottoman Empire that no Christian army had entered it since 1434.*

Sofia fell to Gourko's army; then, on January 9, General Radetsky took possession of the Shipka Pass once and for all, driving the Turks to the south passes, capturing the village of Shipka and taking an astonishing 32,000 prisoners and ninety-two artillery pieces. The Russian losses were considerable (nearly 5,500 casualties), but Suleiman

---

*Even in the Russo-Turkish War of 1829, the Russians had taken possession of Tatar Bazardzhik and Philippopolis but were unable to penetrate Sofia's defenses.

Pasha's defeat was so total that he abandoned his plan to fall back on Adrianople, truly the gateway to the capital, for a stand.

MacGahan had to rise from his sickbed in Bucharest, leave Barbara and his son once again, and depart for the Balkans, crossing with Radetsky's triumphant army, and moving on to Kazanlik on January 19, where he wrote his first dispatch of 1878: "The Russian army has within the last twenty days developed an amount of energy and shown a degree of activity for which nobody was prepared. . . . It is probably known that the Turks have been trying during the last two weeks to obtain an armistice by requests made at St. Petersburg, and also to the Grand Duke Nicholas."

Although personal health, harrowing personal incidents, and moments of magnified personal intrepidity were common correspondent fare in the war dispatches of the day, MacGahan did not mention his latest mishap with his already weakened leg. Soon after joining Radetsky's force in the Shipka Pass, he had again been thrown from his horse and rolled down an incline; in his pain and incapacity, he had to be lashed to a gun carriage for the remainder of the passage along the Shipka's treacherously frozen trails. Moreover, he was still tormented with intermittent fever, that undiagnosed "Danubian" fever that was said to rise as a miasma out of the marshes of the great river.

The Russian approach to Adrianople created something close to panic in England. On January 23, the British cabinet ordered Admiral Hornby to take his six ironclads of the Mediterranean fleet, anchored at Besika Bay for six months, through the Dardanelles as a reminder that England wished to be consulted about an armistice. Parliament was asked to vote six million pounds for military purposes if a show of force became necessary. But the orders to Admiral Hornby were soon countermanded, and the ships steamed back to Besika Bay at the suggestion of the British ambassador at Constantinople.

The Russians, meanwhile, answered the jittery British by moving a portion of the army further southward; Skobelev marched a force as close as Chatalja, west across the straits from the Ottoman capital. The war fever flared anew. The London music-hall song, the one that added the word *jingo* and *jingoism* to the language, erupted with renewed popularity:

> We don't want to fight;
> But by jingo, if we do,
> We've got the men, we've got the ships,
> We've got the money, too.

Once again able to mount a horse, MacGahan arrived in Adrianople on January 26 to find the city "in the quiet possession of Skobelev," and abandoned, despite its strong defenses, by its military commander Eyoub Pasha and his army of some twenty thousand men. MacGahan wrote of seeing thousands of wagons and refugees passing through Adrianople on their way to Stamboul, ancient core of Constantinople, abutting on the Bosporus and the Sea of Marmara: "When asked where they were going, very few of these people could answer. They only knew that they must get away as fast as possible, and they were so distracted with terror, that when their arabas [carriages] broke down even in the streets of Adrianople, they left their baggage and hurried away without it, most of the women on foot, no shoes, half-starved, exhausted."

Skobelev's triumphal entry into Adrianople had been that of a welcomed conqueror: Crowds of people flowed out to meet him, flowers and weaths were strewn in his path, and Bulgarian women flocked to kiss his hands and boots. He had departed Kazanlik on January 15 and had pushed his force 275 miles in twenty days. MacGahan reported their stopping at one village where Skobelev set all the bakeries working round the clock to produce twelve thousand loaves of bread for his troops.

Of his journey southward from Shipka Pass, MacGahan wrote that the countryside had the aspect of a graveyard—silent, cold, dead, with but one type of inhabitant and that reminiscent of the denizens of bloody Batak:

> I forgot; there is some sign of life, and that is those strange savage animals, the Bulgarian dogs, half wolf, half dog, apparently, that may now be seen everywhere . . . living in fields and along the roads, wandering about without masters and without homes in a wretched forlorn way that is striking. . . . They live on the bodies of the cattle and horses that have fallen and died by the wayside, and sometimes on even finer fare! . . . They have their death list, too. One sees numbers of them along the road, some shot and speared by the Cossacks out of mere sport, others starved, or poisoned by the carrion on which they feed, the greater part frozen to death by the fierce storm in spite of their great fur coats.

The road south formed a sad and dreary journey, marked at almost every step by the corpses of dogs, horses, oxen, frozen stiff in every attitude of exhaustion and suffering. The human dead were everywhere too. MacGahan found the body of a child of four or five, lying in the snow as if asleep. He got down from his horse, thinking the child might still have a flicker of life. "I laid my hands on the little face," he wrote, "and it was hard and cold as ice. There were no marks of violence, and she had evidently frozen to death."

The child haunted his *Daily News* copy later on when, closer to Adrianople, he stumbled upon lodgings out of the cold in an abandoned Turkish peasant shack where the Cossacks had left a wood fire burning. He found, to his inexpressible delight, that the old house contained a tiny bathroom, the water in huge earthen jars already heated by a cunning contraption connected to the fireplace. "A luxurious bath so handy as this, after a long day's ride through the snow and cold, is a thing not to be found anywhere else but in Turkey. There are no people in the world but the Turks who understand the art of living," he wrote in a glow afterward. Following the long bath, he made tea, roasted a piece of mutton on the blazing hearth, and spread his blanket on a wooden divan. He wrapped his fur cloak about him and tried to sleep, the only sound that of his horse tethered outside munching on his hay: "There is no happiness without alloy," he wrote. " 'There's a poison drop in man's purest cup.' In spite of the warm bath and the blazing fire, the imprint of that icy little face was almost as distinct on my hand after five hours as when I touched it to see if it were not perhaps alive."

On January 17, MacGahan witnessed the arrival in Adrianople of the Grand Duke Nicholas and his entourage of Russian officers and Turkish officials. Terms of the peace were as yet unknown among the few remaining correspondents, but MacGahan was certain that, while the Turks were objecting more or less to all the conditions impressed on them by Russia, the one item preventing an agreement was the matter of Bulgarian autonomy. Of the Turks, he wrote, "They are willing to cede Kars and Erzeroum, willing to grant the complete independence of Rumania and Serbia, the free passage of the Straits to the Russian fleet, and war indemnity, but not the autonomy of Bulgaria."

He was equally certain that Russia would remain inflexible on the Bulgarian issue even though, he said, she fully expected the peace conditions to be "discussed and maybe modified by Europe":

Although she means to force the Turks to consent to these things in principal, she expects to refer to Europe for their confirmation and application. In this way Russian diplomacy offers no hold to the English government to seize as a pretext for war. Even Lord Beaconsfield will hardly attempt to go to war to prevent Bulgarian autonomy, the only question on which the Russians are inflexible.

Late on January 31, the armistice was signed, and the terms of the instrument were remarkable. As Francis Vinton Greene observed, they showed "that the Turks at last despaired of receiving active assistance from England, without the *hope* of which they would never have undertaken the war, and had determined to throw themselves wholly upon the mercy of the Russians."

The armistice terms included Bulgarian autonomy "with a national Christian government and a native militia"; independence for Montenegro, Rumania, and Serbia with territorial indemnities; administrative reforms in Bosnia and Herzegovina; and a war indemnity.

3
"The measured tramp, tramp, tramp"

In the first two weeks of February, MacGahan ranged between Adrianople, Kadiköy (headquarters of Mukhtar Pasha, commanding the Turkish defenses of Constantinople), and Skobelev's headquarters at Chatalja. The armistice increased the apprehension of England's intervention in the war, and MacGahan was compelled to write and repeat that "in the case of a declaration of war by England, Skobelev, who now has four divisions, can throw the whole force on the heights behind Constantinople in forty-eight hours."

Skobelev's proximity to the Ottoman capital was such, MacGahan added, that "Constantinople may be virtually considered in the hands of the Russians." He continued:

> They have the self-restraint not to enter, that is all. Skobelev, while going over the lines of delimitation the other day, was near enough to see the place. He and the whole of his staff, with the escort, sat on their horses and gazed on the capital for some minutes. There was some disappointment expressed that they should not have been allowed to march in, but all are in general very glad the war is over.

For an instant on February 12 it appeared the war might not be over after all. On that date the British fleet in the Aegean steamed through the Dardanelles toward Constantinople, the British government insisting, in a classic display of gunboat diplomatic language, that the show of force was necessary "to protect the lives and property" of their subjects in the capital. Despite Turkish remonstrances, the fleet passed through The Straits, and when the news arrived in St. Petersburg, the czar telegraphed the grand duke, authorizing him to enter Constantinople with a part of his force, the reason given to likewise protect the lives and property of Christians living in the city.

The result of these unsubtle moves was the agreement obtained by the grand duke from the sultan to permit the Russians to occupy the village of San Stefano on the Sea of Marmara, six miles from the walls of Constantinople. The grand duke and his staff, Skobelev, a large force of Cossacks, and miscellaneous officers and troops traveled by rail from Adrianople to San Stefano arriving there on the 24th. Skobelev established his headquarters at St. George, twelve miles north of the town.

MacGahan, in a telegraphed dispatch to the *Daily News* on February 12 said again of Skobelev: "He can put two divisions on the high ground just behind Constantinople in thirty-six hours."

From San Stefano, MacGahan wrote at length on February 26 of the sensitive situation. The dispatch was of particular interest in depicting, through hearsay, both the grand duke's and Skobelev's attitude toward a possible fight with England:

> Mr. Gladstone seems to fear the danger of the army escaping from the control of cooler hands at St. Petersburg. There is not the slightest danger of this. There has not been a move without orders. The aversion of the Grand Duke for the continuation of the war was shown in a somewhat amusing way. . . . The Grand Duke, who was excited and indignant at the situation, asked Skobelev, it is said, what he thought of it. The latter, with the reckless indifference which characterizes him, replied, "For my part, Monseigneur, I think we shall have to fight England." "Oh, but you are a madman," exclaimed the Grand Duke in a half-angry manner, turning from him and spitting as every Russian peasant spits when anything displeases him. It is the highest expression of displeasure or anger.

For the next several days, MacGahan was able to enjoy the spectacular view that San Stefano afforded over the Sea of Marmara: boats and caïques sailing on its emerald-blue water and groups of Russian soldiers sunbathing and swimming. While visiting General Ignatiev's villa, MacGahan could see from the windows the minarets of Santa Sophia.

At last, at five o'clock in the afternoon of March 3, the Treaty of San Stefano was signed, and it became the responsibility of MacGahan and Frank Millet to collaborate on the last major dispatch of the war, to be telegraphed from Constantinople to the *Daily News*.

For days, the correspondents wrote, the uneasiness over the impending treaty signing had been like standing on the lip of a volcano. But finally, in a house by the seaside in San Stefano, a place shaken by the gales that tore across the Sea of Marmara, secretaries of both diplomatic bodies worked all night preparing the document for the signatories. After the signing the grand duke dashed off in his carriage to where his troops were formed on high ground close by the seacoast near the San Stefano lighthouse. After riding between their lines, the grand duke halted on a ridge where he could see the entire review, and formally read the announcement of peace. "I have the honor to inform the army that, with the help of God, we have concluded a Treaty of Peace."

MacGahan and Millet wrote:

> Then another shout burst forth from 20,000 throats, rising, swelling, and dying away. There was a general feeling of relief and satisfaction. I must say, however, that the news of peace was not greeted with anything like the wild excitement and enthusiasm caused by the Emperor's proclamation of war at Kischenev last April. . . . There were the men who had toiled over the slippery mountain paths, scantily fed, thinly dressed, dragging the heavy guns across the valley, finding, after their struggles with cold, hunger, and fatigue, a desperate enemy ready to resist them on every hilltop. . . . These were the men whose courage, devotion, and unparalleled endurance will go down in history.

The correspondents noted that little more than a rifle-shot distance away "stood the enemy they had found worthy of their steel," the Turks standing in small groups on neighboring hills, interested spectators of the grand duke's ceremony.

Following the formal announcement to the army, a solemn Te Deum was conducted by the priests to the kneeling soldiers of the czar, and nearly all his generals except Skobelev (who remained at Chatalja), together with such guests as the Austrian, French, Prussian, Swiss, and American military attachés—the latter being Lieutenant Francis

V. Greene—and the five correspondents who remained with the Russian army of the eighty who had begun the campaign at Ploeşti.

MacGahan and Millet ended their dispatch:

> Never has a peace been celebrated under more dramatic and picturesque conditions, or with more impressive surroundings. The two armies, face to face, the clearing storm, the waning light of day, the rush of the wind, and the near wash of the wave mingling with the chant of the priests and the responses of the soldiers and the road of the Sea of Marmara swelling and falling. The landscape, always of great beauty, now formed a wonderfully appropriate background to the picture. Across the fretting chafing waters of the sea, the dome and slender minarets of St. Sofia came up sharply against the sky, the dominant points in the interesting silhouette of distant Stamboul. Away to the south, the Prince's Island rose like great mounds, dark and massive, against the distant Asiatic shore, and behind them we knew was hidden the English fleet. Above and far beyond, the white peak of Mount Olympus unveiled for a moment its majestic summit as the rays of the ruddy sunset were reflected from the snow-covered flanks.

The Te Deum ended, the army filed past the grand duke with a swinging stride; night fell rapidly, and MacGahan and Millet left the San Stefano lighthouse hill to press on to Constantinople to send their dispatch: "As we rode down into the village, we could hear the joyful shouts still ringing in the air, and the measured tramp, tramp, tramp, going off in the darkness. So ends the war of 1877–78."

4
"This joyless, parasitic existence"

After the peace protocol and collaborative dispatch with Frank Millet, MacGahan was reunited with Edwin Pears in Constantinople and spent several weeks with the *Daily News*'s resident correspondent at his summer residence on the island of Prinkipo in the Sea of Marmara. Pears remembered MacGahan as "greatly weakened by his work," and since typhoid was raging in the capital, felt that the healthful atmosphere of the island might do much to revivify his American friend. "He was the delight of all members of the family," Pears wrote, "and especially of one of my boys, who knew almost by heart his *Northern Lights*, a story of his adventures in the Arctic Seas. . . . The two would sit on the edge of a pond in my garden and construct fleets of paper boats and amuse themselves, MacGahan getting stronger every day. After some three weeks' stay he went to Pera, frankly against my advice, with the intention of remaining a few days."

"Don't you ever feel the need to write to me? Are you not in the least interested in knowing whether we are still alive, Paul and I?" Barbara asked in an exasperated letter to her husband dated April 12 from Bucharest. It was now over a month since the treaty signing at San Stefano, and as she and her son waited in the Rumanian capital to be reunited with her wandering husband, her funds running low and her patience lower, she was forced to write: "If things have reached this point, we might as well be frank and say so, rather than leave me in this eternal suspense. You did wire me that you were expecting developments but this is hardly an explanation of this silence of two months."

She wrote twice again within six days of her April 12 letter, not yet at wit's end—indeed, she clearly had her wits about her in striking back at MacGahan's comparison of her with other women, and she was mercilessly blunt—"My cards are on the table"—in informing her absentee husband of his failed duties to her and his son.

These letters, in excellent French, have survived and are revealing of Barbara's strength, stamina, and determination. They also reveal a sadly realized sense of hopelessness.

Her April 14 letter is worth quoting at length:

> I am taking pen in hand this evening to talk a little sense to you, dear friend. Don't take this amiss and don't look for hidden motives when everything is sincere. Hear me out: this style of living can't go on. It's not that I want to reproach you for being so far from me for months on end; but I see after all that you are too accustomed to living alone, too uncaring about all that concerns Paul and me to be sincerely and irrevocably attached to us. . . . Love on your part is past, habit has not been able to replace it; you are attached to us only through a certain point of honor that you have imagined yourself. . . . I gave myself to you without reserve and I knew well what I was getting into, so I have no one to blame but myself for what has happened. You have no duty toward me. Toward Paul you get off easy by agreeing to support him until I am able to meet all of his needs. If it were not for Paul, I perhaps would not have the strength to struggle against this crazy love that I still have

for you, but in view of his future I must settle on something to cease this joyless, parasitic existence that brings happiness to neither one of us. . . . Please don't suspect that I am engaging in some hidden intrigue. My cards are on the table. I have loved only you for seven years and I will never really love any other man.

On the 18th, after remonstrating with MacGahan for calling her "a goose," apparently in a long-overdue letter from him from Constantinople ("It's distinguished and it's encouraging," she said, "especially for me in case I should want to persevere with you"), she inserted a stiletto: "The way you compare me to other women leads me to believe that you are not neglecting any opportunity to acquire all the experience possible in this connection in order to be able to judge me with competence."

By the end of the month, she was writing: "I beg of you to send me some of your money to live on. . . . I am in grave need of money at present. I no longer have anything."

At last, on May 5, six days after this message, MacGahan sent a telegram to her asking her to "take only the most necessary belongings," to bring Paul, and to come join him. By the 14th, she and her son had rooms at the Hotel Constantinople, and MacGahan managed to take three days off to be with his family. Barbara recalled that "we were inseparable, riding over the town, having lunch and dinner in restaurants, taking the horse tramway to Kadikoi." Here, MacGahan asked her to bring Paul and stay, since it was a safe distance from the city. Barbara was horrified at the idea of living in the "wilderness" where it would take her husband forty-five minutes to reach her by train or boat in an emergency, and she refused.

But MacGahan's sense of danger was correct. That spring and early summer of 1878 was a disquieting time for a foreigner to be living in Constantinople. Strange rumors stalked the ancient streets: that village grindstones were whirring at night, sharpening swords for the slaughter of all non-Muslims in the city; that the sultan had been assassinated; that bashi-bazouks were about to fall on Pera, the European district of the capital called "the pig's quarter" by some of the more fanatic Muslims; and that all the Christians—"the herd"—in Pera would soon have a taste of the yataghan.

It was not only a disturbing time, but an unhealthy one: refugees pouring into the city brought in their wake smallpox, typhoid, typhus, hideous diseases without description and many without cure.

With his wife and son installed in reasonably comfortable quarters in Pera, MacGahan made arrangements with Eugene Schuyler to have working space in Schuyler's apartment in the American legation in the central part of the city, in close enough proximity to his family to be home a few hours each day as well as overnight. He shared these quarters with Lieutenant Francis V. Greene, who was busy working on his notes for a history of the war just concluded. While away, MacGahan had given two thousand francs to Barbara with instructions that, "in case of disorders," she and Paul were to flee to Scutari* on the Asiatic side of the Bosporus, one of the "hiding places," together with Odessa, Galatz, and Trieste, devised by Pera's Europeans in case of attack.

MacGahan was still in the employ of the *Daily News* and had a certain amount of work to do, principally to keep watch on events in Constantinople and the Russian army's preparation to return to its homeland. The latter duty enabled him to travel frequently to Skobelev's headquarters in San Stefano, a few miles southwest of the capital.

The famous young general inevitably drew the correspondents to his side. He was nearly always accommodating in offering some outrageous opinion on the war and the peace, in particular the Russian decision not to risk British intervention by invading Constantinople. It was said that the sultan, Abdul Hamid, "took special interest in the megalomaniac speeches of the Russian general" and that the Ottoman ruler saw Skobelev as a valuable pawn in his political game of playing England and Russia against one another.

Frederic Villiers was a frequent visitor to Skobelev's headquarters and remembered the Russian as an eccentric figure, "with a clean-shaven head, yellow beard that seemed to cover the upper part of his tightly buttoned gray overcoat," his high Russian boots always splashed with mud, his personal quarters strewn with books. (Three books he was reading in San Stefano were a history of the American Civil War, a life of Napoleon, and MacGahan's *Campaigning on the Oxus*.)

In joining Skobelev for a meal, Villiers was led from the general's headquarters tent to a cooking line a few paces distant, where Skobelev personally inspected the twenty cooks, each man holding in front of him a pannikin of ragout which he and Villiers tasted. "The rations of the men should be good enough for the generals," Skobelev liked to say.

---

*Scutari was made famous in the Crimean War as the location of the military hospital in which Florence Nightingale and her band of nurses ministered to the terrible casualties coming down from the battle zone.

Edwin Pears also came to know Skobelev—whom the Turks had named *Ak Pasha* (White Pasha) for his white uniform and horse, renowned on the battlefields of northern Bulgaria. Pears said Skobelev's great-grandfather was a Scotsman who had taken service in Russia and that Skobelev was proud of his British ancestry. "He spoke English like an Englishman," Pears wrote, "and claimed that he had read all the six volumes of Wellington's dispatches and believed him to have been the greatest strategist of modern times." Skobelev also told Pears that every Russian was born with the belief that it was the destiny of his country to take possession of Constantinople.

XVI
A Death in Galata

1
"Amid much laughter"

Once plans for the forthcoming Berlin conference were being verbalized in diplomatic circles, MacGahan intended to cover the momentous meeting of the European powers for the *Daily News* and perhaps the *Herald* as well. He knew that the arbitration in Berlin would change, perhaps radically, the stipulations of the Treaty of San Stefano and wanted to be there to chronicle the events, in part for his own purposes. MacGahan had expressed his most immediate ambition to such close friends as Millet and Pears to return to England immediately after the Congress of Berlin, there to write a great work. It would be, he said, a complete history of the Eastern Question and a history of the separate nationalities whose fate depended upon its solution. He planned to terminate this vast work with a detailed review of the Russo-Turkish War and its diplomatic aftermath.

But, in fact, during his stay at the American consulate with Schuyler and throughout his periodic trips to San Stefano to visit Skobelev and to Pera to be with his wife and son, MacGahan's health continued to fail. He suffered from persistent chills, fever, headaches, and loss of appetite, all symptoms he tended to shrug off for Barbara's peace of mind as a bout of "gastric fever." The fever was intermittent, but it was taking longer and longer to recover from it. "He ate quinine by the spoonful," fellow correspondent Frederic Villiers said.

He was still a young man, but the long campaign in Bulgaria had devastated his health and energy, sapped him in the same way it had taken the robust Forbes completely out of action in the latter stages of the war. MacGahan limped like an old man, his broken and rebroken ankle swollen and discolored. His hair had thinned to baldness on top; his beard had streaked with gray and white. He was weak, worn out, used up, and he often told Barbara it was time for him to "quit this arduous business." He had made a name and believed a literary career of some kind lay ahead, perhaps in America but more likely in England, France, or perhaps even Russia. Few men of his age, or any other, had seen so much in so short a time. A career of but seven years' duration, a bit more, and wars in France, Turkestan, Spain, Bulgaria—and an arctic voyage! What man, certainly what American, could claim more than this? What man not yet thirty-four years old could match such a record and be called, as he was called by Bulgarian peasants, a "savior" of a country?

The past seven years were fuel for a lifetime of more sedentary living. There were books in those experiences, and innumerable stories and tales for the lecture circuit and for children and grandchildren.

In mid-May, while her husband was off to San Stefano in search of Skobelev, Barbara traveled by steamer to Byuk Dere on the Bosporus, where the Russian legation was located. There she enjoyed a reunion, after a seven-year separation, with her "favorite brother," John, a junior officer on the corvette *Taman*. It was a revivifying visit for her, walking the seashore, enjoying excursions aboard John's ship in the cool, bracing air.

With MacGahan's return to Constantinople Barbara persuaded him to take rooms in an apartment in Pera with her so that she and Paul could be truly reunited with him. They moved to their new quarters at #9 Broussa Street on May 26.

Thus they were together, although they slept in separate rooms, perhaps to protect Barbara from his as yet undiagnosed illness, and the relationship continued to be strained. Even so, "for a few more days we were happy," she would write of this last two weeks of her husband's life. "MG told me in those days that people were asking him if he was not sick, finding him looking so badly. I laughed, saying it was not important what other people were saying, as long as he felt well." He told her he had a "gastric fever" of some kind, that there was nothing to be concerned about.

In his "office" in the American legation headquarters, MacGahan found a telegram awaiting him which authorized his preparation for assignment in Berlin, where the Congress was to meet. There came too a message from the *Daily News*'s manager, John Robinson, apparently asking the correspondent for an accounting of his expenses since his arrival in the Ottoman capital. MacGahan apologized for the "heavy bills" and said he was "wrestling with the accounts," in particular the telegraph bills, bribes paid at the telegraph office, and payments to Frank Millet, Cecil Buckland, and other correspondents who were assisting in the *Daily News*'s postwar and peace negotiation coverage.

On the last day of May, MacGahan learned that his friend, the young American lieutenant, Francis Vinton Greene, had fallen seriously ill with typhoid fever after a visit to Skobelev's headquarters at San Stefano. Treated first at the British Marine Hospital in Galata, in the old commercial quarter north of the Golden Horn, Greene was later removed to the care of Eugene Schuyler at the American consulate in the capital. It was in Schuyler's house that MacGahan undertook to help nurse his American comrade, spending a bedside vigil with Greene, doing what little could be done with warm blankets and cold cloths to ease the officer's chills and fever.

Little was then known of typhoid, but the bacterium certainly followed the enormous refugee population that swarmed south from the battle zones into Constantinople, where glutted sewage systems and contaminated water and foodstuffs carried any number of dread diseases.

"I asked him to be cautious," Barbara related later, "when he was caring for Mr. Greene, but he would not listen to that. He spent most of the day with Mr. Greene and even stayed one night at the consulate when Mr. Greene felt worse and MG did not want to leave him alone with the servants."

On June 1, MacGahan rose early, visited Green briefly, then met Barbara and Paul at the steamer dock for the journey to Byuk Dere. Barbara recalled that her husband was, even then, feverish, but said there was a cooling breeze on the Bosporus that day, and while she felt slightly seasick, he and their son drank iced lemonade and stood at the rail enjoying the brief voyage.

They arrived at Byuk Dere at noon, visited the Russian embassy, and, joined by John Elaguine, had lunch at the Hotel Bellevue, MacGahan eating "with a big appetite," Barbara remembered, "macarone and hamburgher," and "amid much laughter and banter," drinking champagne toasts with her brother.

In their room at the Bellevue that night, Barbara produced a volume of Grimm's fairy tales in French, and MacGahan read to Paul until the boy fell asleep. "MG could play and speak with Paul better than I," Barbara said. "He never tired of the noise and childish conversation."

MacGahan complained of a severe headache and went to bed. Barbara brought cold towels for him and opened the windows for whatever breeze might be produced. That night they heard sailors singing evening prayers on board the *Taman*. "This sonorous choir of men's voices and the solemn tune of the prayers, dispersing far on the Bosporus, made a pleasing impression on me," she wrote.

MacGahan, despite a restless night, felt better the next day and, upon arriving back at Pera, separated from Barbara and his son to visit Greene and attend to *Daily News* business. Barbara and Paul had dinner alone, and when her husband returned that night, he brought with him a quantity of quinine he had purchased and took it, she said, "in big doses." He could not sleep and came to her bedroom to kiss the sleeping Paul. "I asked him to lie down in my bed near Paul," she said, "and offered to go to his bed, but he refused."

She saw him for the last time the next morning, Monday, June 3, as he went off to the consulate to visit Schuyler and the still weak but recovering Francis Vinton Greene.

2
"I lost my senses"

MacGahan did not return to his family that Monday. During the day he went to the consulate and dined later in the day with Frederic Villiers in the hotel of the English club in the Grand rue de Pera. Villiers remembered many years later that his American colleague had no appetite and could eat only a few strawberries.

That evening, MacGahan sent a note by courier to Barbara that he was investigating another rumor that the sultan had been assassinated—this time by poison. (The gossip proved false.) He said he would spend the night at the consulate.

On Tuesday she received another note from him which said that John Robinson had ordered him to Berlin and that she should begin packing so they could leave on Saturday. He said a doctor had given him some "strong medicine" and that he could not come to her that evening.

On Wednesday, Barbara's increasing sense of foreboding over her husband's health sharply rose when a courier delivered yet another message from MacGahan; in this one, which she would later describe as "delirious," her husband said he was sick and had consented to let Edwin Pears move him to the British hospital at Galata. The message

MacGahan, looking much older than his 33 years, cropped from another version of the group photograph of the correspondents gathered in Constantinople in early 1878. (MacGahan Papers)

THE WESTERN UNION TELEGRAPH COMPANY.

Blank No. 1.

This Company TRANSMITS and DELIVERS messages only on conditions, limiting its liability, which have been assented to by the sender of the following message. Errors can be guarded against only by repeating a message back to the sending station for comparison, and the Company will not hold itself liable for errors or delays in transmission or delivery of Unrepeated Messages. This message is an UNREPEATED MESSAGE and is delivered by request of the sender under the conditions named above.

ANSON STAGER, Vice-Pres't, Chicago.

WILLIAM ORTON, Pres't,
A. R. BREWER, Sec'y, } New York.

Dated 187

Received at Toledo O June 11th 78 – 810am

To Macgahan

Toledo Ohio.

We are inexpressibly grieved to state that J. A. Macgahan died on Sunday in British Hospital Constantinople – Every possible care was shown to him = Receive our fullest sympathy

Robinson

32 London

Mᴮᵘ – SD – α

Telegram to the correspondent's mother in Toledo, Ohio, from John Robinson of the *Daily News*, announcing MacGahan's death. (MacGahan Papers)

begged her not to come there yet, to keep Paul and herself away from the possible contagion of his illness which, he said, might be typhoid.

"I understood then," she wrote, "that he was hiding the truth from me. There was nothing dangerous or infectious in 'gastric fever.' But I had to wait." She knew too of the epidemic of typhus—a far more virulent disease than typhoid fever—that was raging in the Russian camp at San Stefano, where her husband had spent so much time in recent weeks.

Early on June 6, Barbara, probably with the assistance of Edwin Pears or Eugene Schuyler, paid a visit to the surgeon treating her husband, a Dr. Patterson, head of the English hospital in Galata. He told her MacGahan had "severe typhoid fever," and she remembered him saying the disease "was concentrated in MG's brain." The English physician also told her that her husband had passed a very bad night—so much touch and go that he, his assistant, and several nurses had stayed the night at the hospital, fearing MacGahan might die.

Barbara, with the help of her brother, found a room a short walk from the hospital on Kutchuk Hendeck Street in Galata for herself and Paul, and began a lonely vigil. Because of the contagion, she was not allowed to see her husband and was dependent upon Dr. Patterson and the hospital staff, whom she questioned several times a day, for information. From her own recollections of these painful days, it appears she was not told by hospital authorities that MacGahan was suffering from typhus, not typhoid, but Barbara found out. She wrote later of her belief that her husband had contracted the disease during a visit to a Russian army hospital where victims of the disease were pouring in from San Stefano and dying.

Frederic Villiers, on about June 8, learned of MacGahan's hospitalization but had no notion of the seriousness of his friend's illness. He journeyed to San Stefano on the 9th to keep a dinner engagement both he and MacGahan had with Skobelev and reported what he knew to the Russian general. Upon hearing Villiers's report, Skobelev exclaimed, "I know MacGahan thoroughly. I fear he must be seriously ill not to keep an appointment with me. I am going to send a telegram to find out how he is."

After dinner, Villiers later recorded, the response came from the capital informing Skobelev, "MacGahan seriously ill. Unconscious." With the general's permission, Villiers left San Stefano the next morning on Skobelev's white stallion, galloping to the capital over a roadway sodden from the incessant rain that had been falling for nearly a week. Skobelev waited briefly, then donned civilian clothes for the short rail trip to Constantinople.

To Barbara, the reports from Dr. Patterson and his staff were a frustrating mixture of contradictory news. On Friday, June 7, she was told MacGahan had improved and had eaten a bit of meat when the doctor visited him at 10 A.M. But that night she learned her husband had suffered convulsions similar to grand mal, had become comatose in his fever, recovered briefly and asked for her, and then had relapsed into unconsciousness.

"I lost my senses," Barbara recalled. "I did not admit the possibility of death."

On the 8th, Dr. Patterson assured her that although MacGahan had suffered another dangerous convulsion and now lay unconscious, she should not give up hope. Her husband was strong and resolute and had led a moderate life, the surgeon told her.

In his memoirs, Edwin Pears stated that the British medical staff at the Marine Hospital did everything in its power to save MacGahan's life, everything then available to medical science in combating a plague as hideous in its tenacious grip on the frailties of the human body as typhus.

This was the scourge of antiquity, the pestilential, putrid, jail, or hospital fever, commonly following in the ruck and waste of war, its germ borne by body lice. Those stricken often died of the supervention of heart failure, or of meningitis, or deepening coma.

Throughout the afternoon of Saturday, June 8, and on Sunday morning no change was reported in MacGahan's condition, and during her walks from her room to the hospital, Barbara wrote later, she maintained confidence he would recover. "I knew he would be weak a long time, so I planned to take him to Byuk Dere, where we could both rest from all our troubles."

At about six that evening she heard a sharp rap on the door of her apartment. Her landlady asked her to come to the landing below. There a man whom she did not recognize stood waiting. He had come from the hospital to tell her that MacGahan had died, without gaining consciousness, an hour before.

The date was Sunday, June 9, 1878. Had he lived three days longer, he would have reached his thirty-fourth year.

3
"Esteemed by all who knew him"

Barbara's recollections many years later of MacGahan's death took on a stoic, almost clinically passionless tone. She did not attempt to probe deeply into the emotions of the moment. Perhaps, despite her protestations to the contrary, she knew from the beginning of it the hopelessness of her husband's illness; perhaps, too, the love she felt for him in the early years of their relationship had been blunted and made no keener in the intervening years before she finally wrote of that rainy day in June in Galata.

She was escorted to the hospital and described the place where MacGahan had died: "In a big room with white painted walls on the third floor were standing near the door two screens and behind them a bed, the pillow to the wall. There he was lying. . . . He was still warm. I got the senseless hope that he had not died, but the doctor would not let me long console myself. He really was not alive, his soul had flown away, but he was lying there quietly, as in sleep."

The next morning, now accompanied by her brother, Barbara saw MacGahan for the last time before his corpse was removed for burial. "His face was the same," she recalled. "He seemed to have a child-like expression, like someone without troubles, that same wonderful profile, long eyelashes. He had not begun to decompose. I said goodbye to the dear man, whom I had loved for the past seven years."

Neither Frederic Villiers nor Skobelev arrived in Galata before MacGahan's body had been removed. Edwin Pears remembered how the Russian general, warned of the contamination of the death room, pushed a hospital guard aside at the door and knelt beside the vacant bed, bursting into tears.

In London, two days after his correspondent's death, *Daily News* proprietor John Robinson cabled the MacGahan family in Toledo: "We are inexpressibly grieved to state that J.A. MacGahan died on Sunday in British hospital Constantinople. Every possible care was shown to him. Receive our fullest sympathy." Robinson also cabled Edwin Pears, instructing him to arrange for MacGahan's funeral at the newspaper's expense and to order a marker to be placed on the grave.

On June 11, the funeral mass was conducted by Dominican monks of Constantinople, and while Barbara and Paul were present for these obsequies, she could not bring herself to attend the burial at the Catholic cemetery at Feirkeni on a hillside on the outskirts of Pera. Later describing herself as "prostrated with grief," she was escorted from the mass by her brother before the closed coffin was removed for burial.

The procession to the gravesite was led by Michael Skobelev; pallbearers included Frederic Villiers, Frank Millet, Edwin Pears, and Eugene Schuyler. Embassy representatives from several countries were also present, including the American minister; officers from the U.S. warship *Dispatch* lined up in full dress uniform; and a large number of Russian officers, resplendent in their braid, orders, and medals, stood solemnly with the others. Skobelev wept openly and only with great difficulty recovered his composure.

Barbara, who later visited the grave, said the cemetery of Feirkeni lay "in a wilderness of utterly neglected graves, half buried in wild reeds and uncared-for shrubs." One poignant touch, she recalled, was the honeysuckle, white jasmine, roses, and pansies planted around his grave by his steadfast friend, the humanitarian Viscountess Strangford.

The *Daily News* marker later placed on the grave carried a message with a subtle editorial: "Here lies J. MacGahan, an American citizen, who died in Constantinople June 9, 1878, from typhus, whilst acting as correspondent of the Daily News of London. Esteemed by all who knew him, for his earnestness, simplicity, manly character and advocacy of the Eastern Question on Christian side."

On the day of his burial at Pera, the New York *Herald* carried a column and a half story on MacGahan's death on page seven of the newspaper, together with a five-inch editorial. The headline of the news story ran:

DEATH OF MR. MACGAHAN
The Gallant Correspondent of the
Herald and Daily News

A HERO AND A MARTYR
Many Kind Words from Sympathiz-
ing Hearts.
Last Hours and Resting Place.

Except for describing MacGahan's grave as "overlooking the rushing waters of the Bosporus and the sunlit sea of Marmara," the *Herald* story was mundane, remarkable only for its incomprehensible errors. It was perhaps a mordant footnote to MacGahan's career that the newspaper which gave him his start seemed to know so little about him, not so much as his actual first name—the *Herald* story consistently referred to him as "John" A. MacGahan. In the sketch of his life that accompanied the news of his death and burial occurs one short sentence containing four errors of fact: "Mr. John A. MacGahan was born in St. Louis in 1846, and was, therefore, thirty-two years of age."

The *Herald* editorial had a chauvinistic tone and naturally failed to mention that MacGahan's signal work in the Balkans was accomplished for the *Daily News* of London and despite the *Herald*'s initial lack of interest in the story:

> In his achievements as a correspondent with the Russian army through this war he has shown the world the kind of journalists that we produce on this side of the ocean; and in those famous letters in which he pictured the Turkish butcheries in Bulgaria he served the cause of humanity in intensifying that indignation which left the Russian for a time free to deal with the barbarous Osmanli.

The *Daily News*'s announcement of their correspondent's death emphasized MacGahan's knightly character:

> In person he was handsome, with a bold physique, capable of great endurance. His disposition was generous and manly, and his manners quiet and unassuming. In all his instincts he was chivalrous and in all his actions just and honorable. No enterprise ever daunted him, whether it was one in which he hoped for personal reward or one in which he would suffer that others might profit by his efforts.

No one at the time of his death or in later years could provide a more thorough portrait of MacGahan than such encomiums as these. All who wrote of him seemed to share Edwin Pears's simply stated obituary: "He was a keen observer, absolutely fearless and withal of a kindly disposition and charming manner, which won for him the friendship of all whom he met."

Frank Millet, when he wrote of MacGahan in 1884, touched on MacGahan's fleeting fame in his native country and lent to the American's career an aura of martyrdom:

> His whole career was one of unselfishness and sacrifice for others. For the Bulgarians he gave up his life. That young nation reveres his memory as their noblist champion. They have done appropriate honor to his name.
>
> The remoteness of the field of his usefulness and his own sensitivity to publicity are reasons why he was less known in America than he should have been. The least we can do to honor a countryman who died a martyr to the cause of human liberty, is to give his remains a place in the soil of his own State and country.

4
"How will it ever end?"

After MacGahan's death, Barbara came under the care of Dr. Patterson, Edwin Pears, Mr. Smythe (director of the Ottoman Bank in the capital) and her brother John. A few days following the funeral and upon the invitation of the Russian ambassador, she and Paul moved their meager belongings from their rooms in Pera into the Russian legation at Byuk Dere.

In cash, she recorded in later years, she had precisely thirteen hundred American dollars plus the two thousand French francs MacGahan had given her as emergency money in the event she and Paul had to leave Constantinople hastily in a time of postwar upheaval. John Robinson of the *Daily News* sent her a draft for one hundred pounds to assist her in leaving Turkey and resettling, her sister Natalia wrote and offered to send her twenty-five rubles monthly, and soon after the news of MacGahan's death spread to Europe, *Golos* offered her a permanent staff position at one hundred rubles (about seventy-five dollars) a month, which she quickly accepted.

In the weeks she and Paul spent at Byuk Dere, Skobelev often came to visit. The first time, she remembered, he "sobbed like a child in speaking of MacGahan." He was persistent in attempting to persuade Barbara to let him enroll Paul in the Corps of Pages, highest standing Russian military school in St. Petersburg. This institution, he told her, enjoyed the special patronage of the czar, and its cadets entered the elite Guard Corps, spending their military life in imperial court circles. Barbara opposed this well-intentioned plan of Skobelev's, however, and when she traveled on to St. Petersburg in September to begin her staff work on *Golos*, she left Paul in the care of Elaguine family members in Moscow.

A month after the correspondent's death, Patrick A. MacGahan, then a young lawyer living in Ohio, wrote Dr. Patterson in Galata asking for details of his brother's death. On July 31, Patrick wrote to Barbara, declaring his surprise in learning she and his brother had married and saying that Jan had never mentioned this to him, nor that he had a son. He suggested that Barbara meet him in London, where he would assist her to "decide her course of action" and suggested she might eventually like to move to America.

"His letter was goodhearted and frank," Barbara recorded in her memoirs. "He said that his mother was grief stricken, but that he hoped in time it would be a consolation for her to meet me, and that the boy would take in her heart the place of her favorite son."

Even before she met him, Barbara decided to confide in her husband's brother and wrote Patrick at length, describing in painful detail her stormy relationship with MacGahan. "I sent him the whole story of our life together during the last seven years, and let him decide if he still wanted to meet me in London," she wrote.

Patrick was apparently undaunted by Barbara's forthright disclosures. That winter he met Barbara and Paul in London and arranged for her to meet John P. Jackson, manager of the London office of the New York *Herald*. The result of this timely introduction was Barbara's acceptance of an offer to be the paper's St. Petersburg correspondent.

Patrick, perhaps interceding for Barbara in the event monies were due her for her husband's work, also obtained from John Robinson an accounting of MacGahan's services for the *Daily News*. On October 3, 1878, Robinson wrote Patrick MacGahan: "Supposing that his [MacGahan's] engagement with us began on July 3, 1876, and terminated on June 9, 1878—say 102 weeks—the amount of his salary would have been 2040 pounds."

From this accounting, MacGahan had earned the equivalent of one hundred dollars a week for his *Daily News* work, and Robinson's figures seemed to show that all salaries due MacGahan had been paid.

Back in August, as she prepared to leave Byuk Dere for London, thence to travel to Moscow to visit her family and to St. Petersburg to begin her *Golos* work, Barbara wrote: "The story of my past is now over. All for me is covered with complete darkness, complete incertitude."

Despite the assurances of her family and friends, she agonized over her future and Paul's. "Where shall I go?" she wrote, "and how shall I make a living? How will it ever end? My poor boy!"

Epilogue

In St. Petersburg that fall following MacGahan's death, Barbara had the honor of being elected an honorary member of the Panslovanic Society of Russia. Only two other women received this tribute: the widow of Fyodor Dostoevsky and Olga Novikov, a writer on the Eastern Question and on other Slavic causes.

Two years after her husband's death Barbara made her first trip to America. At the continued urging of Patrick, who relayed the appeals of his mother that she wanted to meet her daughter-in-law and grandson, Barbara and Paul, accompanied by a niece, Elise Elaguine, and Barbara's Rumanian friend, Catherine Moscou, arrived in New York in June. Patrick registered the party at the Grammercy Hotel, took them on a whirlwind tour of New York, Niagara Falls, and Albany, then escorted them to Toledo.

Barbara made no mention in her memoirs of the long-awaited meeting with Esther MacGahan.

While in America, *Golos* assigned her to write a "history" of the American presidential election, from the nomination of delegates in Chicago until the elected president took his oath of office in Washington. Barbara thus witnessed most of the campaign of James A. Garfield and his election, and, extending her assignment, covered his short time in office and the aftermath of his murder. The last of her series of articles for *Golos* had to do with the execution of Garfield's assassin, Charles Guiteau.

Coincidentally, Barbara had contact with another assassinated president, William McKinley, although at the time of the contact, McKinley was governor of Ohio. An undated letter survives from Governor McKinley to Mrs. J. A. MacGahan, 787 Park Avenue, New York City, written from the State of Ohio Executive Chamber in Columbus. The letter expresses McKinley's appreciation for a message Barbara apparently wrote him after hearing him speak at an "Ohio Society dinner." The governor wrote: "It gave me great satisfaction to name your husband with the other distinguished men whom Ohio has produced. His great career has been an inspiration to me as I am sure it will continue to be to the young men of the country."

In all, Barbara remained in America three years, serving as resident correspondent for *Golos* until the paper's demise in 1883.

That year she and Paul journeyed to Russia for a nine-month visit. Upon returning to America, she settled in Brooklyn, and in 1892 she enrolled Paul in Columbia University.

By now Barbara had several assignments and earned a good living with her correspondence. She wrote for the New York *Herald* and served as U.S. correspondent for *Russkya Viedomosti* and the St. Petersburg daily *Novosti*, together with several Russian monthly papers and magazines. When in Europe she wrote for the Brooklyn *Eagle*, New York *Times*, New York *Herald*, Philadelphia *Press*, Pittsburgh *Dispatch*, Zanesville, Ohio, *Signal*, Cleveland *Leader*, and Toledo *Commercial*, and contributed to such magazines as *Lippincott's*, *Frank Leslie's*, and *Harper's Monthly*.

In 1894 she returned to Russia for the last time and in July of the year had one of her life's memorable experiences. With arrangements made through an exchange of letters, she traveled by carriage to Yasnaya Polyana, a few miles from Tula, and there interviewed Count Tolstoy. During the course of this overnight visit, she presented to Tolstoy the book *Progress and Poverty* and some other works by her friend Henry George, the American economist and reformer, and learned that Tolstoy was already a believer in George's single-tax theory.

Barbara never remarried. She died of cancer in February 1904, and was buried at Mount Olivet Cemetery in Brooklyn. The services were conducted by the priest at St. Nicholas Russian Orthodox Church in Manhattan, a church she had helped found and which to this day contains a stained-glass window in her memory.

Paul MacGahan, only son of Barbara and Januarius, lived a long and active life. While he had virtually no personal recollection of him, he was devoted to his father's memory. The youngest of Paul's children, retired psychologist John A. MacGahan, says his father "made intermittent attempts to collect copies of J.A.'s publications and various biographical notices in reference books, but in the last analysis he was far more under his mother's influence and I conclude that his interest in his father was mostly a reflection of her interest in J.A."

While born fifteen years after his grandmother's death, John MacGahan describes her as "a very strong and positive woman," basing this statement on her writings and career after her husband's death, her influence on her only son, and Paul's testimony as passed on to his children. "My grandmother and her son were very close," John MacGahan states, pointing out that Paul did not marry until the year after his mother's death. He adds: "They did not maintain close geographical contact; he moved in his own circles and had his own friends . . . but she was a very dominant person and exerted great influence over my father."

Paul MacGahan graduated from Columbia University in 1896 with a

Barbara MacGahan with son Paul, about 1880-81. (MacGahan Papers)

Barbara in later years. (MacGahan Papers)

Stained-glass window in Brooklyn church "In Memory of Barbara MacGahan."
(MacGahan Papers)

Frank Millet (standing) and MacGahan, studio photograph probably taken in Bucharest in 1876. (Bullard, *Famous War Correspondents*)

Jonathan MacGahan with the bust of his great-great-grandfather in Batak, People's Republic of Bulgaria, 1978. (MacGahan Papers)

MacGahan Street today in Sofia, People's Republic of Bulgaria. At left is Barbara E. MacGahan, granddaughter of the correspondent, and Aileen MacGahan O'Meara, great-granddaughter of Januarius.

Statue of the correspondent in New Lexington, Ohio. (Dale L. Walker)

Grave of MacGahan, with duplicate of Batak bust at left, in New Lexington, Ohio. (Dale L. Walker)

degree in electrical engineering and worked in this field until his retirement from the Westinghouse Corporation. He married Carolyn Campbell Crowell in 1905, a union that endured happily until her death in 1957. They had four children: Barbara, Pauline, William, and John.

Paul retired in 1944 and took up painting, earning considerable renown as a landscapist of the Catskill Mountains. He died of a heart attack at age eighty-five on October 15, 1959.

General Michael Skobelev did not long survive his American friend. He returned to Russia from the Balkans a hero and in 1881 commanded the Russian army in central Asia which conquered the Tekke-Turkoman tribes, a campaign notable for a particularly sanguinary battle fought at an outpost named Geok-Tepe, a victory which again brought Skobelev's name into public prominence.

The American army attaché in St. Petersburg, Francis Vinton Greene, met Skobelev in his headquarters camp in Bokhara during the Geok-Tepe campaign. For both men the reunion must have been a poignant one. Greene had witnessed many of Skobelev's exploits at Plevna and had written a balanced but admiring account of the work of this notable young commander. Greene noted that Skobelev had not lost his taste for reading military history, finding him poring over the English language history of the destruction of the British army in Afghanistan in 1842, a tale that surely warmed the Russian's heart.

Certainly the two must have talked about their mutual friend MacGahan.

Skobelev served for a time as governor of Minsk, and on July 7, 1882, while staying at the Hotel Deseaux in Moscow, he died, perhaps of heart disease, at the age of thirty-nine. (It was said his heart had been weakened by a shell fragment which struck him at Plevna during a night attack in November, five years before.) Although he had sometimes embarrassed his superiors, including the czar, with his recklessness deeds and statements, he was given the funeral of a national hero.

An ardent pan-slavist to the end, Skobelev had said: "My motto is short—love of country, freedom, science, and Slavs! On these four piers we can erect a political power which shall make us fear neither our friends nor our enemies."

Archibald Forbes wrote of Skobelev:

> We lived in considerable intimacy during the earlier days of the Russo-Turkish campaign, and in my haste, I set Skobelev down as a genial, brilliant, dashing—lunatic. Presently I came to realize that there was abundant method of a

sort in the superficially seeming madness; and I ended in holding, as I still hold, that Skobelev came nearer being the heaven-born soldier and inspired leader of men than any chief of whom I have had personal cognizance.

The place Skobelev occupied in the minds of his countrymen is perhaps best stated in the last entry of Fyodor Dostoevsky's *A Diary of a Writer*: "I repeat: 'If one fears England, one should sit at home and move nowhere!' Therefore, let me exclaim once more: Long live the Geok-Tepe victory! Long live Skobelev and his good soldiers! Eternal memory to those valiant knights who 'were eliminated from the rolls.' We shall record them on our rolls."

General Konstantin Kaufmann also died in 1882.

Eugene Schuyler continued in the diplomatic service, becoming consul general in Rome and later in Bucharest and in Greece. He translated Tolstoy's *Cossacks* and wrote books as varied as a life of Peter the Great and a treatise titled *American Diplomacy and the Furtherance of Commerce*. In 1889 he was sent to Cairo as consul general, but his health failed, and he died in Venice in 1890 at the age of fifty.

Archibald Forbes's career continued through two more campaigns after his recovery from the "Danubian fever" in England. They were two of the "small wars" of British colonialism: the Second Afghan War of 1878 (which included the celebrated march by Lord Frederick Sleigh Roberts and his force from Kabul to Kandahar and the uncelebrated disaster to the British force at Maiwand) and the Zulu War of 1879. After the battle of Ulundi which ended the Zulu campaign, Forbes returned home worn out after a decade on the move for the *Daily News*—France, Spain, Serbia, Bulgaria, India, Burma, Afghanistan, and South Africa.

In the twenty years which followed, Forbes turned to full-time writing, lecturing, and spinning tales of the wars and battles he had seen. He was a fixture and a welcome one at the various clubs and military organizations of London. He wrote prolifically: tales of British soldiers at Corunna and Waterloo, in the Sepoy Mutiny and the Crimea; biographies of Sir Colin Campbell, Sir Henry Havelock, and Charles G. "Chinese" Gordon; histories of the Black Watch regiment and of England's two Afghan wars; and books with titles guaranteed to take the reader down the high road to vicarious adventure: *Glimpses through the Cannon-Smoke; Barracks, Bivouacks and Battles; Camps, Quarters and Casual Places; Soldiering and Scribbling;* and *Czar and Sultan.*

He wrote often of the eminent men, in particular soldiers, he had known: Kaiser Wilhelm I, von Moltke, Marshals Bazaine and MacMahon, U. S. Grant, Sherman, Sheridan, Lords Wolseley of Cairo and Roberts of Kandahar, Evelyn Wood, Todleben, and Skobelev ("all in all, the most remarkable man I have ever known"), and he wrote often on the trade of the war correspondent. Of his own choice of a career, he wrote in typically Forbesian purple:

> It is possible that had I declined I might have been a happier man today. I might have been a haler man than I am at forty-five, my nerve gone, and my physical energy but a memory. Yet the recompense! To have lived ten lives in as many short years; to have held once and again in the hollow of my hand the exclusive power to thrill the nations; to have looked into the very heart of the turning-point of nations and of dynasties! What joy equal to the thrilling sense of personal force, as obstacle after obstacle fell behind one conquered, as one galloped from the battlefield with tidings which people awaited hungeringly and tremblingly!

Once writing a long essay entitled "War Correspondence as a Fine Art," Forbes later amended his opinion, writing with prescience: "It is now an avocation, at once simplified and controlled by precise and restraining limitations. In all future European wars, by an international arrangement, the hand of the censor will lie heavy on the war correspondent."

And in his many books and magazine articles he wrote often of MacGahan, even maintaining staunchly that "it is absolutely true that there was a large faction in Bulgaria on both sides of the Balkans prepared to agitate for the offer to MacGahan of the chiefhood of the future principality." And, in two final, touching, tributes to his great American friend, Forbes said: "Of all the men who have gained reputation as war correspondents, I regard MacGahan as the most brilliant, " and, "I do not believe that any two men loved each other more than MacGahan did me and I did MacGahan."

Just as the character of Gilbert Torpenhow in Rudyard Kipling's *The Light That Failed* is believed to have been patterned after Frederic Villiers, "the Nilghai" of the same novel may have been inspired by Archibald Forbes: "the chiefest, as he was the hugest of the war correspondents. . . . there was no man mightier in the craft than he, and he always opened the conversation with the news that there would be trouble in the Balkans in the spring."

Twice married and father of two daughters, Forbes died at the age of sixty-two in London on March 30, 1900, after a lengthy illness which emaciated him and caused him moments of feverish delirium. John

Robinson, manager of the *Daily News*, visited Forbes three days before the correspondent's death and found his friend lying on his bed, eyes wide open and bulging from his gaunt face. Suddenly Forbes sat bolt upright and shouted, "The guns, man, don't you hear the guns?!" He may well have been reliving the Great Assault on Plevna, which he had witnessed twenty-three years past.

A most poignant epitaph for both Forbes and his profession was the remark in his entry in the *Dictionary of National Biography*: "His readiness to prophesy no less than to judge suggests a rashness in forming opinions, inseparable perhaps from the profession that he followed."

Five days after Forbes's death, Osman Ghazi, defender of Plevna, died in Constantinople.

General Joseph Gourko died in 1901.

Francis David "Frank" Millet, who had served as a drummer boy in the American Civil War, continued his life of adventure. He returned to Bulgaria in 1891, voyaging seventeen hundred miles down the Danube in the American traveler Poultney Bigelow on an assignment for *Harper's Magazine*. Millet served again as war correspondent in the Spanish-American War and became an accomplished artist and raconteur. He is supposed to have said that if he could choose the manner of his death, it would be to die in battle. But he perished on the *Titanic* in 1912.

James Gordon Bennett, MacGahan's employer and chief nemesis in the first five years of the Ohioan's frenetic career, and a man who seemed to personify Joseph Pulitzer's mordant comment that every reporter was a hope, every editor a disappointment, died on May 14, 1918.

Francis Vinton Greene resigned from the army in 1886 to practice civil engineering but returned for service as a colonel, later major general, in the Spanish-American War, serving in the Philippines. He was New York City police commissioner in 1903 and retired in 1915. He wrote several books, including a noteworthy history, *The Russian Army and Its Campaigns in Turkey, 1877–78*. He died in New York City in 1921.

Frederick Villiers, regarded as having witnessed more warfare than any man of his century, from the Serbian War of 1876 through World War I, over four decades of battle, died in London in 1922 at the age of seventy.

* * * *

In 1884, Hon. H. C. Greiner of the Ohio legislature sponsored a resolution in which Ohio lawmakers petitioned the U.S. secretary of the navy to send a warship to Constantinople for the purpose of "conveying home the remains of Mr. J.A. MacGahan." Soon after this, Greiner, a Perry County native, heading a committee of six senators and representatives of the Ohio legislature, arrived in Washington to visit Navy Secretary William Chandler to discuss the resolution. With Chandler in New York to greet the returning Adolphus Greeley arctic expedition, Greiner called on his Perry County friend General Philip Sheridan who readily agreed to join the delegation, introduce them to the secretary upon his return, and assist them in urging their case.

From Barbara MacGahan's unpublished memoir, we know she was present for this momentous meeting with Secretary Chandler. She recalled that in fifteen minutes every detail had been arranged: the USS *Quinnebang*, already anchored off Constantinople, would take MacGahan's remains as far as Lisbon, then transfer the sealed coffin to the paddle steamer *Powhaten*, which would bring it to New York Harbor.

After receiving the coffin from the *Quinnebang*, the *Powhaten* steamed from Lisbon Harbor on July 30, heading for Madeira, thence across the Atlantic to New York. A black-hulled vessel bristling with cannon, the *Powhaten* carried, in addition to MacGahan's coffin, parrots from the coast of Africa, a monkey, and a gazelle. The animals were all gifts to New York's Central Park zoological collection.

On August 27, the *Powhaten*, her flag at half-mast, reached New York and was saluted by every vessel from Sandy Hook to the harbor. There, in short order, MacGahan's remains were transferred to a government yacht which took them on to the Brooklyn navy yard. Awaiting the yacht were the correspondent's widow, the navy secretary, Secretary of War Robert Todd Lincoln, and Navy Commander Winfield Scott Schley. Also present were members of the New York Press Club, which escorted the horse-drawn hearse from the Battery to City Hall, the route lined with spectators who had read of the event for weeks in the New York papers.

The coffin, covered with an American flag, was placed on heavily draped trestles in the Governor's Room of City Hall, and one New York newspaper, under the headline "LAST TRIBUTES TO MACGAHAN" gave this account of the ceremony:

> No sooner were the gates opened than a long line of people began to pass by the coffin, being kept in order by a detail of police. . . . Two superb wreaths of flowers, one at either end, bore long satin ribbons, on which were inscribed "From the New York Press Club," and "From the Journalists of New York." The body lay in state until 4:30 when it

was taken to the Pennsylvania depot by pallbearers repre-
senting the New York Press Club, Herald, Journal, Sun,
World, Star, Staats-Zeitung, Truth, Times, Telegraph,
Tribune, and AP.

A New York *Star* reporter wrote: "In this utilitarian age, in which is
unhappily associated with the world a reprehensible ingratitude, it
was somewhat cheering to find great deeds remembered and a great
character fitly honored."

MacGahan's remains were next taken by train to Columbus, where
the flag-draped coffin again lay in state, this time in the capital ro-
tunda, with a military guard of honor. With the reburial ceremony
scheduled several days hence in New Lexington, the remains were
shipped briefly to Zanesville and kept in the Calvary Cemetery vault
there until time to move the coffin for the last time.

On September 12, 1884, religious services were conducted by Bishop John A. Watterson at 8:30 A.M. at St. Rose Church in New Lexington
(in which about one-twentieth of those present could be accommodated). The coffin was then escorted by a platoon of Grand Army of
the Republic veterans, marching with swords reversed, to the brick-
lined vault on a knoll in Maplewood Cemetery, where a crowd of several hundred waited, including the correspondent's mother, brother,
son, and widow; Gen. Philip Sheridan; more than sixty newspapermen
from across the country; foreign dignitaries; Ohio Governor George
Hoadley; members of the Ohio state legislature, and H. C. Greiner,
serving as marshal for the occasion.

After the placing of a cross of flowers on the coffin by the Zanesville
Press Club, military and religious rites, a eulogy and the reading of an
original poem by Col. W. A. Taylor, MacGahan was laid to rest for the
last time.

Only rarely over the next century would national attention be
drawn to MacGahan or to his grave. In December 1896, a letter and
enclosure was sent out to one thousand American newspapers in an
effort to obtain funds to erect a statue of MacGahan in New York City.
"The MacGahan Statue Fund," headquartered at 29 Park Row, listed
Murat Halstead as its chairman, Francis V. Greene, treasurer, and
such names as Francis D. Millet and Julius Chambers on its letterhead.
Editors around the country were asked to "awaken interest in the
movement" by giving prominence to the article enclosed, addressed
"To the Press and People of the United States." It was explained that
the statue would be designed by Charles H. Niehaus, "gifted American

sculptor," and a crude drawing of the work was enclosed in the mailing. It depicted a figure in high boots, hat, lapelled jacket and tie, sitting on a rock, hands on his knees, pencil and notebook poised.

The campaign apparently failed to raise enough money to commission the sculpture.

In October 1900, through the efforts of the teachers of Perry County, a heart-shaped granite boulder was placed on the grave, lettered with MacGahan's name, date of birth, and death, and embellished with a simple cross.

On Tuesday, July 4, 1911, the largest crowd ever gathered in Perry County (estimated at ten thousand) were awakened at 5 A.M. by a thirteen-gun salute that heralded a day's activities that would culminate with a grand ceremony and the unveiling of a monument at Mac-Gahan's grave. Even President William Howard Taft had been invited and, in declining, had written: "As an Ohioan, as an American, I am proud of the career of MacGahan, a son of Perry County. The world owes much to him for his undaunted courage and for his peerless powers of description and the convincing truthfulness of his narratives. Ohio may well give him high place in the gallery of her heroes, and no true American can deny him the tribute of this admiration."

In the speech making during "Sleepless Week"—the period preceding the unveiling of the monument—Judge Maurice H. Donohue of the Ohio Supreme Court spoke on the irony of Turkey's great nemesis and Bulgaria's great savior being born in humble circumstances in rural Ohio, and Col. William A. Taylor read another original ode to MacGahan's memory.

Among the Bulgarian dignitaries present that day, one Svetozar Tonjorov spoke of MacGahan's heart-rending description of entering the devastated village of Batak, where, Tonjorov said: "the entire population of between three and four thousand men, women and children had sought refuge in the large village church from the methods of the Turkish 'pacifiers.' . . . Among the victims was Dimitri Tonjorov, a kinsman of mine, who as village teacher shared the fate of his pupils in that desecrated Temple of the Redeemer."

Another ceremony took place at the grave on July 4, 1929, when Hon. Simeon Radev, Minister of Bulgaria to the United States and special representative "to the tomb of MacGahan" of His Majesty King Boris III of Bulgaria, visited New Lexington. A parade of Company F, 166th U.S. Infantry, took the minister, his staff, several congressmen, and other dignitaries to the grave, where the ceremonies began with an address by Hon. John B. Barbee, mayor of New Lexington. Ambassador Radev made a brief address and laid a wreath on the grave, and the New Lexington band played the Bulgarian national anthem and the "Star-Spangled Banner." The ceremony ended with a rifle volley and a playing of taps.

On June 12, 1944, the centenary of MacGahan's birth, a touching tribute took place at the grave site, sponsored by the National Bulgarian-Macedonian Organization, and another was held on June 8, 1958, when nearly five thousand people (including Paul MacGahan, in his last public appearance) came to see the Bulgarian organization place a wreath on the tomb. In this instance, the entire ceremony was recorded to be broadcast over the "Voice of America" program behind the Iron Curtain.

On June 3, 1978, nearly the centennial of the correspondent's death, a more modest ceremony took place in New Lexington, organized by Dr. George Tabakov of Akron, a Bulgarian émigré who was a leader in creating the MacGahan Bulgarian-American Foundation based in Ohio. The centennial observance included a march to MacGahan's grave with American and Bulgarian flags flying. Former Ohio governor Frank Lausche made an address, and Father Christo Christov of Akron conducted the Eastern Orthodox memorial service.

But despite these tributes, after Paul MacGahan pulled the lanyard that unveiled his father's monument in Maplewood Cemetery that July 4, 1911, another shroud seemed to descend over the name J. A. MacGahan. The name lives on in the sense that it is embalmed, with brief biographical data, in specialized references (some encyclopedias, biographical dictionaries, *A Treasury of Great Reporting*); in histories of foreign correspondence, of the Bulgarian atrocities, and of the Russo-Turkish War; in biographies of James Gordon Bennett; and in autobiographies of Edwin Pears, John Robinson, and Archibald Forbes. MacGahan's own books are to be found only by diligent search and command high prices from rare-book dealers. His life lies, for the most part, in the long-forgotten pages of the New York *Herald* and London *Daily News*, both defunct and sources available only to the person willing to spend hours in the library before a microfilm reader.

The fact is that Januarius MacGahan, at least in his own country, is a forgotten man. Perhaps Frank Millet put his finger on part of the reason for this—"the remoteness of his usefulness." America has never had reason to extend to MacGahan any special gratitude.

Bulgarians, on the other hand, have continued to remember the name. Charles F. Wingate, a friend of Barbara MacGahan, had an experience with this in 1893 and left a letter describing the incident. At the World's Columbian Exposition in Chicago, Wingate came across the Bulgarian exhibit, met a tall, handsome gentleman there, and struck up a conversation with him. The Ohioan asked the exhibit official if he were a native of Bulgaria and if he had ever heard of Januarius MacGahan. He got this response: "I shall answer that by inquiring if you are an American and if so, if you have ever heard of Washington, Lincoln or Grant. What you think of these immortal heroes, we think of MacGahan."

Peter Dimitrov, who accompanied the correspondent and Eugene Schuyler from Constantinople to Bulgaria that fateful summer of 1876, published in 1901 a brief book with a long title, *Spomeni po Izsledvaniata na Turskite Svirepstva pri Potoushenieto na Bulgarskoto vustanie pres 1876* (Memories of the inquiry about the atrocities committed by the Turks in crushing the Bulgarian uprising of 1876 and the outcome of the inquiry). The book, published to commemorate the twenty-fifth anniversary of the April revolt, gave MacGahan credit for revealing to the world the agony of Bulgaria under Turkish suzerainty. Dimitrov especially remembered MacGahan's dispatch on the massacre at Batak, writing that "when he read the story to me and Mr. Schuyler, our eyes were filled with tears."

In other books commemorating the April revolt of 1876, Bulgarian writers have maintained that it was MacGahan's "letters" to the *Daily News*, followed by Gladstone's fiery pamphlet, which produced over five hundred resolutions at public meetings, helped collect immense sums of money for the relief of the stricken Bulgarian villages, sent there humanitarians such as the Viscountess Strangford and her volunteers, and inspired others to speak out publicly against the Turks. Among these were, in England, Oscar Wilde, Algernon Swinburne, Charles Darwin, John Bright, and Thomas Carlyle; in France, Victor Hugo, de Vestine (of *Le Figaro*), journalist Auguste Vacquerie, and Emile le Garardin; in Russia, F. M. Dostoevsky, Ivan Turgenev, D. I. Mandeleev, Peter Kropotkin; in Italy, Garibaldi.

In the Bulgarian National Library in Sofia today there are to be found copies of MacGahan's *Turkish Atrocities*, translated by Stefan Stambolov and published in 1880, and copies of the collected *Daily News* dispatches of 1877–78. As recently as 1966, a new translation of MacGahan's atrocity dispatches was published. It is a superior book by Theodor Delchev Dimitrov and contains an introductory essay on the correspondent, reintroducing him to a new generation of Bulgarians. The National Library in Sofia also has copies of the popular book, *Veliki blagodeteli na bulgarskia narod* (Great benefactors of the Bulgarian people) by P. M. Mateev, published in 1934. This book deals with the lives and works of such non-Bulgarian figures of the 1876–78 period as Pears,

Schuyler, Lady Strangford, and MacGahan—seventy-five pages on MacGahan alone together with a full-page portrait of the American newspaperman.

Two of the three volumes of the *First Bulgarian Encyclopedia*, compiled by Louka Kassurov (1854–1915), have entries on MacGahan. In volume I, published in Plovdiv (formerly, Philippopolis) in 1899, one page out of the total of fifty-five devoted to the April rising is on the correspondent—"A good-natured American who found everywhere signs of inhumanities that are beyond description." The special entry on MacGahan in volume II published in 1905 covers a page and a half and begins, "A famous correspondent, born in 1844 in Northern America (Ohio) of Irish parentage. He played an important role for the liberation of Bulgaria."

The Bulgarian Encyclopedia in one volume, compiled by N. G. Danchov and Ivan G. Danchov and published in 1936, characterizes MacGahan as "a famous American correspondent, who played a significant role in Bulgaria's liberation."

The latest such reference work, called *The Concise Bulgarian Encyclopedia*, published by the Bulgarian Academy of Sciences in 1969, contains in volume III this entry:

> MACGAHAN, Januarius Aloysius (1844–1878), an American journalist. In 1876 he was sent to Bulgaria by the British paper "The Daily News" to inquire into the position of the Bulgarian people after the crushing of the April uprising. MacGahan gave detailed information about the cruelties committed by the Turks. This information was influential in helping to win the sympathies of democratic public opinion.

In addition to these written histories, Bulgarians remember Mac-Gahan in other ways. The American's portrait hangs in the district museums at Pazardzhik and in public buildings in Panagyurishte and Batak along with those of Penayot Volov, Georgi Benkovski, Todor Kableeshkov, Vassil Petleshkov, Pavel Bobekov, Raina Popgeorgieve, and other leaders of the April revolution.

In Sofia, Plovdiv, Pazardzhik, Panagyurishte, Perustitsa, and Batak, there are streets named for MacGahan, Schuyler, and Lady Strangford.

In 1971, the present writer received a letter from Bozhidar Kunt-schev, a student in Bulgarian philology at the University of Sofia. The letter was in response to a question as to MacGahan's renown, if any, in Bulgaria today. Kuntschev wrote: "The name of MacGahan is widely known in this country. Numerous articles are published about him on the occasion of the anniversary of the Liberation of Bulgaria; his name is mentioned in all Bulgarian histories, and there are streets bearing his name in a number of towns as well as here in Sofia."

MacGahan Street in Sofia is located in a working class neighborhood, Hadzi Dimitar. It is a small street, neatly laid out, of one- and two-story homes. The street names of the Hadzi Dimitar district are all of cultural heroes and revolutionaries of Bulgarian history.

There is yet another monument. On the first anniversary of MacGahan's death, June 9, 1879, in an address delivered before the Grand Assembly of the Slavonic Society of St. Petersburg, a certain Professor Oreste Muller announced that, "according to a decision of the Bulgarian National Assembly, there will be on June 9 a Requiem Mass sung in the cathedral of Tirnova in memory of the man so universally beloved by the Slavs, Januarius MacGahan."

The cathedral of Tirnovo lies at the foot of Shipka Pass, an exquisitely beautiful church of golden cupolas built as a memorial to the events of August 9–21, 1877, when 3,773 Bulgarians and Russians died and the Turks lost 10,000 men before the Russian General Radetsky came with reinforcements to hold the pass from Suleiman Pasha's armies.

MacGahan is remembered in prayers there to this day.

In Ohio, there is a delightfully meandering road, S.R. 13, between Athens, home of glorious old Ohio University (founded 1802) and MacGahan's hometown of New Lexington. The road winds through a countryside not all that much changed from that of the correspondent's day when he must have seen much of it afoot or on the back of a farm horse. It wanders past plowed fields and frame farmhouses; past red brick homes with wooden porches and porch swings; past villages with names like Chauncey, Redtown, Glouster, Jacksonville, and Trimble; past the Wayne National Forest; and into Perry County and more villages—Corning, Rendville, Oakfield, Moxahala.

In New Lexington, at the corner of North Main and East Brown streets, stands a sturdy, gingerbread-colored, brick county courthouse, built in 1887 in the ornate Victorian style of turrets, weathervanes, and fortresslike dominance.

Stand on the front steps of the Perry County Courthouse and look directly across Main Street, and you will see Januarius MacGahan walking toward you.

The statue of MacGahan, in full stride, pen in one hand and notepad in the other, is a larger-than-life representation of the correspondent by Lubomir Daltchev, an acclaimed Bulgarian-American sculptor, whose work in New Lexington was unveiled in June 1984—the centennial of MacGahan's reinternment at Maplewood Cemetery. Commissioned by Dr. Tabakov's MacGahan Foundation, Daltchev produced a statue from pocked, volcanic-looking reddish stone of the correspondent in action. The facial likeness, though undetailed, is true to existing photographs, down to the bald pate and grimly determined mouth and eyes.

On the statue's base are the words

JANUARIUS MACGAHAN
1844   1878
Champion of Bulgarian Freedom

East Brown Street will take you to Maplewood Cemetery if you watch for a weathered sign nailed to a telephone pole a short distance behind the old courthouse and follow the narrow, wooded road southwest. The cemetery is crisscrossed by brick paths, wide enough for a single automobile's passage. To find MacGahan's grave, ask any caretaker—all of them know it instantly as it is the chief attraction there for out-of-towners.

The grave faces one of the narrow brick roadways and is dappled by the sun filtering through a profusion of maple trees. Near the main marker is the old stone, decorated with a simple cross, placed there in 1900. To the right is a cannon of unknown date and origin. To the left is a huge bust on a pedestal—object of some controversy when it was placed there a few years ago. This grim and blockish work, a head that resembles Lenin far more than it does MacGahan, is a gift to the city of New Lexington from the People's Republic of Bulgaria. It is a duplicate of a bust outside a museum in Batak, that Balkan village of mournful memory that was the locus of some of MacGahan's most incendiary dispatches on the "atrocities."

The centerpiece of the gravesite is that striking marble marker on its massive plinth and just as young Bulgarians in the Hadzi Dimitar district of Sofia must wonder about the street with the strange name, so must the visitor to Maplewood be awed by that beautifully simple— yet so enigmatic—white monument.

Here in a restful, tree-shaded Catholic section of a rural Ohio graveyard on the fringe of Appalachia, is a tomb carrying this eloquently plain inscription:

MacGAHAN
LIBERATOR OF BULGARIA

Notes

Part I
Chapter I
1

The 1911 tomb dedication ceremony at New Lexington is described in detail in *The MacGahan Monument: A Dedication at New Lexington.*

2

Perry County history: Files of the Perry County *Tribune*, New Lexington; also data supplied by the Ohio State Historical Society, Columbus; Wingate MS, and packet marked "Biographical Materials, Miscellany," MacGahan Papers.

MacGahan family history: A detailed family genealogy with biographical data on the correspondent's parents and his early life is to be found in the packet "Biographical Materials, Miscellany," MacGahan Papers.

JAM Christian name: Ostrander, "Penman of Independence."

P. H. Dempsey recollections of JAM: MacGahan Papers; also "Biographical Materials, Miscellany."

JAM letters to his mother from Huntington, Indiana: MacGahan Papers.

Walter J. Blakely recollections of JAM: MacGahan Papers; see also packet "Pre-1870 Letters."

JAM meeting with Gen. Philip H. Sheridan in 1868: This is based on speculation by Walter Blakely in March 1901, twenty-three years after the correspondent's death. (Blakely Letters, MacGahan Papers.)

3

Until 1982 when John A. MacGahan, grandson of the correspondent, located a misplaced mass of family papers, details of the 1869–71 period of JAM's life were exasperatingly sketchy. The gap has been filled in great detail by these archives which include a number of diary-like letters from JAM to his mother from Brussels, the art colony at Écouen, and Paris, with chatty letters to Frances and Walter Blakely. Also included in these papers is a sketchy and gap-filled but nonetheless valuable daily diary JAM began in January 1871, and kept up, if desultorily, through the campaign on the Amu Darya and the march to Khiva in 1873. See JAM diary, and packet "Pre-1870 Letters," MacGahan Papers.

JAM contrast of Germans and French: Many years later, Barbara MacGahan inserted a note on this long letter from the Rhine: "To some extent, after the Franco-Prussian War and the Commune, M. modified his views of the French character."

4

JAM activities on the eve of the Franco-Prussian War: Letters to his mother and the Blakelys, JAM Diary and "Pre-1870 Letters," MacGahan Papers.

JAM assignment with the New York *Herald*: Walter Blakely speculation in 1901, Blakely Letters, MacGahan Papers; also "Biographical materials, Miscellany."

Chapter II
1

Nineteenth century developments in journalism and rise of war correspondence: Bullard; Hohenberg; Knightly; Matthews; and Stein.

Forbes on Lord Wolseley, "paramount duty": Forbes, "War Correspondence as a Fine Art."

William Howard Russell: Atkins; Bullard; and Furneaux, *The First War Correspondent*.

2

Forbes: See especially his *Souvenirs of Some Continents*, "War Correspondence as a Fine Art," *My Experiences*, and *Memories and Studies*; also Bullard's excellent chapter on Forbes in *Famous War Correspondents*.

"Telegraph freely," George W. Smalley, William H. Russell, and Holt White: Furneaux, *News of War*; also Atkins; Bullard; and Matthews.

Causes of the Franco-Prussian War and JAM's joining Bourbaki's army: Horne; Howard; JAM diary, MacGahan Papers.

Chapter III
1

Bourbaki and opening events of the Franco-Prussian War: Horne, *The Fall of Paris*; Howard.

2

JAM's Bordeaux letter of March 1871 is to be found in the Barbara Elaguine MacGahan Papers. See attached to this letter a note reading, "The following letter is the first written after he joined the *Herald* staff. Its modest yet exuberant tone is characteristic."

JAM and Victor Hugo: The account of the visit to Hugo is found in JAM Diary, MacGahan Papers. The entry is undated, but the interview with Hugo appears to have occurred on about February 20, 1871. Although the story would seem to have been important, I have been unable to find evidence that it resulted in a published dispatch in the *Herald*. In all likelihood, the novice correspondent's interview notes were used by others, since Hugo's name and observations appear repeatedly in *Herald* columns on the war at this stage.

March 6 dispatch: This document, written in ink in a large, looping, and very readable hand—in contrast to later dispatches in which his writing became increasingly difficult to decipher—is among but a handful of original JAM dispatches to survive and is found in the packet marked "Franco-Prussian War and Commune of Paris (1870–71)," MacGahan Papers.

The Commune: Horne; Howard.

JAM to Montmartre: JAM Diary, MacGahan Papers.

3

"Heavy interpreting": Bullard.

Dombrowski career, in Commune, death: Horne; Howard.

"Riding with Dombrowski" letter: It is dated "June 1" and was written to Walter Blakely. "Franco-Prussian War" packet, MacGahan Papers.

JAM arrest, Washburne account: JAM Diary, MacGahan Papers; Bullard; Washburne. See also Washburne's letter in the New York *Daily Tribune* for July 6, 1878, wherein the former minister claims MacGahan held "friendly relations with the military and civil leaders of that movement [the Commune] of anarchy and blood." Washburne also states, "It is safe to say that he had a more intelligent knowledge of all that was taking place at the time than any man in Paris. From him and Dr. Hosmer, as well as from Mr. Southworth, I obtained from day to day much valuable information which enabled to me keep *au courant* with the passing events. Mr. MacGahan was everywhere and taking great hazards. . . . As an American journalist he was everywhere well received by the Communards, but had any suspicions arisen against him, his life would not have been worth a pin's fee."

Commune mopping-up operations, Gallifet: Horne.

JAM's post-Commune summary: Blakely Letters, "Franco-Prussian War" packet, MacGahan Papers.

Chapter IV

1

JAM and Livingstone: JAM Diary, MacGahan Papers. See also O'Connor.

Roving commission, Odessa: JAM Diary and letter fragment in packet marked "Miscellaneous Letters, Documents," MacGahan Papers.

Yalta and "quiet, dreamy" description: Excerpted from an eighteen-page "letter," presumably for the *Herald*, written on thin, fragile notepaper, which survives intact in the "Miscellaneous Letters" packet, MacGahan Papers.

First encounter with Varvara (Barbara) Elaguine: Derived from Barbara Elaguine MacGahan's unpublished memoir (written in 1897) of her life with JAM (BEM file, MacGahan Papers).

"One of the ladies": JAM diary, MacGahan Papers.

2

Elaguine family history: From Barbara Elaguine MacGahan's unpublished manuscript (undated, edited by her son, Paul MacGahan in 1956) titled "The Twilight of the Czars: Absolutism and Its Effects in Russia," BEM file, MacGahan Papers.

Barbara Elaguine's appearance: Derived from her description of herself (1897 memoir) and from photographs in the MacGahan Papers.

Barbara and sister Natalia, Barbara's initial reaction to JAM: 1897 memoir, BEM file, MacGahan Papers.

3

Barbara, JAM, in Odessa, St. Petersburg: 1897 memoir, BEM file, MacGahan Papers.

Sherman tour: JAM diary, MacGahan Papers; scattered references to it in letters to his mother, Walter Blakely, "Miscellaneous letters" packet, MacGahan Papers.

Alabama Claims, Geneva: JAM diary, MacGahan papers; see also Morley for details. JAM's role, as with the Sherman tour, is unclear.

The *Herald* coverage of these events is extensive, but as with the Hugo interview, it appears that JAM's duties were more of a news-*gathering* and note-taking variety, with the dispatches written by others, perhaps by the paper's editors in New York from the data collected by several correspondents.

Patrick A. MacGahan: JAM diary, MacGahan Papers.

4

Paris letter to Barbara: BEM file, MacGahan Papers. Barbara's "this fatal letter" reaction to it may be found in her unpublished 1897 memoir of her life with JAM.

Barbara and JAM in Paris: 1897 memoir, BEM file, MacGahan Papers.

5

JAM meeting with Bennett, Hosmer: JAM diary, MacGahan Papers; Bullard; O'Connor.

Louis Napoléon funeral: JAM diary, MacGahan Papers.

January–February 1873, Paris to St. Petersburg: BEM Papers.

Preparations for Khiva expedition: The letter from JAM to his brother Patrick is in the packet marked "Khiva (Turkestan)," MacGahan Papers.

Barbara on JAM preparations and her reaction to the expedition and to Bennett: 1897 memoir, BEM file, MacGahan Papers.

Eugene Schuyler: See his *Turkistan*, also the opening pages of JAM's *Campaigning on the Oxus*.

Chapter V

1

The James Gordon Bennetts: Carlson; O'Connor.

2

Prince Tchinghiz: Schuyler.

Vambéry: JAM Diary, MacGahan Papers.

Connolly and Stoddart in Bokhara: English; Macrory.

Kaufmann portrait and early work in Turkestan: Becker; Boulger.

Turkoman tribes: MacGahan, *Campaigning on the Oxus*.

Orenburg letter: The letter to Walter Blakely is found in the "Khiva (Turkestan)" packet, MacGahan Papers.

3

From Kazala across the Kyzyl Kum to Irkibai: MacGahan, *Campaigning on the Oxus*. Indeed, the entire story of MacGahan's experiences in seeking, finding, and riding with Kaufmann's forces in Turkestan, the account of the fall of Khiva, and the subjugation of the Turkoman tribes is best drawn from his remarkable book, with additional material from such sources as Becker, Boulger, Burnaby, Curzon, and Schuyler. MacGahan's dispatches from central Asia that were used in the *Herald* are, probably as a result of editorial work in New York, a strangely sketchy and unsatisfactory record of the campaign.

4

JAM riding in pursuit of Kaufmann: Schuyler.
Schuyler on hearing of JAM's adventure: Schuyler.

Chapter VI

1

Fall of Khiva: Becker; Curzon; MacGahan, *Campaigning on the Oxus*. MacGahan entered Khiva on June 10, 1873, but his cursory dispatch, dated June 11, did not appear in the *Herald* until August 4 and gave no hint of his Arabian Nights adventures in journeying to the ancient citadel. His dispatch merely summarized the negligible Russian casualties, revealed the number of slaves set free by Kaufmann's decree, and pictures Khiva as a "dirty, squalid town" and the Khan's palace as "shabby." (See Snyder and Morris.)

"I say, American": Unpublished MS titled "Sojourn of the Turkestan Division at Khiva, Our Return From Khiva; Appearance in the Midst of Us, of an American During Our Affair on the Amou-Daria," in the MacGahan Papers. This remarkable twenty-six-page document, unsigned and undated (but written about 1873), is in fair English and was written by an officer with Kauffman's forces at Khiva.

Skobelev at the Hazavat Gate: Knox.

Zuleika: MacGahan, *Campaigning on the Oxus*. For a far different opinion of the comeliness of Khivan women, see Burnaby.

Muhammad Rahim: Burnaby; MacGahan, *Campaigning on the Oxus*.

The Russian encampment at Khiva, banquet: "Sojourn of the Turkestan Division" MS, MacGahan Papers.

Chapter VII

1

Letter from American Geographical Society: Dated July 8, 1873, in the "Khiva (Turkestan)" packet, MacGahan Papers.

The Turkomans, campaign against the Yomuds: MacGahan, *Campaigning on the Oxus.*

2

Results of campaign: Boulger; MacGahan, *Campaigning on the Oxus.*

Skobelev character, career: Harcave; Hodgetts; Nemirovitch-Dantchenko.

JAM letter to Russian officer: "Sojourn of the Turkestan Division" MS, MacGahan Papers.

3

Barbara MacGahan and reunion with "M.G.": 1897 memoir, BEM file, MacGahan Papers.

Bennett banquet and gold watch affair: 1897 memoir, BEM file, MacGahan Papers.

Letters to Barbara from Key West and New York: Packet marked "Miscellaneous Letters, Documents," MacGahan Papers.

Account of Geographical Society lecture: New York *Herald*, February 17, 1874.

Request for leave of absence: 1897 memoir, BEM file, MacGahan Papers.

Chapter VIII

1

London, book contract, Stanley visit: 1897 memoir, BEM file, MacGahan Papers.

Athenaeum review: Quoted in the New York *Herald*, July 12, 1874.

JAM letter from Estella: This was addressed to Walter Blakely, dated October 12, 1874 (packet marked "Carlist War in Spain," MacGahan Papers).

St. Stanislaus medal: Described in the Charles J. Wingate MS, an unpublished memoir of an American friend of JAM, MacGahan Papers.

Carlism, First Carlist War: Holt.

Letter to Barbara from Écouen: Packet marked "Letters from Carlist War to Varvara," MacGahan Papers.

2

Biarritz: 1897 memoir, BEM file, MacGahan Papers.

3

Don Carlos biography, character: Holt.

Barbara MacGahan during JAM's absences, birth of Paul: 1897 memoir, BEM file, MacGahan Papers.

4

In Bayonne: 1897 memoir, BEM file, MacGahan Papers.

JAM letters to Barbara from Estella and elsewhere in Spain: Packet "Letters from Carlist War to Varvara," MacGahan Papers.

Barbara and account of JAM imprisonment: 1897 memoir, BEM file, MacGahan Papers.

5

End of Carlist campaign: Holt.

Item on arctic expedition: New York *Herald*, November 23, 1874.

Chapter IX

1

Bayonne: 1897 memoir, BEM file, MacGahan Papers.

Attitude toward James Gordon Bennett: Although Barbara Mac-Gahan left a full record, particularly in her 1897 memoir, of her thoroughgoing disgust and distrust of Bennett and what she considered the *Herald* editor's lack of appreciation for her husband's work, except for oblique references—a few of them slightly negative—MacGahan left no such record, even in his letters to her and to such friends as the Blakelys. Clearly MacGahan felt an indebtedness to Bennett for his blossoming career. The roving commission after the Franco-Prussian War and the Khivan and Carlist campaigns did, after all, demonstrate a strong confidence in the young correspondent's talents. Barbara, in turn, tended to confuse her husband's failure to discharge his familial responsibilities with Bennett's insistent assignments of new work to a man Bennett had on the full-time *Herald* payroll.

Assigned to *Pandora* expedition: Bullard.

2

"Having the honor to represent Mr. Bennett": MacGahan, *Under the Northern Lights*. Unless otherwise noted, the account of the *Pandora* voyage is derived from this source.

Captain Alan W. Young: Bullard.

Sir John Franklin and Franklin Northwest Passage expeditions: Loomis, in his brilliant biography of the American arctic explorer Charles Francis Hall.

Sampson, Low accounting: Documents in the packet marked "Miscellaneous Letters, Documents," MacGahan Papers.

3

Disko, Upernivik, Cary Islands, Beechey Island: MacGahan, *Under the Northern Lights*.

4

McClintock letter to Bennett: Copy in packet marked " 'Pandora' Expedition," MacGahan Papers.

Young letter to Bennett: Copy in " 'Pandora' " packet, MacGahan Papers.

JAM meeting with Bennett: 1897 memoir, BEM file, MacGahan Papers.

End of *Pandora*: For the account of the subsequent (1876) and penultimate voyage of *Pandora*, I am indebted to Spink & Son, Ltd., the famous numismatists of London for the data sent me, written by Rev. S. Salter, Cheltenham College. Reverend Salter's history of the fate of *Pandora* was written for Spink & Son as an explanation of the arctic medal awarded to the thirty-three members of her 1876 crew. (The crew received this distinction because the 1876 voyage was officially commissioned by the British Admiralty, while the first, MacGahan's, was "purely a private venture.") In the summer of 1879, the *Pandora*, now rechristened *Jeanette* (after Bennett's sister), steamed from San Francisco Bay to her fate. Her commander was Lt. George De Long of the U.S. Navy, and her mission was a run for the pole via the Bering Strait. She was last sighted in September that year, and for two years she dropped from sight as if off the edge of the world. In 1881, locked in pack ice in the delta of the Lena River of Siberia, *Jeannette* sank, crushed by abrading floes. De Long and all but three of his crew perished in their makeshift encampment. See Guttridge.

Part II
Chapter X
1

Burnaby meeting: 1876 memoir, BEM file, MacGahan Papers; Burnaby.

Burnaby's death: Alexander.

Bennett's secretary's letter, *Dauntless*: "Miscellaneous Letters, Documents," MacGahan Papers. This letter, dated November 29, 1875, is marked "Confidential."

Letter to mother: "Miscellaneous Letters, Documents," MacGahan Papers. The letter is undated—as is the exasperating fact of many of JAM's hasty messages to family and friends, and even in many of the letters to Barbara which have survived.

2

Bulgarian revolt, history: David Harris; MacDermott; Shannon.

Atrocity reports within Bulgaria: Chilingirov MS, "The Bulgarians about MacGahan," author's files. This unpublished study, written in 1970 by Bulgarian historian Dobrimir Chilingirov of Sofia, traces MacGahan's place and importance in the history of the 1876 revolt.

"Dark rumors" and Edwin Pears: London *Daily News*, June 8, 23, and 30, 1876; and MacGahan, *The Turkish Atrocities in Bulgaria*, 1876.

Disraeli flippancy: Shannon.

Punch on the Bulgarian atrocities: David Harris.

Le Charivari cartoon: Wirthwein.

Victoria on the bashi-bazouks: Longford.

The bashi-bazouks: Herbert.

"Monstrous exaggeration": Typical of the British press's reaction to

Edwin Pears's "dark rumors" reports is that of the *Saturday Review,* September 16, 1876.

3

JAM's connection with the *Daily News*: 1876 memoir, BEM file, MacGahan Papers.

Times (of London) declines JAM's services: *The History of 'The Times'.*

"I fear I am no longer impartial": this and all subsequent quotations from JAM's dispatches from the Bulgarian villages are taken from the *Daily News* or from MacGahan's verbatim reproduction of them in his *The Turkish Atrocities in Bulgaria,* 1876.

Batak: MacGahan, *The Turkish Atrocities;* Chilingirov MS, author's files. See also David Harris; Shannon; Wirthwein.

Schuyler on burning of Batak church: Wirthwein.

JAM's reportage, *Daily News* circulation: A recent scholar of the period, R. T. Shannon, points out that while it was an unusual feature of the 1876 atrocities that their disclosure caused such agitation in England, there was certainly nothing new about either the insurrection or the reprisals. "Both were endemic features of Ottoman administration," Shannon says, proceeding to point out that the Bulgarian murders were not even unusually extensive, quoting one source which gives these estimates of Christians massacred in Turkish territory in the nineteenth century at the instigation or with the connivance of Turkish authorities:

1822: Greeks, especially in Chios—50,000 dead.
1850: Nestorians, Armenians, in Kurdistan—10,000 dead.
1860: Maronites, Syrians, in Lebanon and Damascus—12,000 dead.
1866–68: Cretans, in Crete—number of dead not cited.
1876: Bulgarians, Bulgaria—15,000 dead.
1894: Armenians, in Armenia and Sassum—120,000 dead.
1896: Armenians, in Constantinople—2,000 dead. (See Shannon.)

JAM on Sir Henry Elliot and Benjamin Disraeli: In alleging the English ambassador at Constantinople to be "the friend and champion of the Turk" and that Sir Henry Elliot saw his duty "to defend the Turks through thick and thin and to shut his eyes to the atrocities," MacGahan told the truth. Elliot's Turkophilia caused him to accept the Porte's assurances that the atrocity stories were monstrously exaggerated, and this message he confidently conveyed to his government. He was ill throughout much of 1876 too, and this may have had a bearing on his lethargic failure to pursue the matter. Disraeli could never accept the *Daily News* stories as anything but gross sensationalism. He despised the liberal paper for its always harsh treatment of his policies. See Blake.

2

Eastern Question: David Harris; Pim; Shannon; Wirthwein.
Schuyler on Cossacks: Quoted in Wirthwein.
"Soldiers of the Czar": Chilingirov MS, author's files.

Chapter XI

1

Effects of JAM's Bulgarian dispatches: Pears.
Julius Chambers letter: Packet marked "Turkish Atrocities in Bulgaria," MacGahan Papers.
Victoria's reaction: David Harris.
Disraeli reaction: Ensor; Longford.
Elliot denunciation: Ensor.
Manchester Guardian, Times (of London), *Saturday Review, Spectator*: Quoted in Shannon.
Edmund Ollier: *Cassell's Illustrated History of the Russo-Turkish War.*
Forbes on JAM dispatches: Forbes, *Souvenirs of Some Continents.*
Gladstone at Hawarden: Blake; Morley.
Reaction to Gladstone's *Bulgarian Horrors*: Blake; Ensor; Morley. In the *Daily News* of September 14, 1876, while the Bulgarian atrocities, Eastern Question matters, and Gladstone's pronouncements were the subjects of many columns, only a tiny notice was carried on Lord Beaconsfield's dream: "The Imperial assemblage to be held in Delhi on the 1st January 1877, for the purpose of proclaiming Her Majesty's title of Empress of India, will be attended by upwards of seventy native potentates." Of particular interest to American newspaper readers at this time was the news from Madrid on September 8 that William Marcy "Boss" Tweed had been arrested in the port of Vigo and charged with embezzlement in America of the sum of six million dollars.
Gladstone supporters: Morley.
Events in Constantinople: Wittlin.

2

Marston letter: "Turkish Atrocities" packet, MacGahan Papers.
Correspondents at Six Powers Conference: Wirthwein.

Barbara to Constantinople: 1896 memoir, BEM file, MacGahan Papers.

Russia declares war: Cowles; Hozier.

JAM at Jassy: 1896 memoir, BEM file, MacGahan Papers.

JAM dispatch from Kischenev: London *Daily News*, April 28, 1876. All of MacGahan's *Daily News* war dispatches were included in the *The War Correspondence of the 'Daily News,' 1877–78* volumes published by Macmillan (of London) in 1878. None of the many correspondents whose work is included in it receive credit by name. Indeed, Archibald Forbes and MacGahan are the only two correspondents mentioned by name at all by the editors, and that on the title pages only. In the preface to volume I, it is stated: "Owing to the large number of the Special Correspondents whose letters are now republished, and in order that each of them may have credit for his own labors, a conventional sign has been appropriated to each correspondent and prefixed to his letters, by which his writings may be distinguished." Thus, some of the dispatches are marked with an asterisk, some with a dagger, some with double colon(::), small triangle, small square, etc. More puzzling yet, *no key* to these various symbols is provided! It is only by serious study of the books that one is able to identify the various contributors. Forbes (*) and MacGahan (†) are fairly easy to pin down; Edwin Pears is designated by ‡, and Frank Millet by +. The others remain unknown. What was accomplished by this Byzantine system, especially since so many of the *Daily News*'s correspondents were names of some consequence to the reading public, is also unknown.

"There is nothing in my experience": Forbes, *Souvenirs of Some Continents*.

"Incomparable Archibald": Bullard.

Forbes biography: Bullard; Forbes's own autobiographical writings in such books as *Souvenirs of Some Continents, Memories and Studies in War and Peace*.

Forbes in Franco-Prussian War: Forbes, *My Experiences of the War between France and Germany, Memories and Studies of War and Peace*; see also Bullard.

Forbes meets JAM at Jassy: Forbes, "War Correspondence as a Fine Art," also his chapter on JAM in *Souvenirs of Some Continents*. Jassy (Iaşi), five centuries old at the time of the Russo-Turkish War, had the ironic distinction of a long history of burnings and sackings by Tartars, Turks, and Russians. A treaty signed there in 1792 marked the end of the second major Russo-Turkish war during the reign of Catherine II.

Letter of Forbes to Barbara: The letter fragment is to be found in the packet marked "Varvara Nicholavna Elaguine," MacGahan Papers.

Forbes later included the content of this letter in his chapter on JAM in *Souvenirs of Some Continents*.

Forbes maxim and "The journalism of both worlds": Forbes, *Memories and Studies of War and Peace*.

Forbes on "copious telegraphy," the "pony express" system to Kronstedt: Hohenberg.

Use of Bucharest telegraph office: Forbes, "War Correspondence as a Fine Art."

JAM's "trusty coachman" and "took his chances": Told by Forbes in *Souvenirs of Some Continents* and in an undated newspaper clipping in the "Russo-Turkish War" packets, MacGahan Papers.

4

JAM in meeting Skobelev: London *Daily News*, May 20, 1877.

Skobelev biography, character: Curzon; Hozier; Furneaux, *The Breakfast War*; Nemirovitch-Dantchenko.

Greene on Skobelev: Greene, *Sketches of Army Life in Russia*.

Forbes on Skobelev: Forbes, *Souvenirs of Some Continents*.

Villiers's background and his account of his meeting with JAM at Tatar Pazardzhik is found in *Villiers, His Five Decades of Adventure*.

JAM letter to his mother from St. Petersburg is dated March 17, 1877: See "Miscellaneous Letters, Documents" packet, MacGahan Papers. There is a noticeable lack of reference in the letter to Barbara and their son, Paul. Indeed, in none of the few letters of JAM that have survived from this period of his career are his wife and son mentioned.

Chapter XII

1

Butler on the Russo-Turkish War: Butler, "The War Campaign and the War Correspondent."

Mobilization, the contending armies: Greene, *The Campaign in Bulgaria; 1877–1878*; Knox.

Drew Gay: Gay.

Russian common soldier: Greene, *The Campaign in Bulgaria*.

Turkish common soldier: Hozier.

Villiers witnesses opening shot: Villiers.

JAM dispatches: Taken variously from the *Daily News* under dates listed, or from *The War Correspondence of the 'Daily News,' 1877–78*.

2

Description of Cossacks and equipment: Hozier.

3

Shipka Pass: For accounts and data on all major engagements of the war, in addition to the dispatches of the *Daily News* correspondents, see also Greene, *The Campaign in Bulgaria*; Hozier; Maurice; Ollier.

On Gourko: Greene, *The Campaign in Bulgaria*; Hozier.

Brackenbury on JAM: Quoted in Hozier.

Bulgarian reprisals: Lt. Gen. Valentine Baker Pasha, *War in Bulgaria*. Baker (1827–87), younger brother of Nile explorer Sir Samuel Baker, served with the 12th Lancers in South Africa and the Crimean War, traveled (like MacGahan and Burnaby) through central Asia, and became a polished writer and a notable authority on cavalry tactics. His promising career in the army ended in 1875 when he was convicted of "indecently assaulting" a young woman in a railway carriage. He was dismissed from the army and in 1877 took service under the sultan as a major general of gendarmerie, later given command of a division in the Balkans. In 1882 he entered the Egyptian service, again in command of police. He commanded troops at Tokar and El Teb in the Sudan War and remained in command of Egyptian police until his death from heart disease at Tel-el Kebir in 1887.

4

Forbes on Gourko's passage of the Balkans and on Bulgarian reprisals against the Turks: Quoted in Hozier.

Brackenbury: Quoted in Hozier.

Forbes on Bucharest, JAM: Forbes, *Souvenirs of Some Continents*.

JAM in Bucharest with Barbara and Paul: 1897 memoir, BEM file, MacGahan Papers.

Chapter XIII

1

"Beware of Plevna!": Herbert.

"Occupy Plevna": Greene, *The Campaign in Bulgaria*.

Osman Nuri Pasha and Plevna before the battle: Gay; Hozier; Ollier; Villiers.

Reverse at Bukova and Janik Bair: Hozier.

Krudener defeat on July 30: Greene, *The Campaign in Bulgaria*; Hozier; Ollier.

Forbes's ride: Forbes, *Souvenirs of Some Continents* and recounted several times by Forbes in his autobiographical books. Barbara Mac-Gahan, in an unpublished memoir written many years later, wrote: "Forbes was a more brilliant writer but far below M. [MacGahan] in personal character. He was neither truthful nor trustworthy and he never could have returned to the Russian army after he left under the plea of sickness. His story of riding 80 miles in one night to take his dispatch to the telegraph office was pure fabrication." BEM file, Mac-Gahan Papers.

2

JAM on the July 30 assault: In his estimates of the Russian loss in the battle, MacGahan's guess of 33 percent of 24,000 engaged was close. Later estimates put the Russian strength at about 30,000 and the casualties at 25 percent.

3

Wellesley on the czar's handling of the press: Hozier.

The czar: Alexander II (1818–81), who succeeded his father, Nicholas I, in 1855, was a reform-minded ruler whose most important act was the emancipation of the serfs in 1861. He was assassinated by a member of a terrorist group called The People's Will.

Frederick Boyle: Boyle gently rebuked the Russians and told his side of the story in a book, *Narrative of an Expelled Correspondent*, published in England in 1877.

4

Greene on meeting JAM: Greene, *Sketches of Army Life in Russia*.

Russian losses at Lovtcha: Greene, *The Campaign in Bulgaria*.

Skobelev's "Order of the Day" and "Leave me at once!": Nemirovitch-Dantchenko.

Prince Imeretinsky's Official Report: Knox.

Forbes informs Skobelev, Sr.: Furneaux, *The Breakfast War*.

Prince Charles of Rumania: He was a Prussian of the house of

Hohenzollern-Sigmaringen leading the combined Russo-Rumanian forces against the Turks in Bulgaria. See Cowles.

Chapter XIV

1

Keys to Turkish position: Greene, *The Campaign in Bulgaria*.

2

Czar and retinue: Cowles.
Krishin casualties: Greene, *The Campaign in Bulgaria*.

3

Gortalov's death: Nemirovitch-Dantchenko.
"A carnage rarely witnessed": Hozier.
Greene on Skobelev in the Great Assault: Greene, *The Campaign in Bulgaria*.
Casualties in the Great Assault: Furneaux, *The Breakfast War*; Greene, *The Campaign in Bulgaria*.
Todleben: Eduard Ivanovitch Todleben (1818–84) won his great renown for his defensive works at Sebastopol during the Crimean War. He was subsequently to receive command of the entire Russian army and was created a count.
War correspondents as lecturers: Furneaux, *The Breakfast War*.
Forbes on MacGahan "still limping": Forbes, *Souvenirs of Some Continents*.

4

JAM in Bucharest after the Great Assault: 1897 memoir, BEM file, MacGahan Papers.
Butler's review of *The War Correspondence of the 'Daily News'*: Butler, "The War Campaign and the War Correspondent."

5

Osman Pasha's reply to surrender request: Hozier.
Details of the last sortie and of Osman's surrender: *War Correspondence of the 'Daily News'*; Greene, *Campaign in Bulgaria*; Hozier; Ollier.

Chapter XV

1

Frank Millet in Plevna: *War Correspondence of the 'Daily News.'*
Villiers after Plevna: Villiers.
Millet on MacGahan's injury: Quoted in McCarthy and Robinson.
JAM letter to Robinson: "Russo-Turkish War" packet, MacGahan
Papers.
Barbara MacGahan, "Maybe our young enjoyment": 1897 memoir,
BEM file, MacGahan Papers.

2

Forbes lecture, "jingo" song: Furneaux, *The Breakfast War.*
Greene on armistice terms: Greene, *The Campaign in Bulgaria.*

3

For details on the treaty signing and events at San Stefano, JAM's
and Frank Millet's dispatches form the best eyewitness account. See
War Correspondence of the 'Daily News'.

4

Pears on JAM: Pears.
Barbara MacGahan letters from Bucharest: These letters, which she
apparently retrieved after her husband's death, are in the BEM file,
MacGahan Papers.
Abdul Hamid: Wittlin.
Villiers at Skobelev's headquarters: Villiers.
Pears on Skobelev: Pears.

Chapter XVI

1

Treaty of San Stefano: The Congress of Berlin of July 1878 did, in
fact, nullify much of the Treaty of San Stefano, placing Russia in the
somewhat ignominious position of a military victor whose gains were
parceled out by those not involved in the conflict. Great Britain, represented by Lord Beaconsfield, and Austria-Hungary were the powers
most insistent on revision. Bismarck served as the "honest broker"—

chairman of the Congress. The other signatories were France, Italy, and, of course, Russia and Turkey.

JAM's plans to write "a great work": 1897 memoir, BEM file, Mac-Gahan Papers.

"Quinine by the spoonful": Villiers.

JAM's accounting to Robinson: Letter in the packet marked "Death of MacGahan (1878)," MacGahan Papers.

JAM's last days: Barbara MacGahan's 1897 memoir, BEM file, Mac-Gahan Papers, is the best and most poignant source. See also Pears; Villiers.

2

JAM's loss of appetite, Villiers with Skobelev on hearing news of JAM's illness: Villiers.

Pears on JAM's fatal illness: Pears.

3

Aftermath of JAM's death: 1897 memoir, BEM file, MacGahan Papers.

Robinson cable to MacGahan family: Preserved in the Papers, "Death of MacGahan (1878)" packet, MacGahan Papers.

New York *Herald* obituary: June 11, 1878.

London *Daily News* obituary: June 11, 1878.

Pears's remarks: Pears.

Frank Millet assessment: Charles J. Wingate MS, MacGahan Papers.

4

Barbara MacGahan after JAM's burial: 1897 memoir, BEM file, MacGahan Papers.

Robinson letter to Patrick MacGahan: In the "Death of MacGahan (1878)" packet, MacGahan Papers.

Epilogue

Barbara MacGahan's life and career after JAM's death: 1897 memoir, BEM file, MacGahan Papers; also letters to author from John A. MacGahan, Barbara MacGahan's grandson, February 12, 1973, and December 23, 1975.

Paul MacGahan's life and career: Information supplied by John A. MacGahan, son of Paul MacGahan, letter to author, January 13, 1976.

Greene on Skobelev: Greene, *Sketches of Army Life in Russia*.

Death of Skobelev: Furneaux, *The Breakfast War*.

Skobelev, ardent Panslavist: Nemirovitch-Dantchenko.

Forbes on Skobelev: Forbes, *Memories and Studies in War and Peace*.

Forbes on JAM, "taken all in all": Forbes, *Memories and Studies in War and Peace*.

Forbes, "It is possible": Quoted in Bullard's chapter on Forbes.

Forbes on JAM's "chiefhood" and final tributes to JAM: Forbes, *Souvenirs of Some Continents*. Barbara MacGahan added some fuel to Forbes's claim that MacGahan might have become ruler of Bulgaria had he lived. In her unpublished memoir of her life with the correspondent she wrote: "He was a desirable candidate and it had been seriously planned that he would be ruler of the new nation. Not being a native of Bulgaria had not created personal animosities. A German or Frenchman would have had political affiliations, while a Russian was out of the question. It is most interesting to consider how he could have administered the position."

Forbes and MacGahan: Despite Forbes's often magniloquent postmortem magnanimity toward MacGahan, there were critics who saw Forbes benefiting from MacGahan's work without proper credit while the Ohioan was alive. Barbara MacGahan seems to have regarded Forbes as something of a poseur. Within a month of MacGahan's death, a writer at the New York *Herald* (perhaps John P. Jackson, a correspondent Bennett seemed to be grooming as another Stanley or MacGahan) wrote under the heading "In Memory of MacGahan": "I cannot help thinking that Mr. Forbes might have spoken of Mr. MacGahan's services before he had died. Mr. Forbes has been lecturing in England about the Bulgarian campaign ever since October or November, but I have never heard that he ever mentioned Mr. MacGahan's name in connection with the 'Daily News' correspondence. And yet but for Mr. MacGahan, it is certain that neither Mr. Forbes nor the 'Daily News' would have been able to reap so much glory. To Mr. MacGahan's immense influence with the Russian generals is due much that the 'Daily News' accomplished through Mr. Forbes. Many of Mr. MacGahan's brilliant letters to the 'News' were popularly credited to 'Forbes' (and he was careful not to correct the report), and part of the reputation which the latter won is due to Mr. MacGahan. Mr. Forbes' letters would have been read by Mr. MacGahan's friends with infinitely greater pleasure if he had in his lectures given the fellow worker on the battle fields of Bulgaria at least a just share of the honors due him." (New York *Herald*, July 7, 1878.)

Death of Forbes: *Dictionary of National Biography—Supplement*, Bullard; Furneaux, *The Breakfast War*; and McCarthy and Robinson *The 'Daily News' Jubilee*.

Return of JAM's body from Constantinople: 1897 memoir, BEM file, MacGahan Papers; also a vast number of New York and Ohio newspaper clippings, most undated, in a scrapbook in the MacGahan Papers.

New York *Star* report: August 27, 1884.

December 1896 letter and statue drawing: Copies of both are in the "Miscellaneous Letters, Documents" packet, MacGahan Papers.

Taft letter: Dated June 20, 1911, "Miscellaneous Letters, Documents" packet, MacGahan Papers.

Tonjorov remarks: *The MacGahan Monument*.

1929 ceremony: A copy of the program and various undated clippings on the ceremony are in the "Miscellaneous Letters, Documents" packet and scrapbook, MacGahan Papers.

1958 ceremony and "Voice of America" broadcast: In August 1943, the U.S. Office of War Information wrote Paul MacGahan asking him to give a talk on the "Voice of America" that, while not appealing directly to King Boris, would give him a warning. The letter to Paul MacGahan stated, "Your name is well known among Bulgarian intellectuals who are deeply grateful to your father. I think a firm, friendly word from you might be very helpful." Paul MacGahan gave the broadcast, saying, in part: "Now all that stupendous military force, borne on wings, loaded on ships and carried in the hands of countless stalwart men, is converging toward you. The Nazis and Fascists are going down to destruction. Do you wish to go down with them? If you stay with them, terrible catastrophe faces you. You will be subjected to disasters not unlike those of which you complained when my father was in Bulgaria." ("Miscellaneous Letters, Documents" packet, MacGahan Papers.)

1893 incident at Chicago World's Fair: Wingate MS, MacGahan Papers.

Dimitrov on JAM, and Bulgarian accounts of JAM's life and contributions to the country: Chilingirov MS, author's files.

Bozhidar Kuntschev: Letter to author from Sofia, Bulgaria, January 6, 1971.

Tirnovo mass to JAM: O. Muller MS, MacGahan Papers.

Bibliography

I Manuscripts

MacGahan Papers. This mass of papers, in the possession of the grand-children of the correspondent, include MacGahan's letters to his wife, mother, and American friends; some handwritten dispatches for the New York *Herald* (including a lengthy one from France during the Franco-Prussian War); his book contracts; expense account of his Khivan journey; and clippings, photographs, scrapbooks, and documents of miscellaneous interest.

The papers are divided into thirteen packets:

Pre-1870 Letters
Franco-Prussian War and Commune of Paris (1870–1871)
Varvara Nicholavna Elaguine
Khiva (Turkestan) and *Campaigning on the Oxus* (1873)
Carlist War in Spain (1874)
Letters from Carlist War to Varvara (1874)
"Pandora" Expedition and *Under the Northern Lights* (1875)
Turkish Atrocities in Bulgaria (1876)
Russo-Turkish War and Aftermath (1877–1878)
Miscellaneous Notes, Documents: Constantinople (1878)
Death of MacGahan, Aftermath, Tributes (1878 passim)
Biographical Materials, Miscellany
Miscellaneous Letters, Documents

Of particular value in the balance of the MacGahan Papers are the following manuscripts and letters:
JAM Diary, 1871–73.
"Sojourn of the Turkestan Division at Khiva, Our Return From Khiva; Appearance in the Midst of Us, of an American During Our Affair on the Amou-Daria": This is an undated (but about 1873), handwritten, twenty-six-page account in English by an unknown officer of the Russian army under General Konstantin Kaufmann at the siege of Khiva.

Charles J. Wingate MS: A memoir by an American friend of Mac-Gahan's covering the early life of the correspondent.

Walter J. Blakely Letters: These consist of letters preserved by

Blakely from MacGahan beginning in the St. Louis period through the voyage of the *Pandora* to arctic waters.

Letters of Januarius A. MacGahan to his mother: A valuable and revealing handful of letters, invariably signed "From your affectionate son, Januarius."

O. Muller MS: This manuscript is of a long address by Prof. Orestes Muller of the University of St. Petersburg to the Pan-Slavonic organization in St. Petersburg in the year of MacGahan's death, 1878. It contains valuable observations on the correspondent which Muller appears to have derived directly from Barbara MacGahan—who was given an honorary membership in the organization upon her return to Russia following her husband's death.

Barbara Elaguine MacGahan Papers. In addition to her diaries (in Russian and French) and number of letters and notes, these papers include two invaluable manuscripts:

"The Twilight of the Czars: Absolutism and Its Effects in Russia," and unpublished MS of Barbara MacGahan's autobiography and Elaguine family history, edited by Paul MacGahan in 1956.

Untitled Memoir, a handwritten autobiography of Barbara MacGahan which she wrote in 1897.

Chilingirov MS. This unpublished manuscript, titled "The Bulgarians about MacGahan: A Survey," was written in Sofia in 1970 by Dobrimir Chilingirov and sent to the author via the ambassador from Bulgaria in Washington, D.C.

Correspondence. With Dr. L. Guerassimov, ambassador, People's Republic of Bulgaria, Washington, D.C.; Boschidar Kuntschev, University of Sofia, Bulgaria; Theodore Delchev Dimitrov, Geneva, Switzerland; John A. MacGahan, Exton, Pennsylvania, and Haines Falls, New York; William H. MacGahan, Bloomingdale, New Jersey.

II Periodicals

Columbus (Ohio) *Dispatch*
Cleveland Plain Dealer
New York *Herald*
New York *Star*
New York *Times*
New York *Tribune*
Perry County (Ohio) *Tribune*
Somerset (Ohio) *Press*
The Times (London)
Illustrated London News

The London *Daily News*
The Literary Digest
The Bookman
The Manchester Guardian
The Nineteenth Century
Munsey's Magazine
The Athenaeum (London)
The Spectator (London)
Century Magazine
McClure's Magazine
The Outlook
Macmillan's Magazine
Catholic Home Messenger
The Idler (London)
The Elk's Magazine

III   Books and Articles

Alexander, Michael. *The True Blue: The Life and Adventures of Col. Fred Burnaby, 1842–1885.* London: Rupert Hart-Davis, 1957.

Anderson, Dorothy. *The Balkan Volunteers.* London: Hutchinson, 1968

Anderson, Harold M. "The American Newspaper: The War Correspondent." *The Bookman*, March 1904.

Arline, Henry N. "Januarius Aloysius MacGahan." *Catholic Home Messenger*, January 1959.

Arter, Bill. "The Liberator from New Lexington." *The Columbus Dispatch Magazine*, September 9, 1962.

Atkins, J. B. *Life of Sir William Howard Russell.* 2 vols. London: John Murray, 1911.

The Avita Fraus of Russia. London: W. Ridgway, 1877.

Baker, Lt. Gen. Valentine Pasha. *War in Bulgaria: Narrative of Personal Experiences.* 2 vols. London: Sampson, Low, Marston, Searle & Rivington, 1879.

Becker, Seymour. *Russia's Protectorates in Central Asia: Bukhara and Khiva, 1865–1924.* Cambridge: Harvard University Press, 1968.

Blake, Robert. *Disraeli.* New York: St. Martin's Press, 1967.

Boulger, Demetrius C. *Central Asian Portraits.* London: W. H. Allen & Co., 1880.

Boyle, Frederick. *The Narrative of an Expelled Correspondent.* London: Richard Bentley & Son, 1877.

Bullard, F. Lauriston. *Famous War Correspondents.* Boston: Little, Brown, 1914.

Burnaby, Fred. *A Ride to Khiva*. London: Cassel & Co., n.d.

Butler, William F. "The War Campaign and the War Correspondent." *Macmillan's Magazine*, March 1878.

Carlson, Oliver. *The Man Who Made News: James Gordon Bennett*. New York: Duell, Sloan and Pearce, 1942.

Compton, Roy. "Mr. Frederic Villiers." *The Idler*, September 1897.

Cowles, Virginia. *The Russian Dagger*. New York: Harper & Row, 1969.

Curzon, George H. *Russia in Central Asia*. London: Frank Cass & Co., 1967 (first published in 1889).

Dostoievsky, F. M. *The Diary of a Writer*. Vol. 2. Translated and annotated by Boris Brasol. New York: Scribner, 1949.

Ensor, R. C. K. *England, 1870–1914*. London: Oxford University Press, 1936.

Forbes, Archibald. *Barracks, Bivouacks and Battles*. London, 1891.

———. *Camps, Quarters and Casual Places*. London, 1896.

———. *Czar and Sultan*. Bristol: J. W. Arrowsmith, 1894.

———. *Glimpses through the Cannon Smoke*. London, 1880.

———. "Is the War Correspondent a Necessity of Civilization?" *The Idler*, September 1897.

———. *Memories and Studies of War and Peace*. 2 vols. Leipzig: Bernard Tauchnitz, 1895.

———. *My Experiences of the War between France and Germany*. 2 vols. Leipzig: Bernard Tauchnitz, 1871.

———. *Souvenirs of Some Continents*. London, 1885.

———. "War Correspondence as a Fine Art." *The Century Magazine*, December 1892.

———. "A War Correspondent's Reminiscences." *The Nineteenth Century*, August 1891.

Friends or Foes? London: P. S. King, 1878.

Furneaux, Rupert. *The Breakfast War*. New York: Crowell, 1958.

———. *The First War Correspondent: William Howard Russell of The Times*. London: Cassell & Co., 1945.

———. *News of War*. London: Max Parrish & Co., 1965.

Gay, J. Drew. *Plevna, Sultan, and the Porte*. London: Chatto and Windus, 1878.

Gladstone, William E. *The Bulgarian Horrors and the Question of the East*. London, 1876.

Greene, Francis V. *The Campaign in Bulgaria, 1877–78*. London: Hugh Rees, 1903.

———. *Sketches of Army Life in Russia*. New York: Scribner, 1885.

Guttridge, Leonard F. *Icebound: The Jeannette Expedition's Quest for the North Pole*. Annapolis: Naval Institute Press, 1986.

Harcave, Sidney. *Years of the Golden Cockerel*. New York: Macmillan, 1968.

Harris, David. *Britain and the Bulgarian Horrors of 1876*. Chicago: University of Chicago Press, 1939.

Harris, Frank. *My Life and Loves*. New York: Grove Press, 1963.

Hart, Charles. "A Mass for MacGahan." *The Elks Magazine*, May 1936.

Herbert, William V. *The Defence of Plevna*. London: Longmans, Green & Co., 1895.

The History of 'The Times': The Tradition Established, 1841–1884. London, n.p., 1939.

Hodgetts, E. A. B. *The Court of Russia in the Nineteenth Century*. 2 vols. London: Methuen & Co., 1908.

Hohenberg, John. *Foreign Correspondence: The Great Reporters and Their Times*. New York: Columbia University Press, 1964.

Holt, Edgar. *The Carlist Wars in Spain*. London: Putnam, 1967.

Horne, Alistair. *The Fall of Paris*. New York: St. Martin's Press, 1965.

_____. *The Terrible Year: The Paris Commune 1871*. New York: Viking Press, 1971.

Howard, Michael. *The Franco-Prussian War*. New York: Macmillan, 1962.

Hozier, Capt. Sir Henry M. *The Russo-Turkish War*. 5 vols. London: William Mackenzie, n.d.

In Memory of Januarius A. MacGahan, 1844–1878, Liberator of Bulgaria. New Lexington, Ohio: n.p., 1929.

Kinnear, John B. *The Mind of England on the Eastern Question*. London: Chapman & Hall, n.d.

Knightley, Phillip. *The First Casualty*. New York: Harcourt Brace Jovanovich, 1975.

Knox, Thomas W. *Decisive Battles since Waterloo*. New York: Putnam, 1887.

Longford, Elizabeth. *Queen Victoria*. New York: Harper & Row, 1964.

Loomis, Chauncey C. *Weird and Tragic Shores*. New York: Knopf, 1971.

MacDermott, Marcia. *A History of Bulgaria, 1393–1885*. New York: Praeger, 1962.

MacGahan, J. A. *Campaigning on the Oxus and the Fall of Khiva*. New York: Harper & Brothers, 1874.

_____. *The Turkish Atrocities in Bulgaria*. London: Bradbury, Agnew & Co., 1876.

_____. *The Turkish Atrocities in Bulgaria.* Translated into Bulgarian and English and with introduction by Theodore Delchev Dimitrov. Geneva, n.p., 1966.

_____. *Under the Northern Lights.* London: Sampson, Low, Marston, Searle & Rivington, 1876.

The MacGahan Monument: A Dedication at New Lexington. Columbus, Ohio: Ohio Historical Society, April–July 1912.

Magnus, Philip. *Gladstone: A Biography.* New York: Dutton, 1954.

Masaryk, Thomas G. *The Spirit of Russia.* Vol. 3. New York: Barnes & Noble, 1967.

Matthews, Joseph J. *Reporting the Wars.* Minneapolis: University of Minnesota Press, 1957.

Maurice, Maj. F. *The Russo-Turkish War, 1877.* London: George Allen & Unwin, 1905.

McCarthy, Justin, and Sir John R. Robinson. *The "Daily News" Jubilee.* London: Sampson, Low, Marston & Co., 1895.

Morley, John. *The Life of William Ewart Gladstone.* 3 vols. London: Macmillan, 1903.

Nemirovitch-Dantchenko, V. I. *Personal Reminiscences of General Skobeleff.* London: W. H. Allen & Co., 1884.

O'Connor, Richard. *The Scandalous Mr. Bennett.* New York: Doubleday, 1962.

Ollier, Edmund. *Cassell's Illustrated History of the Russo-Turkish War.* 2 vols. London: Cassell & Co., 1897.

Ostrander, Stephen. "Penman of Independence: Januarius Mac-Gahan," *Timeline* [Ohio Historical Society], June–July, 1987.

Pears, Sir Edwin. *Forty Years in Constantinople.* New York: D. Appleton & Co., 1916.

_____. *Turkey and Its People.* London: Methuen & Co., 1911.

Pim, Capt. Bedford. *The Eastern Question, Past, Present and Future.* London: Effingham Wilson, Royal Exchange, 1877.

Prior, Melton. *Campaigns of a War Correspondent.* London: Edward Arnold, 1912.

Schuyler, Eugene. *Turkistan: Notes of a Journey in Russian Turkistan, Kokand, Bukhara and Buldja.* New York: Frederick A. Praeger, 1966.

Shannon, R. T. *Gladstone and the Bulgarian Agitation 1876.* London: Thomas Nelson Sons, 1963.

Snyder, Louis L., and Richard B. Morris, eds. *A Treasury of Great Reporting.* New York: Simon & Schuster, 1949.

Stein, M. L. *Under Fire: The Story of American War Correspondents.* New York: Julian Messner, 1968.

"A Veteran Campaigner." *The Outlook,* April 19, 1922.

Villiers, Frederic. *Villiers: His Five Decades of Adventure.* 2 vols. New York: Harper & Brothers, 1920.

The War Correspondence of the 'Daily News,' 1877–78. London: Macmillan & Co., 1878.

Washburne, Elihu B. *Recollections of a Minister to France.* 2 vols. New York: Scribner, 1887.

Wirthwein, Walter G. *Britain and the Balkan Crisis, 1875–1878.* New York: Columbia University Press, 1935.

Wittlin, Anna. *Abdul Hamid: The Shadow of God.* London: The Bodley Head, 1940.

Index

Boldface numerals = photograph or drawing; italicized numerals = map; fn = reference in footnote; n = reference in Notes section.